MW01017414

Aboriginal Justice and the Charter

Law and Society Series
W. Wesley Pue, General Editor

The Law and Society Series explores law as a socially embedded phenomenon. It is premised on the understanding that the conventional division of law from society creates false dichotomies in thinking, scholarship, educational practice, and social life. Books in the series treat law and society as mutually constitutive and highlight scholarship emerging from the interdisciplinary engagement of law with fields such as politics, social theory, history, political economy, and gender studies.

A list of titles in the series appears at the end of the book.

David Leo Milward

Aboriginal Justice and the Charter
Realizing a Culturally Sensitive
Interpretation of Legal Rights

UBCPress · Vancouver · Toronto

21 20 19 18 17 16 15 14 13 12   5 4 3 2 1

Printed in Canada on FSC-certified ancient-forest-free paper
(100% post-consumer recycled) that is processed chlorine- and acid-free.

Library and Archives Canada Cataloguing in Publication

Milward, David Leo, 1974-
   Aboriginal justice and the Charter : realizing a culturally sensitive interpretation of legal rights / David L. Milward.

(Law and society, ISSN 1493-4953)
Includes bibliographical references and index.
Also issued in electronic format.
ISBN 978-0-7748-2456-9

   1. Native peoples – Legal status, laws, etc. – Canada. 2. Native peoples – Civil rights – Canada. 3. Indian courts – Canada. 4. Canada. Canadian Charter of Rights and Freedoms. 5. Criminal justice, Administration of – Canada. I. Title. II. Series: Law and society series (Vancouver, B.C.)

KE7709.M56 2012   342.7108'72   C2012-904141-6
KF8205.M56 2012

Canadä

UBC Press gratefully acknowledges the financial support for our publishing program of the Government of Canada (through the Canada Book Fund), the Canada Council for the Arts, and the British Columbia Arts Council.

This book has been published with the help of a grant from the Canadian Federation for the Humanities and Social Sciences, through the Awards to Scholarly Publications Program, using funds provided by the Social Sciences and Humanities Research Council of Canada, and with the help of the University of British Columbia through the K.D. Srivastava Fund.

UBC Press
The University of British Columbia
2029 West Mall
Vancouver, BC V6T 1Z2
www.ubcpress.ca

For Mary and Leo,
the best parents anybody could ever hope for.

And for my niece Naomi,
whose joyful spirit never fails to give me hope.

Contents

Foreword

David Milward, a law professor of Cree ancestry at the University of Manitoba, has undertaken a remarkably difficult task in *Aboriginal Justice and the Charter*. In these pages, he considers the broad range of issues necessary to make a case for the creation of free-standing Aboriginal justice programs, conceived and administered by Aboriginal communities themselves. Milward examines various Aboriginal concepts of justice, keeping an eye out for the difficulties inherent in reconstructing ideas and practices long since pushed underground by the colonizers. However, since Canadian Aboriginal peoples (First Nations, Métis, and Inuit) are subject to Canadian law, as Milward writes, it is not entirely clear on which grounds they might create and operate their own justice initiatives.

To get at this problem, he advocates the concept of the culturally sensitive interpretation of legal rights as articulated by the Royal Commission on Aboriginal Peoples in *Bridging the Cultural Divide*.[1] Milward makes the assumption (he is aware that it is contentious) that Aboriginal communities can exercise broad jurisdiction over criminal justice under section 35(1) of the *Constitution Act, 1982*.[2] The idea is that the Canadian Charter of Rights and Freedoms might be reinterpreted so as to provide greater room for the operation of Indigenous methods of justice.[3] These ideas, together with the *R. v Oakes* tests for constitutional justification, as refined by the decision in *Dagenais v Canadian Broadcasting Corporation,* Milward suggests, could constitute the grounds that would allow non-hierarchical accommodation when constitutional rights come into conflict (for example, Aboriginal rights to criminal jurisdiction versus legal rights).[4]

This interpretation implies a blending of older Indigenous teachings and Canadian legal principles. Since Aboriginal peoples within Canada have now lived for a century and a half or more under some form of common law, many have syncretic notions of natural law and Aboriginal law, and expectations of the law have also changed. Milward poses the question of whether Indigenous law can evolve to meet contemporary needs in light of the accommodation of traditional practice and Canadian common law standards. He thinks it can.

Conventionally, there is a division of labour in writing about Aboriginal law, including those who write about law as it concerns Aboriginal peoples and communities within Canadian legal orders. This group is primarily, but not entirely, composed of legal scholars who examine case law, with a smaller contingent coming from history, anthropology, and, perhaps more recently, literary and cultural studies, and who explore the social and cultural ramifications of Canadian law for Aboriginal people and society at large.

Members of an altogether different group write about the historical practice of law within Aboriginal communities. Scholarly attempts to reconstruct Aboriginal legal orders started seventy-five years ago with the pioneering work of a team consisting of legal scholar Karl Llewellyn and his anthropologist colleague E. Adamson Hoebel. Writing within the legal realist tradition, they analyzed fifty cases of Cheyenne dispute resolution, based on the memories of elders, to extract the legal genius of the culture. The resulting seminal work, *The Cheyenne Way,* was published in 1941.[5] However, the work of studying what appeared to be vanishing legal concepts and practices primarily fell to anthropologists who remained interested in the diversity of approaches to justice in non-Western societies. For a long time, the topic seemed unimportant and unnecessary to the Canadian public. Unlike their approach to colonialization in India and Africa, there had been no intention on the part of the British to rule through local elites, a circumstance that would require that regional juridical practices be recorded in writing. In North America, at least following the War of 1812, there was no comparable incentive. I must point out that there were exceptions – senior Aboriginal people adjudicated cases involving whites in the Oregon Territory before the creation of the international border in 1846, for example, and mainstream courts have accounted for Aboriginal law in rulings involving Aboriginal-white crime. In any case, a visit to the law library at the University of British Columbia reveals rows of books about the laws of African and Indian peoples but little about those of North American Aboriginal people. Surprisingly few scholars have considered historical concepts and practices with regard to Canadian law concerning Aboriginal people. David Milward is one of these, and more studies appear to be on the way.

More recently, legal scholars, often Aboriginal community members themselves, have begun to undertake their own examination of these historical practices. Some have attempted to integrate the ideas inherent in mythology and the behaviour of culture heroes into their interpretations, arguing that these stories constitute the ancestral laws. Notably, legal scholars Val Napoleon and John Borrows are among those attempting to apply Aboriginal narrative to interpreting legal orders, and there is now a younger generation, trained by Napoleon, Borrows, and others, following in their footsteps. Meanwhile, Milward has noted the scarcity of published material on historical Aboriginal practices. But he has read much of what there is, and it has informed his own thinking. He does not attempt to recreate Cree law in *Aboriginal Justice and the Charter*. However, he notes that he has applied his understanding of his own culture and the ways in which Cree people might approach justice. His combination of talents, in particular, his law school training in common law and his cultural knowledge, strengthen his work.

Milward's project is not prescriptive. He acknowledges that at each step there will be considerable differences in points of view, tenaciously and sometimes combatively held. But he hopes to provide a pragmatic position and describes himself as midway between the polar positions established in Canadian discourse about Aboriginal issues, somewhere between the arguments of the incommensurability of Canadian and Aboriginal perspectives advanced by Taiaiake Alfred and the reactionary and sometimes dismissive position of Tom Flanagan, an academic and former federal Conservative advisor.[6] Milward positions himself with Borrows, as hopeful but cautious about the capacity of Canada to hear Aboriginal voices and to move thoughtfully towards a greater recognition of Aboriginal ideas. In an unusual move, he makes his own case based on what he regards as appropriate compromises, considers what the objections might be, and systematically provides his responses to these objections. He hopes to spark an informed conversation within the communities and among legal scholars and practitioners.

Although he is a self-described centrist pragmatist, Milward's work is timely and is a welcome change from the timidity regarding Aboriginal justice reform that has characterized Canada for far too long. There has been very little serious consideration of advancing Aboriginal justice programs beyond small-scale diversionary justice programs or sentencing circles that incorporate Aboriginal practices and concepts late in the legal proceedings. This timidity is often matched with dangerous jumps in logic, faulty assumptions, and inadequate preparation when Aboriginal practices are engaged in cases involving Aboriginal crime.

Although I do not wish to suggest that it is commonly the case, I have been dismayed on a few occasions to receive phone calls from police or other officials who are about to enter into a sentencing circle and are baffled about what it is about or what their role will be. (I do not mind receiving these calls if anyone has this in mind – I am glad to help when I can.) And I have been puzzled by some of the assumptions behind sentencing circles. For example, in the Coast Salish territory in which I live, cases have arisen in which people of Coast Salish origin, but who have no contact with their ancestral community, have been brought into Aboriginal sentencing circles following an admission of guilt. This seems to me to violate a core principle that a culturally specific sentencing circle must consist of people with some common understandings and ideally with real connections to the same group of people.

Milward's approach addresses another vital issue, which is the incorporation of generic Aboriginal concepts into the legal practice of specific communities. In one instance, I spoke at a First Nations-sponsored conference on Aboriginal law where the Maōri family group conferencing model was presented. The packaged program was adopted for reasons of convenience by a First Nation interested in establishing a process for what it hoped would eventually be its own legal system. However, very quickly, the discourse shifted, and what had been adopted for expediency became thought of as an ancestral system. It perhaps did reflect something of a historical system, but it was Maōri and not Coast Salish. Milward indicates that although there are features in common between perhaps all historical Aboriginal approaches to justice, there are also local variations, which are highly specific and resonate with local people in ways that generic programs likely do not. Milward's suggestions could potentially lead to circumstances in which the stop-gap justice concepts, which are sometimes ill thought out and even foreign, would no longer be integrated into justice programs. Instead, communities could systematically build their own programs.

A systematic, localized approach to rebuilding a justice system with a strong connection to historical practice would also have the benefit of eliminating the need for under-the-table, sometimes dangerous experiments in justice. Many such programs are underway in Canada, too many to easily track. An example concerns a panel of elders, military veterans, who adjudicated a case of rape perpetrated by another veteran. Their redress, I am told, was to strip the rapist of membership within the veterans' organization. Communities have in some instances created their own new processes for dealing with rape, but these are based on local cultural understandings. These experiments have the benefit of creating local control and of keeping rapists from entering into a Canadian criminal justice system that removes them from community oversight, only to return them much later and badly damaged by their time in jail. Yet all of these efforts, even if thought through, have an *ad hoc* quality.

Milward writes of the possibility that his proposals, if put into practice, would simply lead to the *indigenization* of mainstream law. Critics have argued against the mere substitution of Aboriginal authority for Canadian authority or of Aboriginal people for non-Aboriginal people. These critics claim the effect would simply be to re-inscribe the mainstream common law system onto a purportedly Aboriginal system. A primary objection concerns the question of whether or not the Charter would apply directly to any new Aboriginal systems. Milward recognizes that this issue could emerge, but he argues that there is more to consider. First, he notes that communities can create their own charters that would be more directed towards local values. These could be carefully crafted to reflect not just historical practices but also the current reality on the reserve and the feelings within the band population off reserve. Consider, for example, the conflict between the common law concept of the right to silence and Aboriginal concepts of truth speaking. As Milward writes,

> The possibility of the Charter's application engages a tension between individual rights and Aboriginal justice traditions that emphasizes collective well-being. This tension can be sharp indeed. Some Aboriginal societies had truth-speaking traditions whereby those individuals accused of misconduct were obligated to explain themselves to their Elders. What if an Aboriginal man in a contemporary community accused of wrongdoing invokes the Charter right to silence and therefore informs his Elders that he does not have to speak to them because of the Charter. Does this decision mean that nothing will be done about what the man did? Does it mean that the conflict in the community will remain unresolved? What if he admitted that he did the wrongdoing to the Aboriginal police officers who were employed by the community to keep the peace? What if the officers forgot to inform him of his right to counsel under the Charter? Does this fact mean that there may be evidence concerning the man's responsibility for the crime that will be excluded due to Western notions of limiting the state's power to preserve individual freedom?

Milward argues that one approach is to maintain the right to silence during the police investigation but to make operative the truth-seeking principle "once matters reach adjudication to determine the truth of allegations of criminal misconduct."

What of judicial neutrality? Should justices be members of communities in which they preside? On the surface, this practice would seem to be an insurmountable problem in small communities. Milward deploys the doctrine of necessity as a way out of this dilemma:

> The right to natural justice presents difficulties on account of the doctrine that a judicial authority not be personally connected to any party to the proceedings. The practical effect of this doctrine may be the perpetual disqualification of community court judges given the often closely-knit nature of smaller Aboriginal communities. There is, however, a real need for fairness in criminal proceedings in Aboriginal communities since power dynamics and relationships can be abused to the severe disadvantage of either Aboriginal accuseds or victims. The resolution that is proposed is based on a generous understanding of the doctrine of necessity that can shield community court judges from being perpetually disqualified from

hearing disputes. So long as community court judges are actually being fair in the discharge of their duties, natural justice will not be violated. If the parties have any concerns about a community court judge's fairness, Aboriginal courts of appeal and the requisition of recorded reasons also provide possible safeguards.

Another potential objection to Milward's approach is that Aboriginal communities would be pushed into recreating mainstream legal apparatus, including police, bailiffs, and so on, in order to match up with surrounding non-Aboriginal jurisdictions. This, too, is a valid objection, which Milward carefully considers and reveals how it might be overcome.

However, what might happen following the creation of free-standing community legal systems is not entirely a theoretical question. It is also an empirical one. Consider that Canadian First Nations and other Aboriginal groups have lived historically, and continue to live today, all along the international border with the United States. From the east coast to the west, Mi'kmaq, Anishinabe, Lakota, Cree, Interior Salish, Coast Salish, and Nuu chah nulth, among others, are nations whose members live side by side in Canada and the United States. The communities on the American side have tribal courts that have been scrutinized by various scholars interested in the extent to which they reflect local values, are co-opted by the state, or are engaged in the creation of their own new, non-"traditional" Aboriginal state.

My own studies of the northwest Washington State intertribal court system in the 1990s reveals that the extent to which communities connect to their own historical practice is quite varied but that legal analysis commonly misses the localization of what might be mistaken for mainstream ideas. Indeed, a publication of the American Bar Association considered these courts to be merely inadequate versions of the mainstream system. These Washington State tribal courts arose out of the necessity to manage their salmon harvest, which had been newly regained following treaty litigation in the 1970s, but grew into a wider scope of criminal law. Tribal officials initially downloaded legal boilerplate from a variety of sources in order to gain jurisdiction (which would be absent without tribal code), but they quickly adapted code to their own needs and understandings. They also tailored legal procedure to fit with local historical practices and the expectations of community members.

Interestingly, culturally similar tribes have created quite different tribal code, showing that interpretations of historical practice need not and cannot be understood narrowly. In one instance, a tribe created a code that mandated that abused children be removed from their family and placed under the oversight of the tribal authority. This decision followed from the argument that constituent families are the historical core unit of the larger community and that families sometimes act to protect their collective interests rather than those of individual members. Families sometimes shield the perpetrator rather than protecting the child. A neighbouring tribe, acting on the same understanding of historical social organization, wrote a code that defined family broadly (and in conformity with historical practice) and *restricted* the removal of children from the oversight of the family, so defined. A child might be placed in the custody of someone other than the parents, but he or she must stay within the family. These studies support Milward's contention that the creation of local Aboriginal legal systems need not be understood as merely poor imitations. Still, as Milward notes, others will disagree.

Further, I have argued that when legal systems operate in theory only, an undue emphasis is placed on hypothetical distinctions and abstractions. The northwest intertribal courts, in contrast, have had to deal with the real world of conducting jurisprudence – forcing code writers and tribal authorities to focus on the achievable and on the pragmatic. I spoke once with a tribal council of a recently federally recognized US tribe about their own historical cultural practices as they related to law while they were preparing to establish a tribal court. The councillors were openly concerned, worried, and some were even a bit frightened by the authority they were establishing and the effect this power would have on their own lives and on those of their families and the other constituent families. They sought to deal realistically with problems such as the potential influence on the court by dominant families, which is the sort of issue that Milward considers in his text.

As I have indicated, Milward's project avoids the traps into which so many fall. One is the too easy comparison to restorative justice (as in the case of the community that adopted the Maōri family group conferencing model, a version of restorative justice, as its own). Aboriginal historical practices have features in common with contemporary restorative and transformative justice concepts, but these are not the same. A similar trap in a related field is facile comparisons between the mainstream environmental movement and Aboriginal ideas of the people's place within the land and seascapes. The differences between these positions have been played out in widely noted public conflicts between environmentalists and Aboriginal peoples, but there have been no similar public events concerning justice. The idea that Aboriginal justice is a forerunner of restorative justice persists. There are commonalities, but they are not the same.

There is a paradox here. Aboriginal ideas about justice are thought to both significantly or even entirely overlap with the restorative justice ideas coming from mainstream society (once a pet of Justice Canada), but they are also thought to be entirely distinct from the common law. A recurring feature of many publications about Aboriginal justice is the listing of binary oppositions. These lists suggest that European-derived law is punitive and individualistic – emphasizing the protection of private property, for example – and that Aboriginal law is the opposite. These binaries have slowed down a serious consideration of the relationship between Aboriginal and Canadian systems of justice. And since Aboriginal justice systems arose before any contact with Europeans, they cannot reasonably be thought to be opposites or to have originated in opposition to each other. Milward points out that Aboriginal systems did have punitive practices for the general welfare of the community and that the common law, meanwhile, is not solely punitive.

One highly touted argument for Aboriginal justice systems is the potential for emphasis on healing and spiritual-based practices, as opposed to punitive impersonal common law. Milward wades directly into this debate, although I think his tendency is to support the proposition. He does not sidestep the problems, though. Emma Laroque, Sherene Razack, and others have raised concerns about the emphasis on healing in cases of sexual assault. They write that this emphasis trivializes the harm and signals to offenders that the consequences of their actions for themselves will be minimal. Milward adds to this idea that healing might not be possible if the defence acts to have evidence excluded or if a harsh cross-examination of witnesses occurs.

I have my own concerns about claims of healing in justice systems that have been partial (such as sentencing circles), underfunded, and short-lived. In these cases, the justice system lacks the social and financial capital to undertake the long and difficult task of healing. There is less cause for concern with fully established systems that have a chance to gain legitimacy within the communities they service. However, this will not happen unless the programs are able to withstand the sources of abuse of justice. An important feature of Milward's proposals is that they offer insight into the most pressing questions facing present-day Aboriginal communities and how justice systems might address these issues. He mentions, in particular, violence against women and the domination of council and the justice system by large families and community elite. Justice systems that are able to exist under these stresses would, I think, very likely gain legitimacy among community members. As has been widely documented, Aboriginal peoples of Canada have considerable distrust of the Canadian legal machinery, including police, courts, and justices. There are sound reasons for this distrust. And although one outcome of the colonial experience has been the distrust of members' own community band council and administration, the addition of a free-standing justice system will be central to establishing the totality of institutions. Evidence from US tribal courts suggests that these institutions can gain acceptance internally. The development of a full set of community-directed institutions, including justice, may be a step towards overcoming members' alienation.

There are several possible reasons put forward to explain the limited attention given to the possibility of establishing band justice systems. Justice Department officials have suggested to me that Canada is too large, and the bands too small, for an efficient delivery of legal services. Attention has been turned elsewhere, with concerns for the residential school abuse now taking centre stage within a Truth and Reconciliation Commission. Community leaders are directing their efforts to the creation of sustainable economic development. And public attention – and the attention of Aboriginal leaders – has focused on a whole cluster of other urgent concerns, including what to do about various proposed oil pipeline projects intended to cut directly through First Nations lands. The failure of Canada to assist in establishing safe and reliable water supplies on northern reserves continues to be a national embarrassment, as is the suicide rate on some reserves, and the public and sometimes violent clashes over the ownership of land in Caledonia, Ontario, and elsewhere. In British Columbia, the disappearance of some six hundred Aboriginal women from the streets of Vancouver and the highways heading north remains an open wound. Meanwhile, the refusal of the Missing Women Commission of Inquiry and society at large to take seriously the systemic racism so obviously at the core of this problem has led grassroots activists such as Gladys Radek to organize mass protest marches to Ottawa. These issues, and many more, including the slow grinding of land claims through the federal and provincial courts, has absorbed the strength of a generation of leaders and the community members trained as lawyers.

Milward is not distracted. He calls for a greater financial, legal, and political commitment than Canada has heretofore demonstrated through the current creation of underfunded projects that have led to incomplete social institutions and a pilot-project mentality. There is now a considerable history of projects that have failed to gain the support of community members. I must add that, to a very considerable degree, the Canadian experiments in Aboriginal justice have failed precisely because of the timidity I previously mentioned. Since they are partial, they fail to provide adequate protection for community members, who rightly look askance. Of particular concern is the fear that female community members have experienced regarding their own community's new programs. In one instance in British Columbia, a pilot justice project collapsed because rape victims were put into the hands of elders serving as counsellors who were family members of the perpetrator. In this case, there was an inadequate understanding of the exercise of power and of the social organization of the community by those engaged in the creation of the program. And on the north shore of Greater Vancouver, women of the Squamish First Nation have publicly and loudly protested what they regard as gendered bias in access to community housing. They have expressed their notion that there should be a retrenchment – a retreat from the development of community self-governance infrastructure when it creates vulnerability.

David Milward gives central place to his concerns about the possibility of rank and file community members being dominated by an elite and of women being exploited by men. He expresses the view that this is a clear danger in Canadian Aboriginal communities, and he points to specific ways to deal with these problems while developing justice systems. A problem has been, to my mind, that Canadian justice initiatives have stopped midstream, at just the wrong place, which, as the Squamish women have said, will leave people in jeopardy. Rather than retreating from the institutional development of Aboriginal communities, Milward suggests a move forward, to building justice institutions that might be able to protect the interests of community members from their own elite, from predatory men, or from any other individual, group, or faction. He raises the question of domestic violence against women and shows how women's concerns can be addressed by an Aboriginal justice system.

It does not seem to be fully clear to Canadian justice authorities that there is utility in participating in the development of self-directed Aboriginal justice or, at least, in standing aside while this happens. For some years now, representatives of the Canadian government have claimed that Aboriginal ideas of justice would be helpful in transforming the beleaguered mainstream system. They have primarily meant the application of Aboriginal concepts to restorative justice projects. The neo-colonial Canadian state and many citizens within it remain fearful of Aboriginal people and their institutions, while simultaneously being fascinated. In British Columbia, fear of Aboriginal self-government has slowed the modern-day treaty process. Similarly, fear and misunderstanding stands in the way of Aboriginal justice. *Aboriginal Justice and the Charter* shows how a much bigger step may be contemplated and taken.

Bruce Granville Miller
Department of Anthropology, University of British Columbia

Acknowledgments

Special thanks go to Gordon Christie, Michael Jackson, Douglas Harris, Bruce Miller, Darlene Johnston, Ted Palys, and Joanne Archibald for their invaluable feedback on earlier versions of the manuscript. The author also wishes to thank Renisa Mewani and June McCue for their valuable input in the process of researching this book. Special thanks also go to the peer reviewers for helping the manuscript become the very best that it could be. Special thanks also go to the editors of UBC Press – Randy Schmidt in particular – for their hard and patient work in bringing this book to fruition.

The author also wishes to thank his family, both immediate and extended, for all their love and support over the years, especially his parents, Leo and Mary.

Aboriginal Justice and the Charter

1
Introduction

By way of introduction, I am of Cree descent and a member of the Beardy's and Okemasis First Nation in Saskatchewan. When I first entered law school, my hope was to become a lawyer fighting for Aboriginal rights, such as the fight for land reclamation, the honest recognition of treaties, our constitutional rights, and all the rest of it. But then my first year of legal studies showed me a new path. For reasons that I still cannot quite put my finger on, first-year criminal law quickly became my favourite course. Furthermore, as I was growing up, I had lived in an urban Aboriginal community in Calgary, where many of the issues that I discuss in this book were affecting the lives of those people around me, many of my friends included. Some of my old friends I have lost to suicide, others have taken their turns in the prison system, and one was even designated as a dangerous offender deemed fit for indeterminate detention. These two realities suddenly coalesced into a new career objective. I wanted to become a defence lawyer helping my people defend themselves against the Canadian justice system. My pursuit of this career objective, however, encountered a hitch when a difference of opinion between a provincial law society and my first legal employers escalated needlessly, in my honest opinion, and I became part of the collateral damage.

Initially, my subsequent pursuit of graduate legal studies was simply a way to try and get back into the legal profession after I had fallen on some hard times. My subsequent success, coupled with encouragement from my master's degree supervisor, Catherine Bell, however, convinced me that I could join the legal academy and that I had plenty to talk about. In the course of my studies, I began to contemplate in earnest some sincere questions about the interaction of Aboriginal peoples with the Canadian criminal justice system. In particular, my thoughts were directed to the question of how the Canadian Charter of Rights and Freedoms might apply to Aboriginal justice systems.[1] And so the seeds were sown for the focus of my graduate studies, of which this book is an end product.

The subject of the book is self-determination for Aboriginal peoples over criminal justice, an idea that has been around for decades. Self-determination as an abstract concept sounds simple enough: "The principle of self-determination refers to the right of a people to determine its own political destiny."[2] The principle is also recognized under international human rights law. The United Nations' *International Covenant on Economic, Social and Cultural Rights* states: "All peoples have the right of self-determination. By virtue of that right they freely determine their political status and freely pursue their economic, social and cultural development."[3] The right of Aboriginal peoples to self-determination is also recognized in international law. For example, the *Declaration of the Rights of Indigenous Peoples* reads in part:

> Recognizing the urgent need to respect and promote the inherent rights and characteristics of indigenous peoples, especially their rights to their lands, territories and resources, which derive from their political, economic and social structures and from their cultures, spiritual traditions, histories and philosophies ...
> Convinced that control by indigenous peoples over developments affecting them and their lands, territories and resources will enable them to maintain and strengthen their institutions, cultures and traditions, and to promote their development in accordance with their aspirations and needs.[4]

The idea of self-determination seems fairly straightforward or at least straightforward enough that it can be enshrined in international legal instruments. An issue that is a good deal more complex is the realization of Aboriginal self-determination within a domestic jurisdiction such as Canada, where Aboriginal peoples remain a clear minority that lacks economic or political power and whose members are often interspersed among non-Aboriginal Canadians within both rural and urban settings. It should therefore not be surprising, given the complexity of the Canadian situation, that the subject of Aboriginal self-determination in Canada has generated a good deal of academic debate. Aboriginal scholars such as Taiaiake Alfred and Jeff Corntassel have argued that arrangements that involve working within a state framework do not truly amount to self-determination, are recipes for continued colonialism, and are not conducive to revitalizing Aboriginal cultures and dealing with the social problems faced by Aboriginal peoples.[5] Some non-Aboriginal scholars such as Alan Cairns and Thomas Flanagan have vigorously argued against Aboriginal self-determination.[6] Their arguments suggest that it is impractical for Aboriginal peoples to carve out separate political entities within Western democracies, that it would be destabilizing for existing social orders, and that self-determination is not required for dealing with Aboriginal social problems. Then there are Aboriginal scholars who may be thought of as taking positions that can be situated somewhere in between. Dale Turner and John Borrows have argued for visions of self-determination that do not altogether eschew participation within, or harmonization with, a Canadian state framework but still involve Aboriginal peoples' attaining considerably more control over their institutions, governance arrangements, and law than they now have.[7] It is not my intention to participate in this debate, at least not directly, although I think that much of what I will propose in this book falls into the "in between" camp.

Of course, Aboriginal demands for self-determination include demands for greater control over criminal justice for a number of reasons.[8] An important background is that the current criminal justice system, with its heavy reliance on incarceration, has resulted in the drastic over-incarceration of Aboriginal peoples in Canada – a problem that has been well documented and studied for at least the past two decades.[9] A recent statistical analysis reveals that Aboriginal persons have consistently comprised 17-19 percent of all adult admissions to Canadian federal penitentiaries for the past decade, even though Aboriginal peoples represent only 3.8 percent of the Canadian population.[10] The statistics are even more appalling when it comes to admission to provincial jails. In 2007-08, Aboriginal persons comprised 21 percent of all admissions to provincial jails in Newfoundland and British Columbia, 35 percent in Alberta, 69 percent in Manitoba, 76 percent in Yukon, 81 percent in Saskatchewan, and 86 percent in Northwest Territories.[11] These large percentages persist despite the fact that Aboriginal peoples are clearly a small minority, constituting 3.8 percent of Canada's population as of 2006.[12] The notion of using contemporary adaptations of past Aboriginal justice practices with parallels to restorative justice as more constructive alternatives to incarceration is an important impetus behind Aboriginal demands for greater control over justice. It has therefore not been surprising that much of the literature in the field has focused on this theme, holding up visions of Aboriginal justice as an ideal that is yet to be realized. It is not to say that the topics that get emphasized are unimportant, far from it. My point is that it may have had an unfortunate consequence in that other important aspects of Aboriginal justice that need to be explored have been left relatively neglected. For example, how is Aboriginal self-determination over justice going to work if we actually succeed in achieving it? How can it be implemented? Can it play out on the ground in such a way that it eventually accomplishes its stated goals?

There is one particular question surrounding the future of Aboriginal justice that I focus on in this work. What happens when interested parties insist on applying the Canadian Charter of Rights and Freedoms to Aboriginal justice systems? This question has been raised before but very often in a hypothetical framework and without anything resembling a concrete and earnest search for tangible solutions.[13] The possibility of the Charter's application engages a tension between individual rights and Aboriginal justice traditions that emphasize collective well-being. This tension can be sharp indeed. Some Aboriginal societies had truth-speaking traditions whereby those individuals accused of misconduct were obligated to explain themselves to their Elders. What if an Aboriginal man accused of wrongdoing in a contemporary community invokes the Charter right to silence and therefore informs his Elders that he does not have to speak to them because of the Charter. Does this decision mean that nothing will be done about what the man did? Does it mean that the conflict in the community will remain unresolved? What if he admitted that he did the wrongdoing to the Aboriginal police officers who were employed by the community to keep the peace? What if the officers forgot to inform him of his right to counsel under the Charter? Would this mean that there may be evidence concerning the man's responsibility for the crime that would be excluded due to Western notions of limiting the state's power in order to preserve individual freedom? Would it mean that nothing would be done about what happened? Clearly, the possibilities can be alarming for an Aboriginal community that wants to revive past methods of justice for contemporary use in order to remedy the social problems associated with Aboriginal criminality and over-incarceration.

There are also concerns surrounding what may happen if there is no individual rights regime to regulate the exercise of Aboriginal self-determination. The old ways of proving oneself as a worthy leader in Aboriginal communities have been eroded to a large degree. People often become leaders in Aboriginal communities nowadays by mimicking the ways of Canadian leaders. Members of contemporary communities often compete with each other for power and money. Will those individuals in power, including those involved in the justice system, abuse their advantages to the detriment of the people they are supposed to be serving? What does this possibility mean for resolving conflicts in the community? Does it mean that innocent people will be persecuted by being punished for things they never did? Does it mean that the powerful can use law enforcement authorities to intimidate community members? Will it leave vulnerable people, such as women and children, unsafe in their own communities? Maybe the Charter will be helpful after all if it can prevent these abuses from happening. However, using the Charter in the first place brings us back to the original concerns about applying the Charter to Aboriginal justice. The tension is palpable. How is it to be addressed?

In 1996, the Royal Commission on Aboriginal Peoples published a number of reports that considered various solutions for the problem of strained relationships between Aboriginal peoples and the Canadian state. One such report, *Bridging the Cultural Divide,* focused on Aboriginal justice issues.[14] The report explores a broad array of issues, including the tension involved in applying the Charter to Aboriginal justice systems. The report suggested

addressing this tension by using the concept of a culturally sensitive interpretation of legal rights, which essentially means reinterpreting legal rights
under the Charter to better reflect Aboriginal justice traditions while still
leaving in place meaningful safeguards against the abuse of collective power.
The report did offer a few brief suggestions about how the culturally sensitive interpretation of legal rights could work, but it did not purport to engage
in any in-depth search for specific proposals. The field of Aboriginal justice
has since returned to its near exclusive focus on sentencing initiatives and
parallels to restorative justice. This book strives to pick up where *Bridging
the Cultural Divide* left off. It puts culturally sensitive interpretation into
action by exploring specific proposals with reference to a number of specific
rights in the Charter.

This exercise will by its very nature engage in a sort of legal syncretism.
Some of the proposals reached as a part of this exercise will resemble features of common law systems. For example, I will suggest that Aboriginal
communities can design their own court systems in a culturally sensitive
manner. The judge's role would for the most part be restricted to ensuring
that the participants do not behave in a coercive or exploitative fashion,
thus addressing recent critiques that have been directed against restorative
justice and Aboriginal justice initiatives alike. Judges, however, would not
interfere with the parties' resolution, so long as they had participated in the
process fairly and had reached a genuine consensus on a resolution. The
law of the Aboriginal community – not Canadian criminal law – would
thus govern disputes. I will also suggest that cultural perspectives can be
incorporated whenever Aboriginal police forces need to engage in warrantless searches for evidence. This is partly what I meant when I said that I did
not intend to directly participate in the debate on what Aboriginal self-
determination means or on what its nature should be. These proposals may
very well be dismissed by Alfred and others as mere Indigenization, not truly
amounting to self-determination. There is, however, no single vision of
self-determination, as the work of Aboriginal scholars such as Borrows and
Turner suggests. My view is that the pursuit of a culturally sensitive interpretation of legal rights, and the proposals that are explored in this book,
can be situated somewhere between the visions of Alfred and Flanagan.

And, indeed, other proposals may also be quite controversial from a
Canadian legal standpoint. For example, I suggest that the right to silence
need only be applicable during the stage of police investigation. Truth-
speaking traditions can become operative once matters reach adjudication
in order to determine the truth of allegations of criminal misconduct, civil
libertarian objections notwithstanding. Another suggestion involves
Aboriginal communities' using judicial corporal punishment in instances
where restorative resolutions are deemed inappropriate and as a punitive

sanction that avoids the worsening effects of incarceration. The Charter bars corporal punishment as a cruel and inhumane punishment. I will argue that an Aboriginal accused can undergo corporal punishment on the basis of a full and informed waiver of the right against cruel and unusual punishment.

Before I begin the discussion in earnest, there is an issue about my methodology that I need to address. A reader with any degree of academic proficiency will notice that I rely on secondary research instead of primary research, which in this context means collecting first-hand opinions on justice from Aboriginal peoples themselves in order to articulate Aboriginal visions of justice. There are a number of reasons for this reliance. The first one is an honest recognition of my own limitations. As a lawyer, I was trained to interview clients in anticipation of a court case. I do not, however, have the training of an anthropologist, or an ethnohistorian, to seek out primary accounts of Aboriginal justice both past and present. Second, there are plenty of good secondary sources by experts who have already made this effort and spoken with Aboriginal peoples about their approaches to justice. I submit that these examples can blur the line between secondary and primary sources as secondary representations of primary information. It is my sincere hope that these representations faithfully recount how some Aboriginal peoples have envisioned and practised justice and, therefore, that they provide a meaningful basis for me to proceed with my own discussions. Third, I have a certain personal knowledge of Aboriginal spirituality, culture, and justice, through my own lifetime spent within my community. At the same time, I am not an Elder or a carrier of oral history. My preference whenever possible has been to rely on sources from experts with better experience and qualifications than myself who have gone out and spoken directly with Aboriginal peoples. Fourth, even if I had conducted primary research, there is always the risk that I may not have ended up getting the kind of content that I was hoping for. This last point will be demonstrated when I describe towards the end of this book the efforts made by John Borrows, Alfred Scow, and DeLloyd Guth to conduct their own primary research. After I had reviewed the available secondary literature, I concluded that there was enough material available to enable a meaningful discussion of the issues raised in this book.

As a final note, I would like to advise the reader that I am not claiming to be setting out what justice has to look like for all Aboriginal communities. My purpose has simply been to spur some much needed discussion on issues that will have to be addressed in the future. Now I will begin by providing some background, by flushing out the differences between various models of justice in order to articulate Aboriginal visions of justice.

2
Aboriginal Aspirations for Justice

The discussions in this chapter will animate much of the remainder of this work. It is my intention in this chapter to provide an overview of Aboriginal demands for self-determination over criminal justice and of what many in Aboriginal communities hope to accomplish through greater control over justice. This background canvasses the contrasts and similarities between what we know about past Aboriginal justice practices, restorative justice, and Western approaches to justice with adversarial and punitive emphases. There are reasons for providing this background. Restorative justice is often presented as being a more constructive approach to dealing with crime than adversarial and punitive approaches. This perception provides considerable impetus behind Aboriginal demands for jurisdiction over justice as Aboriginal communities often portray their own justice practices, many of which parallel restorative justice, as effective alternatives. This theme will resonate throughout this book. It is not to say that such pursuits are above criticism. There are indeed many criticisms against restorative justice and Aboriginal justice initiatives, and these critiques will be covered later on in the book, especially in Chapter 6. The intention for now is to present Aboriginal aspirations with respect to justice as an ideal. The possible contemporary significance of Aboriginal justice practices with distinctly punitive emphases will also be explored. An explanation of Western approaches to justice and the rationale behind them follows in the next section.

Western Approaches to Justice
Traditional Western models of justice are often characterized by at least two emphases, the use of punitive sanctions to address crime and the use of adversarial procedures to resolve disputes. The discussion begins with the first emphasis. Western justice systems make frequent use of punitive sanctions such as incarceration to address criminal behaviour. To be fair, incarceration is often reserved for more serious offences or for particularly recidivist

offenders. Western justice systems also use other measures such as probation and fines, but even these sanctions are classified as punishments.[1]

There are several justifications for punishing crime, and they are not necessarily consistent with each other. One justification is deterrence. Deterrence as an objective can be subdivided into two different types of deterrence. Specific deterrence focuses on the individual offender who has committed a crime. It is meant to communicate to the offender the fact that the punishment is a direct consequence of the crime, and therefore it seeks to dissuade the offender against committing further crimes. General deterrence uses the punishment of an individual offender to send a message to society at large. The offender's punishment is used to dissuade other members of society from committing the same crime. Both general and specific deterrence strive to protect society by threatening punishment in order to dissuade against future crime.

Another justification is known as the "just deserts" theory of punishment. An offender has caused harm by committing a crime, and so retributive pain must be inflicted upon the offender in proportion to the moral gravity of the crime. There is a well-known theoretical tension between deterrent and retributive justifications of punishment. Deterrence has a utilitarian emphasis. Punishment should be enough to deter the offender, or other members of society, from repeating the crime. Punishment should not exceed what is necessary to achieve the social net gain of decreasing crime. Retribution as an end in itself has the potential to inflict more punishment than is necessary or less than what is required. Just deserts theories emphasize the moral agency and rationality of the offender. Since the offender chose to engage in harmful behaviour, retribution must be inflicted upon the offender in proportion to the moral gravity of the crime. Therefore, utilitarian theories wrongly use the offender as a means to a social end and end up denying the autonomy and rationality of the offender as a moral agent.[2] Theodore Blumoff argues that in light of this tension, the goal of articulating and sustaining an intrinsically consistent theory of punishment is ultimately unattainable.[3] Both of these sentencing justifications, despite their theoretical inconsistency, are present in section 718 and section 718.1 of the *Criminal Code,* which read:

> 718. The fundamental purpose of sentencing is to contribute, along with crime prevention initiatives, to respect for the law and the maintenance of a just, peaceful and safe society by imposing just sanctions that have one or more of the following objectives:
>
> a) to denounce unlawful conduct;
> b) to deter the offender and others from committing offences;
> c) to separate offenders from society, where necessary;
> d) to assist in rehabilitating offenders;

e) to provide reparations for harm done to the victim or the community; and

f) to promote a sense of responsibility in offenders, and acknowledgement of the harms done to victims and the community.

718.1. A sentence must be proportionate to the gravity of the offence and the degree of responsibility of the offender.[4]

One can see in section 718(b) the utilitarian objective of deterrence. One can also see in section 718(a) and section 718.1 reflections of the just deserts theory. Keep in mind also that rehabilitation is also a sentencing objective in this provision, which is indeed a primary goal of restorative justice. However, it will be seen that a point that many restorative justice proponents make is that rehabilitation is frequently in competition with other sentencing goals such as deterrence and retribution. Their point of contention is that the goals of deterrence and retribution are prioritized reflexively and routinely for far too many offences and for far too many offenders, where perhaps the legal system should be giving greater consideration to rehabilitative possibilities.[5]

In section 718(c), there is a third justification that is specific to incarceration, the incapacitation of the offender. The public is protected against further harm from the offender by forcibly confining the offender. It is motivated by the same concern as deterrence. Deterrence, however, is premised on the idea that the offender and other members of society can be dissuaded against future misconduct. The incapacitation rationale in section 718(c) is conceptually different in that it deems that the offender will not respond to the message of deterrence, at least not for the time being, and therefore physical separation becomes necessary. It is not to say that both rationales cannot inform the same sentence handed out for an offender. Incapacitation may protect society through physical separation in the interim. The term of imprisonment, during its duration and upon its expiry, hopefully triggers specific deterrence by communicating to the offender that the punishment is occurring, and has occurred, for the misconduct. In summary, Western justice systems respond to crime with punitive sanctions that can be motivated by a number of objectives that are not necessarily consistent with each other.

The second emphasis of Western justice systems is their reliance on adversarial procedures, which require an impartial adjudicator to decide the issues of culpability and punishment. Each party to a prosecution competes with the other party through various means such as giving evidence in support of their cases, cross-examining adverse witnesses, and making legal and factual arguments to persuade the judge that its position is the correct one. The accused is usually represented by a defence lawyer, while the state is usually represented by a public prosecutor. The judge then renders a decision based upon the evidence presented and the arguments that have been made after both parties have had a fair chance to present their cases.[6] Adversarial procedures apply to either a trial to determine guilt or innocence or to a sentencing hearing, which is subject to the parties' reaching a suggested agreement (for example, a plea bargain). An overview of restorative justice as it applies to criminal conflicts will now be provided, along with comparisons to Aboriginal approaches to justice.

Restorative Justice and Comparisons to Aboriginal Justice

As of yet, there is not a universally accepted definition of restorative justice. What follows thus is a summary of the essential features of restorative justice. Restorative justice envisions a horizontal process whereby persons with a stake in a conflict negotiate a resolution, unlike the adversarial system whereby a judge imposes the resolution (vertical decision making). Those "persons with a stake in a conflict" are not restricted to the parties involved directly in the legal matter should the dispute proceed to adversarial court. That group can include a wider circle of persons who have been affected, even indirectly, by the conflict.[7]

In the adversarial justice system, the interests of the victim are collapsed into the state's interests in prosecuting crime. The prosecutor speaks to the harm done to the victim before an adversarial court. This process has been criticized as deflecting attention away from the fact that in many crimes it is the individual victim, and not the state or society at large, that has suffered tangible harm and has a legitimate interest in obtaining redress from the offender.[8] The horizontal emphasis of restorative justice provides the victim with an opportunity to participate directly in the process. A restorative resolution will ideally include the victim's agreement and will satisfactorily address the victim's interests such as personal safety and their healing from any traumas.[9]

One reason that Aboriginal justice is often likened to restorative justice is that many Aboriginal societies in the past have held councils to negotiate resolutions to conflicts. Typically, these councils have involved the presentation of material gifts to the victim, or the victim's kin, as reparation for the offence. These gifts were often accompanied by apologies or acknowledgments of responsibility. The acceptance of the gifts signified the resolution of the conflict and the restoration of community harmony. This practice is known to have occurred among the Cree,[10] the Anishinabe,[11] the Navajo,[12] the Dene,[13] the Twanas, the Clallams, the Puyallups, the Nisquallys,[14] the Mi'kmaq in New Brunswick,[15] the Coast Salish in British Columbia,[16] and the Iroquois.[17]

A key goal of restorative justice is repairing relationships and furthering harmony between those affected by the conflict.[18] An integral part of this emphasis on relationship reparation is the reintegration of the offender back into the community as he corrects his behaviour and strengthens his relationships with those around him and with those he has affected with his behaviour. John Braithwaite and Stephen Mugford hold that there is more than one facet to reintegration. One facet emphasizes the role of community members who provide support and encouragement to the offender as he reforms. Another facet, and one that is not necessarily incompatible with the other facet, is that those who have been adversely affected confront the offender so that he understands the gravity of his actions and develops motivation to change.[19] Restorative justice pursues a resolution that aims to facilitate this reintegration. Restorative resolutions therefore often emphasize alternatives to incarceration, such as requiring the offender to perform community service, make restitution to the victim, and participate in counselling programs to address problems such as substance abuse or anger management.[20]

The ceremonial feasts of the Lake Babine people, called *balhats*, combined several themes that parallel restorative justice. First, the aggrieved party had to present gifts to the offending party along with a declaration of what the offender had done wrong. The challenge was for the offending party to provide reparation to the aggrieved party in the form of material wealth with interest. The reparation was accompanied by a public affirmation of proper and expected behaviour and a final recounting of the infraction after which it was never to be mentioned again. These elements blended together to mark reconciliation and an end to the conflict. The ultimate goal was the strengthening of social relationships within the community.[21]

There are parallels between Aboriginal conflict resolution and restorative justice. Both emphasize reparation with the aggrieved party and improved relationships in the community. Both restorative justice and Aboriginal justice are presented as more constructive alternatives to dealing with crime, and this perspective, in turn, has fuelled a number of criticisms against traditional Western approaches to crime. The discussion will now examine in detail those criticisms and will consider, where appropriate, their relevance to Aboriginal peoples.

Criticisms against Western Punitive Approaches

Deterrence Unrealized

Restorative justice proponents frequently claim that faith in the threat of imprisonment to deter crime is misguided.[22] Classical theory holds that the effectiveness of deterrence rests on three essential components: the certainty that a punishment will be assessed as a consequence of committing a crime, the swiftness with which the punishment will be assessed afterwards, and the severity of the punishment itself.[23] The efficacy of each of these components has been called into question. Some scholars argue that there is a profound lack of empirical evidence to support any claim that increasing the severity of sentences will enhance general deterrence.[24] The small amount of research that has been done to assess the effects of sentence severity on general deterrence has not demonstrated a correlative relationship between the two.[25] Other research has also failed to demonstrate that the deterrent effects of incarceration are greater than those of noncarceral sentences.[26] It has also been frequently argued that the prospect of jail will often have no deterrent value for certain persons. These include people in disadvantaged circumstances who lack legitimate opportunities and therefore have little if anything to lose by committing crimes and those who are socialized into, and whose livelihoods depend on, criminal lifestyles.[27] Criminal sanctions may also lack deterrent effect on those who act out impulsively or in a moment of inflamed emotions [28] or on those who determine that they can commit crimes without getting caught.[29] Deterrence may also decrease for some people who envision and desire tangible benefits for themselves from committing crime (for example, money).[30]

It is not to say that deterrence is entirely a hollow shell. Some studies show that it is the certainty that and swiftness with which something will be meted out to a criminal as a consequence of committing an act, rather than the particular severity of that something (for example, the length of the prison term), that has any real deterrent value.[31] Silvia Mendes qualifies this notion to an extent. She suggests that the something still has to be at least significant if certainty and swiftness are to truly realize any deterrent potential. Otherwise, the mere fact of a certain and swift arrest, without a meaningful sanction, will not have much persuasive value for prospective criminals.[32] Be that as it may, the deterrent value provided by certainty and swiftness may be reduced in some contexts. Some studies have shown that certainty and swiftness may have little impact on substance abuse crimes.[33] Certainty and swiftness may lose deterrence for repeat offenders[34] and certainly for repeat drug offenders.[35] Negative peer associations can undermine the deterrent value of certainty and swiftness, either because those peer associations can encourage criminal behaviour or because knowledge that social peers have committed crimes and gotten away with them can encourage a risk assessment that optimistically minimizes the fear of getting caught and convicted.[36] A study by Alex Heckert and Edward Gondolf concludes that neither severity nor certainty was sufficient to deter domestic batterers from reoffending.[37] Critics suggest not only that the deterrent value of imprisonment is questionable but also that imprisonment makes matters worse.

Makes the Offender Worse

David Cayley argues that prison life involves harsh conditions that harden inmates. Placing a convict among other convicts creates conditions whereby a convict has to harden himself, and be willing to commit violent acts without hesitation, in order to survive and convince the other convicts to leave him alone. Prisons have counter-cultures in which the conventional rules of society are turned upside down. Defiance, lack of respect for authority, and violent behaviour become the norms. Once a person has done enough time, the painful effects of being separated from society wear off. Convicts frequently become acculturated and habituated into prison life such that they are unable to adapt to life outside of prison and even prefer to remain behind bars.[38] This outcome has been verified to some degree by empirical studies that have demonstrated that in comparison with a suspended sentence, imprisonment increases the probability of offender recidivism,[39] even for those offenders who previously had a high stake in conforming to societal norms and avoiding arrest.[40] Stuart Kinner and M.J. Milloy add: "Although complete data on recidivism in Canada are not publicly available, studies suggest that the majority of ex-prisoners reoffend, typically within two years. Illicit drug use is a key, modifiable risk factor for recidivism."[41]

The worsening effect has also been observed among Aboriginal inmates, at least in an anecdotal sense, if not in an empirical sense. Rupert Ross describes one of his personal conversations this way:

> In that regard, I remember an Aboriginal woman at a justice conference complaining about the use of jail. She felt that jail was a place where offenders only learned to be more defiant of others, more self-centred, short-sighted and untrusting. Further, because they had so many daily decisions taken away from them, she felt that their capacity for responsible decision making was actually diminished, not strengthened.[42]

Judge Heino Lilles states:

> Jail has been shown not to be effective for First Nation people. Every family in Kwanlin Dun [Yukon] has members who have gone to jail. *It carries no stigma and therefore is not a deterrent. Nor is it a "safe place" which encourages disclosure, openness, or healing.* The power or authority structures within the jail operate against "openness." An Elder noted: "jail doesn't help anyone. A lot of our people could have been healed a long time ago if it weren't for jail. Jail hurts them more and then they come out really bitter. In jail, all they learn is "hurt and bitter."[43]

Jail does temporarily assure public safety by separating the offender from society for the duration of the prison term. Mark Carter states: "The benefits of incapacitation, such as they are, are the only guarantees."[44] The problem is that those terms are usually temporary. There remains the potential danger that the offender has been worsened by the experience of imprisonment after release, with significant probabilities for reoffending.[45] Jo-Anne Fiske and Betty Patrick argue that incarceration can "aggravate rather than allevi-ate" social tensions in small Aboriginal communities. Their consultations with members of the Lake Babine Nation in British Columbia led them to believe that imprisoning violent or sexual offenders can leave community offenders feeling unsafe after the offenders are released.[46]

Prisons are also some of the best recruiting grounds for street gangs.[47] This is a phenomenon that is particularly worrisome for Aboriginal peoples. Many Aboriginal criminals are already members of existing Aboriginal gangs or are prime candidates for recruitment when they are incarcerated.[48] The Criminal Intelligence Service of Canada describes the origins of Aboriginal gangs as follows:

> In Alberta, Aboriginal-based gangs that once existed primarily in prisons for protection purposes have now recognized the financial benefit of trafficking hard drugs (for example, cocaine) on reserves. Many of the gangs have ready access to weapons, including firearms, that has resulted in a number of incidents of violence.[49]

Mark Totten estimates that "twenty-two percent of known gang members are Aboriginal, and that there are between 800-1,000 active Aboriginal gang members in the Prairie provinces."[50] He argues that sending Aboriginal youth to prison will only entrench them further into criminal lifestyles, precisely because of prison gang structures.[51]

Mere Political Gesture
Another argument is that reliance on imprisonment does not involve any rational consideration of whether it actually works but, rather, demonstrates an effort to score political points with a public that fears the spread of crime and wants the assurance of safety.[52] Cayley provides an example of this perception. Douglas Hurd, a minister in Margaret Thatcher's government, commenced a policy starting in 1987 that emphasized restraint in the use of prison and encouraged the use of community-based alternatives. This policy led to a dramatic decrease in the British prison population, while those of Canada and the United States were increasing just as dramatically. It was carried out administratively, well away from the public eye. However, things changed after the notorious kidnapping and murder of two-year-old Jamie Bulger by two pre-adolescent boys. Hurd's legislative reforms were repealed in favour of a "tough on crime" policy. The British prison popula-tion skyrocketed afterwards. Penal policy went from being a quiet adminis-trative exercise to a highly political commodity.[53] Cayley also views American "get tough on crime" and "war on drugs" policies in a similar light.[54] He

asserts that such policies represent efforts to score political points with the public by showing that "something has been done" but that lawmakers do not rationally consider whether such a policy effectively reduces crime.[55] Justice E.D. Bayda also condemns such policies as "politicians pandering to public fears and stereotypes in order to get re-elected."[56] The reason that "something has been done" is misguided is that it does not get to the bottom of why crime occurs in the first place.

The Root Causes of Crime

A common criticism against a reliance on imprisonment is that it fails to address the underlying causes of criminal behaviour. There is a plethora of literature in fields such as criminology and sociology that argues that social conditions in a community have a strong role in the probabilities of crime among its members. Growing up in an abusive home environment increases the chances of children, and adolescents, later becoming involved in lives of crime, including violent offences and drug-related offences.[57] When male children witness the abuse of their mothers in the home, it significantly increases their chances of becoming intimate abusers later in life, both of their partners[58] as well as of their children.[59] Being at risk for mental health problems stemming from abuse while young also increases the risk for involvement with the criminal justice system.[60]

Many studies have found a correlation between community poverty and higher crime rates.[61] This link is apparently true even for the most serious of offences, including homicide offences.[62] Poverty and lack of employment opportunities have also been found to have a positive correlative relationship with gang membership.[63] Lack of education also increases the chances of falling into a life of crime.[64] Conversely, greater education and literacy decrease the chances of young persons getting caught up in criminal lifestyles.[65] Poverty also increases domestic violence because it leaves battered women with fewer resources to obtain independence from abusive partners.[66]

There are other social contributors as well. Hard drug use has also been found to increase the chances of involvement with the justice system[67] as well as propensities towards violent crime.[68] Having experienced racial discrimination has also been found to increase involvement with crimes of violence.[69] These problems can be multi-layered. A study by Carter Hay and others argues that community poverty exacerbates the effects that an unstable family environment can have on the level of crime.[70] Preeti Chauhan and N. Dickon Reppucci's study asserts that poverty, coupled with the exposure to violence while young, whether its growing up in an abusive environment or witnessing it first-hand, can increase one's propensity towards juvenile violence.[71] Poverty has been found to increase the probability of substance abuse, and both poverty and substance abuse, in turn, increase the probability of criminal behaviour.[72]

A fact of Canadian history is that its Aboriginal peoples were subjected to harmful processes of colonization, which included military conquest,[73] the acquisition of Aboriginal land bases through treaties,[74] and policies of assimilation that attempted to force Aboriginal peoples to abandon their own cultures in favour of Euro-Canadian lifestyles by criminalizing cultural activities such as the potlatch.[75] An especially harmful part of the history of colonization was the forcing of Aboriginal children to attend residential schools.[76] Many were physically and sexually abused and, thus, passed this intergenerational trauma on to their descendants.[77] Many were forced to abandon their languages and cultures. Many left school not having acquired the skills or education to gain meaningful employment, thus contributing, along with economic colonialism and ongoing workplace discrimination, to the impoverishment of Aboriginal communities.[78] What colonialism against Aboriginal peoples has done has been to introduce the previously mentioned social contributors to crime into Aboriginal communities and to ensure that these factors have persisted as an enduring legacy generation after generation.

Annie Yessine and James Bonta's study, which is based on a comparison of Aboriginal and non-Aboriginal youth under probation in Manitoba, argues that Aboriginal youth are incarcerated far out of proportion to their representation in the population because they come from disadvantaged social backgrounds that involve poverty, unstable family settings, and negative peer associations (for example, youth gangs).[79] In his study, James Waldram interviewed many Aboriginal federal inmates in the Regional Psychiatric Centre in Saskatoon, the Saskatchewan Penitentiary, the Stoney Mountain Penitentiary, and Rockwood Institution, which are both in Winnipeg. Many inmates in their interviews attributed their incarceration to various contributors, including severe poverty, racial persecution, and substance abuse, along with having been violently and/or sexually abused in their home environments, having experienced a loss of connection to their own culture, or having suffered a loss of positive self-esteem as Aboriginal persons.[80] Colonialism has likely introduced an additional social contributor to crime that is specific to Aboriginal peoples. It has cut off many Aboriginal communities and their members from ethical and spiritual teachings from their cultural past that could have acted as a social restraint against criminal behaviour.[81]

This theory speaks to why restorative justice is held out as a better alternative than incarceration. Jail fails to address the root causes behind why an offender commits crime. The ability to deter, either the specific offender or society at large, through more severe sentences is questionable to say the least. The certainty and swiftness of punishment may have deterrent value but not in certain contexts. Many Aboriginal peoples find themselves in social contexts in which deterrence, whether it is dependent on certainty, swiftness, or severity, has little value. These contexts include crimes fuelled by poverty, substance abuse, intergenerational trauma, negative peer association (for example, gangs), and domestic violence. Prison not only provides no deterrent to many Aboriginal peoples who come into the system, but it also makes matters worse by entrenching many of them further into lives of crime. Restorative justice discussions aim to flush out these underlying causes and then to explore more constructive solutions to them.[82] Daniel Kwochka states: "Aboriginal traditions suggest that the acts are no more than signals of disharmonies in relationships, and it is the disharmonies that should be focused upon."[83] Once the causes are discovered, then healing can begin for the offender, the victim, and others affected by the crime.[84] The next criticism takes issue with how retributive justice addresses victim harm.

Does Not Serve the Victim
Western justice systems often collapse the harm done to the victim into the state's interest in prosecuting crime. The victim does not tend to have any direct involvement in the proceedings, while the prosecutor speaks to the public interest as a surrogate victim before the court. Also, restorative justice provides a better alternative by providing a crime victim with a direct opportunity to speak to his or her fears, concerns, and interests in the course of the process and in an atmosphere of safety and honesty. By incorporating the victim's dialogue into the process, the victim's interests and concerns will be addressed by the resolution.[85] As will be explained in more detail later in this book, restorative justice claims to be a better approach to inspiring contrition and responsibility in the offender. It is seen as being integrally bound up with the victim's participation in the restorative process. Cayley expresses it this way:

> If contrition is possible for the offender, it is the victim's suffering above all that is likely to trigger it. If healing and reconciliation are possible for the victim, then it is the humanization that occurs when an offender acknowledges and tries to atone for what he has done that is most likely to bring it about. In this respect each holds the key to the other's liberation from the continuing thrall of whatever violence has occurred.[86]

By including victim participation and reaching a resolution that directly accounts for the individual victim's interests, restorative justice claims to better serve the victim than state-administered punishment. The victim also benefits if the process effectively addresses the offender's behaviour. A key potential benefit is the victim's safety, even after the victim has suffered serious violence.[87]

Does Not Promote Responsibility

The Canadian justice system, due to the prospect of imprisonment or other punishments, provides procedural safeguards to the accused such as requiring the Crown to prove the accused guilty beyond a reasonable doubt. These safeguards are themselves cause for criticism for restorative justice proponents. Restorative justice does not aspire to punish for its own sake but, rather, to heal the offender and correct behaviour. This goal leads to the reintegration of the offender, which in turn is part of the broader agenda of restoring relationships and harmony in the community.[88] A problem, assuming that the accused did commit the crime, manifests when the procedural safeguards are exploited to garner an acquittal or otherwise nullify the charges. The accused does not have to accept any responsibility, and the opportunity to strengthen community relationships is lost.[89] Even if the accused is convicted, there will still be problems with encouraging offender responsibility. The sentence is given by a judge, which is often accompanied by a lecture. However, chances are the offender will never see that judge again. Neither the punishment nor the lecture is likely to deliver any meaningful message to the accused.[90]

Restorative justice, it is said, has a greater potential to inspire contrition and responsibility in the accused. The victim, and perhaps other members of the community as well, have the opportunity to describe how the offender's actions have affected them. The offender is forced to face up to the consequences of the behaviour. This action, in turn, can lead to contrition, remorse, and an acceptance of responsibility. It can instill a genuine desire on the part of the offender to change his or her ways and make right by those who have been affected. This shift, in turn, provides a stronger assurance that the accused will complete any rehabilitative measures that are agreed upon, such as counselling and community service.[91] Restorative justice does not necessarily present a softer option than jail. The meeting with the victim (and perhaps others affected by the crime) and the rehabilitative measures that are employed can make a restorative justice resolution just as, or even more, onerous than a prison term.[92] If the standard justice system does not address the victim's concerns or further an offender's acceptance of responsibility, then community relationships remain fractured. This possibility forms the basis of the next criticism.

Does Not Promote Relationship Reparation

Adversarial justice processes, such as the right to cross-examine witnesses or to present submissions in contradiction of the other party, are also a target for criticism by restorative justice proponents because of their competitive emphasis. This competitive emphasis is held to be counter-productive to repairing and strengthening relationships in the community, which represents one of the key aspirations behind Aboriginal demands for self-determination over justice. Canadian criminal procedure is often seen as culturally inappropriate and incompatible with Aboriginal processes. The imposition of adversarial procedures has had the effect of suppressing Aboriginal legal orders along with processes that had nurtured community relationships. Aboriginal control over justice, in theory, aspires to reinvigorate traditional processes that had emphasized harmony and relationship reparation in place of imposed adversarial processes that do not have cultural legitimacy with Aboriginal peoples.[93]

Restorative Justice Is More Effective
A frequently made claim is that by successfully changing the offender's behaviour and addressing its underlying causes, restorative justice can be more effective in addressing criminal recidivism. Restorative justice proponents can garner some pretty impressive statistical evidence in support of such claims. One study found that youth who participated in selected victim-offender mediation programs in California and Tennessee re-offended at a 32-percent lower rate than that of those who did not participate.[94] A study of community justice committees in Arizona found that youth who completed the program were 0.64 times as likely to reoffend relative to those youth who did not complete the program.[95] A study of a program in Australia found a 38 percent reduction in driving while intoxicated and in violent offences by juveniles.[96] Success does not stem only from juvenile crime. Meta-analyses of restorative justice programs both juvenile and adult in Australia, Canada, and the United States have consistently found a substantial aggregate reduction in recidivism relative to non-restorative approaches.[97]

Restorative justice has also been successfully applied to serious crimes that would normally warrant incarceration. In Ottawa, the Collaborative Justice Program applies restorative approaches to offences regardless of the seriousness, such as robbery, intoxicated driving causing bodily harm or death, and sexual offences. Of those individuals who completed the program in the years 2002 to 2005, 15.4 percent reoffended within a year after completion and 32.3 percent within three years of completion. A comparison group of offenders reoffended at rates of 28 percent within the first year and 54 percent within three years.[98] Kathleen Daly's study of a program in South Australia that deals with sexual offences in youth found that those who completed the program reoffended at a lower rate (48 percent) than those who were dealt with through the standard court process (66 percent).[99]

Remarkable successes have occurred in Aboriginal contexts as well. A juvenile justice program in the Northern Territory of Australia, for example, was able to report an 89 percent successful completion rate, and only one of thirty-two participants from 2003 to 2006 had reoffended.[100] Rupert Ross describes the success of the Hollow Water Healing Circle Program, which dealt with pervasive sexual abuse in a Manitoba Aboriginal community: "Out of the forty-eight offenders in Hollow Water over the last nine years, only five have gone to jail, primarily because they failed to participate adequately in the healing program. Of the forty-three who did, only two have repeated their crimes, an enviable record by anyone's standards."[101] A follow-up evaluation found that the number of recidivists remained at two, even after another sixty-four had gone through the program.[102]

These results fuel another criticism, which is the notion that the high costs of incarceration are just not worth it. As of 2006, it has cost the federal government annually $110,223 to keep one male inmate, and $150,867 for one female inmate, confined in a maximum-security institution. The annual cost per inmate amounts to $70,000 for medium- and minimum-security institutions.[103] The Prison Justice Day Committee found that in the 2004-05 fiscal year, Correctional Services Canada used 71 percent of its budget to keep 31,500 offenders in custody, while 14 percent was spent supervising 120,500 offenders in the community.[104] An Australian study in 2004 found that the daily cost of holding somebody in secure custody was $253, but it cost only $12 for them to participate in community corrections.[105] Parliamentary Budget Officer Kevin Page has estimated that Prime Minister Stephen Harper's legislative enactment that will replace the double credit against sentence for time spent in pre-trial custody with a straight one-to-one credit will cost an extra $618 million each year and an additional $1.8 billion in construction costs.[106]

Consider these statistics in light of the success of the Family Group Conferencing Program in New Zealand, which drew upon traditional Māori principles of mediation. Judge F.M.W. McElrea reported that admissions to youth custody facilities dropped from 2,712 in 1988 to 923 in 1992-93. Half of the facilities were closed as a result. Youth prosecutions dropped by 27 percent from 1987 to 1992.[107] Mandeep K. Dhami and Penny Joy note that in a diversionary program in Chilliwack, British Columbia, an average of 12.45 hours was spent for each participant in comparison to an average of 34.5 hours for an offender in the standard justice system.[108] They go on to explain: "The insufficient funding of RJ initiatives in Canada is particularly difficult to accept in light of the large amount of money that the federal and provincial governments save through diversion cases from the traditional system into RJ programs. Volunteer-run, community-based programs are both efficient and cost-effective."[109] The argument is that restorative approaches represent the better demand on resources.

Certainly, there is some justification to a rhetoric that essentializes past Aboriginal justice practices as holistic healing and relationship reparation, while essentializing Western justice systems as adversarial and punitive. It must be noted, however, that some Aboriginal justice practices were at a considerable distance from what is associated with restorative justice. The potential relevance of these practices to contemporary visions of Aboriginal justice will now be considered.

Aboriginal Punitive Approaches

Restorative justice themes were not the only elements of Aboriginal justice. Many Aboriginal societies also had significant punitive inclinations. Mary Ellen Turpel-Lafond and Patricia Monture-Angus describe banishment as the most severe remedy under Aboriginal justice systems, since it involved "the end of social and cultural life with one's community."[110] This form of punishment was indeed a common thread among Aboriginal societies, often a last resort for someone who just would not respond to previous efforts at correction.[111] The uses of banishment varied. The Dene used banishment if satisfactory resolutions could not be reached regarding the most serious offences, those dealing with the proper handling of game animals and extramarital sexual relations. Such retribution was practically a death sentence because a single individual was highly unlikely to survive on his own in the Arctic.[112] The Cheyenne did not usually intend that banishment be permanent. It was used in a manner analogous to common law legal systems' use of quantums of prison terms and parole-hearing determinations. Terms of banishment could be lessened if there were mitigating circumstances such as provocation or intoxication. Chiefs and military societies could also lift banishment if they deemed that the killer demonstrated sufficient penitence such that his return would not jeopardize community safety.[113]

There were, however, plenty of other sanctions with a harshly punitive emphasis among Aboriginal communities. A point that seems to be overlooked is that while many Aboriginal societies did have a restorative orientation, these practices were integrally bound up with systems of private vengeance, at least in cases that involved instances of homicide (intentional or not). Although the precise practices varied, the kin of the victim generally had the right to seek the death of the killer if they were not given sufficient compensation. The victim's kin were expected to negotiate in good faith, and acceptance of adequate compensation was expected. Nonetheless, what we see is a fairly common emphasis on retributive killing, subject to whether negotiated compensation worked out.[114] The Osage of the Mississipi Valley, for example, also made a point of addressing a potential problem with retributive killing. The family against whom a revenge killing was carried out could in turn claim a right to seek revenge. This possibility could conceivably lead to a destructive cycle of violence. An aggrieved family could therefore substitute a member of an enemy tribe in place of the actual murderer, which could help channel the demand for vengeance in a relatively more productive direction.[115]

Among the Iroquois, a woman (and only the woman apparently) who committed adultery would be flogged publicly.[116] The Iroquois also punished the practice of witchcraft with execution.[117] In Tlingit society, incest, marriage with a slave, prostitution, and witchcraft were punishable by death since these types of conduct brought shame on a Tlingit clan.[118] The Cheyenne also used corporal punishment. On one occasion, members of the Fox Soldier society beat a man who had inflicted an arrow wound on another man's arm that resulted in its amputation.[119] The Cheyenne also used public whipping to punish individuals for theft and for bringing a non-Cheyenne person into the tribe without permission. The Cheyenne also punished sexual offences and the violation of marital taboos with "cropping," which meant the severance of an ear or the nose.[120] Other tribes are said to have used "cropping" to punish individuals for adultery, including the Utes, Comanches, Creeks, Wyandots, Shawanoese, Ottawas, Miamies, Putawatimies, and Weas.[121] Among tribes in what is now Washington State, a cuckolded man could slay an adulterer without fear of reprisal from the adulterer's kin. Among some groups, the wife could also be killed without reprisal from the wife's kin.[122] Among the Sanpoil or Nespelem, a headman could assess the use of whipping for retaliation against crimes including "murder, stealing, perjury, improper sexual relations, and abortion."[123]

The Choctaw provide an interesting example of how the practice of corporal punishment can evolve in response to different social influences. Choctaw clans often used flogging for offences committed by their own members. Floggings were relatively private affairs that stayed within the clan. The idea was to encourage compliance with community standards, not retribution. This practice, however, evolved after extensive contact with American settlers. Corporal punishment was still practised frequently in many American states during the nineteenth century. The Choctaw's use of such punishment had evolved to emulate the American approach. Choctaw corporal punishment went from being a relatively private chastisement to a much more public ritual, with the intention of communicating deterrence, and retribution, to the Choctaw people at large. This practice continued, at least publicly, until the tribal government in that territory was disbanded in 1906.[124]

Public shaming of an offender was also a practice among some Aboriginal groups. Sometimes shaming was part in parcel with reintegrating the offender with the community. It was counterbalanced by other considerations, such as affirming that the offender remained a valued member of the community and marking the end of the conflict. These considerations were certainly a part of the Lake Babine traditions, for example. However, shaming practices in other societies may have had a distinctly punitive emphasis, with deterrence or retribution as the objectives. Consider the following example from the Dene:

A minor offence might be a small theft. For example, elders reported that when youths stole some bannock, they were ridiculed and shamed. The person from whom they stole would pin the bannock on their jackets and everyone in camp would know they had stolen it and would laugh at them. This was considered to be a "deterrent"; it was unlikely the youth would repeat his or her theft because they would not want to face ridicule again.[125]

The Anishinabe sometimes responded to repeated theft by compelling the thief to wear a special costume to signify his transgressions through a public humiliation.[126]

It was common for past Aboriginal justice systems to include peacemaking discussions and reparations alongside more punitive elements. Punitive sanctions often encouraged co-operation with community resolutions or provided last resorts when previous efforts at correction did not succeed. Michael Cousins says that, for the Iroqouis, private vengeance was a last resort only when other methods of "putting things right" between the victim and the murderer, and between their clans, had not succeeded.[127] The Aboriginal community of Strelley, West Australia, used various responses to crime, including reconciliation meetings, community service, public admonition, public shaming, fines, banishment to a neighbouring community, and corporal sanctions.[128]

To summarize, some past Aboriginal justice practices had strong parallels to restorative justice. It is fair to say that community reconciliation was often the primary emphasis of Aboriginal justice systems. This understanding will be germane to many of our subsequent discussions, since the use of restorative type processes is an important impetus behind the Aboriginal pursuit of control over justice. The practices that were restorative in nature were not, however, the sum and total of past Aboriginal justice. Some Aboriginal justice practices were harsh and punitive. Certainly, some of these practices were part of systems that emphasized reconciliation and were used either as encouragements or last resorts. Some practices, however, were often of such a forceful or retributive nature that they were considerably distant from restorative justice. The potential contemporary relevance of these practices will also be relevant to some of our subsequent discussions, particularly the discussion in Chapter 9 on the Canadian Charter of Rights and Freedom's right against cruel and unusual punishment.[129]

Contemporary Aboriginal responses to crime, even if jurisdiction over justice is obtained, are unlikely to rely upon restorative measures to the complete exclusion of punitive measures. It is erroneous to think of punishment and restorative justice in purely oppositional terms. Christopher Bennett stresses that while a criminal justice system can accommodate restorative ideals such as apology and victim restitution, it should not compromise other important functions such as retribution and public denunciation.[130] Some scholars argue that restorative justice is really about alternative approaches to punishment. A restorative resolution can impose onerous burdens and restrictions on an offender. It is punishment, but with a greater emphasis on rehabilitation and reintegration. Restorative resolutions are often backed by the prospect of punitive sanctions in the regular justice system in order to encourage compliance with their conditions. They also provide a backup when an offender fails to comply with the terms of a restorative resolution.[131] Restorative and standard punitive approaches should be seen as complementary instead of oppositional. Each can fill in the gaps of the other to provide a comprehensive system of responding to crime.[132]

Even its most enthusiastic proponents do not propose a complete reliance on restorative justice. They often concede that some offences are so serious and some offenders so dangerous as to be inappropriate for applications of restorative justice and that some offenders simply will not respond to corrective efforts. Their point is that in Western justice systems, imprisonment is relied upon reflexively and uncritically for far too many offences.[133]

It is also clear that restorative justice relies in no small measure on voluntary participation. A victim's refusal to participate can be a significant stumbling block to a restorative process since their absence or opposition means that any discussions or potential agreements will be missing the input of a vital stakeholder.[134] Daniel Kwochka concedes that the victim's refusal to participate "tend(s) to militate against proper and full reconciliation," but he holds that it is not necessarily fatal.[135] For the Hollow Water program, the victim was encouraged, but not required, to attend the sentencing circles that were held outside the court system. If the victim did not attend, the circle could proceed with pursuing a resolution that emphasized the offender's rehabilitation and reintegration.[136]

Even more critical is the offender's participation. It has been held that a fundamental prerequisite to applying restorative justice is the offender's willingness to accept responsibility for, or otherwise admit to, the commission of the offence. If an offender truly wants to assert his or her innocence, it may be entirely appropriate for the case to go ahead within the adversarial system.[137]

It is not a matter of one approach to justice occupying the entire field. Both punitive and restorative approaches can, and necessarily would have to, exist side by side in a dual-system approach. The real question is how much space in the same field should each occupy relative to the other. It was common for Aboriginal societies to use both reconciliatory and punitive approaches as complementary parts of an integrated system. If Aboriginal communities do adapt traditions with restorative emphases, they will necessarily have to use punitive measures as well. Aboriginal communities may find themselves unwilling to dispense with prison altogether for certain offenders or certain offences. Judge Heino Lilles has pointed out that Elders' sentencing advisory panels have occasionally recommended terms of incarceration that have exceeded what the Crown had recommended.[138] Another possibility is the revival of traditional sanctions such as public shaming or corporal punishment as deterrent sanctions and as "short and sharp" punishments that have cultural significance for Aboriginal offenders but avoid the long-term effects that have been associated with imprisonment.

Corporal punishment may offend some peoples' notions of treating criminals humanely because of the physical pain involved and the possibility of lasting injuries or scars. Correctional Services Canada, for example, states that Canadian use of corporal punishment as a criminal sanction ended in 1972 and that it is degrading to human dignity.[139] The idea of corporal punishment may not be as outrageous as some people might think. Michael Fay, an American citizen, was sentenced to public caning in Singapore in 1994 after he was caught spray painting and egging several cars and was found to be in possession of stolen public property. President Bill Clinton and thirty-four American senators sent a petition for leniency to the Singaporean embassy. The American public was to no small degree of a different opinion. Many Americans flooded American radio stations, newspapers, and the Singaporean embassy with both letters and phone calls expressing support for the caning. A public opinion poll also indicated that 38 percent of Americans were in favour of the use of corporal punishment.[140] Jon Huntsman, a former ambassador to Singapore, questioned whether the use of such a sanction was appropriate for an American system that values political dissent, freedom of expression, and the rights of appeal during the criminal justice process. He also explained the role of cultural differences in Singapore's use of caning: "Culturally, it's a far different equation. It is a very traditional, Confucianist society in which the family is still the most important unit ... a society that believes in the well-being of the whole, not necessarily the individual."[141] On that note, it is conceivable that corporal sanctions, if they have a basis in past practices, could gain currency in a contemporary Aboriginal community. A community may want to revive such sanctions with the goal of deterrence and/or public denunciation as an alternative to jail. An Aboriginal community may want to use corporal sanctions as part of the restorative resolutions or as a supplement to the terms of incarceration. This is certainly a controversial issue because, despite how one feels about judicial corporal punishment, it still engages not only Canadian law and policy but also international standards of human rights. What I will say for now is that I will engage with this issue more fully in Chapter 9 of this book. The question now is whether Aboriginal communities should have the legal autonomy (that is, the jurisdiction) to realize these visions of justice. The next chapter will provide a basic overview of the situation in Canada.

3
The Current Situation in Canada

The purpose of this chapter is to examine the extent to which Aboriginal approaches to justice have been accommodated in Canada. Legislative and executive allowances are mostly limited to adaptations of sentencing processes, diversionary programs for limited ranges of offences, and correctional programming for convicted offenders. Constitutional Aboriginal rights are also interpreted narrowly, providing Aboriginal peoples with very little legal leverage to demand more from Canadian leaders. This limitation leads into the latter half of the chapter, which will explore the motives of Canadian judges and politicians for sustaining this status quo. However, first, we begin with an overview of legislation relevant to Aboriginal approaches to justice.

Canadian Legislation and Aboriginal Justice

Legislative allowances to Aboriginal peoples when it comes to justice do not suggest a very encouraging picture. The *Indian Act* gives an Indian justice of the peace jurisdiction over a limited number of summary offences, including trespassing on Indian reserves (section 30), removing certain cultural objects situated on reserves (section 91), and removing natural resources from the reserves (section 93).[1] Section 102 creates a general offence for violating a provision of the *Indian Act* or any other federal legislation. Section 107(b) confers jurisdiction in order to enforce band council bylaws using fines and/or imprisonment, although the bylaws themselves are subject to disallowance by the minister of Indian affairs under section 82(2).

Another legislative allowance for Aboriginal perspectives on justice is section 718.2(e) of the *Criminal Code*, which reads in part:

A court that imposes a sentence shall also take into consideration the following principles: ...

(e) all available sanctions other than imprisonment that are reasonable in the circumstances should be considered for all offenders, with particular attention to the circumstances of Aboriginal offenders.[2]

In *R. v Gladue,* the Supreme Court of Canada stated that this provision was enacted in response to alarming evidence that Aboriginal peoples were incarcerated disproportionately to non-Aboriginal people in Canada.[3] Section 718.2(e) is thus a remedial provision, enacted specifically to oblige the judiciary to reduce incarceration of Aboriginal offenders and to seek reasonable alternatives for Aboriginal offenders.[4] Justice Peter Cory adds:

> It is often the case that neither Aboriginal offenders nor their communities are well served by incarcerating offenders, particularly for less serious or non-violent offences. Where these sanctions are reasonable in the circumstances, they should be implemented. In all instances, it is appropriate to attempt to craft the sentencing process and the sanctions imposed in accordance with the Aboriginal perspective.[5]

A judge must take into account the background and systemic factors that bring Aboriginal people into contact with the justice system, such as poverty, substance abuse, and "community fragmentation," when determining a sentence.[6] A judge must also consider the role of these factors in bringing a particular Aboriginal accused before the court.[7] A judge is obligated to obtain that information with the assistance of counsel or probation officers using a report or through other means. A judge must also obtain information on community resources and treatment options that may provide alternatives to incarceration.[8]

Certain offences, and offences committed under certain circumstances, could render an Aboriginal accused ineligible for a community-based sentence under section 718.2(e). *R. v Wells,* which revisited section 718.2(e), holds that a community-based sentence will not be appropriate if an offence requires two or more years of imprisonment.[9] Mitigating factors can reduce an otherwise appropriate term of imprisonment to less than two years, thereby making an Aboriginal offender eligible for community-based sentences. However, if a judge decides that an Aboriginal offender is a danger to the public, that offender will not be eligible for community-based sentences. It would be a stretch, to say the least, to view this provision as a legislative concession of substantive jurisdiction to Aboriginal communities. The chapter now provides an overview of other accommodations of Aboriginal justice initiatives in Canada.

Aboriginal Justice Initiatives in Canada

One contemporary adaptation of Aboriginal perspectives on justice is the sentencing circle, which involves the offender, the victim(s), the family members of those involved, as well as any interested members of the community, assembled together in a circular seating arrangement. Justice personnel such as lawyers, probation officers, the judge, and counselling professionals will often participate as well. The circle often commences with a smudging ceremony or similar rite. A spiritual symbol, often a feather, is then passed around to one participant at a time. The person who currently holds the symbol has the opportunity to speak to matters being considered by the circle. The symbol is then passed on to the next person in the circle. This process continues until a consensus is reached on the appropriate resolution.[10] Examples of communities that have engaged in this practice include the Kwanlin Dun in Yukon,[11] Hollow Water in Manitoba,[12] and the Innu at Sheshashit and Davis Inlets.[13]

There is no *Criminal Code* provision that authorizes or even mentions the holding of sentencing circles. Whether a judge will allow a sentencing circle as part of the sentencing process is a matter of judicial discretion.[14] A judge is not bound by the recommendations of the circle. The judge can impose a harsher sentence if he or she concludes that the recommendations do not provide a fit sentence.[15] Indeed, a trial judge's adoption of the circle's recommendation can be appealed if it involves a sentence that does not give sufficient emphasis to deterrence (for example, incarceration).[16]

Diversionary programs allow offenders to resolve their cases outside of the court system. The usual first step is that a prosecutor approves an offender for participation in a program based on certain criteria such as whether the offence is a minor one, the offender has not previously been through the program, and the accused is willing to accept responsibility for the offence. Note that diversionary programs often allow an accused to accept responsibility for an offence without prejudicing his or her right to plead not guilty at a later time. The court then typically adjourns the case for a period of months or even in excess of a year. The offender is then required to perform certain tasks or meet conditions with a view towards correcting his or her behaviour. In diversionary programs with an Aboriginal emphasis, these tasks can include attending counselling for certain types of behaviour, meeting with the victim(s) under appropriate conditions in order to resolve differences, completing the performance of community service hours, participating in cultural activities, and meeting with Elders for spiritual guidance. If an offender successfully completes the required steps, then the prosecutor will withdraw the charge on the next court date. If an offender does not complete the requirements and the prosecutor is not willing to provide an additional opportunity, the case is returned to the court system.[17] Such diversionary programs are usually confined to minor offences, and cases are subject to approval by Crown prosecutors.[18]

Canada has also established a small number of courts designed specifically for Aboriginal offenders. The Cree Court in Saskatchewan is presided over by Provincial Court Judge Gerald Morin. The court holds session in a circuit of three different Aboriginal communities in and around Prince Albert. Aboriginal offenders attending the court have the option of having the proceedings conducted in the Cree language. Judge Morin speaks with each offender, asking blunt questions that probe for the root causes of the behaviour as he tries to ascertain whether a non-custodial sentence may be appropriate.[19] The New Westminster First Nations Court, presided over by Judge Buller Bennett, the only female Aboriginal judge in British Columbia, has a similar orientation. Everybody in the courtroom can provide input with respect to the sentence when court is in session. The emphasis is again on ascertaining what is behind the offender's behaviour and how to deal with it. Judge Bennett also conducts regular review hearings following the initial sentence in order to determine the individual's compliance with the conditions and his or her behavioural progress.[20]

There is also the Teslin Tlingit Council peacemaker court system in Yukon. The Tlingit people have traditionally been divided into clans. Each clan has a separate peacemaker court. A Tlingit who is charged with a summary of- fence may be eligible for diversion. The requirements for diversion are worked out between the accused and the Elders of his or her clan. A justice co-ordinator acts as a facilitator between the clan Elders and the court. For any offences not dealt with by diversion, the clan Elders are allowed to act in an advisory capacity. The clan Elders hear submissions from Crown and defence counsel and are allowed to read a pre-sentence report that provides background information on the accused. The judge then explains what the available sentencing options may be. The case is then adjourned. The clan Elders then work out a recommendation for sentencing, which the judge is not obligated to accept.[21] Most recommendations are accepted, and this in turn has meant a 50 percent decrease in property crime, a 75 percent decrease in break and enters, a 50 percent decrease in assaults, and a 35 percent decrease in overall crime within the first few years of implementation.[22]

Another court is the Aboriginal Persons Court in Toronto, Ontario. There are two main functions of this court. One is to explore restorative resolutions for Aboriginal offenders through the sentencing process, pursuant to *Gladue*. A caseworker from Aboriginal Legal Services in Toronto will assist the court at the request of the judge, the defence counsel, or the Crown prosecutor. The caseworker will investigate the background and life circumstances of Aboriginal offenders, prepare a report detailing this information, and may also provide recommendations for a sentence.[23] The court's other function is a diversionary process called the Community Council Program. Even serious offences or repeat offences that could merit jail time can be diverted. Once approved by a Crown prosecutor, the offender meets with members of the Community Council, a group of selected volunteers from Toronto's

Aboriginal community. The council then works out a plan of rehabilitation and acceptance of responsibility with the offender. Successful completion leads to the charge being withdrawn.[24]

The Peacemaking Court of the Tsuu T'ina nation near Calgary, Alberta, was presided over by Judge Leonard Mandamin, an Anishinabe. This court had an expansive diversionary program, from which only sexual assault and homicide offences were excluded. The offender would meet with selected Elders, who would then work out a plan of rehabilitation and responsibility. Successful completion led to the withdrawal of the charge. Otherwise, the case was returned to court and resolved by the standard justice system. Judge Mandamin could authorize the offender's participation, even over the objections of the Crown prosecutor.[25]

Once the criminal process has been concluded and the Aboriginal offender has been convicted and sentenced, there is still another type of accommodation, which can occur while the offender is serving his or her prison term. A brief explanation of the Canadian penal system and its correctional programming is in order first. Federal penitentiaries are for those offenders who are sentenced to a term of imprisonment of two years or more. Provincial jails are for offenders serving terms of less than two years.[26] In both types of institutions, correctional programs are often available that emphasize rehabilitation and the gradual reintegration of offenders into the community once they are released. The types of services available to inmates in these programs include educational upgrading classes, anger management counselling, substance abuse treatment, and life skills training. The availability and types of these programs apparently varies considerably from institution to institution. The programs are also both less available and less accessed within provincial institutions due to the much shorter incarceration terms.[27]

Section 80 of the *Corrections and Conditional Release Act* mandates that Correctional Services Canada (CSC) shall "provide programs designed particularly to address the needs of aboriginal offenders."[28] One approach to fulfilling this mandate has been to provide programs that are tailored to include the inculcation of Aboriginal cultural values. Another approach has been to facilitate inmate participation in cultural activities, such as pipe ceremonies and sweat lodges. These services are often delivered by Elders or other members of the Aboriginal communities with similar cultural authority. The availability of culturally sensitive programs varies greatly from institution to institution.[29] The rationale behind these approaches is that the CSC identifies the loss of cultural identity as the underlying cause of Aboriginal criminality.[30]

When the National Parole Board grants parole, the delivery of correctional programming continues. The early stages of parole are often spent in a residential correctional facility – a halfway house. A halfway house, while not a prison, requires the offender to reside there and not be absent save under specific exceptions (for example, supervised absences or employment). It is meant as a transitional phase in an offender's parole, neither full incarceration nor full freedom in the community, with the goal of gradual reintegration into the community. Many of the services previously mentioned as being available in federal penitentiaries are often available in halfway houses as well.[31] There are indeed a number of halfway houses designed specifically to provide culturally sensitive services for the reintegration of Aboriginal offenders. These include the Forensic Behaviourial Management Clinic for sex offenders in Winnipeg, the Stan Daniels Centre in Edmonton, the Waseskun House in Montreal, and the AIM House in Vancouver.[32]

Aboriginal justice initiatives in Canada are subject to definite limitations. One limitation is that they are confined to those cases in which an Aboriginal accused has pleaded guilty (for example, sentencing circles and correctional programs) or otherwise accepted responsibility (for example, diversion). If an Aboriginal accused contests the allegations, then Canadian legislation requires adversarial procedures. There are indications, which will be explored in later discussions in this book, that at least some Aboriginal communities may want even their fact-determining processes to have restorative or inquisitorial aspects rather than an adversarial emphasis. This focus limits the capacity of Aboriginal communities to design their justice systems in such a way as to reflect cultural difference.

Another limitation is offence bifurcation whereby Aboriginal approaches to justice generally remain inapplicable to more serious offences. The precise parameters of this bifurcation vary greatly from court to court and from program to program. Aboriginal peoples may want to expand their initiatives beyond what is allowed by the present offence bifurcations. The obvious reason is the current over-incarceration of Aboriginal peoples. Calls for greater Aboriginal control over justice are motivated in large degree by a desire for autonomy to develop community-based alternatives to incarceration. This lack of autonomy can clearly manifest during a sentencing circle. When Aboriginal communities reach a consensus about a sentence, the implementation is at the discretion of a judge who is not a member of the community. Judges have frequently not accepted circle recommendations.[33] Offence bifurcation limits the capacity of Aboriginal communities to implement their visions of justice that reflect cultural difference since accommodation is extended only for certain categories of offences.

Canadian legislators, executive officials, and judges are willing to accommodate Aboriginal approaches to justice, but usually only within certain limitations. The following sections of the chapter will reveal that Aboriginal peoples have rights recognized under the Canadian Constitution but that these rights provide a weak foundation for challenging the status quo since they are most often interpreted narrowly.

Aboriginal Rights under the Constitution

The basis for constitutional Aboriginal rights in Canada is section 35(1) of the *Constitution Act, 1982,* which reads: "The existing aboriginal and treaty rights of the aboriginal peoples of Canada are hereby recognized and affirmed."[34] There are at least three distinct categories of rights under this provision: inherent Aboriginal rights, land title (which will not be discussed here since any connection between land title rights and criminal jurisdiction may be tenuous at best), and treaty rights.

Inherent Rights to Cultural Practices

The first step a court must take in adjudicating an inherent rights claim is to determine how the right is to be characterized. Chief Justice Antonio Lamer wrote in *R. v Van der Peet:* "To characterize an applicant's claim correctly, a court should consider such factors as the nature of the action done pursuant to an Aboriginal right, the nature of the governmental regulation, statute or action impugned, and the tradition, custom or right relied upon to establish the right."[35] The practice that is claimed as a right must be phrased in specific, as opposed to general, terms and be cognizable to the Canadian common law system.[36] The Supreme Court of Canada, for example, ruled in *R. v Pamajewon* that an inherent rights claim to Aboriginal self-government would cast the judicial inquiry at a "level of excessive generality."[37] Claiming a right to a separate justice system would therefore be unacceptable. What may instead be acceptable is claiming rights to individual practices within that justice system. Possible examples include the right of an Aboriginal society to banish an offender permanently or a right to inflict corporal punishment for repeated theft. It is also not enough to show that Aboriginal peoples in general have engaged in the practice. The practice must be specific to the Aboriginal society claiming the right.[38] The Court has also since emphasized that inherent rights are communal rights. A practice claimed as an inherent right must have the purpose of ensuring the continued existence of an Aboriginal society. An inherent right "is not one to be exercised by any member of the aboriginal community independently of the aboriginal society it is meant to preserve. It is a right that assists the society in maintaining its distinctive character."[39]

Once the practice is properly characterized, the next test is that only practices, traditions, and customs that were integral to distinctive Aboriginal societies before contact with Europeans are protected as inherent Aboriginal rights under section 35(1).[40] For the Métis, a distinctive group of Aboriginal peoples with ancestral ties to both First Nations and European settlers, the temporal threshold is when Canada assumed legal control over their territories as opposed to when the Europeans made first contact.[41] It is not enough for the practice to have been significant to an Aboriginal society before contact. It had to have been "integral" to that society before contact – that "it was one of the things that truly made the culture what it was."[42] Practices that developed solely in response to contact with Europeans are excluded.[43] The test is a restrictive one. As such, Chief Justice Lamer stated: "In assessing a claim for the existence of an Aboriginal right, a court must take into account the perspective of the Aboriginal people claiming the right ... It must also be recognized, however, that the perspective must be framed in terms cognizable to the Canadian legal and constitutional structure."[44] Conclusive evidence of the practices is not required in order to establish a successful claim. The evidence only needs to demonstrate which practices originated before contact.[45] The practice need not be distinct to only one particular Aboriginal society. The inquiry is whether the practice is integral to a "distinctive," as opposed to "distinct," Aboriginal society. Distinct means unique. Distinctive means "different in kind or quality; unlike."[46]

R. v Sappier; R. v Gray is another landmark case on inherent rights that tries to delineate more clearly the "integral to a distinctive culture" test. First, the Court tried to clear up any misunderstandings over this statement in *Van der Peet*:

> To recognize and affirm the prior occupation of Canada by distinctive ab-
> original societies it is to what makes those societies distinctive that the court
> must look in identifying aboriginal rights. The court cannot look at those
> aspects of the aboriginal society that are true of every human society (for
> example, eating to survive), nor can it look at those aspects of the aboriginal
> society that are only incidental or occasional to that society; the court must
> look instead to the defining and central attributes of the aboriginal society
> in question. It is only by focusing on the aspects of the aboriginal society
> that make that society distinctive that the definition of aboriginal rights
> will accomplish the purpose underlying s. 35(1).[47]

If a practice is directed solely towards survival (for example, obtaining sus-
tenance), it does mean that the practice cannot be integral to a distinctive culture. The test also does not require that the practice go to the core of a society's identity, which would make the threshold stricter than was intended in *Van der Peet*.[48] The test also does not require that the practice be a "defin-ing feature" of an Aboriginal society or that an Aboriginal culture would be "fundamentally altered" in the absence of the practice. This only serves to erect "artificial barriers" to the recognition of inherent Aboriginal rights.[49] The Court also explains that the word "culture" in the context of the *Van der Peet* tests means the way of life of a particular Aboriginal society prior to contact and includes "means of survival, their socialization methods,

their legal systems, and, potentially, their trading habits."[50] The test also requires that there be continuity between the practice before contact and the practice as it manifests today. There need not be an unbroken chain of continuity. The practice may have ceased for a period of time, then resumed, without offending the requirement for continuity. The test will also permit some modification of the practice so that it can be exercised in a contemporary manner.[51]

Inherent Aboriginal rights are not frozen in the form in which they were limited by law when the *Constitution Act, 1982* came into force. In other words, laws and regulations can now be found unconstitutional if they have imposed limitations on the exercise of Aboriginal rights, even if they were in force prior to the *Act* coming into force. This can include situations where a law or regulation has the effect of not allowing Aboriginal peoples to exercise their rights in their "preferred manner."[52] The Supreme Court of Canada has also made it clear that the "integral to a distinctive culture prior to contact" test governs Aboriginal claims to rights involving governance.[53]

The Court's jurisprudence subjects the recognition of inherent Aboriginal rights to a series of strict tests. If efforts to obtain effective control over criminal justice are stonewalled by Canadian authorities, an Aboriginal community would have to take on the onerous burden of litigating multiple claims to all of the individual justice practices that would form part of its justice system. This reality makes the constitutional recognition of comprehensive Aboriginal justice systems through litigation too costly and impractical for Aboriginal communities.

Litigating for rights to justice practices may also frequently fail to satisfy the *Van der Peet* tests, given their stringency. Russell Lawrence Barsh and Sákéj Henderson criticize the "central and integral" test as an arbitrary and fallacious concept that fails to recognize how everything within a culture is interconnected and interdependent. This false dichotomy gives judges a flimsy pretext to excise much of what could merit protection under section 35(1) as merely "incidental."[54] Some claims to justice practices may fail to meet the pre-contact threshold, while others could be deemed merely incidental instead of central and integral. The jurisprudence on section 35(1) tips the scales heavily in favour of the Canadian state. As restrictive as these tests are, Aboriginal rights are also subject to constitutionally justifiable infringement by the Canadian state.

Justifiable Infringement

Section 35 is not part of the Canadian Charter of Rights and Freedoms, but it is in another part of the *Constitution Act, 1982*.[55] Section 35 rights are therefore not subject to justifiable limitation under section 1 of the Charter (more on section 1 later). Nonetheless, the Court has noted that the words "recognized and affirmed" mean that section 35 rights are not absolute. They are still subject to justifiable limitation.[56] The first stage of the limitation test is whether there is a *prima facie* infringement of an Aboriginal right. Chief Justice Brian Dickson stated in *R. v Sparrow:*

> To determine whether the fishing rights have been interfered with such as to constitute a prima facie infringement of s. 35(1), certain questions must be asked. First, is the limitation unreasonable? Second, does the regulation impose undue hardship? Third, does the regulation deny to the holders of the right their preferred means of exercising that right?[57]

In *R. v Gladstone*, the Court affirmed that an Aboriginal litigant does not have to satisfy all three of these tests to demonstrate a *prima facie* infringement. A negative finding on one of the tests will only be one factor to be considered.[58]

The next stage is deciding whether there is a valid legislative objective for infringing the Aboriginal right. In *Sparrow*, the Court stated that "the public interest" is too broad and vague to qualify as a valid objective.[59] Conserving natural resources and preventing the exercise of Aboriginal rights in a way that would cause harm to the general population or to Aboriginal peoples themselves are valid objectives.[60] The Court expanded on this idea in *Gladstone* and stated that legislative objectives are valid if they are directed at either "the recognition of the prior occupation of North America by aboriginal peoples" or "at the reconciliation of aboriginal prior occupation with the assertion of the sovereignty of the Crown."[61] Providing for non-Aboriginal access to a fishery to ensure "regional and economic fairness" is an example of a valid legislative objective directed towards reconciliation between prior occupation and Crown sovereignty.[62] In *Delgamuukw v British Columbia,* the Court affirmed that general economic development is a valid legislative objective for purposes of the test of justifiable infringement.[63]

The next stage is whether the measures in pursuit of the objective are justified. This decision is influenced by *Guerin v The Queen*.[64] In *Guerin*, the Supreme Court of Canada found that the Crown owes fiduciary duties to Aboriginal peoples in particular circumstances.[65] Chief Justice Dickson incorporated the notion of fiduciary obligation first introduced in *Guerin* into the *Sparrow* justification test: "[T]he honour of the Crown is at stake in dealings with Aboriginal peoples. The special trust relationship and the responsibility of the government vis-à-vis Aboriginals must be the first consideration in determining whether the legislation or action in question can be justified."[66] He also adds:

Within the analysis of justification, there are further questions to be addressed, depending on the circumstances of the inquiry. These include the questions of whether there has been as little infringement as possible in order to effect the desired result; whether, in a situation of expropriation, fair compensation is available; and, whether the Aboriginal group in question has been consulted with respect to the conservation measures being implemented.[67]

These tests also represent a potential concern in that Canadian governments can limit the space for Aboriginal approaches to justice so long as they satisfy the tests. How the tests for justifiable infringement would apply in such a context has not yet been addressed by the courts. One can see that it would involve a very complex analysis of competing concerns such as the state's interest in preserving public safety and deterring crime and Aboriginal interests in cultural legitimacy and justice. The results that would come from an analysis under the *Sparrow* tests of justifiable infringement are far from clear at this point. Matthias J. Leonardy suggests that Canadian governments may not be able to satisfy these tests.[68] Aboriginal peoples can make out a *prima facie* violation since Canadian legislation may deny Aboriginal peoples their preferred means of practising justice. Canadian governments trying to assert the application of the full gamut of criminal legislation over Aboriginal peoples take matters closer to a broad "public interest" objective and therefore invite a finding of vagueness. He also suggests that Aboriginal over-incarceration means that Canadian governments cannot satisfy the minimal impairment test. One must be cognizant, however, that these issues have not yet been tested and that courts must treat constitutional issues in relation to the specific fact patterns that come before them.

Treaty Rights

If a treaty is reached between an Aboriginal society and Canada, the rights enjoyed by the Aboriginal group under the terms of that treaty modify or replace their inherent rights under section 35(1). The Supreme Court of Canada has articulated a number of principles of treaty interpretation that apparently favour the Aboriginal signatories as follows:

1. "[A] treaty is a solemn agreement between the Crown and the Indians, an agreement the nature of which is sacred."[69]
2. "[R]elations with Indian tribes fell somewhere between the kinds of relations conducted between sovereign states and the relations that such states had with their own citizens ... [A]n Indian treaty is an agreement *sui generis* which is neither created nor terminated according to the rules of international law."[70]

3. The treaties "should be given a fair, large and liberal generous construc-
   tions [sic] in favour of the Indians."[71] This, in turn, requires that ambiguities
   and uncertainties be resolved in favour of the Aboriginal signatories.[72]
4. Treaties "must ... be construed, not according to the technical meaning
   of [their] words ... but in the sense in which they would naturally be
   understood by the Indians."[73]
5. Treaties should be "interpreted in a flexible way that is sensitive to the
   evolution of changes" in practices that are the subject of treaty rights
   (for example, evolving methods of hunting or fishing).[74]
6. It is implicit that treaty rights include those activities that are "reasonably
   incidental" to those expressly mentioned in a treaty.[75]
7. "[T]he honour of the Crown is always at stake in its dealings with Indian
   people. Interpretations of treaties and statutory provisions which have
   an impact upon treaty or aboriginal rights must be approached in a manner which maintains the integrity of the Crown. It is always assumed
   that the Crown intends to fulfill its promises. No appearance of 'sharp
   dealing' will be sanctioned."[76]

Bruce Wildsmith argues that historically the British – and Canada post-
Confederation – understood the treaties as respecting Aboriginal peoples'
autonomy over their internal affairs.[77] As the Court stated, "[t]he whole
emphasis of Treaty 8 was on the preservation of the Indian's traditional way
of life."[78] With reference to Treaty 6, the Court stated: "It [British Crown]
also allowed them autonomy in their internal affairs, intervening in this
area as little as possible."[79] The Court also noted a letter written by the lieutenant governor of Manitoba and Northwest Territories, Alexander Morris,
to the federal government:

> I then fully explained to them the proposals that I had to make, that we did
> not wish to interfere with their present mode of living, but would assign
> them reserves and assist them as was being done elsewhere, in commencing
> to farm, and that what was done would hold good for those that were away.[80]

In Wildsmith's view, this historical context and the principles of treaty interpretation mean that the treaties recognize Aboriginal autonomy over
internal dispute resolution.[81]

Another example of this recognition is provided by Sákéj Henderson.
Article 6 of the Wabanaki Compact of 1725, reached between the Wabanaki
people and Great Britian, reads:

> If any Controversy or difference at any time hereafter happen to arise be-
> tween any of the English and Indians for any reall or supposed wrong or

injury done on either side no private Revenge shall be taken for the same but proper application shall be made to His Majesty's Government upon the place for Remedy or induse there of in a due course of Justice. We submitting ourselves to be ruled and governed by His Majesty's Laws and desiring to have the benefit of the same.[82]

The last sentence could come across as submission to the colonial legal regime. However, it appears within a clause that only makes specific mention of disputes arising between the Aboriginal peoples and the Crown but makes no mention of a dispute between members of the same Aboriginal society. For Henderson, a proper application of the principles of treaty interpretation means that the British recognized that the Mi'kmaq retained authority over disputes between their own members.[83]

Gordon Christie, however, cautions us that treaty interpretation is not always tipped in favour of the Aboriginal signatories.[84] In *R. v Marshall (no. 1)*, Justice Ian Binnie stated: "The Court's obligation is to "choose from among the various possible interpretations of the *common* intention [and at the time the treaty was made] the one which best reconciles" the Mi'kmaq interests and those of the British Crown.[85] This principle, while seemingly fair, can potentially work at cross-purposes with the other principles of interpretation that favour Aboriginal signatories. Justice Binnie concluded that the Mi'kmaq's right to trade the products that came from their hunting and fishing was limited to the attainment of a "moderate livelihood," which included "food, clothing and housing, supplemented by a few amenities" but did not include the accumulation of wealth. This understanding reflects a reconciliation of the interests of the Mi'kmaq and the Crown and their common intention as of 1760.[86] Christie criticizes this conclusion as referring only to present-day conservation policies, and as giving insufficient consideration to the fact that the Mi'kmaq at the time of the treaty would not likely have understood the truck house clause as implying a limit on the amount of wildlife products that they could bring in for trade.[87]

Another example of how the reconciliation principle can work to the detriment of Aboriginal signatories can be seen in *R. v Badger*.[88] The Supreme Court of Canada interpreted Treaty 8 as permitting the Aboriginal signatories to hunt and trap for food only so long as it did not conflict with "visible, incompatible land use." It is interesting to note that immediately after this interpretation was articulated, the Court acknowledged that "[t]he promise that this livelihood would not be affected was repeated to all the bands who signed the Treaty" by the commissioners who negotiated Treaty 8.[89] John Borrows criticizes this conclusion as allowing non-Aboriginal economic development to always continue in disregard for promises made to the Aboriginal signatories. It always allows non-Aboriginal economic interests to trump constitutionally protected treaty rights.[90]

Henderson identifies other concerns. Treaty rights are subject to the same tests for justifiable infringement that were used in *Sparrow*.[91] He views this as being inconsistent with the nature of treaties as solemn agreements, as the Court perpetuating a "colonial legal consciousness," and as the Court endorsing legislative and executive discrimination against Aboriginal peoples.[92] In *R. v Marshall (no. 2)*, Justice Binnie states: "[R]egulations that do no more than reasonably define the Mí'kmaq treaty right" do not infringe a treaty right.[93] This statement means that "regulatory limits that take the Mí'kmaq catch below the quantities reasonably expected to produce a moderate livelihood or other limitations that are not inherent in the limited nature of the treaty right itself have to be justified according to the Badger test."[94] Henderson criticizes this principle as allowing governments to unilaterally limit treaty rights without even having to meet a justification test.[95]

While there is a strong argument for treaties to recognize Aboriginal rights to criminal jurisdiction, there is also reason for caution. A guarded appraisal can sense danger in certain principles of treaty interpretation that are not generous to Aboriginal signatories. John Borrows argues that Canadian courts have many times recited the principles of treaty interpretation as a matter of routine, but without applying them in any fashion that may genuinely resolve ambiguities in favour of the Aboriginal signatories, without giving meaningful recognition to Aboriginal understandings of the treaties, or without holding the Crown to its duties of honour.[96] The position put forward by the Crown during treaty rights litigation becomes the default position, and this position places an all but impossible burden of proof on Aboriginal litigants.

One can perhaps see this notion at work in both *Marshall (no. 1)*, *Marshall (no. 2)*, and *Badger*. Consider the principle of reconciliation with the Crown's interests. Will the exercise of treaty interpretation bring into the analysis the Crown's interests in preserving order in society and protecting the public? Will this exercise, in turn, legitimate the process of narrowing the treaties' recognition of rights to Aboriginal justice practices? It is impossible to tell at this point how the Supreme Court of Canada would interpret the various treaties when confronted by these questions. But the principle of reconciliation – and how this principle was used during *Marshall* and *Badger* – gives reason for concern. The fact that Canadian governments can "reasonably define" and justifiably infringe treaty rights also leaves cause for concern. Just how far would the court take these principles if Aboriginal communities were to litigate claims to rights to their own justice systems? Would the Court then state that existing criminal legislation and current accommodations such as diversionary programs reasonably define or justifiably infringe treaty rights to past justice practices?

A few observations are also in order regarding modern self-government agreements. The treaty between the Nisga'a, the federal government of

Canada, and the provincial government of British Columbia recognizes Nisga'a jurisdiction over public order, peace, and safety.[97] The Nisga'a may prosecute violations of Nisga'a laws, but they can only use sanctions recognized for summary offences under the *Criminal Code*.[98] Under section 14 of the *Act Relating to Self-Government for the Sechelt Indian Band (Sechelt Act)*, the council of the Sechelt band may punish the violation of any law made by the band government upon summary conviction.[99] Similar provisions that emphasize enforcing local laws through summary conviction are also found in the *Tsawwassen First Nation Final Agreement Act*.[100] These are examples of modern agreements with apparent limitations on traditional justice practices. With modern treaties, the Canadian courts will likely impute a greater degree of education or understanding, and less linguistic difficulty, to the Aboriginal signatories.[101] As such, the absence of linguistic barriers or difficulties in understanding will mean that principles such as resolving textual ambiguities in favour of the Aboriginal signatories will not be invoked in interpreting modern treaties. The text of a modern treaty, if it imposes any limitations upon criminal justice practices, will be determinative if those limitations are spelled out in clear language that is relatively free of ambiguity. Of course, section 3 of the *Sechelt Act* expressly stipulates that the act does not affect inherent or treaty rights. Even so, Leonardy suggests that this stipulation reflects an effort on the part of the federal government to contain an Aboriginal government within parameters resembling those of a municipal body.[102]

Section 35(1) of the *Constitution Act, 1982* does recognize Aboriginal rights as constitutional rights. This provision conceivably provides recognition of Aboriginal substantive jurisdiction over criminal justice. However, the Supreme Court of Canada's interpretations of this provision do not leave a lot of cause for optimism. In the end, Aboriginal rights under the Canadian Constitution are interpreted very narrowly. The present picture is such that if Aboriginal peoples were to pursue substantive jurisdiction over criminal justice through constitutional litigation, such efforts are rather unlikely to succeed. Aboriginal peoples are therefore left without a solid constitutional foundation with which to challenge Canadian policies that accord only limited accommodations. Whether we consider legislators, executives, or the judiciary, it is apparent that Canadian allowances for Aboriginal approaches to justice are quite limited. The motivations and policies that maintain this state of affairs is the subject of the next set of discussions.

Political Obstacles
It is now time to explore the motives and policies behind minimizing the legal space for Aboriginal visions of justice. Judicial interpretations of section 35(1) rights are narrow. Possible motives include the subordination of Aboriginal rights to state sovereignty and a preference that the issues be

resolved by political negotiations instead of litigation. Canadian politicians, in turn, are motivated to sustain the status quo because of political pressure to avoid the appearance of being "soft on crime" and, by extension, to avoid the appearance of Aboriginal offenders obtaining lenient sentences unavailable to non-Aboriginal offenders.

Judicial Doctrine and the Status Quo

More than one explanation can be suggested for the current state of Aboriginal constitutional rights jurisprudence. One suggestion is that the jurisprudence is deliberately designed to leave Canadian sovereignty intact and unchallenged by Aboriginal rights. Inherent rights have been interpreted restrictively, rendering litigation for self-determination rights costly and impractical. Principles of treaty interpretation appear to be generous towards Aboriginal signatories at first blush but also contain strands that leave cause for concern. The reconciliation principle, in particular, leaves concern for how generously courts would interpret the treaties in the contexts of self-determination and criminal jurisdiction.

It is interesting to note that "sovereignty" is a word frequently used in Supreme Court of Canada decisions on Aboriginal rights. In *Sparrow*, Chief Justice Dickson explained:

> It is worth recalling that while British policy towards the native population was based on respect for their right to occupy their traditional land, a proposition to which the Royal Proclamation of 1763 bears witness, there was from the outset never any doubt that sovereignty and legislative power, and indeed the underlying title, to such lands vested in the Crown.[103]

Chief Justice Lamer stated in *Delgamuukw* that section 35(1)'s purpose is to reconcile the prior presence of Aboriginal peoples with the assertion of Crown sovereignty.[104] In *Haida Nation v British Columbia*, Chief Justice Beverley McLachlin stated that the honour of the Crown requires that Aboriginal rights be "determined, recognized, and respected" and that the Crown must negotiate a just settlement of unresolved Aboriginal claims through a treaty-making process.[105] Nonetheless, she also maintained the principle that sovereignty remains vested with the Crown, although it is subject to the duty to act honourably.[106] Numerous scholars have argued that these legal principles reflect a deferential stance that deliberately reinforces Canadian sovereignty at the expense of Aboriginal claims to governance rights and minimizes the capacity of Aboriginal rights to upset the status quo.[107]

Another possible explanation is not so much that the Court is unsympathetic to Aboriginal aspirations but, rather, that the Court questions its own fitness to resolve the issues. Political negotiations are suggested as a better route than litigation for resolving Aboriginal claims. Catherine Bell suggests that the Court has been conscientious of potential backlash against its decisions and therefore pushes such issues "back into the political arena" because "consensual resolution is preferred to the imposition of perceived chaos."[108] Justice Michel Bastarache of the Supreme Court of Canada stated:

> I think the Court is not the right forum for determining how the native rights will blend in with the rights of other citizens in the country, and with citizenship and all of those other issues, and I wish there was a way that most of these things could be determined through negotiation. I don't really believe that the Court is going to be able to be the final arbitrator in that area.[109]

Justice Gérard La Forest, speaking in the context of Aboriginal land title claims, asserted that "the best approach in these types of cases is a process of negotiation and reconciliation that properly considers the complex and competing interests at stake."[110] This rationale may have some justification in that the honour of the Crown does require Canadian governments to pursue a just settlement of unresolved claims, and the test of justifiable infringement typically imposes on the Crown the duty to consult with Aboriginal peoples before pursuing actions that will adversely affect their rights.

This approach suffers from a certain flaw, however. It is difficult to overlook the fact that current accommodations of Aboriginal justice practices, which are the products of negotiations between Aboriginal communities and Canadian leaders, remain minor. The existence of Crown duties of consultation has apparently done little to assist Aboriginal communities in obtaining extensive accommodations of their approaches to justice. The fundamental problem is that the prospect of meaningful negotiations is hampered by a certain reality, despite any preference the Court may have for negotiated solutions and despite the existence of a legal duty to consult that is owed to Aboriginal peoples. The reality is that the Supreme Court has framed Aboriginal rights with significant restrictions that preserve state sovereignty, which has allowed Canadian political leaders to sustain the status quo because Aboriginal peoples are left in a weak negotiating position.[111] The discussion will now explore the political motivations behind perpetuating a minimal level of accommodation.

The Political Inertia against Aboriginal Justice Reform

The reason Canada accords only limited accommodations to Aboriginal visions of justice is that extensive support for Aboriginal community-based alternatives may be politically controversial. "Tough on crime" policies are intended to win political support from the public. To be fair, Western democracies have often recognized the merits of restorative justice and have often implemented restorative justice programs to reflect such recognition.[112] However, such concessions only go so far. Western justice systems have a stake in the use of imprisonment for more serious offences in order to avoid losing public support by appearing to be soft on crime, and this position can translate into a hesitancy to implement alternatives, even if they may prove more effective.[113] David Garland argues that "tough on crime" policies devalue the role of research and efficacy evaluations in comparison with other areas of policy, like wildlife conservation, for example.[114]

And, indeed, voting publics in Western democracies often demand hefty prison terms. Public opinion surveys in the 1990s have indicated that approximately 80 percent of voters in Australia, Canada, the United Kingdom, the Netherlands, and the United States feel that existing sentences are too lenient.[115] Subsequent reports have confirmed that this attitude has persisted in Canada well into the new century. A recent report indicates that at least two-thirds of Canadians support the current Tory government's approach of increased police presence and increased sentences for crime.[116] A particularly lenient individual sentence can indeed provoke public outcry. In Ontario, Anthony and Irene Goodchild's marriage had been falling apart, partially because of Irene's infidelity. Anthony was feeling suicidal and confronted Irene with a shotgun on the night in question. This situation culminated in Anthony fatally discharging a shotgun blast that struck Irene in the neck. Anthony pleaded guilty to manslaughter and received one year of jail, followed by parole and then probation.[117] David Paciocco describes the ensuing outrage:

> The public was appalled. The Sudbury open-line talk shows were abuzz with callers, letters to the editor were sent off, and protests were staged. The sentence, for many, brought the administration of justice into disrepute. It is easy to understand why this sentence was considered to be outrageous. Members of the public would conclude that it was simply too lenient to act as a deterrent to other potential offenders. They would wonder why the cost of killing a human being is less than a year in jail, followed by parole and then probation. What kind of message is this sentence giving? The public would be disturbed that within a year there would be a killer walking in its midst. How does this protect society? Of equal importance, the public would feel that the sentence simply fails to express its outrage at the crime. Symbolically, it devalued the life of Irene Goodchild.[118]

Sometimes the public demand for stiffer sentences is also fuelled by a perceived need to get tough on particular categories of crime. A frequent political response to crimes that have gained public notoriety for being prevalent and/or serious is to increase the imprisonment terms for those offences. Examples in Canada include street racing,[119] auto theft,[120] possessing or trafficking crystal meth, the end of accelerated parole eligibility (one-sixth instead of one-third of one's sentence) for white collar crimes,[121] and an ongoing effort by Stephen Harper's Tory government to impose mandatory minimum sentences for drug-trafficking offences involving gangs or violence.[122]

Public demands on the Canadian state to respond to crime with incarceration and lengthier terms of incarceration present a powerful obstacle to any realization of Aboriginal control over justice. Past Aboriginal justice practices did not always have a restorative emphasis. Nonetheless, those practices that do resemble restorative justice retain an important contemporary significance in the effort to deal with the problem of Aboriginal over-incarceration. A reasonable conclusion is that Canadian politicians are reluctant to extend greater accommodations for fear of losing public support after giving the appearance of being "soft on crime." A study by Julian Roberts and Loretta Stalans has verified that public opinion surveys have consistently demonstrated strong support for applying restorative approaches to less serious crimes (for example, minor property offences) but that support falls off dramatically when it comes to applying restorative approaches to more serious offences, such as violent or sexual crimes.[123]

This reaction reverberates in the level of accommodation towards Aboriginal approaches as well. Even as Aboriginal peoples are subject to over-incarceration and all of the social ills of which over-incarceration is a symptom, they are powerless to pursue their own solutions to the problems beyond the parameters set by the Canadian state. This reality reflects their relative powerlessness as a political minority.[124] Chris Andersen argues that contemporary Aboriginal justice initiatives in Canada reflect an effort by the Canadian political hegemony to indirectly regulate Aboriginal crime and contain Aboriginal aspirations for greater control over justice within certain parameters that in substance leave the status quo intact.[125] Aboriginal justice initiatives display a veneer of community empowerment and accommodation of cultural difference. It is the Canadian state, however, that provides the funding and therefore calls the shots and sets the parameters of the justice initiatives. These parameters include the provisions that Aboriginal accuseds must plead guilty or otherwise accept responsibility and that the justice initiatives will usually only cover the less serious offences that the standard justice system would itself be willing to deal with using community-based sentences (for example, probation and conditional sentences). The Canadian state thus accommodates Aboriginal justice initiatives only to the extent that its own interests happen to converge with those of Aboriginal communities. Once this convergence is no longer there – for example, when Aboriginal communities may want to apply their own approaches to offences that the standard justice system would want to deal with by incarceration – then the accommodation will stop.

Section 718.2(e) has apparently sparked some public controversy in Canada. There were certainly plenty of scathing newspaper editorials directed towards the provision in the years following its enactment.[126] Rachel Dioso and Anthony Doob performed a study to gauge Canadian public opinion on section 718.2(e).[127] They admitted that their sample of survey participants was not necessarily representative of Canada as a whole. Survey participants who viewed the justice system as being too lenient were significantly more likely to view section 718.2(e) negatively (mean = 9.4, with a higher number on the scale indicating a supportive attitude) in comparison to those who viewed current sentences as being about right (mean = 11.3) and those who viewed sentences as being too harsh (mean = 12.7). One has to wonder how the Canadian public at large would view section 718.2(e) given that public opinion surveys still indicate that a substantial majority in Canada consider the justice system to be too lenient.

Policies that rely extensively on imprisonment, as applied to everybody, end up having a very adverse impact on Aboriginal people, who are powerless to challenge such policies as a political minority. For the politicians, addressing the harsh penal policies that are applied to Aboriginal peoples in any truly meaningful fashion would give the especially unpalatable appearance of being lenient towards Aboriginal offenders and offering them concessions that the non-Aboriginal majority do not enjoy. Canadian authorities are able to impose their will in this fashion due to judicial deference that promotes state sovereignty at the expense of Aboriginal self-determination.

This reality is acutely demonstrated in the tragic story of Christopher Pauchay, a member of the Yellow Quill Cree nation in Saskatchewan, and his two young daughters. Pauchay was home alone with Kaydance, aged three, and Santana, aged one, during January 2008. The temperatures during the night in question were close to minus 50 degrees Celcius. Pauchay was drunk that night and refused the offer of his brother-in-law to take care of the girls, asserting that he could look after them himself. One of the girls was apparently hurt. Christopher, while intoxicated, decided to try and bring them to his sister's house in order to get help. At some point, he became separated from the girls and only managed to arrive at a neighbour's house during the early hours of the next morning. He was overcome with frostbite and hypothermia. Eight hours later, he recovered enough to remember the night before and asked about his daughters. This realization set off a frantic search. Both girls were found frozen to death beneath snowdrifts, wearing only t-shirts and diapers.[128]

A sentencing circle was held, with the result that the Yellow Quill Elders as well as the chief of the reserve, Larry Cachane, wanted Pauchay to undergo spiritual healing and rehabilitation instead of going to prison.[129] Some of the reactions to the tragedy within the Yellow Quill community itself reflect Aboriginal philosophies on how to deal with harmful behaviour. The girls' grandmother, Irene Nippi, said in an interview: "I was worried about my grandchildren. I did not want them to leave this world in vain. I hope there's change now that happens – a lot of changes like no alcohol and counseling and stuff to be brought in here. Our old teachings should be brought back."[130] Community members' responses provide examples of how an individual tragedy can signal the pressing need to address issues affecting the community at large. Pauchay's stepmother, Jo Anne Machiskinic, said she felt angered that a tragedy such as this one had to happen before the community was alerted to the need to address problems of alcohol abuse. Elder Howard Walker called the tragedy a "wake-up call to society."[131] Tim Quigley, a law professor at the University of Saskatchewan, emphasized during an interview with the Canadian Broadcasting Corporation that a sentencing circle would actually be a much more difficult ordeal for Pauchay than a standard sentencing hearing because he would have to listen to community members describe to him how his actions have affected their lives.[132]

Efforts to have Pauchay's case resolved through a sentencing circle and non-custodial alternatives inspired a significant number of scathing newspaper editorials across the country. Mindelle Jacobs, for example, writes:

> Nothing will bring back his children, Kaydance, and Santana. At the same time, nothing will be accomplished by concluding such a horrific crime merits a mere community sentence. In this case, accepting responsibility and expressing remorse isn't enough. There has to be some expression of societal contempt for such behaviour and a non-custodial group hug just doesn't cut it.[133]

John Mohan, the chief executive officer of the Siloam Mission in Winnipeg, emphasized the viewpoint that harm to the victims demands retribution:

> A just society should consider circumstances and intent when determining sentencing. But what is too often overlooked in cases like these is justice for the victims. To deem someone not criminally responsible or absolve them of consequences because they were drunk or not treating their mental illness devalues both their crime and the people wronged. Valuing and ensuring justice for victims may do far more to restore sanity to our communities than deflected responsibility or a lenient sentence could.[134]

Such opinions have not just come from newspaper columnists either. This rather strongly worded opinion letter was sent to the *Winnipeg Sun:*

I read that the defence team for Christopher Pauchay (the father that killed his two children by blindly stumbling about the freezing prairies with them both dressed in nothing but diapers and a light shirt) is asking for him to be sentenced by a native sentencing circle. I truly hope the judge sees what bull this is and puts him away for the prescribed time in a real jail. It stated that he has accepted his responsibility – big deal. If I go out and rob a bank and not kill anyone I'm still going away to jail. Maybe being Scottish I should ask for the ancient punishment of banishment. I'm sure that this would teach me a lesson. Let's get real.[135]

The presiding judge, Barry Morgan, rejected the sentencing circle recommendations and gave Pauchay a sentence of three years imprisonment, in part because he was not convinced that Pauchay fully understood his role in the girls' deaths.[136] It must be kept in mind that Judge Morgan, as an impartial judge, was not allowed to craft the sentence according to the dictates of public outrage or passions. His job is to apply Canadian law on the appropriate sentence for criminal negligence causing death, which carries a maximum term of life imprisonment under section 220(b) of the *Criminal Code* and very often requires at a minimum a term of incarceration.[137] It must nonetheless be kept in mind that the law he was applying was Canadian law, enacted by elected Canadian legislators. This case, leaving aside for a moment the merits of what Christopher Pauchay may or may not have deserved as a negligent father, demonstrates how Canadian attitudes towards crime and justice can manifest hostility towards Aboriginal restorative approaches. The legal and political realities are such that Canadian law is applied as a matter of course so as to trump approaches that Aboriginal communities may want to use to address crime.

Conclusion

The legal and political space for Aboriginal approaches to justice within Canada is rather minimal to say the least. Canadian accommodations are limited for the most part to less serious offences and to when an Aboriginal offender is prepared to plead guilty or accept responsibility. There is an acute political inertia against any further accommodation since it can give the especially undesirable appearance of affording a leniency in the sanctioning of Aboriginal offenders that is not available to non-Aboriginal offenders. Aboriginal constitutional rights have been interpreted restrictively, leaving Aboriginal peoples with a poor foundation upon which to press for more extensive accommodations from the Canadian state. Any efforts by Aboriginal peoples to reclaim substantive jurisdiction over criminal justice, whether it involves constitutional litigation, negotiations that are marked by obvious disparities in bargaining power, or other possible methods, will obviously face immense challenges. Let us imagine for a moment, however, that such challenges are overcome and that Aboriginal peoples have a broadly recognized constitutional right to substantive criminal jurisdiction. There is an important issue that will need to be considered, one that involves greater collective power for Aboriginal communities. With this power, there is also an increased potential for abuses of collective power against Aboriginal individuals. Should the power of Aboriginal collectivities be emphasized so that they can promote harmony, traditional values, and responsibilities? Should the rights and liberties of the Aboriginal individual be emphasized instead to prevent power abuses by Aboriginal leaders? Such possibilities invite an apparent tension.

The remainder of this discussion will proceed on a certain assumption, namely, that Aboriginal peoples have a broad jurisdiction over criminal justice in their own communities and that it is a jurisdiction that is legally and judicially recognized under section 35(1) of the *Constitution Act, 1982*. This assumption may seem dubious since gaining such jurisdiction would depend in no small part on persuading the Supreme Court of Canada to depart from the stringent *Van der Peet* tests. There is at present no indication that such a development is forthcoming. However, it is a necessary assumption that makes possible many of the subsequent discussions in this work.

4
Addressing the Tension

The goal of this chapter is to describe in general terms the problems that the Canadian Charter of Rights and Freedoms presents for Aboriginal approaches to justice.[1] By its very nature, the Charter engages a tension between collective power and individual liberty.

Collective Power versus Individual Liberty

The General Tension

Any society is faced with a fundamental issue when developing a system of governance. A society may deem individual liberty and the freedom to pursue self-interest to be of paramount value. This decision implies limiting collective power over the individual. Another society may deem that empowering the collective to pursue the good of the whole is of paramount value. Protecting individual rights against collective power becomes correspondingly of less value. There is a tension between the two concepts.[2] Emphasizing one will be at the expense of the other. Societies often try to accommodate both concepts, although, in practice, their legal and political systems can end up placing greater emphasis on one relative to the other. The two concepts may be thought of as opposite ends of a spectrum, whereby any given society may end up at its own place on the spectrum.

Western democracies have tended to adopt approaches that favour the individual liberty end of the spectrum. Classical liberalism is one example of such an approach.[3] Loren Lomasky describes classical liberal theories of rights as follows:

> Liberals take rights very seriously; they are the heavy artillery of the moral arsenal ... For one viewing from outside the liberal church, this insistence on respect for rights will seem somewhat mysterious, if not bordering on fanaticism. Rights block the realization of otherwise alluring social ends – for

example, those of a redistributive nature intended to advance overall welfare or equality. They also impede paternalistic interventions designed to prevent individuals from doing harm to themselves.[4]

This tension between collective power and individual rights is relevant to the issue of Aboriginal control over justice in two specific contexts. One context is a conflict between Western liberal emphases on individual liberty and Aboriginal traditions that emphasize the collective good. The other context is a conflict between the crime control and due process models of criminal justice. The first context is dealt with in the next section.

Aboriginal Collective Values versus Western Individual Rights
Pre-colonial Aboriginal societies can be said, within very general terms, to have placed a greater relative emphasis on the good of the collective. The Dene of the Canadian north, for example, had very strict rules concerning the hunting of game and the distribution of the products of the hunt. Failing to distribute meat so as to ensure that everyone was provided for or failing to observe spiritual taboos so as to ensure the availability of game were violations of customary law. Particularly serious or repeated violations could lead to an individual's permanent exile from the community because he or she had endangered the well-being of the entire community.[5]

Western liberal democracies have placed a greater emphasis on individual rights relative to Aboriginal customary law. This preference has drawn criticism from Aboriginal academics. Gordon Christie opposes the imposition of legal structures that reflect Western liberalism on Aboriginal communities.[6] Liberal theory emphasizes the autonomy of the individual – the individual pursuit of the good life. This emphasis in turn is reflected in a legal structure that emphasizes individual freedom, autonomy, and rights. Aboriginal concepts of pursuing the good life are quite different. The individual is understood in the context of broader relationships with the Aboriginal community and its other members. Aboriginal cultures promote values of responsibility to the community and to others. An individual was expected to contribute to the good of the collective and often even to subordinate self-interest if doing so would enhance collective well-being.

In Western democracies, the relationship between the individual and the community is displayed in very different terms. An example can be seen in the different viewpoints regarding the distribution of material goods. Western notions of private property emphasize the rights of the individual holder to exclude others from possession, even the state under normal circumstances. The state may acquire public property, levy taxes in order to acquire funds to finance public policies, and thereby achieve some redistribution of wealth. Nonetheless, an individual may use whatever resources are left to him or her, after taxation and perhaps state acquisition, to acquire as much property as he or she desires and can afford. The individual is usually not under any legal obligation to use his or her material goods to look out for the well-being of others, even when he or she is aware of the homelessness or starvation of others. Charity and philanthropy are at the discretion of the individual property holder.

Many Aboriginal societies, by contrast, placed a heavy emphasis on ensuring that the material needs of everyone were seen to and a corresponding de-emphasis on the individual acquisition of material wealth. Jesuit Father Ragueneau said of eastern Aboriginal peoples:

> No hospitals [shelters] are needed among them, because there are neither mendicants nor paupers as long as there are any rich people among them. Their kindness, humanity, and courtesy not only make them liberal with what they have, but cause them to possess hardly anything except in common. A whole village must be without corn, before any individual can be obliged to endure privation. They divide the produce of their fisheries equally with all who come.[7]

The Lake Babine utilized their *balhat* ceremonies as a method of achieving the equitable distribution of wealth. Chiefs and other notable authorities used *balhats* to distribute goods to other community members in displays of generosity. It was also during *balhats* that material goods were provided to community members who needed them.[8] Steven Wall argues that these kinds of cultural differences may continue to reverberate to the present day, such that there remains a latent and ongoing tension between individual liberal rights and Aboriginal collective rights.[9] The specific example that he gives is that an Aboriginal government may hypothetically permit individual members to dispose of individual pieces of land that they reside on in an effort to enhance their own material well-being (for example, the sale of land). Wall contends, however, that such a possibility may be unlikely since it can threaten the land base of the Aboriginal community, thereby setting up a tension between the collective good and individual freedom.

According to Christie, it is the Elders of an Aboriginal community who pass on collective values from generation to generation in a system of non-coercive transmission. The imposition of liberal legal structures amounts to oppression in that it fails to respect the collective autonomy of Aboriginal communities, promotes the pursuit of individual self-interest at the expense of Aboriginal cultural values of responsibility, and disrupts the system of non-coercive transmission.[10] Mary-Ellen Turpel-Lafond has expressed concerns that the Charter may invite Aboriginal individuals to invoke Charter rights against their own governments, and such action can "break down community methods of dispute-resolution and restoration, or place limits on the re-establishment of such methods."[11]

On the other hand, Roger Gibbins warns us of dangers involved with an absence of individual rights protections in contemporary Aboriginal communities:

> The Charter takes on additional importance when we realize that individual rights and freedoms are likely to come under greater threat from Indian governments than they are from other governments in Canada. This is not because Indians are particularly insensitive toward individual rights, although the desire to protect collective rights could well encourage such insensitivity. The threat to individual rights and freedoms comes from the size and homogeneity of Indian communities rather than from their "Indianness" per se. Indian communities tend to be small and characterized by extensive family and kinship ties, and it is in just such communities that individual rights and freedoms are most vulnerable.[12]

With Aboriginal communities, it is not just a simple dichotomy between the collective and the individual. There is an additional layer or dimension. As Gibbins' excerpt makes clear, contemporary Aboriginal communities are often characterized by strife between rival clans or families. These families often compete with each other for political power and control over monetary resources. When a family wrests the reins of power for itself, it often exploits that power to the benefit of its own members and to the exclusion of rival families.[13]

Real concerns surrounding Aboriginal self-determination are the allegations of corruption surrounding the current chief and council system under the *Indian Act* and fears that it will become worse should such institutional arrangements gain expanded powers or not be accountable to another authority, such as Ottawa.[14] Bill Wuttunnee, founding chief of the Assembly of First Nations, once said in an interview:

> One guy in Saskatchewan recently borrowed $550,000 to run for chief, and then bribed voters; he gave them straight cash. On the Red Pheasant reserve, the chief and council blew $4 million of the federal government's Treaty Land Entitlement money, and there was no way anyone could stop it. You can't report it to the police, and who has money for a lawsuit?[15]

A task force in Alberta that interviewed in 1998 over 300 status Indians and Métis concluded that many Aboriginal persons at the time were not supportive of self-government for fear of corruption, lack of accountability, nepotism, and misconduct during band elections.[16] One could say, of course, that the *Indian Act* system, or any variation thereof, is not truly representative of Aboriginal governance ideals. This is a point I will return to later in this chapter.

In 1997, Judge John Reilly heard a case of domestic assault that occurred in the Stoney Reserve in Alberta. Judge Reilly interpreted section 718.2(e) as allowing him to order the provincial Crown to investigate allegations of corruption and intimidation on the reserve, as they would be part of the background circumstances of the Aboriginal offender before his court.[17] He described at length the various allegations that had been made by Stoney people against Chief John Snow, including his spending much of the community's resources on the Nakoda Lodge tourist facility to the neglect of education and social programs, misusing the Nakoda Lodge to his own benefit and the benefit of his family, selling off millions of dollars worth of timber from Stoney lands to outside corporations while his own people derived no benefit, exercising a family monopoly on the nation's monetary resources, frequently firing educational staff in order to destabilize education on the reserve, and deliberately destabilizing education in order to assure his own dominance.[18] Judge Reilly suggested that corruption lay at the heart of crime on the Stoney Reserve:

> The "ghetto mentality" is an attitude of hopelessness in which people are resigned to the fact that there will never be enough for everyone and survival requires getting enough for yourself, no matter what the cost to others. There is a powerlessness that results in weak people dominating weaker people as the only way that they can feel any sense of self worth. This results in family violence, school violence, and violence in the community.[19]

There is an apparent tension here. On the one hand, vesting greater power in Aboriginal communities, unchecked by individual rights standards, enables those communities to subordinate individual autonomy. The examples described earlier also make it clear that greater power can have a corrupting influence. The additional dimension of familial rivalry means that the abuse of power over the individual can take on a particular shade. If a family wrests the reins of power for itself, that family can set the "collective goals" for the Aboriginal community at large. The pursuit of such "collective goals" can end up leading to the benefit of the dominant family and to the neglect or even persecution of rival families. On the other hand, vesting Aboriginal individuals with individual rights can frustrate the pursuit of collective goals by a community, assuming that such goals genuinely reflect the desires of most of the community and not just of a dominant family. Such frustration results because Aboriginal individuals are legally empowered to challenge the pursuit of such goals as well as the application of community law. It is in this context that the debate over collective power versus individual rights is relevant to Aboriginal control over justice. The second context has to do with the nature of criminal justice.

Crime Control versus Due Process

Herbert Packer describes two different models of criminal process: the crime control model and the due process model.[20] Each embodies two different sets of values that compete with each other in regard to how the criminal process is structured and what goals the process pursues. The crime control model attaches primacy to maximizing the efficiency with which the process detects crime and then apprehends, convicts, and punishes offenders.[21] The ultimate objective is the punishment at the end of the process. Packer's starting point is that deterrence is utilitarian in that it strives for the social benefit of decreased crime. It tries to use the certainty of punishment following the commission of a crime to persuade people *a priori* against committing a crime. This end, however, should not be the exclusive goal of punishment. If it were, then the preventative aspect could only be realized by the absolute certainty of punishment following the commission of a prescribed act. This certainty can only be assured by not allowing the accused to claim any exculpatory justifications (defences) for the act. Taking the assurance that far is not desirable in Packer's estimation because it leaves the criminal law without a firm foundation for assessing blame and because it leaves citizens unable to plan their actions with such certainty as to avoid "entanglement with the criminal law." Packer argues that exculpatory justifications and the prospect of punishment following the commission of prescribed acts should be combined together in a harmonious system of punishment that promotes crime control. It not only strives to prevent crime *a priori* but also strives to guide and persuade citizens towards moral and law-abiding habits. The idea is that it is made clear to citizens that certain types of conduct will lead to criminal sanction, while others will not.[22]

If crime control is prioritized, it comes at the expense of legal rights during the criminal process. This is because legal rights compromise the efficiency in detecting and then sanctioning offenders that is valued by the crime control model.[23] For example, rights to search and seizure and against arbitrary detention can limit the ability of police to gather evidence. The rights to silence and to counsel can limit the ability of the police to interrogate suspects. The presumption of innocence and the right to silence make it harder for the state to procure a conviction during trial.

The due process model places reliability as the paramount value instead of efficiency. Efficiency, if taken too far, can lead to erroneously punishing an innocent individual. The process must instead ensure that there is a reliable foundation upon which to justify punishing an accused. For example, frailties and inconsistencies in the evidence must be revealed by cross-examination. Confessions should be reliable, freely given, and not the product of coercion or deception. The presumption of innocence must oblige the state to adduce enough reliable evidence to justify convicting the accused.[24] Packer argues that there is a tension between the two models.

Prioritizing one comes at the expense of the other. Too much efficiency can be a recipe for tyranny. Too much reliability can endanger society by limiting the capacity of its legal system to deal with crime.[25] This aspect of criminal process blends with the tension between Aboriginal collective values and individual rights to produce a particularly acute tension that is specific to Aboriginal aspirations for control over justice.

The Tension Involved with Aboriginal Control over Justice
The tension between the crime control and due process models is tied in with the collective good versus individual liberty dichotomy. In so far as societies want to preserve their collective security, they would want to enhance the efficiency with which their criminal justice systems can detect, investigate, and then prosecute criminal activity. It has been argued, for example, that in the wake of 11 September 2001, Western democracies have been tempted to make strong moves in favour of crime control to address the threat of terrorist activity, even at the considerable expense of individual rights.[26] Other scholars have stressed the need for due process safeguards in order to protect individual liberty against wrongful conviction, intimidation, and other abuses of power by authorities.[27]

These issues are also relevant to Aboriginal aspirations for control over criminal justice. If Aboriginal societies were to make contemporary use of punitive sanctions, such as public shaming and corporal punishment, the objectives behind them could be deterrence and public denunciation of crime. They would have a crime control emphasis. Restorative justice methods, even though they eschew reliance upon imprisonment, can also be thought of as having a crime control emphasis.

Kent Roach articulates a contrary view. He describes Packer's two models as overly simplistic and constructs two additional models. One is the punitive model of victim's rights, which shares similarities with the crime control model and opposes the due process model for similar reasons. There are two key differences, however. One, it is no longer a state interest in preserving public order that is pitted against an accused's rights. It is the rights of the victim, for sanction against the wrong done to that individual victim and against further re-victimization within the criminal process, that are pitted directly against an accused's rights. Second, it is reflexively critical of the crime control model in that it highlights the failures of the system to prevent the victimization of individuals, whether it involves a failure to encourage the reporting of a criminal action, a failure to prevent a second victimization within the process itself, or a failure to enhance actual security for potential victims (for example, security cameras and neighbourhood watches). Roach's other model is the circle model, which is essentially a description of restorative justice and its critique of the punitive inclinations found among Western justice systems.[28] Roach argues that restorative justice is an entirely distinct model from the crime control model because the latter is more punitive, it focuses on retribution for the past instead of future reparation, and it lacks emphasis on victim interests by comparison.[29]

Despite Roach's insistence on depicting restorative justice as a separate model, restorative justice can be understood as having a crime control emphasis if a more flexible understanding of crime control is adopted than was originally intended by Packer. Recall Kathleen Daly's position that retributive and restorative justice systems both assess punishments but with different goals.[30] Restorative justice prescribes punishment with a view towards rehabilitation and reintegration. Restorative justice strives for crime control but in a different way. It strives to reduce crime by dealing with the root causes of crime, reforming an offender to prevent future recidivism and improving relationships within the community at large.[31] In this light, Aboriginal traditions with parallels to restorative justice do have a certain crime control emphasis. And this crime control emphasis does tie in with the pursuit of collective goals in Aboriginal communities.

Aboriginal customary law and value systems have generally been depicted as emphasizing the good of the community as a whole, at least relative to the individualistic emphasis of Western liberal rights. Aboriginal justice practices that have a crime control emphasis, whether they be public shaming, corporal punishments, or restorative resolutions, can be used to further the objectives of Aboriginal customary law and values. They can address the underlying causes of Aboriginal criminality. They can rehabilitate Aboriginal offenders. They can further harmony and co-operation in Aboriginal communities. They can deter Aboriginal individuals from violating customary law. They can inculcate traditional values in Aboriginal people, offender and otherwise.

In contrast to these objectives are the Western standards of legal rights that value a sphere of autonomy surrounding the individual upon which the state should not intrude. This notion often takes the form of civil liberties such as freedoms of expression, association, and religion. This sphere of individual autonomy takes on very particular features in a criminal justice context (that is, the due process model). These features include rights against unreasonable search and seizure, the presumption of innocence, the right to silence, the right to a fair trial, the right to have a case heard before an impartial judicial authority, and others.

The presence of both Aboriginal methods of justice and liberal legal rights during the criminal process within the same social field can produce a particularly acute tension that is not easy to address. If Aboriginal individuals apply for the enforcement of liberal legal rights against an Aboriginal justice system, it can lead to those individuals not being subject to any process or any sanction at all. Examples could include findings that the police had conducted an illegal search of the accused's premises or that they had violated the right to counsel. A potential result is that the evidence will be excluded, meaning that no case can be made against an Aboriginal accused. This result can frustrate the realization of collective goals. Jonathan Rudin and Dan Russell state:

> The difficulty with allowing Charter challenges against alternative dispute resolution systems is that, at their core, these challenges represent philosophical disagreements between members of the community. The person initiating the Charter challenge is seeking to have the community's justice system conform to fit the prevailing Canadian norms of causality and criminality. The success of the individual's Charter claim would lead to the destruction of the collective attempt to create an alternative system that responds to the needs of the community as a whole.[32]

On the other hand, consider what may happen if an Aboriginal justice system prioritizes the collective good over individual liberty to the point of not including any sort of checks and balances. Suppose that an Aboriginal justice system prioritizes the promotion of collective harmony, the deterrence and denunciation of crime through traditional punitive sanctions, and the reduction of crime. If Aboriginal community leaders prioritize these goals, then they may desire to enhance the power of their justice system to subject the Aboriginal individual to the will of the collective. This decision can lead to a corresponding de-emphasis on individual rights – on the presence of any checks and balances – because they limit the power of the collective over the individual. With greater power over the individual comes greater potential for abuse of that power. Examples can include punishing an Aboriginal individual who is not factually guilty of an offence or coercing the individual into consenting to a particularly harsh and onerous resolution. The tension is not an easy one to address. However, that is not to say that we should not try. This chapter will now take a particular approach to addressing this tension.

Culturally Sensitive Interpretations of Legal Rights

The concept being advanced in this book is one of reinterpreting the legal rights of the Charter in order to be more accommodating towards Aboriginal justice practices. The Royal Commission on Aboriginal Peoples states: "[T]he Charter must be given a flexible interpretation that takes account of the distinctive philosophies, traditions and cultural practices of Aboriginal peoples."[33] This approach of culturally sensitive interpretations of legal rights commends itself as a workable method of addressing the tension. It tries to bring in the best of both worlds. It aspires to prevent legal rights from altogether eroding justice practices grounded in Aboriginal cultures that have emphasized the collective good while also providing an Aboriginal individual with culturally sensitive and meaningful modes of redress against potential abuses of collective power. There are, however, at least two objections to this approach. The first one is discussed in the next section.

Continued Colonialism

It could be argued that culturally sensitive interpretations of legal rights is itself a colonial imposition since it requires Aboriginal justice practices to adjust themselves to bear some resemblance, even if limited, to Western standards of rights protections. It is therefore inconsistent with self-determination – an objective that this book affirms. If Aboriginal community leaders want a justice system that heavily favours collective power, without any safeguards against abuses of collective power, this system will certainly represent an exercise of self-determination. It may not, however, be well advised.

If Aboriginal communities obtain self-determination over criminal justice, individual rights must be accounted for somehow, and culturally sensitive interpretations of legal rights as a voluntary exercise of self-determination represent a workable option. Consider this article on an Aboriginal police force in Saskatchewan:

> Saskatchewan's first self-administered police force was formally established in May, and polices the Carry the Kettle, Little Black Bear, Okanese, Peepeekisis and Star Blanket First Nations east of Regina. It has received the first blow to its public image after receiving a complaint from a family after a teenager's arm was broken while in custody. Colleen Stevenson, who lives on the Carry the Kettle First Nation, wants to know how her 15-year-old son, Timothy, suffered a broken arm while in custody of the File Hills First Nations Police. "I don't see how a man in a uniform with an obligation to protect the community is out there inflicting pain, breaking bones," she said.
>
> Timothy Stevenson was with another person when he was arrested last week. He was kept in custody for 12 hours and said he was denied medical attention. He was never charged with any offence. Police Chief Ralph Martin, who oversees seven officers, confirmed that the injury occurred while the teen was in custody. He has met with the family to discuss the case, but the police force has made little information about the incident public. In response to this lack of information, Timothy Stevenson's grandfather, Delmar Runns, alleges the poor treatment of a resident is not an isolated incident. "I think, for myself, we should go back to the RCMP, because the tribal police are overreacting," Runns said. "They're overdoing it."
>
> The province's public complaints commission says it's aware of the allegation about the teenager, but hasn't received a formal complaint. It could investigate itself or turn the matter over to an outside police force.[34]

Note how these perceived abuses of power have led to at least one local individual demanding that outside authorities take matters over to set them right. If contemporary Aboriginal justice systems are to enjoy the support of community members, some allowance has to be made for individual rights and the prevention of power abuses. Self-determination must embrace some form of rights protection, and culturally sensitive interpretations of legal rights represent a workable method for realizing it. There is, however, another objection that is closely related.

No Longer Tradition?
Culturally sensitive interpretations of legal rights, by their very nature, involve incorporating laws and practices that were not previously features of Aboriginal traditional law. Can blending both Aboriginal and Western legal concepts still be thought of as reflecting Aboriginal beliefs and value systems? Can it still be called Aboriginal traditional law? One could answer no, which does not necessarily have to be an undesirable answer from the perspective of Aboriginal peoples, especially if Aboriginal communities themselves decide to pursue this route. Law is neither an isolated nor a static unit. Law is a dynamic phenomenon. Our knowledge of Aboriginal history prior to contact may be limited. Even so, can any Aboriginal people (or any other society for that matter) confidently assert that their laws and practices have remained exactly the same throughout the ages, notwithstanding interactions with other Aboriginal groups, whether through trade, migrations, or other forms of interaction? An example may be in order. The basis of Iroquois traditional law is the Great Law of Peace. In simple terms, the Great Law set out the governing structure of the Iroquois confederacy. The clan mothers selected the chiefs. The chiefs resolved disputes and governed the general affairs of the confederacy. They could be deposed if the clan mothers decided they were not doing a good job or if they behaved in a manner that was not befitting their position. The cornerstones of the great law of peace were (1) peace; (2) responsibility (to the people as a whole); and (3) reason. Peace was more than the absence of war, it was a state of mind that each member of the confederacy was to strive for so that the confederacy could reach for, and sustain, a state of genuine harmony. The origins of the great law of peace were tied to a figure known as the peace maker. He was Huron by birth. He spent years preaching the message of the Great Law of Peace until it gained general acceptance among the Iroquois, whose existence had previously been marked by violent feuding.[35]

The peace maker may be identified as a point of genesis for Iroquoian law. However, we know little of Iroquois law prior to the peace maker. The violent feuding may suggest complete lawlessness beforehand, but do we know that for certain? Were the warring factions feuding out of a sense of obligation to seek honour or from a sense of vengeance? What the peace maker does signify is that the Iroquois people made a choice to depart from the status quo and accept a new law. There may have been initial divisions among the Iroquois over the Great Law, with some individuals initially being reluctant to embrace it. In the end, the Iroquois did not cling to the past but, instead, adopted something new, something that had not been "traditional," because it better met the needs of their time.

If Aboriginal societies willingly and selectively draw upon Western legal concepts, it can merely amount to another step in the millennia-old evolution of law among Aboriginal peoples. Of course, one could persist with the objection that it still practically represents an obligation to depart from what had been traditional law. Canadian legal and political institutions, enjoying far greater power, have the leisure of according only minor accommodations of Aboriginal perspectives on justice. Aboriginal peoples, by comparison, can find themselves under considerable pressure to acquiesce in Canadian state policy that insists on the full-scale application of the Charter. The fact of the matter is that culturally sensitive interpretations of legal rights may at least provide a better alternative for preserving Aboriginal justice traditions than the usual insistence on the full application of the Charter. Culturally sensitive interpretations of legal rights provide an opportunity for Aboriginal communities to pursue a balance on terms that are acceptable to the communities, as opposed to the unilateral application of the Charter. Principles in Canadian constitutional law, as we will see in later discussions, may be such that the Canadian state cannot necessarily force Aboriginal peoples to accept the full application of the Charter. Aboriginal law can still remain Aboriginal law if Aboriginal peoples choose to selectively incorporate Western legal concepts according to their contemporary needs.

There is reason to believe that some form of formal rights protections may be relevant to the needs and realities of contemporary Aboriginal communities. Aboriginal peoples live in a far different world than the one they lived in prior to contact. It is a world that is marked by different technologies and different economics and, therefore, one that is thoroughly suffused with relationships of hierarchy and power. This situation presents challenges for present-day Aboriginal governance.[36] Robert Porter argues that a critical issue for modern Aboriginal sovereignty is infighting and competition for economic opportunities.[37] Such behaviour includes competition for revenue from economic development – for example, casino profits – which, in turn, spurs competition for political power. With greater political power comes greater access to economic opportunities.

This competition for political power and economic opportunities can have implications for justice in Aboriginal communities. Suppose that a particular family or faction secures economic and political power to become the elite of an Aboriginal community. A potential concern then is that the elite can use justice processes to oppress their rivals and to maintain their elite position. There are numerous documented instances of powerful elites around the world using their resources to corrupt the administration of justice to their own benefit. Examples include allegations of corporate executives receiving preferential treatment from law enforcement officials to avoid the inspection of their business activities,[38] of organized criminals bribing police and other public officials to avoid prosecution,[39] of organized criminals and state officials co-operating with each other in pursuit of mutual profit,[40] of political elites compromising judicial independence to avoid successful prosecution for their own corruption,[41] of political elites using the police to undermine political opponents,[42] of anti-corruption investigators having been sidelined to avoid further investigation,[43] and of police abusing their powers to advance their own material interests.[44]

Of course, it could be said that such social realities do not reflect Aboriginal ideals. The current state of affairs in Aboriginal communities represents an undesirable loss of tradition in the lives of Aboriginal people.[45] How far back, though, can the clock be turned? Yes, Aboriginal traditions of governance, responsibility, and interpersonal relationships may have contemporary relevance for Aboriginal peoples. Those traditions, however, somehow have to make their mark in a social setting (and, yes, one that has regrettably been introduced by colonialism) that lends itself very well to the formation, and perpetuation, of relationships that are marked by inequities of wealth and power. With such relationships comes a greater potential for the abuse of power. Is it a realistic hope that any people, Aboriginal or non-Aboriginal, can completely avoid the need for formal safeguards against governing power in today's world? The selective incorporation of Western legal concepts does not need to amount to an abandonment of tradition. It can amount to an evolution of Aboriginal law that better meets contemporary needs. This approach is complicated nonetheless because it involves synthesizing many different and often contradictory legal principles. How to realize such an approach is the subject of the next chapter.

5

Realizing the Culturally Sensitive Interpretation of Legal Rights

Canadian Law and the Culturally Sensitive Interpretation of Legal Rights

An essential consideration involved with realizing the culturally sensitive interpretation of legal rights is the exploration of how the concept may fit within the broader Canadian legal system. To begin with, section 35(1) of the *Constitution Act, 1982* will again be assumed to include Aboriginal rights to criminal jurisdiction.[1] Section 7 of the act reads: "Everyone has the right to life, liberty and security of the person and the right not to be deprived thereof except in accordance with the principles of fundamental justice." The principles of fundamental justice are considered to provide many of the philosophical underpinnings of the criminal justice system. Justice Antonio Lamer (as he then was) had this to say about section 7 in the context of criminal law: "[T]he principles of fundamental justice are to be found in the basic tenets of our legal system."[2] Sections 8 to 14 provide more specific legal rights, such as the right to counsel, the right to a fair trial, the right against arbitrary detention, and the right to be presumed innocent until proven guilty beyond a reasonable doubt. The question becomes how would these legal rights impact upon Aboriginal rights to criminal jurisdiction under section 35(1)? What legal authority would be used to resolve an ensuing conflict?

There are two sources of legal authority that may be relevant to the issue. One is section 25 of the Charter, which, depending on its interpretation, may accord blanket immunity to Aboriginal governments from any challenge based on the Charter.[3] Another is a constitutional doctrine that mandates striking a balance when one constitutional right comes into conflict with another constitutional right. An analysis of section 25 follows in the next section.

Section 25

Section 25 of the Charter reads:

The guarantee in this Charter of certain rights and freedoms shall not be construed so as to abrogate or derogate from any aboriginal, treaty or other rights or freedoms that pertain to the aboriginal peoples of Canada including:

(a) any rights or freedoms that have been recognized by the Royal Proclamation of October 7, 1763; and
(b) any rights or freedoms that now exist by way of land claims agreements or may be so acquired.

The typical understanding of section 25 is that it prevents challenges by non-Aboriginal peoples to the rights protected in section 35 on the basis of the right to equality under section 15 of the Charter.[4] An example is where Aboriginal fishermen have a right of preferred access to fisheries for ceremonial and sustenance purposes. Early academic commentary on this provision suggested that section 25 shielded existing section 35 rights from abrogation or derogation by Charter rights but that it does not otherwise create any new rights.[5] Judicial commentary on section 25, scarce as it is, has confirmed this understanding.[6]

Academic opinions have divided on the question of whether section 25 exempts Aboriginal governments from Charter scrutiny or whether Aboriginal individuals still enjoy Charter rights enforceable against their own governments. Peter Hogg and Mary-Ellen Turpel consider it unlikely that Canadian courts would conclude that section 25 provides blanket immunity to Aboriginal governments from Charter review.[7] The basis for their conclusion is that the main purpose of section 25 has been to shield Aboriginal rights from equality rights claims under section 15 in situations in which Aboriginal persons are given preference over non-Aboriginal persons. Aboriginal self-government was not contemplated by the drafters of the Charter in 1982.

Brian Slattery draws a distinction between the existence of a right to self-government and the exercise of that right.[8] The right of self-government itself would be protected by section 25, but the exercises of that right by Aboriginal governments would be subject to Charter review. This proposition was subsequently endorsed by the Royal Commission on Aboriginal Peoples.[9] Jonathan Rudin and Dan Russell have also endorsed this distinction with specific reference to Aboriginal practices involving crime and justice.[10] Thomas Isaac also argues that section 25 should not be interpreted as an absolute bar against the Charter's application to Aboriginal governance. It should instead be interpreted in a way that balances the rights of Aboriginal individuals with the collective rights of Aboriginal peoples. His reasons for this position are that the underlying purpose of section 25 has been to shield Aboriginal rights from equality rights challenges by non-Aboriginal peoples and that the Supreme Court of Canada has already ruled that section 35 rights are not absolute but, instead, subject to justifiable limitation.[11]

Other commentators insist that Aboriginal governments are immune from the Charter by virtue of section 25. Kent McNeil explains this perspective with reference to the position of the Royal Commission on Aboriginal Peoples:

> In my view, this argument does not take sufficient account of the dual protection offered by section 25. In particular, it does give the word "derogate" adequate weight. If the Charter applies to protect individual Aboriginal persons in their relations with their own governments, this necessarily involves a limitation on the powers of those governments which can only be characterized as a derogation from the right of self-government.[12]

Bruce Wildsmith admits that the question of whether section 25 provides Aboriginal governments with blanket immunity from Charter challenges is difficult to answer. He views section 25 as a trump when a Charter right and a section 35 right come into conflict, effective even where the protection of Charter rights against Aboriginal governments is concerned.[13] He qualifies this conclusion, however, by speculating that Canadian courts may still be motivated to limit the power of Aboriginal governments for the sake of Charter values, albeit by different methods such as by narrowing the construction of a treaty or self-government agreement in question or by using the administrative law doctrine that holds that the power to govern is not to be used unreasonably. Relief by using the Charter itself though would not be one of these methods.[14]

Kerry Wilkins argues strongly that section 25 exempts Aboriginal governments from the Charter. He explicitly questions Slattery's distinction between the existence and the exercise of the right to self-government as follows:

> I confess that I simply do not understand this supposition. To me, a right's scope and power are what define it and give it uniqueness. A right's scope consists of the kinds and range of conduct it protects; its power is the kind and degree of protection that it gives them. When a given activity comes within the protected scope of some particular right, then engaging in that activity just is a way of exercising that right. Imposing external restrictions in it diminishes – derogates from – the scope or the power (or both) of the right itself and, by doing so, rearranges the right's defining coordinates.[15]

Wilkins also constructs a couple of additional arguments to support his position. The first is the position that there is nothing in the legislative history of section 25, or in the few cases dealing with the provision, to support the Royal Commission on Aboriginal Peoples's view. However, this legislative history argument is not very compelling. In *Reference re Section 94(2) of the Motor Vehicle Act, B.C.*, the Supreme Court of Canada attached little weight to comments found in the minutes of the *Proceedings and Evidence of the Special Joint Committee of the Senate and of the House of Commons on the Constitution* that fundamental justice in section 7 meant only procedural justice, and it concluded that section 7 applies to substantive law as well.[16] The Court will not be bound by legislative history if and when it is called upon to interpret section 25 in the context of a conflict between Charter rights and Aboriginal rights to self-government under section 35. Wilkins concedes as much.[17]

Wilkins's next argument is much stronger. It is based on judicial treatment of another interpretive provision of the Charter, which uses almost identical phrasing as section 25. Section 29 reads: "Nothing in the Charter abrogates or derogates from any rights or privileges guaranteed by or under the Constitution of Canada in respect of denominational, separate or dissentient schools." The impact of this provision has been considered by the Supreme Court of Canada. In *Reference re Bill 30, An Act to Amend the Education Act (Ontario)*, the Court held that "s. 29 is there to render immune from Charter review rights or privileges which would otherwise, i.e., but for s. 29 be subject to review."[18] In *Adler v the Queen in Right of Ontario*, the Court stated that section 29 "explicitly exempts from Charter challenges all rights and 'privileges' guaranteed under the Constitution in respect of denominational, separate or dissentient schools."[19] After reviewing these cases, Wilkins reaches this conclusion: "This reading of s. 29, which replicates the reading that most commentators, and the few decided cases, have given to s. 25, leaves little, if any, room for the Royal Commission's alternative."[20] Gordon Christie also argues that adopting Slattery's distinction would be undesirable, since it would narrow the scope of section 35 rights to such an extent that Aboriginal communities would lose their capacity for self-determination and for maintaining their distinctly Aboriginal identity within Canada.[21]

The argument that section 25 is a complete bar against Charter review seems stronger and more consistent with the text. At least one lower court has reached this decision. In *Campbell v British Columbia (A.G.)*, it was found that the right to vote in elections of the House of Commons and legislative assemblies under section 3 of the Charter had no effect on the Nisga'a's self-government agreement.[22] The basis for this conclusion was that any ambiguities that may exist in section 25 would have to be resolved in favour of Aboriginal rights.[23]

Wilkins and others may have the stronger arguments, at least from a purely doctrinal standpoint, and the text of section 25 may seem more consistent with their positions. It is nonetheless quite another matter to say that the Supreme Court of Canada will necessarily interpret section 25 as a complete bar to the Charter's having any application to Aboriginal governments. What is worthy of note is the fact that the odd time that any Supreme Court of Canada justice has ever commented on this issue it has been in favour of the Charter's having some application to Aboriginal governments. Former Chief Justice Brian Dickson was of the view that Aboriginal self-government should not be implemented unless there is "some provision for ensuring that certain laws continue to apply." During an interview, he made it clear that the Charter should be among those laws that continue to apply: "I think it would be a chaotic situation at best if no laws applied to them. It would be disastrous ... I think the Charter should be applicable to all Canadians because it's a great document which we should be very proud of."[24] It is also interesting to note that the Royal Commission on Aboriginal Peoples included Justice Bertha Wilson. The commission had actually construed section 25 as a legal basis for requiring that the legal rights in the Charter be given culturally sensitive interpretations when they are applied to Aboriginal justice systems.[25]

One can see at least an inkling of this idea most recently in the Supreme Court of Canada decision of *R. v Kapp*.[26] The majority of the Court, led by Chief Justice Beverly McLachlin, was content to dismiss an equality rights challenge by non-Aboriginal fishermen against an Aboriginal-specific fishery on the basis of section 15(2) of the Charter, which exempts laws or governmental actions that have as their goal the amelioration of the conditions of a disadvantaged group from equality rights challenges. The majority recognized the importance of outstanding questions such as whether section 25 completely exempts Aboriginal rights under section 35 from Charter scrutiny, but it declined to venture immediate answers:

> A second concern is whether, even if the fishing licence does fall under s. 25, the result would constitute an absolute bar to the appellants' s. 15 claim, as distinguished from an interpretive provision informing the construction of potentially conflicting Charter rights. These issues raise complex questions of the utmost importance to the peaceful reconciliation of aboriginal entitlements with the interests of all Canadians. In our view, prudence suggests that these issues are best left for resolution on a case-by-case basis as they arise before the Court.[27]

Justice Michel Bastarache also dismissed the challenge but relied on section 25 to do so. He was of the view that section 25 shielded Aboriginal constitutional rights from an equality rights provision but was not so eager to conclude that section 25 completely exempted Aboriginal rights from any Charter challenges.[28] Sprinkled throughout his judgment are statements such as "Is this shield absolute? Obviously not"; "There is no reason to believe that s. 25 has taken Aboriginals out of the Charter scheme"; "It is not at all obvious in my view that it is necessary to constrain the individual rights of Aboriginals in order to recognize collective rights under s. 25"; and, lastly,

> I do not believe there are distinct Charter rights for Aboriginal individuals and non-Aboriginal individuals, or that it is feasible to take into account the specific cultural experience of Aboriginals in defining rights guaranteed by the Charter. The rights are the same for everyone; their application is a matter of justification according to context.[29]

The majority stated that they were not willing to make any detailed decisions on the precise scope of section 25, so *Kapp* certainly does not represent a resounding endorsement of Slattery's position.[30] At the same time, they certainly did not race to support Wilkins's position either. What is distinctly noticeable is that any time that a justice from the Supreme Court of Canada has ever commented on the provision, ever since its passing until most recently in *Kapp*, it has been closer in line with the position taken by Slattery and the Royal Commission on Aboriginal Peoples than with the position taken by Wilkins and McNeil. If the Court is ever called upon to directly decide this issue, irrespective of any present or future composition, the justices may be deeply concerned about exempting Aboriginal governments from the Charter.

The question may be whether the Court, if push comes to shove, can as a matter of law interpret section 25 as not providing blanket immunity to Aboriginal governments despite the apparent wording of the provision. The word in section 25 that is truly an obstacle is "derogate." Slattery's distinction between the existence of the right and the exercise of the right may provide a way around this obstacle. The right of self-government itself is not abrogated or derogated from. The exercise of that right must still respect the Charter rights of Aboriginal individuals. This is admittedly a dubious way to finesse the language of the text of section 25, but it may be possible. The Royal Commission on Aboriginal Peoples has also adopted the distinction. As such, the Court may end up adopting this distinction with respect to Aboriginal self-government.

What are even greater impediments to adopting the commission's reading of section 25 are the Court's own precedents on section 29, which do not appear to leave much room for adopting a different interpretation of the very similarly worded section 25. It is not to say that it is impossible though. An important doctrine in Charter jurisprudence is the purposive approach. Chief Justice Dickson describes it in the following way:

> In my view, the analysis is to be undertaken, and the purpose of the right or freedom in question is to be sought by reference to the character and the larger objects of the Charter itself, to the language chosen to articulate.

the specific right or freedom, to the historical origins of the concepts enshrined, and where applicable, to the meaning and purpose of the other
specific rights and freedoms with which it is associated within the text of
the Charter. The interpretation should be, as the judgment in *Southam*
emphasizes, a generous rather than a legalistic one, aimed at fulfilling the
purpose of the guarantee and securing for individuals the full benefit of the
Charter's protection.[31]

In applying this approach, what is important is that every provision in
the Charter is to be interpreted in light of the larger objects of the Charter.
As previously mentioned, the typical understanding of section 25 is that it
shields Aboriginal rights from challenges by non-Aboriginal peoples based
on the right to equality. This interpretation could easily be fitted into the
"larger objects of the Charter" since there is also section 15(2), which protects affirmative action programs from equality rights challenges. Along
with these protections could be grouped section 29. In *Adler,* the Court
elaborated that an underlying purpose of section 29 was to maintain the
protection provided by section 93(1) of the *Constitution Act, 1867.* Section
93(1) permits provinces to legislate in matters of education but not in a way
that prejudicially affects the rights at law of denominational schools. The
Court viewed section 93(1) as an assurance to respect certain rights of the
Roman Catholic minority so as to achieve confederation. The usual understandings of sections 25, 29, and 15(2) could all be thought of as having a
common thread – the provision of special treatment or benefits to historically
disadvantaged groups. This common thread can easily be included in the
larger objects of the Charter. Interpreting section 25 to provide Aboriginal
governments with blanket immunity from the Charter may prove to be a
different story. The Court would already seem inclined to have everyone in
Canada who is protected by the Charter included in the "larger objects of
the Charter."

Indeed, in *Hunter v Southam,* Chief Justice Dickson stated that the goal of
the purposive approach is to secure for individuals the full benefit of the
Charter's protection. The Court could use the purposive approach to say
that section 25 requires a different interpretation in the specific context of
Aboriginal self-government. This different interpretation could be that section 25 does not provide Aboriginal governance practices with immunity
from Charter review since this action would abrogate one of the larger objects
of the Charter, ensuring the protection of individual rights for everyone
within Canada.

In summary, there is the distinct and real possibility that section 25 renders
the whole concept of the culturally sensitive interpretation of legal rights
unnecessary to begin with, if it is interpreted as providing Aboriginal governments with complete immunity from having their laws and actions re-

viewed under the Charter. The arguments in favour of this possibility seem stronger, at least from a purely doctrinal viewpoint, and more consistent with the wording of section 25 itself. However, it is by no means a given that the Supreme Court of Canada will interpret section 25 in this fashion. Any time a Supreme Court of Canada justice has commented on this issue, it has been to the effect that the Charter should still apply to Aboriginal governments. Certain strands in Canadian constitutional jurisprudence also suggest that the Court will be loathe to interpret any Charter provision, section 25 included, in such a way as to leave significant portions of any population residing within Canada without any recourse to the Charter. The possibility of blanket immunity is thus not one that its supporters should necessarily hold their breaths for. If the Court does not interpret section 25 as providing blanket immunity, both Thomas and the Royal Commission on Aboriginal Peoples have suggested that section 25 could provide an instrument to balance the individual rights vision of the Charter with the collective governance philosophies of Aboriginal societies. There are, however, constitutional principles that speak much more directly to the question of resolving a conflict between the legal rights of the Charter and Aboriginal rights to criminal jurisdiction under section 35.

Principles of Constitutional Balancing

If section 25 is not interpreted in such a way as to provide Aboriginal governments with blanket immunity from Charter review, the issue then becomes one of addressing a conflict between two different sets of constitutional rights. The conflict stems from the possibility that legal rights in sections 7-14 under the Charter may demand limitations on the exercise of Aboriginal justice practices under section 35(1). In this scenario, there are principles of Canadian constitutional law that suggest that constitutional rights that come into conflict with each other must be balanced with each other to avoid giving priority to one over the other.

Section 1 of the Charter reads: "The Canadian Charter of Rights and Freedoms guarantees the rights and freedoms set out in it subject only to such reasonable limits prescribed by law as can be demonstrably justified in a free and democratic society." In *R. v Oakes*, the Supreme Court of Canada set out a series of tests for determining whether infringements upon Charter rights are justified under section 1. Chief Justice Dickson states:

> First, the objective which the measures responsible for a limit on a Charter right or freedom are designed to serve, must be "of sufficient importance to warrant overriding a constitutionally protected right or freedom." It is necessary, at a minimum, that an objective relate to concerns which are pressing and substantial in a free and democratic society before it can be characterized as sufficiently important.

Second, once a sufficiently significant objective is recognized, then the party invoking s. 1 must show that the means chosen are reasonable and demonstrably justified ... There are in my view, three important components of a proportionality test. First, the measures adopted must be carefully designed to achieve the objective in question. They must not be arbitrary, unfair or based on irrational considerations. In short, they must be rationally connected to the objective. Second, the means, even if rationally connected to the objective in this first sense, should impair "as little as possible" the right or freedom in question ... Third, there must be a proportionality between the effects of the measures which are responsible for limiting the Charter right or freedom, and the objective which has been identified as of "sufficient importance."[32]

The Supreme Court of Canada case of *Dagenais v Canadian Broadcasting Corporation* has further refined the last prong of the *Oakes* framework, the proportionality test. When the constitutional justification of legislation that infringes a Charter right is being examined under section 1, the proportionality test now mandates weighing the salutary (beneficial) effects of the legislation in comparison to the deleterious (detrimental) effects that the legislation may have on a Charter right. The salutary effects must exceed the detrimental effects if there is to be constitutional justification under section 1.[33]

If laws used by Aboriginal justice systems infringe Charter legal rights, they will have to be justified under section 1 and the *Oakes* test. One could, however, argue that laws under Aboriginal justice systems are themselves grounded in constitutional rights under section 35(1) rights. Nonetheless, such laws would still have to pass muster under a section 1 justification analysis if they infringe the legal rights in the Charter.[34] However, there is recognition in Canadian constitutional jurisprudence that if the law being challenged under section 1 has constitutional dimensions that protect or engage Charter rights, these dimensions can affect the contours of the section 1 analysis. *Dagenais* thus has additional significance by offering an interpretive guideline for when a section 1 justification analysis involves more than one set of constitutional rights in conflict with each other. Chief Justice Lamer stated:

A hierarchical approach to rights, which places some over others, must be avoided, both when interpreting the Charter and when developing the common law. When the protected rights of two individuals come into conflict, as can occur in publication bans, Charter principles require a balance to be achieved that fully respects the importance of both sets of rights.[35]

Dagenais, just as with the proportionality test under *Oakes,* mandates an assessment of the salutary and deleterious effects on constitutional rights when seeking a balance between conflicting constitutional rights. As Chief Justice Lamer states,

[a] publication ban should only be ordered when:

(a) Such a ban is necessary in order to prevent a real and substantial risk to the fairness of the trial, because reasonably available alternative measures will not prevent the risk; and

(b) The salutary effects of the publication ban outweigh the deleterious effects to the free expression of those affected by the ban.[36]

If Aboriginal individuals were to assert their Charter rights against Aboriginal justice systems grounded in section 35(1) rights, Canadian courts may have to engage in a similar analysis. How such an exercise would play out is anyone's guess at this point. There may be a concern in that one prong of the *Oakes* test, while it may not insist on the most minimal impairment possible, will still demand the lack of reasonable alternatives before finding justification.[37] The third prong of the proportionality analysis, however, may require weighing the salutary effects of Aboriginal justice practices against the deleterious effects of legal rights (and vice versa). Canadian courts, if obliged to consider these issues, may have to examine a whole range of factors, such as the need to safeguard against the conviction of innocent persons, the need to prevent the emergence of police states, the need to ensure fairness in criminal proceedings, the cultural beliefs of an Aboriginal group, Aboriginal over-incarceration, as well as others.

There are a number of potential implications that stem from this possibility. First, the law recognizes that constitutional rights are not absolute and can, to some degree, be limited in the pursuit of desirable social ends. This is a theme that will resonate in the following chapters when I propose several specific examples of how a culturally sensitive interpretation of legal rights can work. These proposals will at several points suggest that Charter rights can often be limited or modified for the sake of allowing Aboriginal communities to pursue what they may decide for themselves to be their own collective social goals. Second, the proportionality analysis under *Oakes,* and as refined by *Dagenais,* can facilitate the culturally sensitive interpretation of legal rights. This is because it calls for a non-hierarchical balancing between legal rights and Aboriginal justice laws that may themselves have constitutional dimensions under section 35(1), such that legal rights should not be given clear preference over Aboriginal justice practices. Third, the salutary versus deleterious effects analysis provides a mechanism whereby serious consideration would have to be given to Aboriginal perspectives on justice. Aboriginal perspectives on justice, and the potential benefits of Aboriginal approaches to justice, would have to be considered in the analysis. Principles of constitutional balancing may provide a workable doctrine for realizing culturally sensitive interpretations. Realizing these interpretations in the real world, however, is another matter.

Implementing the Culturally Sensitive Interpretation of Legal Rights

It must be stated at the outset that the culturally sensitive interpretation of legal rights actually involves addressing two different kinds of tension. One source of tension is the conflict between protecting individual liberty through Charter rights and maintaining legal space for Aboriginal traditions that, by comparison, place greater emphasis on the collective good. As previously mentioned, principles of constitutional balancing provide a workable method to address this tension. A more difficult source of tension is the conflict between competing jurisdictions. Assume that Aboriginal communities have jurisdiction over criminal justice. Aboriginal individuals seeking the protection of their liberty against Aboriginal criminal justice systems through the Charter invite the application of legal principles from an outside jurisdiction. This jurisdictional clash may entail Aboriginal laws being modified to ensure compliance with the Charter, a legal document that derives its authority from Canadian federal and provincial jurisdictions.

Indeed, under the Canadian federal government's policy on First Nations' self-government, the Charter must apply to Aboriginal governments.[38] This policy is reflected in provisions in self-government agreements that require the application of the Charter. For example, Chapter 2, Article 9, of the *Nisga'a Final Agreement* reads: "The Canadian Charter of Rights and Freedoms applies to Nisga'a Government in respect of all matters within its authority, bearing in mind the free and democratic nature of Nisga'a Government as set out in this Agreement."[39] Sometimes the precise form varies, but the effect is the same. The *Sechelt Agreement-in-Principle* asserts: "The Final Agreement will provide that the Canadian Charter of Rights and Freedoms applies to the Sechelt government in respect of all matters within its authority."[40] The *Tsawwassen Final Agreement* states: "The Canadian Charter of Rights and Freedoms applies to Tsawwassen Government in respect of all matters within its authority."[41]

This is not the only way to address concerns about preventing power abuses in Aboriginal communities. I would admonish the federal government to be open to alternatives that are more accommodating towards Aboriginal cultures. In 2008, the Canadian Human Rights Commission prepared a report that recommended that section 67 of the *Canadian Human Rights Act,* which barred human rights tribunals from hearing complaints by members of First Nations against their own elected band and councils, be repealed.[42] It was repealed later the same year.[43] The commissioners, in the course of producing the report, consulted with several Aboriginal leaders, organizations, women's conferences, and various Aboriginal individuals, including Elders.[44] It perhaps should not be surprising that the feedback received by the commissioners demonstrated a diversity of viewpoints. Some First Nations representatives saw the need for allowing human rights mechanisms to have force in the communities to prevent power abuses and discrimination. Others opposed the repeal of section 67 on the basis that it was a colonial imposition of external rights standards on Aboriginal rights to governance that are protected under section 35(1) of the *Constitution Act, 1982* and the treaties. Other First Nations representatives expressed the hope that a balance could be reached and that redress against discrimination could be made available to members of First Nations communities, but in ways that accorded respect to First Nations' rights to self-determination and the collective emphasis in First Nations' governance.[45] The Canadian Human Rights Commission elected to adopt a "middle of the road" approach in its final report. Its recommendation to repeal section 67 was not necessarily an insistence that individual rights, as conventionally understood within Western human rights paradigms, would apply in full vigour. The commission stressed that human rights tribunals should be willing to consider the customary laws and traditions of First Nations when hearing complaints by First Nations citizens against their own elected governments.[46] The commission added: "The Commission acknowledges and respects the customary laws and traditions of First Nations. Indeed, as detailed below, the Commission believes that the development of First Nations-created human rights institutions consistent with these laws and traditions should be welcomed and nurtured."[47]

The Commission, in the course of its consultations, noticed a frequent demand that transcended the ideological divisions. Aboriginal representatives, whether they opposed the repeal of section 67, demanded the repeal of section 67, or desired a balance between individual and collective rights, almost uniformly insisted that the subject of applying Canadian human rights legislation to Aboriginal communities should be a matter of consultation rather than unilateral federal policy. The notable exception to this trend was representatives of the Congress of Aboriginal Peoples, an organization representing urban Aboriginal peoples. Their position was that thirty years of inaction was enough and that the immediate repeal of section 67 was needed.[48] A similar argument could be made with respect to applying the Charter to Aboriginal justice systems. The federal government's policy has thus far been a unilateral insistence on the full-scale application of the Charter. I would admonish the federal government to be more willing to consult Aboriginal communities on the subject and to be more flexible with alternatives. If an Aboriginal community drafts its own Charter that takes into account its past methods of justice, and provides meaningful safeguards, the federal government should be willing to accommodate these demands.

This proposition may present a way to address jurisdictional conflict when it concerns Canadian legislators. There remains a problem of jurisdictional tension when it comes to the judicial branch. Recall that principles of constitutional balancing provide a workable solution to the first tension of individual liberty versus collective good. The application of the non-hierarchical approach and the salutary versus deleterious effects analysis itself presents a problem of jurisdictional conflict because claims to Charter rights against Aboriginal justice systems end up being heard in Canadian courts presided over for the most part by non-Aboriginal judges. Both May-Ellen Turpel-Lafond and Patricia Monture-Angus have the same basic objection to this reality. They feel that non-Aboriginal judges would view the issues through their own cultural lenses. Their interpretive exercises would reflect their own Eurocentric biases and their lack of sensitivity towards Aboriginal perspectives.[49] This is a valid objection, but there are at least two possible ways to deal with it.

One possibility is the establishment of a court system for Aboriginal communities. This suggestion, of course, raises the obvious issue of imposing Western legal structures on Aboriginal communities, and it will be considered in more detail in Chapter 6.[50] The point is that court systems presided over by Aboriginal judges provide opportunities for meaningful Aboriginal involvement by striking a constitutional balance between Aboriginal rights to justice jurisdiction and Charter legal rights. It can provide a forum conducive to interpreting legal rights with sensitivity towards the cultural values of Aboriginal communities. In this respect, the American experience has a lesson to offer. An important part of Frank Pommerscheim's writings is the concept of American Indian tribal court systems as interpretive communities.[51] Despite a number of federal statutes imposing restrictions on tribal court jurisdiction, these interpretive communities have the opportunity of blending cultural values and traditions into their adjudications.[52] Pommerscheim describes it this way:

> Tribal courts do not exist solely to reproduce or replicate the dominant canon appearing in state and federal courts. If they did, the process of colonization would be complete and the unique legal cultures of the tribes fully extirpated ... The process of decolonization can *never* lead back to a precolonized society ... this does *not* mean, however, that liberating forces cannot synthesize the best of Indigenous past and present. Confidence, balance, and respect for roots are key elements in this process. The exercise of wise choice among competing possibilities offers the best likelihood for an optimal future. The riprap created by these forces provides an opportunity

for tribal courts to forge a unique jurisprudence from the varied materials created by the ravages of colonialism and the persistence of a tribal commitment to traditional cultural values.[53]

There is a documented example of this phenomenon occurring in a civil context. A Hopi tribal court judge was called on to decide an inheritance dispute in a case in which a Hopi woman had married an Apache man, lived for years outside the Hopi community, but then returned to claim her father's orchard after he passed away. The judge had several Hopi Elders brought in and questioned them as to the applicable traditional law. The judge went to some effort to control the contours of the Elders' testimony so that they were to only explain what the past custom had been for this kind of situation and to avoid commenting on how Hopi tradition might apply to the specific facts before the court. Justin Richland saw this as an effort on the part of the judge to reduce the Elders' testimony on past custom to an abstract and general principle that would resemble common law precedent.[54] In other words, the judge was trying to bridge a difference in form between customary Aboriginal law and common law in Western courts.

James Zion explains further: "What actually takes place in many tribal courts is that customary principles and procedures are applied ... Rather than articulate Indian common law principles in decisions, many tribal judges unconsciously apply tribal values in cases in a way that outsiders cannot see."[55] Larry Nesper, for example, examined cases in the tribal courts of the Lac Du Flambeu Ojibwe, where defendants were charged with hunting and fishing offences. In one instance, the defendant was charged with hunting off-reserve, but he affirmed a traditional understanding of the treaty that the Ojibwe could hunt any animals that were visible from a certain road without it amounting to off-reserve hunting. In another instance, defendants from a hunting party were charged with shooting at a decoy deer set up by enforcement officials. One of the defendants testified that he thought he was shooting at a deer that he had injured earlier in the day during the hunt and thus understood himself to be acting on a cultural and moral imperative to end the suffering of the wounded deer. In these cases, the judges suspended payment of most or even all of the fines levied, subject to good behaviour for the rest of the hunting season. The judges were being creative about affirming the ongoing relevancy and applicability of traditional beliefs and principles even when faced with situations where the defendants were technically guilty of violating a written conservation code.[56]

There is no reason that these kinds of practices cannot be utilized in the pursuit of culturally sensitive interpretations of legal rights. Court systems for each Aboriginal group can interpret legal rights differently to reflect the needs and traditions of that particular group. Mark Rosen states: "Presently, each tribe's courts are empowered to provide their own interpretations of 'due process,' 'equal protection,' 'search and seizure,' and the like, without review from federal courts. The result is that due process means one thing in Manhattan, another in the 25,000 square miles of Navajo land, and yet something else on the Winnebago reservation."[57] For example, in the Navajo court system, an important legal concept is that of *k'é,* which roughly means "talking things out." *K'é,* as a concept, frequently emphasizes that each person who has been affected by a conflict is to have an opportunity to speak to his or her concerns and to speak to how he or she has been affected by the conflict. Of course, this is a theme that also resonates with restorative justice. Raymond Austin emphasizes that *k'é* has also acted as an important interpretive principle for Navajo cases involving due process.[58] Navajo courts in several cases have interpreted *k'é* as allowing Navajo citizens an opportunity to be heard in regard to how their lives and interests will be affected by actions taken or laws passed by the Navajo Nation Council. Failure to provide this opportunity can result in a finding that the Navajo Nation Council laws or actions cannot be upheld under either the Navajo Nation Bill of Rights or the *Indian Civil Rights Act.*[59] Another important concept is that of *hazo'ogho,* which can mean "freedom with responsibility" or "doing things right." Navajo cases have also interpreted this concept to mean that before Navajo accuseds can be subject to sanction by the courts, they must be fully apprised of their rights and possible options available to them. For example, before a guilty plea can be valid, the accused must be clearly apprised of what options are available, the range of sanctions that are possible after a guilty plea, and the fact that entering a guilty plea means fully admitting to guilt as to commission of the offence charged. It is also conceivable that Aboriginal appellate courts, such as those in the American Indian tribal court systems, can become a feature of Canadian Aboriginal court systems and a site for the culturally sensitive interpretation of legal rights.[60]

This concept would address the tension created by jurisdictional conflict in the sense that Aboriginal criminal justice systems would be free to willingly incorporate Charter rights, perhaps in modified forms, into their own laws. The tension would be dissolved by enabling (modified) legal rights to become internal to Aboriginal criminal justice systems so that they no longer remained external. It only represents a partial solution, however, because it must be kept in mind that any such courts, appellate or not, may be subject to being overturned by the Supreme Court of Canada. This solution may be as good as we can be hope for, for now if at all.

Another approach is for Aboriginal communities to draft their own Charters. Communities could perform their own interpretive exercises using the theme of constitutional balancing to produce Charters that both safeguard against power abuse and retain cultural sensitivity. Consider this excerpt from the Royal Commission on Aboriginal Peoples:

The Aboriginal Charter would also serve as an interpretive tool for the courts of the non-Aboriginal justice system in applying the Canadian Charter to the laws and acts of Aboriginal governments. In this way, the concern about having judges of the non-Aboriginal system pronounce on the validity of an Aboriginal nation's laws or acts would be largely alleviated, since the values underpinning such legislation or acts should be readily discernable in its Charter ...

Where a self-government treaty includes an Aboriginal Charter among its provisions, it would appear that courts would be bound to seriously consider the terms of this Charter in interpreting any related provisions of the Canadian Charter.[61]

Such Charters could hopefully invite deference from Canadian courts by demonstrating that safeguarding against power abuse has been taken into consideration and that a sincere effort at constitutional balancing has been made. The Charters could also be used in negotiations in which the federal government can hopefully be persuaded to accommodate Aboriginal alternatives. The next four chapters examine possible scenarios in which the culturally sensitive interpretation of legal rights could work.

6
The Sentencing Process

The remaining chapters will formulate a set of specific proposals for Aboriginal Charters of rights. This exercise is bound to raise controversy since it can be perceived as presuming to set standards of justice for all Aboriginal societies. The perceived imposition of outside standards of justice can indeed be a sensitive issue. Imposing uniform standards of rights protection on all Aboriginal communities is not the intention. The intention is to provide a springboard for further discussion. The concept of Aboriginal Charters of rights has been around for some time, but specific suggestions for what such Charters could look like has not been previously explored. The specific proposals made in this chapter are not intended to bind any Aboriginal communities but, rather, to provide illustrative examples of how culturally sensitive interpretations of legal rights can work. It is conceivable and even encouraged that Aboriginal communities would tailor their own specific Charters to their own traditions and to their own needs.

Nine specific rights will be discussed during this and the next three chapters. They are the right to be heard before an independent judge, the right to natural justice, the presumption of innocence, the right to a fair trial, the right to counsel, the right against unreasonable search and seizure, the right to silence, the right against cruel and unusual punishment, and the exclusion of evidence as a remedy. Each discussion will have four sections. The first will provide an overview of Canadian jurisprudence on that right. The second will describe how that right potentially creates problems for Aboriginal traditions of justice. The third will articulate a proposal for a culturally sensitive interpretation of the right. This section will occasionally draw on comparative insights from the United States and Australia in constructing such interpretations. The fourth will deal with practical or theoretical objections to the proposals.

Before we begin this examination, it is necessary to address another issue. At some previous points in this book, I have stressed that we need to be careful not to essentialize Aboriginal peoples and their methods of justice or reduce them to a simple pigeon hole that perpetuates a questionable dichotomy against Western justice systems. My subsequent treatment of conflicts between Aboriginal methods of justice and Charter rights can come across as engaging in the same kind of exercise.[1] A few points can be offered in response to this concern.

First, I would agree that one must obviously be honest about the diversity that exists between various Aboriginal societies. Nonetheless, one can also notice that Aboriginal approaches to justice sometimes share certain common threads, bearing in mind that the precise details may vary from one Aboriginal society to another. In a sense, this identification of common threads is necessary to enable meaningful explanations of why certain Charter rights can create significant difficulties for many, if not all, Aboriginal societies. Second, at a number of points during subsequent discussions, differences between the justice methods of various Aboriginal societies will emerge. These will be pointed out and explained.

I have one last comment to make about the order of this and the next three chapters. I will not be following what may seem the appropriate chronological order of rights during the investigative stage, the trial phase, and finally the phase of peacemaking and final resolution. Instead, I begin with rights that are pertinent to Aboriginal peacemaking. The reason that I am beginning the discussion with these rights is that it is in the course of these discussions that I set out some suggestions for institutional structures that will also inform further discussion in the ensuing chapters. I then discuss rights during the trial phase, rights during the investigative stage, the right to have evidence excluded, and the right against cruel and unusual punishment. The reason for this order is that sometimes the discussions of the rights to silence and the right to counsel make references back to the proposals that were developed during the chapter on rights during the trial stage. I then finish off with rights during the investigative stage and rights involving final resolution. The discussion proceeds in such a fashion because oftentimes the cart first needs to be put before the horse – in a conceptual sense rather than in a temporal sense – before I can proceed to the next discussion. I now begin with a discussion of rights pertinent to Aboriginal peacemaking.

Right to Be Heard before an Independent Judge

Canadian Jurisprudence
Section 11(d) of the Charter reads:

Any person charged with an offence has the right

(d) to be presumed innocent until proven guilty according to law in a fair and public hearing by an independent and impartial tribunal.

This provision contains at least three different rights. The words "presumed innocent" describe the right to insist that the state establish guilt beyond a reasonable doubt before an accused can be convicted. The word "impartial" speaks to the procedural fairness, or natural justice, of an accused's hearing. These two sets of rights will be dealt with in their own subsequent discussions. The third set of rights is encapsulated by the word "independent," which speaks to a separation of the judiciary from legislative and executive authority as well as to the protection of the judiciary from other sources of outside interference (for example, popular opinion). It is this feature of section 11(d) that will be the focus of the present discussion since it has potential repercussions for how authority in Aboriginal communities is structured.

The Supreme Court of Canada, in *R. v Valente* described the three essential features of judicial independence under section 11(d).[2] The first feature is security of tenure, which means that a judge cannot be dismissed except for just cause, such as corruption or misconduct speaking to bad character. A finding of just cause requires a hearing by an authority that is independent from both the judiciary and the authority that appoints judges (that is, the executive). The judge must have an opportunity to be heard during that proceeding. This bar against dismissing judges but for just cause protects judges from interference and arbitrary dismissal by the other branches of government. The second feature is security of remuneration. The idea is that remuneration for judges should be set at a legally acceptable minimum and not subject to arbitrary lowering or raising by the other branches of government. If the other branches of government could arbitrarily interfere with judicial remuneration whenever they wished, it could appear that judges would have to cater their decisions to the wishes of the other branches of government in order to avoid a scaling down of their judicial salaries. The third feature is administrative independence, whereby the judicial branch has administrative control over matters such as assigning judges to judicial districts and assigning judges to pending cases.

The Supreme Court of Canada has, since *Valente*, refined its jurisprudence on security of remuneration. Before a federal or provincial government can increase or reduce judicial remuneration, it must establish a commission with a mandate to produce a report on judicial salaries and benefits, along with recommendations on what those salaries and benefits should be. The commission must be independent from the executive, legislative, and judicial branches alike. They must also be effective and objective. The recommendations are not binding on the legislative or executive branches, but they must still be given serious consideration. If a government decides to depart from the recommendations, they must justify that departure according to a standard of rationality. Budgetary policies that reduce the salaries of everybody on the public purse will be *prima facie* rational. A policy that affects only judicial salaries will require a fuller explanation. Judges may not negotiate remuneration with the executive or legislative branches since such action would be fundamentally inconsistent with judicial independence. They may, however, simply express concerns about salaries and benefits to governments. Judicial salaries must also be set no lower than a basic and acceptable minimum level for the office of a judge. The reason for this minimum level is the idea that public confidence in the judiciary would be lost if their salaries were so low as to make them appear vulnerable to political manipulation.[3]

In *Mackin v New Brunswick; Rice v New Brunswick,* the Court clarified when there may be a violation of the right to be heard by an independent tribunal. A reasonable person that is fully informed of the circumstances of a dispute brought before a tribunal must conclude both that (1) the tribunal does in fact have institutional independence from other branches of government and (2) the conditions in which the dispute is being heard are such that there is a reasonable perception of institutional independence.[4]

The Conflict

Suppose that an Aboriginal individual for whatever reason suspects that community authorities hearing his or her case are not independent from powerful political forces in the community. If he or she applies to a non-Aboriginal Canadian court for a right to be heard before an independent judge, the application can contemplate that Aboriginal criminal justice systems adopt forms of judicial authority resembling those of common law court systems. At the heart of the conflict is the fact that the application of section 11(d) to Aboriginal communities would involve imposing authority structures that are inconsistent with how Aboriginal authority was structured, even accounting for diversity between different societies. This situation can create difficulties in at least three contexts.

The first context involves Western legal systems that invest a considerable amount of power in the office of the judge. A judge can, within the limits of the law, impose a resolution over the objections of both the state and the accused. Rupert Ross expresses the opinion that investing so much power into such a figure is inconsistent with Aboriginal notions of communal-based power, a dispersion of power to the members of the community at large.[5] Philmer Bluehouse and James Zion contrast a Navajo justice and harmony ceremony with Western adjudication:

> The dynamics of mediation and adjudication are different. Adjudication uses power and authority in a hierarchical system. A powerful figure [the judge] makes decisions for others on the basis of "facts" which are developed through disputed evidence, and by means of rules of "law" which are also contested by the parties ... In sum, adjudication is a vertical system of justice which is based on hierarchies of power, and it uses force to implement decisions.

In contrast, mediation is based on the essential equality of the disputants. If parties are not exactly equal or do not have equal bargaining power, mediation attempts to promote equality and balance as part of its process. It is a horizontal system that relies on equality, the preservation of continuing relationship, or the adjustment of disparate bargaining power between the parties.[6]

This contrast between centralized and decentralized judicial authority in communities has some justification in the ethnographical literature concerning some Aboriginal societies. The Cree and Anishinabe apparently dealt with most infractions through informal negotiations between the relatives of the disputants and subsequent reparations. It was only for the most serious offences, such as murder, witchcraft, and repeated theft, that the community as a whole would sit together as a community council to hear the matter. Even then, it was the community at large that decided what sanction was to be used.[7]

One must be careful, however, of generalizing. It cannot be said that authority concentrated in select individuals was never a feature of any Aboriginal society. Recall that among the Sanpoils and Nespelems, a headman could condemn somebody to whipping for various offences. Consider also the political structure of the Iroquois. The primary unit of social organization in Iroquois society was the clan, an extended family with a shared identity, and an association with an animal totem. The nine clans were the Bear, Beaver, Deer, Eel, Hawk, Heron, Snipe, Turtle, and Wolf. All nine clans existed among the Seneca, Cayuga, and Onondaga nations. Only the Bear, Turtle, and Wolf clans existed among the Oneida and Mohawk nations.[8] The Iroquois were a matriarchal society. The elder women had the greatest say in clan affairs.[9] The clan was itself a political unit. The Grand Council of the Confederacy was composed of fifty *sachems* or chiefs. The Onondaga were represented by fourteen chiefs, the Cayuga were represented by ten, the Seneca by eight, and the Mohawk and Oneida by nine each. The Tuscaroras were placed among the Oneida and Cayuga when they entered the Confederacy nearly three centuries ago. It is through those two nations that they were represented at the Council.[10] When a *sachem* had to be replaced, whether through death, illness, or misconduct, the women of his clan made the initial selection for a new *sachem*. The clan usually had to be unanimous in their selection. The rest of the clans then had to provide unanimous agreement. The Grand Council then had to approve the selection, which was by this time usually a formality.[11]

Cases of witchcraft required a hearing before the Grand Council itself. The reason was that the practice was seen as a threat to the community as a whole. If somebody was caught practising witchcraft, he or she could be killed on sight. If not, the person who observed the practice could bring an accusation before the Grand Council. The accused would then be brought before the council to face up to the accusation. If the accused made a full confession, with a promise to never do it again, a full pardon was granted. If not, then witnesses were examined regarding the facts. If the council was satisfied that the accusation was proven true, the witch was then sentenced to death. The witch was led away to his or her punishment by whoever volunteered to perform the execution, for which there was apparently no shortage.[12]

It is apparent that some Aboriginal societies did concentrate considerable authority in a select few individuals. It may be fair to say that the degree to which power was dispersed to the members of the community at large and away from central authority figures, and the form taken by these authority structures, varied with each particular Aboriginal society. If an Aboriginal society did emphasize dispersed community-based authority, an incompatibility can be seen with requiring appointed judges under section 11(d). The requirement of independent judges can also pose problems in two other contexts.

Another difficulty is that the process by which one becomes a judge and the process by which an Aboriginal person becomes an Elder are different. Each process emphasizes different credentials. Consider the judicature provisions of the *Constitution Act, 1867*.[13] Under section 96, the governor general may appoint the judges of the superior, district, and county courts in each province. Under section 97, judges are to be selected from the provincial bars. Under section 99(2), they face mandatory retirement at age seventy-five. Each of these provisions, if applied to Aboriginal justice processes as a necessary accompaniment of judicial independence, presents problems for Aboriginal conceptions of authority.

Section 96 conceivably represents an interference with Aboriginal self-determination in that the authority to appoint justice authorities lies in the hands of non-Aboriginal individuals and is outside the Aboriginal community itself. Parliament, through the *Indian Act,* obliged Aboriginal societies to adopt a band council system instead of using their traditional governance systems, inspiring critiques of colonial imposition.[14] The application of section 96 could inspire similar critiques because a Canadian authority continues to hold the ultimate decision over who is vested with judicial authority in Aboriginal communities.

Section 97 presents a problem in that it would require a judge in an Aboriginal community to hold membership in the bar. Judicial appointment advisory committees also emphasize that a candidate for a judicial office should have distinguished himself or herself through an outstanding legal career.[15] Aboriginal conceptions of authority do not require this type of formal credential. An Aboriginal Elder typically acquires authority through a combination of seniority and by having lived an exemplary life in accordance with community values. Mary-Ellen Turpel-Lafond and Patricia Monture-Angus state:

> Within aboriginal communities, the equivalent actor to the judge is the Elder. This is not to say that the Elder is the same thing as a judge or assumes that role. Elders are the most respected members of aboriginal communities. Elders are respected because they have accumulated life experiences and hold the wisdom of the community in their hearts and minds. Although it is a qualitatively different value, this respect for a person's knowledge of their culture and language, and for their wisdom, is the equivalent to respect for impartiality in European-based systems.[16]

This emphasis on seniority, exemplary living, and accumulated wisdom often resulted in very specific protocols in some Aboriginal societies. The Lake Babine people, for example, attached authoritative significance to certain names. Possession of the name conferred privileges such as the authority to decide certain matters or the privilege to engage in certain activities during the *balhat* feasts. Possession of the name, however, also required obligations, such as looking out for the economic and spiritual well-being of the community and living an exemplary life. A candidate who aspired towards obtaining a name had to convince the clan holding that name to sponsor him. The conferral of the name was complete when, at a *balhat* feast, the candidate gave away to community members gifts that were commensurate with the prestige of the name.[17]

It is not to say that similar notions of authority are lacking in Western legal systems. The Ontario Judicial Appointments Advisory Committee, for example, stresses that candidates require various qualities such as a "commitment to public service," "politeness and consideration for others," "moral courage and high ethics," and a "reputation for integrity and fairness."[18] The committee demands three or more references to verify that the candidate possesses such qualities.[19] The point is that Aboriginal conceptions of authority focus squarely on a combination of seniority, character, example, and wisdom, but do not place an emphasis on formal legal training or experience. Requiring bar membership may present a problem in that many if not all recognized Aboriginal Elders would not be eligible for a judicial appointment.

Section 99(2) can be problematic for Aboriginal conceptions of authority in that it imposes a cap on participation in justice that from an Aboriginal perspective can seem arbitrary and artificial. Why should an Elder's participation suddenly come to a halt upon reaching a set age? If anything, an Elder's authority to participate in matters of justice would only increase as he or she exceeds that age. In summary, the second context in which section

11(d) creates problems is that it envisions selecting justice authorities with criteria that differ from Aboriginal conceptions of authority. The Royal Commission on Aboriginal Peoples summarizes the difficulties in this way:

> In Aboriginal justice systems, the qualifications for those who are respected as learned in the law are likely to be quite different from those set out in the judicature provisions. The respect accorded the judgment of certain elders does not derive from their being members of a provincial bar, and to the extent that their judgments are based on precedents, they are not found in non-Aboriginal reports. If, as we believe, the Aboriginal right of self-government includes the right to establish justice systems that reflect distinctive Aboriginal values, it makes little sense, as a matter of either constitutional law or policy, to apply provisions that would undermine that purpose.[20]

The third context is that judges and Elders are each seen as exercising different modes of authority. As previously mentioned, a judge can impose a resolution over the objections of the Crown and the accused. The power carried by an Aboriginal Elder is often seen to be of a less coercive sort. The Elder is depicted as more of a spiritual guide and teacher than an adjudicator. The Elder gently inculcates traditional values in a person and provides guidance towards the path to a good life rather than coercing any compliance with expected norms. Rupert Ross describes an example of such behaviour:

> I continually had the impression that most (but not all!) elders were uncomfortable with the coercive role of a Western judge, and because my exposure to traditional teachings over the last few years suggests that their traditional roles were very different indeed. I recall, for instance, an elder who came to the court one day in a small northern community and was introduced to us as such. When the judge turned to him on a particular case and, out of respect, asked him what he would recommend as a proper sentence, his response caught all of us by surprise: he replied that it was not for *him* to tell someone else what was right![21]

Turpel-Lafond and Monture-Angus add:

> Elders are feared as well as respected. The fear does not grow out of the concern that the Elder will punish or hurt you. The fear exists because the Elder knows you, your family and your community. She or he can see your faults clearly and, therefore, to meet with the Elder is to accept that any wrongdoing on your part is, in a sense, known to all. You must confront your own faults along with your virtues. This system emphasizes a

willingness to accept your own lack of wisdom and to learn from the Elder. It encourages responsibility for your behaviour and reflection on how to live harmoniously in a community.[22]

This contrast, as Ross' own excerpt hints, is overly simplistic. The reason is that, depending on the norms of a particular Aboriginal society, an Elder's authority sometimes does have coercive aspects. Cree and Anishinabe Elders, for example, apparently warned offenders either publicly or privately against repeating the same behaviour. As previously mentioned, repeated offences could lead to banishment or public shaming.[23] Michael Jackson describes an example of an Elder's use of authority with a more coercive emphasis. A young Coast Salish woman in British Columbia had been charged with shop-lifting. Her community addressed the matter through a ceremonial dinner that included family members and community Elders. She had been the holder of a ceremonial rattle, which was of importance during longhouse ceremonies. During the dinner, it was made clear to her that her action had brought shame not only to herself but also to her family. The consequence was that she could no longer be the keeper of the rattle for a year. When the provincial court judge was made aware of the seriousness of such a deci-sion within the context of Coast Salish culture, an absolute discharge was granted.[24]

The authority wielded by Elders has often focused on spiritual guidance towards an ideal life. This authority, however, sometimes does have coercive aspects that are specific to each given Aboriginal society. Even so, it is rea-sonable to suggest that many, if not all, contemporary Elders may still feel a certain discomfort at taking on an office that confers powers such as issuing arrest warrants and setting the terms of imprisonment.

The Proposal

There are at least three essential features for the proposal. The first is the protection of independence. Aboriginal communities, instead of the governor general, can appoint their own judges and structure their own appointment processes. They can use judicial appointment advisory committees, but they would not necessarily be required to. They can also decide to use alternative appointment processes that best fit their needs and wishes. Alternatives could include election (which is how some American tribal court judges are appointed) or consensus among the community Elders.

Once appointed, the community court judge is to be protected by the three features of judicial independence: security of tenure, security of re-muneration, and administrative independence. There is a reason for insisting on these features. Some critics suggest that many of today's problems can be traced back to the *Indian Act*'s forcing Aboriginal communities to adopt elected band councils instead of their customary forms of governance. This policy has been blamed for creating a class of powerful Aboriginal elites who do not govern with the best interests of the community in mind and who disrupt the generation-to-generation transmission of traditional values.[25] The critics often suggest that if this aftermath could be undone, and a return made to traditional modes of governance, then emulating the Canadian separation of powers would be unnecessary.[26]

Whatever troubles may be laid at the feet of the *Indian Act,* the fact remains that Aborignial people now live in a world that is far different from the one preceding this piece of legislation. It is again fair to ask just how far back the clock can be turned. An inescapable feature of the contemporary world is the pervasive presence of monetary currency as the medium of exchange, for better or worse. Most, if not all, contemporary Aboriginal communities cannot escape the need to designate individuals with the responsibility for administering monetary resources. For example, Nunavut finance minister Keith Peterson announced a budget of $1.3 billion for the 2010-11 fiscal year.[27] With control over money comes greater power. And with greater power comes an increased capacity to interfere with matters of justice in the community. Threatening to withhold services from somebody involved with a dispute or bribing somebody to give a false account of events are hypothetical examples of how control over money can be abused to corrupt justice in the community. Where community court judges are concerned, the threat of reducing one's salary or withholding payments can interfere with the performance of judicial duties.

There is another reason for insisting on the three features of judicial independence. It does not take much to imagine how familial strife in Aboriginal communities can affect justice processes. Suppose that a powerful family enjoys a monopoly on governing power, law enforcement, and money in a community. Now imagine that the offender is a member of that powerful family, while the victim is a member of a rival, but less powerful, family. The powerful family can exert pressure on the victim to acquiesce in an especially lenient resolution for the offender, or to not pursue any resolution at all, against the victim's wishes. Now imagine instead that the victim is a member of the powerful family, while the offender is a member of the rival, but less powerful, family. The powerful family can exert its power to intimidate those people sympathetic to the offender against attending the process, while ensuring that those people hostile to the offender do attend. A chorus of disapproval is voiced against the offender, pushing for especially harsh measures to be set. The reason for insisting on judicial independence is so that the judge can act as an umpire between the families to ensure that the process and resolution is fair for all concerned. If a judge is to have the capacity to act as an umpire between a more powerful family and a less powerful family, the judge must be protected by the three features of independence and so not be affected by any interference from the more powerful family. Otherwise, the powerful family will be able to dismiss the judge without just cause, threaten a reduction in salary, or otherwise interfere with judicial office. The details of how a community court judge can fulfil the role of umpire will be explained in the section dealing with "natural justice."

Aboriginal communities can also be afforded flexibility in how they enforce these three features of judicial independence. Matters such as remuneration or whether there is cause to dismiss do not always have to be determined by a commission. A hearing to determine cause to dismiss can be heard before the Elders of the community or before the broad membership of the community. Both the judge and those individuals who seek dismissal would have opportunities to present their viewpoints. Once both sides have been heard, the Elders or the community at large (by plebiscite) could then decide whether there is cause to dismiss. Hearings to determine remuneration could be similarly structured, where financial administrators and judges present their concerns regarding salaries and benefits.

The second essential feature for the proposal is knowledge of the local Charter. This concept assumes that an Aboriginal community has its own Aboriginal Charter of rights in place. The idea is that a community court judge does not need a law degree and membership in a Canadian bar as qualifications. The judge need only possess knowledge of the community's Charter. This requirement is not meant to exclude other criteria that Aboriginal communities may want (for example, good character). The point is that knowledge of the local Charter would be the only formal qualification required for purposes of a culturally sensitive interpretation of section 11(d).

The American experience offers a valuable lesson. Not all American tribal courts require their judges to have law degrees or bar memberships. Under the *Absente Shawnee Tribe of Oklahoma Tribal Code,* somebody who has completed an approved paralegal program or who has regularly practised as a lay advocate before the tribal court for five years can qualify as a judge. Attendance at the National Judicial College is mandatory.[28] Under the *Blackfeet Tribal Code,* only a high school education is required.[29] The *Ely Shoshone Tribal Law and Order Code* does not impose any educational requirements but simply insists on good moral character, a minimum age of thirty years, and not being a member of the tribal council.[30] Under the *Hopi Indian Tribe Law and Order Code,* there are no educational requirements for probationary judges. However, these probationary judges must complete a training course designated by the tribal chairman in order to be considered for permanent appointment.[31] The position of chief judge requires a law degree and membership in any American bar.[32] The *Oglala Sioux Tribe: Law and Order Code* calls "for knowledge of the Oglala Sioux Code and court procedures and understanding of State and Federal law and court procedures."[33]

The only insistence is that the prospective judge have knowledge of the local Charter, whether that involves an actual training program, having simply read the Charter, being able to recite it back to the appointing authorities, or providing whatever proof of knowledge an Aboriginal community decides is required. Consider also section 24 of the Charter:

24(1) Anyone whose rights or freedoms, as guaranteed by this Charter, have been infringed or denied may apply to a court of competent jurisdiction to obtain such remedy as the court considers appropriate and just in the circumstances.

(2) Where, in proceedings under subsection (1), a court concludes that evidence was obtained in a manner that infringed or denied any rights or freedoms guaranteed by this Charter, the evidence shall be excluded if it is established that, having regard to all the circumstances, the admission of it in the proceedings would bring the administration of justice into disrepute.

The purpose behind insisting on the use of Aboriginal community judges and requiring knowledge of their local Aboriginal Charters is to create courts of competent jurisdiction for the purposes of section 24 that will enforce these Charters.

This idea may run afoul of the Supreme Court of Canada's commentary on section 24. According to *R. v Mills*, a court having this competent jurisdiction often depends upon a statutory grant of jurisdiction over the offence and the accused, as is the case with provincial criminal courts or appeal courts.[34] Courts of superior jurisdiction in each province have all of the historic jurisdiction of the high court in England, subject to statutory limitations, and are therefore courts of competent jurisdiction under section 24. The superior court jurisdiction will not displace the jurisdiction of other courts of limited jurisdiction.[35] These criteria led to the decision by the Supreme Court of Canada that a preliminary inquiry was not a court of competent jurisdiction under section 24. Culturally sensitive interpretation, however, as well as principles of constitutional balancing envision that Charter standards can be relaxed instead of always being applied with full vigour. Community court judges do not need to be held up to the *Mills* standards of courts of competent jurisdiction. Requiring community court judges to possess knowledge of their respective Aboriginal Charters vests them with competency to enforce those Charters for the purposes of section 24. This discussion may seem more relevant to the exclusion of evidence, which indeed forms one of the sections of Chapter 9. The present point though is to make section 11(d)'s demands for judicial independence less onerous than would often be the case in order to accommodate Aboriginal perspectives on authority in criminal conflicts. Formal qualifications need only include knowledge of the local Charter, not a law degree or a particularly distinguished legal career.

The final feature involves the idea that, beyond the insistence on judicial independence and on knowledge of the local Charter, Aboriginal communities are otherwise free to set whatever qualifications for judges they see fit. One can readily see that good character will always be one of those qualifications. The American Indian tribal codes described earlier all require this qualification. Another example is seen in the efforts that Mohawk traditionalists used during the late 1980s to implement a comprehensive justice system based on Mohawk ideas of justice by drafting the *Code of Offences and Procedures for Justice for the Mohawk Territory at Akwesasne* (*Akwesasne Justice Code*).[36] The code emphasizes mediation whereby appointed justice chiefs resolve conflicts by consensus. Even though the code contains a gradation of offences ranging from serious, to grievous, to minor, imprisonment as a sanction is conspicuously absent from the code. Sanctions include banishment, fines of up to $5,000, reparations of up to twice the amount gained from the offence, probation, and community service.[37] While the code asserts exclusive jurisdiction over the offences listed, it also makes provision for turning over offenders to provincial or federal authorities for certain serious offences.[38] The code was submitted to the Mohawk Nation Council of Chiefs in 1989, but it was apparently never adopted. Article 6, section 9(C) emphasizes moral and spiritual qualities almost exclusively for justice chiefs: "The Justices are selected on the basis of their own exemplary behaviour; impartiality, their ability to be mindful of the code, the moral fibre and needs of the community; as well as having compassion for both the accused and the victims of the offenses committed." The American tribal codes also typically require twenty-five or thirty years as a minimum age. One can imagine other possibilities such as completing a course on local culture, completing a course on mediation and arbitration, and so on.

Even though this proposal suggests that Aboriginal justice systems include community court judges with some features that are characteristic of common law judges and emphasizes a separation of roles between judges and Elders or other culturally significant authorities, these systems can still be structured in such a way as to maximize the room for traditional modes of authority to operate. This can happen in more than one way, depending on a given community's preferences. Persons with traditional authority (for example, Elders) can attend a proceeding in an advisory capacity, much as with sentencing circles. Their advisory capacity can extend not only to the resolution for a particular case but also to their understanding of their customary law. "Advisory" may not be an accurate word for what is envisioned by this proposal. So long as the participants reach a genuine consensus, it becomes binding on the community court judge such that he or she must approve it. Another way to structure it is that the participants can discuss and deal with the matter outside of the court system. Once their meetings produce a consensus, they can come to court to communicate to the judge a binding resolution. This is how the Navajo Peacemaker Court works. Opposing sides are encouraged first to try and settle their matters outside the court system with the assistance of a trained peacemaker. Once they reach an agreement, it becomes binding and is entered as a judgment of the court.[39]

An obvious concern arises when the various participants cannot reach a consensus. However, there is a way to deal with this situation. The community court judge can put two choices to the participants. The first choice is to remand the matter so that the participants have further opportunities to reach a consensus. Judge Barry Stuart explains that sentencing circles deal with a multitude of interests, some of them widely divergent or even oppositional to each other. For this reason, significant discussions leading up to a sentencing circle, and adjournments after a first sentencing circle, are often necessary.[40] The second choice is for the participants to agree that the judge will make a binding decision based on the voiced concerns of all of the participants. In this respect, a community court judge is not so much a full-fledged judge but, rather, more of an arbitrator with some judicial powers who affords the parties maximum opportunity to craft their own resolution. This may seem odd given that ethnographical literature often insists that consensus was a frequent feature of Aboriginal justice processes. The point though is that the choice is up to the community participants. They can adjourn for further opportunities to resolve matters or they can allow the judge to "break the tie" based on the participants' feedback.

Objections

One part of the proposed resolution involves the use of community courts and judges. An objection might be that this approach is not new. We have seen sentencing circles, advisory panels, and diversionary approaches before. Simon Owen, for example, takes a viewpoint towards the interaction between sentencing in common law court systems and restorative justice philosophy that is somewhat different from that of Kathleen Daly, who suggests that retributive justice and restorative justice can complement each other in a comprehensive system.[41] Owen observed many sentencing cases resolved by guilty pleas in Provincial Court no. 102 and the Downtown Community Court, which are both in Vancouver, and the First Nations Court in New Westminster. He found that these courts often engaged in discussions or utilized some practices that shared similarities with restorative justice. For example, the courts often tried to ascertain the reasons behind the criminal behaviour (for example, drug addiction) with a view towards a forward-looking rehabilitation plan. Nonetheless, he found that many of these practices fell well short of what restorative justice idealizes. For example, plea bargains worked out between lawyers, brief submissions to the judge, and brief stilted comments by some offenders come nowhere close to the broader and fuller discussions of what happened that restorative justice promotes. Victim impact statements also fall well short of the goal of empowering direct victim participation in restorative justice. Owen also notes (and it is this point that I focus on) that the requirements of proportionality and uniformity in sentencing, with Canadian sentencing law grounded chiefly in deterrence and retribution, still carries the final authoritative voice on what sanctions will be used. Owen thus sees common law court systems and restorative justice as having an uneasy fit.[42]

How does what I am proposing represent community empowerment or an improvement on the piecemeal accommodation that is embodied in sentencing circles and such? The answer is that there is a very important difference. Aboriginal community courts will apply customary law instead of Canadian law. A reality that has hung over Aboriginal sentencing initiatives is that the judge can veto a proposed resolution. This veto is often used when the judge decides, on the basis of Canadian statutes and precedent, that an offence is too serious to merit community-based resolutions. The proposal described in this book holds that it is the community and their traditional authorities that decide what to do about a given conflict, whether it is jail time, community-based resolutions, banishment, corporal punishment, or even corporal punishment and community-based resolutions used together. It removes the veto of judges who are applying Canadian law. The community and their traditional authorities also explain to the community court judge the customary law, which becomes binding. It is precisely this particular kind of uneasy fit, as identified by Owen, that my proposal is designed to circumvent. It represents a fairly fundamental shift in decision-making power over the substantive matters of applicable law and resolutions and purposefully limits a community court judge's power to regulate procedural fairness only. Of course, the issue of what is the customary law can raise issues unto itself.

A second obstacle concerns the recovery of traditional customary law. George Zdenkowski states: "How is the customary law identified? What is the mode of proof – by anthropologists? If Aboriginal elders provide oral evidence of customary law, can they be cross-examined as experts? Can a trial judge competently rule on the issue?"[43] Resolving these issues may not be as difficult as one would suspect for the purposes of this proposal. Zdenkowski's query presupposes establishing customary law in a court setting that is required to apply state legislation, that often uses adversarial procedures, and that usually insists that alleged matters be proven to a standard of proof (for example, balance of probabilities). If an Aboriginal community has preserved its customary law, is it really necessary to insist on holding that law up to common law standards of evidentiary reliability and standards of proof? Why should an Aboriginal community judge simply not accept the community's representations of customary law at face value? This proposal is after all about community empowerment. There is, of course, the possibility that a community court judge will hear more than one version of community law from the various participants. Even here, the judge can afford the participants the same two choices. They can adjourn for further discussion or they can agree that the judge will come up with a resolution. This latter option involves a judge in making a decision as to resolution and not necessarily deciding who gave the correct version of customary law.

There are more fundamental issues with whether past customary laws can even be recovered for contemporary adaptation. Recall that colonialism has been blamed for the disruption of traditional value systems. For example, residential schools in Canada reflected a policy of forcing Aboriginal peoples to abandon their traditional cultures. A consequence of colonialism may be that a good deal of traditional knowledge may be lost to an Aboriginal community, including traditional law for resolving conflict. One can expect that anthropologists or historians performing ethnographical studies may be able to assist a community in reclaiming its traditional law. The lingering effects of cultural colonialism, however, also present troubling repercussions for any such efforts to recover traditional law. Bruce Miller, an anthropologist, states that there are significant problems in ascertaining what traditional law and practice might have been.[44] For example, he explains that there are difficulties involved with relying on memory culture in an effort to reconstruct the past. In his study, many of the Coast Salish elders that he spoke with "grew up in circumstances that limited their access to justice practices." Many of them attended residential schools that removed them from any opportunity to observe how their communities resolved conflicts. These schools, as well as the government agents, worked to disrupt the practise and transmission of knowledge about their culture between the generations.[45]

It has been suggested that there is something inherently questionable in having Aboriginal knowledge represented by non-Aboriginal scholars, however well intentioned those scholars may be, and that something is inevitably distorted or lost in the process. Roger Keesing, in performing ethnographic work among the Kwaio of Australia, admits as much in this manner:

> Just as the ethnographer can never be an invisible presence, so that author aspiring to let the locals speak for themselves can never do so. As I have argued, it is always we who choose, orchestrate, paste together the pieces for our own rhetorical purposes. And inevitably, as I doubtless have done, we place ourselves in a carefully constructed chiaroscuro of self-justification or self-glorification, however we may proclaim our faiblesse.[46]

Turpel-Lafond also states that academic efforts to describe Aboriginal knowledge reveal more about the cataloguer than about the subject.[47] Linda Tuwihai Smith goes even further and suggests that ethnographic studies of Aboriginal cultures and lore have been a tool of colonialism. The West exercises a monopoly on the representation of collected information about Aboriginal cultures. Academic methodologies and studies reflect Western agendas and interests. They essentialize Aboriginal peoples and contrast them with Western societies. The scholarship justifies the superiority of the West relative to Aboriginal peoples, whether in the imperial past (that is, Aboriginal peoples as savages) or in the present (that is, unable to come up with their own solutions, hopelessly corrupt). Smith's solution is the creation of "Aboriginal research cultures" that require that ethnographic descriptions of Aboriginal cultures be carried out by Aboriginal scholars.[48]

It is possible, notwithstanding the prior objections, that some Aboriginal societies may be able to recover knowledge of their traditional laws and adapt them to customary use. Besse Mainville, for example, relates that traditional knowledge still retains a strong role in the contemporary life of some Anishinabe communities in Canada, in areas such as language, ceremonial observances, and social codes of conduct that regulate proper and expected behaviour in daily life.[49] There is, however, the possibility that other Aboriginal societies, with or without the assistance of anthropologists or historians, may be unable to recover knowledge of what the traditional law once was. There are well-documented concerns that some Aboriginal societies may have irrevocably lost access to their traditional knowledge, including, for example, ecological knowledge[50] and languages.[51] If there are such grave concerns about the irrevocable loss of traditional knowledge in areas such as ecology and languages, one cannot expect traditional law to be immune from such concerns either. In fact, the loss of traditional law as a mechanism of social control can have profound consequences for contemporary Aboriginal communities. Carol LaPrairie argues that the loss of traditional culture, laws, and forms of social bonding among the James Bay Cree has meant that many community members lack respect for each other and have very little sense of shame about causing harm.[52] Harald Finkler also attributes the dramatic rise of crime and disorder among the Inuit in the Canadian north to the breakdown and erosion of traditional methods of social control and their displacement by Western institutions.[53]

If this is the case, it is not necessarily fatal to any meaningful exercise of Aboriginal self-determination over justice. For example, what is to stop an Aboriginal community from setting new customary laws that address contemporary realities? Pat Sekaquaptewa describes what she calls Hopi common law.[54] Hopi tribal courts make their decisions based on a number of sources, written statutory instruments of the Hopi Council, Hopi custom as communicated to tribal court judges by community Elders and other members, and state legislation where no other source of law provides an answer. Hopi court judges always strive to incorporate custom as much as possible in their decisions. Hopi common law, however, does not always include what was customary prior to colonization. It can and does include newer customs that reflect a changed world and a different set of needs. Thus, Hopi common law includes not only elements of the past but also newer elements. She elaborates further in the following quotation:

> It is also important, however, to divide "custom" into "traditional practices" and "current local practices." The Hopi judges have found that these are not always the same, although both may be considered legal and either may be a basis for establishing new legal standards in the tribal common law. No culture is static and the legal norms of all societies evolve. Further, in recent history, at least five Hopi villages have experienced a break-up of the governing clan and society system which has permanently altered traditional clan rights in and power over lands and population. Although I will not go into a detailed discussion here, there are times when Hopi trial judges will seek to discern not only a traditional legal norm but also the current practice as legal norm at the village level. Old law is not always still good law.[55]

A great deal of the discussion has emphasized that the community's proposals with respect to customary law and its resolutions, whether recovered from the past or a reinvention of the wheel, are binding on a community court judge. This idea is subject to an important caveat. Aboriginal community court judges are to serve a purpose beyond merely rubber-stamping all of the proposals that come their way. Community court judges are to hold the participants in the process to standards of natural justice. A proposal put forward by the participants will bind a judge only if that judge is satisfied that the participants have behaved in accordance with the standards of natural justice.

A third objection to my proposal is the fact that community court judges require only knowledge of the local Aboriginal Charter and not any other requirements such as a law degree. This point may raise some eyebrows. In Western legal systems, requiring judges to hold law degrees, bar membership, and a legal career of significant length and achievement gives an assurance that they have the analytical and intellectual capacity to resolve the cases that come into their court. The proposal therefore may seem like it does not demand a very high standard of education or competence from Aboriginal community court judges. However, consider the idea that the insistence that Western judges have certain formal qualifications makes more sense in light of the nature of Western law. Western law takes on various forms such as state legislation, regulations, and judicial case law. Given the way that Western societies choose to structure their laws, it makes sense to require lawyers and judges to learn them through formal educational processes, which is not to say that the seeming complexity and forms of Western law make it better law. My point is simply that Western law is different from what I am contemplating, and this difference may obviate the need for Aboriginal societies to replicate every aspect of adjudication and administration seen in Western legal systems.

If an Aboriginal justice system uses customary law, formal training may not be so much of a concern. Aboriginal customary law may certainly be no less complex, but its methods of transmission and learning (for example, oral teaching) and application utilize different mechanisms. Sákéj Henderson describes the dynamics of customary law in this way:

> At its core, law and its need to be just are not abstract. Behind its arcane theories, artificial reasoning and phrases, law is part of a world full of people who live and move and do things to other people. The law lodge has a rhythm of transformation toward justice, which is guided by an elusive human spirit. Law represents that quest. It is a consciousness that attempts to reason from assumptions and commitments to create imaginary purposes and practical results. It is more than a compendium of written text, called either a constitution or legislative statutes or posited rules. It is more than the underlying conceptions or values or customs expressed in text; more than its manifestations or reflections. Justice is a normative vision of the human spirit unfolding, a product of shared thoughts and consciousness. It is a product of a community's beliefs and imagination. It is the shared consciousness that makes a person feel as if they belong to a community. It is the frontier line between power and imagination. Like all visions, it is subject to the evaluation of the community and to transformation.[56]

Given the nature of customary law, do we really need to insist on formal educational requirements to obtain an assurance of judicial competency? The community communicates its customs, which become binding on the community court judge. An Aboriginal community can choose to structure its laws as written statutes and to insist that its judges hold formal requirements such as a law degree. The point is that Aboriginal communities do not need to be forced to adopt all of the trappings associated with Western judges on account of the Charter. The proposal is a culturally sensitive interpretation in that it maximizes the space necessary for the operation of traditional modes of authority and customary law if a community chooses to go this way. Again, a community court judge becomes more of an arbitrator with some judicial powers rather than a full-fledged judge.

Finally, there is a potential problem in that judicial independence in Aboriginal communities can be compromised from the very start, during the selection process. It is conceivable that more powerful factions can use their influence to ensure that selection processes are tipped in their favour. This problem would have the result that powerful factions have their candidates selected as community court judges. The "ear of the community courts" would already be bent in their favour. There are two ways of addressing this issue. One idea is that perhaps Aboriginal communities can structure their selection processes in order to deal with this issue. If one family is known to be particularly powerful, for example, the number of candidates or nominees that that family can have on the community bench can be limited. Such a mandate, of course, can falter in practice if the powerful family exerts its influence during the very creation of a selection process. There is another way of addressing it.

The next section of this chapter will explore both how community court judges will hold the parties to standards of natural justice and how they will themselves be held to those standards. One of the proposals for achieving this will be the creation of Aboriginal appeal courts. The idea is that if a judge is selected from a powerful family, that judge must uphold natural justice, even if it means deciding cases on their merits against the powerful family without fear of interference. The prospect of an appeal before an Aboriginal appeal court hangs like the proverbial Sword of Damocles so as to oblige the community court judge to uphold natural justice. The next section will now explore the issues involved with applying Charter standards of natural justice to Aboriginal justice systems.

Natural Justice

Canadian Jurisprudence
Judicial independence speaks to shielding judges from interference by political authorities and administrators. Judicial impartiality speaks to a judge deciding a case fairly on its merits in accordance with the binding law instead of his or her own personal prejudices, preferences, and biases. In describing what impartiality requires, the Supreme Court of Canada quoted with approval this commentary on a European human rights convention:

> The often fine distinction between independence and impartiality turns mainly, it seems, on that between the status of the tribunal determinable largely by objective tests and the subjective attitudes of its members, lay or legal. Independence is primarily freedom from control by, or subordination to, the executive power in the State; impartiality is rather absence in the members of the tribunal of personal interest in the issues to be determined by it, or some form of prejudice.[57]

As this excerpt implies, impartiality requires not only deciding a case free of bias but also precluding even the appearance of a judge being biased against one of the parties. The Canadian Judicial Council, which can hear complaints on the conduct of judges and recommend a dismissal where appropriate, set out the following as a standard: "Judges should disqualify themselves in any case in which they believe that a reasonable, fair minded and informed person would have a reasoned suspicion of conflict between a judge's personal interest (or that of a judge's immediate family or close friends or associates) and a judge's duty."[58]

Judicial impartiality imposes the judicial duty to accord procedural fairness to all parties to a dispute. Chief Justice Antonio Lamer stated that procedural fairness in criminal proceedings is a requirement of the principles of fundamental justice under section 7 of the Charter.[59] The Royal Commission on Aboriginal Peoples says of natural justice:

> These rules protect the integrity of the decision-making process in three ways: (1) they ensure that the individual has a right to be heard by the decision maker before the decision is made; (2) they require that justice not only be done but be seen to be done; and (3) they ensure that the individual's case is decided by decision makers who have not pre-judged the case as a result of information received before the hearing or personal relationships with those involved in the case.[60]

The combined requirements of judicial impartiality and natural justice may be problematic for Aboriginal approaches to justice in three ways.

The Conflict

Natural justice standards obviously have a very strong role to play when an accused pleads not guilty and demands a fair trial. This is a whole subject of analysis unto itself and will be discussed in detail in Chapter 7. Charter standards of natural justice also have repercussions for Aboriginal justice practices that resemble restorative justice. Restorative justice idealizes a process with less adversarial competition and less emphasis on formal rules. A "side effect" of this endeavour is that a restorative process can become corrupted if there is a power differential between the participants. Without formal rules to impose consistency and fairness, and without lawyers as advocates, the party with the greater power has a free hand to leverage for a favourable resolution by using its advantage in order to coerce, intimidate, or manipulate the weaker party.[61]

Some commentators have pointed out that the fairness of consensus-based processes is especially crucial in Aboriginal communities. In Aboriginal communities, some of them very small, where everybody may know everybody else and where some will enjoy greater power and influence than others, can it be taken for granted that an accused will be treated fairly? Will a victim be treated fairly in a small community? Mary Crnkovich makes this comment:

"[T]he community" is a relatively homogeneous unit. This assumption overlooks the fact that even relatively small settlements are segmented by such considerations as wealth, gender, family connections, inherited or acquired authority, and so on. Unless these inequalities are acknowledged and attended to, they can easily undermine the equality with which the pursuit of a common good is assumed to endow the sentencing circle.[62]

David Cayley further adds:

A place is not always a community. For many native groups, a settled way of life is no more than two or three generations old. Old family rivalries persist in the new circumstances and are complicated when the new political structure created by elected band councils is overlaid on older patterns of influence and authority. The assumption that there is an identity of interest in these circumstances is questionable.[63]

It raises an interesting dilemma. If small Aboriginal communities adopt the proposal for community court judges, will a community court judge ever be able to preside over a case where he or she is not personally connected one way or another to one of the parties involved? If the Charter's insistence on the appearance of impartiality – along with the Canadian Judicial Council's guidelines, which are implicitly a part of that standard – is imposed upon Aboriginal communities, would it result in community court judges perpetually having to disqualify themselves from hearing cases? Would a community court judge ever be able to hear any case in the community?

One could suggest that community judges be Aboriginal but from a different community. Judge Leonard Mandamin, for example, is Anishinabe, and the T'Suu Ti'na did not appear to have a problem with him presiding over their peacemaker court. However, an Aboriginal community may object, assuming they accept the proposal of community court judges and wish to have their own community members serve as judges. The *Hopi Indian Tribe Law and Order Code*, for example, states a clear preference for members of the Hopi tribe to be judicial candidates. Chapter 3, sections 1.3.3 and 1.3.4 read:

1.3.3 QUALIFICATIONS OF CHIEF JUDGE. Any person (Hopi Preference) admitted to practice before the Supreme Court of the United States, or any United States Circuit Court of Appeals, or the Supreme Court of any state of the United States who is over the age of 30 years and who has never been convicted of a felony, or, within the year just past, of a misdemeanor, shall be eligible to be appointed Chief Judge of the Tribal Court of the Hopi Tribe. The work status of the position shall be full-time.

1.3.4 ASSOCIATE TRIAL JUDGES. Any member of the Hopi Tribe of Indians over the age of 25 years who has never been convicted of a felony or, within the year just past, of a misdemeanor, shall be eligible to be appointed probationary associate judge of the Trial Court of the Hopi Tribe. All pro- bationary associate judges must successfully complete a course of training as a prerequisite to be nominated by the Tribal Chairman for a permanent appointment.

The *Akwesasne Justice Code* likewise insists that justices appointed under the code be members of the Mohawk community of Akwesasne.[64] In this respect, an insistence on the appearance of impartiality may be problematic if it amounts to forcing Aboriginal communities to appoint outsiders as judges against their wishes.

Another potential problem stems from requiring judges not to pre-judge a dispute on the basis of personal knowledge obtained prior to the hearing. The Royal Commission on Aboriginal Peoples suggests that this issue creates difficulties in the following way:

> For instance, many Aboriginal justice initiatives rely heavily on the involve- ment of clan leaders and elders and on the participation of the community at large. The reason for their involvement is precisely because they have personal knowledge of the individual and her or his family. As noted earlier, the application of rules of natural justice depends on a great deal on the tasks to be accomplished by a decision-making body. To the extent that Aboriginal justice systems are healing-based systems, they would naturally want to involve those who know and understand the offender. It is precisely these individuals who can craft decisions that meet the person's needs and develop options that lead to healing and change.[65]

Donald McKay, Jr., stresses that community members will possess more intimate knowledge of both the offender and the victim than would a sen- tencing court judge from outside the community.[66]

The previous discussion on a right to be heard before an independent judge emphasized a separation of roles between community court judges and Elders. The Elders act in an advisory capacity, while the judges accept the proposals so long as the standards of natural justice are upheld. However, this separation of roles may not alleviate entirely the problem involved with prior knowledge of a dispute. It may be practically impossible for a com- munity court judge not to know something of a dispute prior to it's being heard. Rupert Ross asks: "How, we ask, can anyone 'come a stranger' to any case in a tiny community? Doesn't everyone know almost everyone else?"[67]

Even if community court judges are not Elders, an Aboriginal community may want to insist that they still possess a significant degree of cultural and moral authority. Such authority may have a role in the performance of a community court judge's duties and in the active resolution of disputes in the community. Even structuring Aboriginal justice systems to maximize the role of the community and customary law does not necessarily preclude a community court judge's taking an active role in resolving disputes. Elizabeth E. Joh describes a frequent practice in American tribal courts:

> Advocates of the current system point to instances where tribal judges take the disputing parties aside, away from the courtroom, and suggest informal resolutions to disputes. Thus, the tribal court judge is recast in the role of tribal mediator, the traditional elder whose aim is to restore harmony to the group.[68]

Ideally, the community members themselves come up with a resolution. That is not to say that the community court judge cannot lend a helping hand. This "helping hand" can involve the use of personal knowledge of the parties and their dispute to facilitate a resolution. Here again, the insistence on certain standards of natural justice may be highly disruptive, either by perpetually disqualifying community court judges or by preventing them from acting in a constructive role during disputes and against community wishes.

A third problem arises in that natural justice may impose visions of equality that are inconsistent with how some Aboriginal societies are structured. Natural justice strives for equal access to justice and the parties' equal right to convince a tribunal that theirs is the correct position. One may be tempted to think of Aboriginal societies as having egalitarian societies void of social hierarchy. This idea, however, is overly simplistic. Some Aboriginal societies have had very substantial hierarchical features in their social organization. Lake Babine social organization, for example, differentiated between *dineeze'*, those who held names, and the *ts'akeze'*, who were basically commoners. It is not to say that social mobility was non-existent. A *ts'akeze'* could earn a name through the sponsorship of his or her clan and the giving of appropriate gifts at a *balhat*. What is clear is that the *dineeze'* held privileges that the *ts'akeze'* did not, and these privileges concerned justice:

> Shaming practices make clear the social distinctions between those who have names and those who do not ... Nor can persons without a name independently shame a chief; they can, however, appeal to their own chiefs to act on their behalf. Chiefs are obliged to treat everyone with respect and

can be scolded for not doing so. They are to show pity for others; when they do not do so they bring shame to themselves. Similarly, people without names cannot turn to the balhats to reconcile disputes without the assistance of their chiefs, who may prefer to settle such problems outside of the feast system. In fact, reconciling disputes, while a core function of the traditional balhats, is no longer as common inside as it is outside the balhats hall, where delicate negotiations and interventions can take place slowly, without public attention, and with greater ease now that people live closely together.[69]

One can imagine that if standards of justice insist on uniform standards of privileges during justice processes, that insistence may be seen as an external imposition on customary laws that recognize different sets of privileges according to social rank and hierarchy. For example, what if a Lake Babine man without a name invokes natural justice to insist that he has a right to directly present allegations against somebody whom he perceives as having wronged him, when the Lake Babine community may prefer that he seek the endorsement of the appropriate clan chief first?

The Proposal
Before delving into how certain difficulties presented by natural justice can be dealt with, it is helpful to explore how a community court judge can hold community members to natural justice standards in ways that are culturally sensitive. There are two sides to this coin. One is protecting the rights of the offender and the other is the rights of the victim. First though, the discussion will deal briefly with the issue of hierarchy. The existence of hierarchical structures among Aboriginal societies does not necessarily entail incompatibility with natural justice. For example, if a Lake Babine commoner obtains an endorsement from an appropriate clan chief and that clan chief brings the commoner's concerns into the discussions, do we really need to feel concern over the fact that the commoner was not able to participate directly in the discussions? A community judge can accommodate the operation of hierarchies, and their concomitant sets of privileges and procedures, so long as they operate to address legitimate concerns. A caveat may be necessary though. If traditional hierarchies and procedures operate unfairly such that a person is denied any opportunity to have his or her concerns addressed (for example, no clan chief will endorse a legitimate complaint), then a judge may be justified in allowing that person to speak directly to the community court as a last resort. Now the discussion turns to how natural justice can protect the rights of the offender.

As previously mentioned, an accused has a right to procedural fairness under section 7 of the Charter. If an Aboriginal offender lacks support in the community, he or she may be vulnerable to the exploitation of a power differential enjoyed by community factions who are hostile to the offender. This situation can result in a chorus of disapproval against an offender that demands especially harsh sanctions. Joyce Dalmyn observes that such realities have tainted sentencing circles:

> [I]f the feather gets passed around and no-one makes any comment whatsoever, I have heard a judge state, right on the record, "Well it's clear that because nothing has been said, obviously they're not willing to say anything good about this person therefore I can only draw the conclusion that there's no sympathy for this person and I have to use the harshest penalties available to me."[70]

Ross Gordon Green also cautions: "A concern with these community sentencing and mediation approaches is that local involvement should not become a forum for the application of political pressure to the advantage of local elite and to the detriment of politically unpopular or marginalised offenders or victims."[71]

There is a way for a community court judge to deal with this scenario. Where an in-court process is used, a community judge can insist that there must be at least one participating community member who is willing to speak positively on behalf of the offender. There is related precedent for this coming from two American tribal court systems. Chapter 2, section 1-176 of the *Colville Tribal Law and Order Code* requires that "[b]efore imposing sentence, the judge shall allow a spokesman or the defendant to speak on behalf of the defendant and to present any information which would help the judge in setting the punishment." Also, the Supreme Court of the Navajo Nation has stated:

> Before the Navajo people adopted the adversarial system, a Navajo who was charged with allegations against the public order always had the right to have someone speak on his behalf." This long-standing cultural practice, which is imbedded in the Navajo concept of fairness and due process, no doubt, contributed to enactment of 7 N.T.C. § 606 by the Navajo Tribal Council in 1959.[72] This section, while prohibiting the appearance of professional attorneys in the Navajo courts, permitted any defendant to "have some member of the tribe represent him." The same section also provided that if a defendant "has no such representation, a representative may be appointed by the judge.[73]

These statements were made more in the context of lay advocates as a tribal court adaptation of the right to counsel, an issue that will be covered in more detail in Chapter 8. These statements are nonetheless valuable for the general concept that they convey – that an offender not stand alone against an overwhelming consensus of disapproval and that any positive information concerning the offender must be accounted for in reaching a resolution. However, how is natural justice to be enforced if this practice is not observed? One suggestion is that a community court judge can insist that proceedings adjourn until there is a community member willing to come forward and say something positive about the offender. A judge may even consider suspending proceedings *sine die* (indefinitely) until the community is willing to abide by the practice.

This proposal, however, only accounts for discussion processes that occur within the courtroom itself under the watchful eye of a community court judge. Having the participants hold their discussions outside the courtroom setting and then present their resolution to the judge is another model. It is then obviously more difficult for a community court judge to monitor the fairness of this type of discussion. Judge Claude Fafard expresses his reservations in the following quotation:

I guess I want to ensure some consistency you know, because you have several accused charged with the same or similar offenses, I want to make sure that the dispositions are fairly consistent, but I guess the greater thing is that it affects so many different people in that one community, that I'm almost afraid of some political influence. Because it touches on so many people, and I just sort of felt that maybe I should be there to ensure that politics doesn't get involved, that you don't have a powerful family dictating to a weaker family, that kind of thing.[74]

Ross Gordon Green suggests that mediators provide an "outside of court" alternative: "[T]rained and experienced community members could eventually perform the facilitation function currently performed by judges during circle sentencing."[75] This is indeed a feature used by the Navajo Peacemaker Court whereby peacemakers, who are trained in mediation and Navajo culture, oversee the out-of-court discussions between disputants.

However, there are other ways to ensure that there is fairness. A community court judge still has a role when a resolution is brought for his or her approval. If the offender appears to be consenting to a rather harsh resolution, then the community court judge can be under a duty to make certain inquiries. Knowledge that the offender is on the other side from a more powerful family or that the resolution is severe in relation to an apparently minor offence can also trigger a duty to make inquiries. The inquiries can include whether the offender's consent to the resolution is genuine and whether the offender has been subjected to coercion or intimidation outside the courtroom setting. The judge might also inquire as to who was present during the discussions with a view towards ascertaining whether there was anybody present who was friendly or sympathetic to the offender. The judge might also inquire whether positive information about the offender has been presented during the discussions. If the judge is not satisfied that the offender is being treated fairly, he can likewise adjourn proceedings or suspend them *sine die* until natural justice is observed. Much of the discussion in this work centres on offender rights. This particular discussion on natural justice, however, must also consider the rights of victims.

Protecting the rights of an accused against the power of the state may not be the only consideration when it comes to the application of the Charter to criminal justice. Theoretically, at least, the constitutional rights of a crime victim can come into conflict with the constitutional rights of the accused. This situation can lower the threshold of protection for the accused's rights. Consider this excerpt from *R. v Lyons:*

> Nor do I find it objectionable that the offender's designation as dangerous or the subsequent indeterminate sentence is based, in part, on a conclusion that the past violent, anti-social behaviour of the offender will likely continue in the future. Such considerations play a role in a very significant number of sentences. I accordingly agree with the respondent's submission that it cannot be considered a violation of fundamental justice for Parliament to identify those offenders who, in the interests of protecting the public, ought to be sentenced according to considerations which are not entirely reactive or based on a "just deserts" rationale. The imposition of a sentence which "is partly punitive but is mainly imposed for the protection of the public" ... seems to me to accord with the fundamental purpose of the criminal law generally, and of sentencing in particular, namely, the protection of society. In a rational system of sentencing, the respective importance of prevention, deterrence, retribution and rehabilitation will vary according to the nature of the crime and the circumstances of the offender. No one would suggest that any of these functional considerations should be excluded from the legitimate purview of legislative or judicial decisions regarding sentencing.[76]

The protection of society from crime is therefore a legitimate purpose of sentencing that must be taken into account in determining whether there has been a violation of the right to life, liberty, and security of the person and the right not to be deprived thereof except in accordance with the principles of fundamental justice, under section 7 of the *Charter*.

This can mean that the rights of a victim under section 7 can come into direct conflict with the accused's section 7 rights. For example, *R. v Mills* involved a constitutional challenge to *Criminal Code* provisions that limited the availability of third party records to an accused.[77] The court applied

Dagenais v Canadian Broadcasting Corporation to a conflict between the right to full answer and defence (that is, to use the records for cross-examination) and the victim's right to privacy in relation to the records, which are both protected under section 7 of the Charter.[78] In weighing this conflict, the Court looked at many factors, including the need to prevent the conviction of innocent persons, the use of evidence of questionable probative value that could distort the search for truth during a trial, and the importance of confidential information to a trust-like relationship.[79]

Another facet of this principle is that the prosecution, and not just the accused, is entitled to procedural fairness during criminal proceedings. The prosecution, supported by the power of the state, would not normally be susceptible to coercive tactics on the part of the accused. The prosecution participates fairly in the process on behalf of the victim and can pursue measures to protect the victim, either in final resolution (for example, a peace bond or jail term) or in the interim (for example, no contact condition as a part of bail release). Restorative justice idealizes the direct participation of the victim in the process itself, which has the effect, however, of removing the state from the process as the surrogate participant. Aboriginal justice practices that resemble restorative justice may therefore engage a victim's rights under section 7 if they do not provide adequate protection to the victim.

Restorative justice idealizes providing a crime victim with the opportunity to speak to his or her fears, concerns, and interests in a safe atmosphere and in complete honesty. By explicitly incorporating the victim's dialogue into the process, the victim's interests and concerns will be addressed by the resolution. One advantage that restorative justice has over traditional sentencing practices is an increased capacity to inspire contrition and responsibility in the offender, which is integrally bound up with the victim's participation in the restorative process. By including victim participation and reaching a resolution that accounts for the victim's concerns and interests, restorative justice claims to provide a result that serves the victim better than state-administered punishment. By effectively addressing the offender's behaviour, the victim also stands to benefit. The benefits can include the victim's safety, even after the victim has suffered serious harm (for example, domestic violence).[80]

There are critiques, however, that suggest that the ideal can prove flawed and unrealistic in practice. There are some crimes that, by their very nature, involve a considerable power imbalance between offender and victim. Sexual assault and domestic assault are obvious examples that occur frequently in some Aboriginal communities. There is the frequently expressed fear that trying to apply restorative justice or Aboriginal peacekeeping to these kinds of offences will only replicate and reinforce the pre-existing power dynamic that exists between the offender and the victim.[81] Annalise Acorn points out that domestic abuse often follows patterns of apology (by the abuser) and forgiveness (by the victim) that sustain a relationship of power over the victim.[82] Restorative justice replicates this pattern with its expectations of apology and forgiveness. Without having to face retribution or a permanent severance of the relationship, the restorative process can end up reinforcing this relationship of power whereby the abuser continues the pattern of abuse against the victim.

Acorn also argues that the very nature of the restorative process itself is intrinsically tipped in favour of the offender. If the process brings out the offender's life circumstances and reasons that the crime was committed, it can generate a certain emotional momentum towards favouring the offender. It can encourage a feeling of fellowship towards the offender, a desire to welcome the offender back in as the prodigal son, which ends up prioritizing the offender's suffering over that of the victim.[83] This dynamic in turn generates pressure on the victim. The victim will be expected to extend understanding and forgiveness to the offender on the road to repairing relationships. Those people involved in the process may frown upon the victim for not meeting this expectation. If the victim will not comply, she is seen as acting against her own interests, against the interests of the broader community, imposing isolation upon both herself and the community, and sabotaging a legitimate effort to promote harmony.[84] The standardized expectations of restorative processes favour the offender over the victim. This point has also been reinforced by Emma Cunliffe and Angela Cameron, who performed a textual analysis of several written decisions involving judicially convened sentencing circles in Canada. Their analysis found that the text of the judgments placed inordinate emphasis (in their view) on the needs and situation of the offender, with at best scant or peripheral mention of the victims' dialogue or interests and at worst none at all.[85]

As previously mentioned, Aboriginal communities are often infused with power relationships that can corrupt restorative processes. Such imbalances can compound the difficulties involved with applying restorative justice to offences that involve a significant power differential between the offender and the victim. The vulnerability suffered by victims of crime during such processes can be multilayered and especially intense.[86] One of Sherene Razack's concerns with the use of community-based sentencing in Aboriginal communities is that it reflects gender imbalance in those communities.[87] Aboriginal communities are suffused with patriarchal power structures that replicate Canadian forms of governance. It is male Aboriginal leaders who pursue community-based sentencing initiatives to the benefit of male Aboriginal offenders who commit crimes against Aboriginal women and children. Razack explains:

In the Northwest Territories, the Status of Women Council has also been clear that women's relationship to community is fraught with contradictions. The Council's report on violence identifies as problematic community denial of abuse, alcohol used as an excuse for violent behaviour, and the fact that "some of our worst abusers may be community leaders."[88]

Aboriginal Elders have to this point been presented as idealized participants that communities will depend on in realizing their visions of justice. Certainly, there are times when Elders use their knowledge, wisdom, and status with sincere intentions of making a positive difference. For example, a study conducted in northern Saskatchewan shows that Cree and Dene Elders' approaches to counselling and healing were effective in both reducing beatings against domestic violence victims and in mitigating the trauma and symptoms experienced by victims after abuse.[89] Experience has unfortunately borne out that there are times when individual Elders have fallen short of conducting themselves in accordance with expectations, and such lapses have had serious repercussions for justice processes. Bruce Miller relates that such abuses of power have plagued the South Vancouver Island Justice Education Project.[90] Elders, often from powerful families, would try to convince female victims to acquiesce in lighter sanctions for offenders under the project rather than going through the usual justice system. Their tactics included attempts to inspire guilt, attempts to persuade in favour of dropping the allegations, threats of witchcraft to inflict harm, or threats to send the abuser to use physical intimidation. Some women felt that the problem was exacerbated by the fact that some of the Elders were themselves convicted sex offenders, which left them wondering how seriously their safety and concerns would be addressed. The ultimate result was that the project was terminated in 1993. As another example, an Elder named Neil Hall was recently convicted of sexual assault because he abused his position as a spiritual counsellor at the Winnipeg Remand Centre to coerce a female inmate into giving him oral sex on several occasions.[91]

As Aboriginal peoples, we certainly hope that Elders can live up to the standards that are expected of them, especially when it comes to something as important as participation in the justice process. No society, however, Aboriginal or non-Aboriginal, can fully escape the need to address those occasions when their leaders fail their mandate and fall short of expectations. Any given society will have to somehow provide for holding its own leaders accountable. Theresa Nahanee, in a submission to the Royal Commission on Aboriginal Peoples, has argued that the Charter needs to have at least some degree of applicability to Aboriginal communities. Part of her concern stems from the fact that conflict resolution in Aboriginal communities will frequently have to address problems such as domestic violence and the sexual abuse of women and children. The reliance on Elders as agents of

Aboriginal justice objectives such as healing and spiritual guidance can be problematic when a significant number of the Elders themselves may have histories as physical and sexual abusers. This situation is a recipe for power imbalance and for power abuses during justice processes and thus necessitates the ongoing application of the Charter.[92]

If restorative justice or peacemaking processes do not operate with fairness to the victim, implications for rights to fair procedure under the Charter certainly follow. The concerns, however, do not end with procedural points but may also extend to the resolution. Another one of Acorn's key points is a caution against an assumption in restorative justice theory about the sincerity of an offender's display of contrition and his or her acceptance of responsibility. This assumption may be unduly optimistic. Her argument is that restorative process has devolved into a set of standard expectations, a constantly repeated and rehearsed script of displaying remorse and contrition, apologizing to the victim and others affected by the crime, and demonstrating the offender's promise to mend his ways. As such, it is open to the offender to manipulate the process to his benefit by effectively playing the expected role. The offender can play the script to escape a harsher sanction. In the end, restorative justice does not necessarily promote a genuine acceptance of responsibility.[93]

The objective of playing to the script, of course, is to escape from the heavier sanction that the standard justice system would assess. Thus, restorative justice is truly softer justice, or so goes the criticism. Mary Crnkovich explains that Inuk accuseds in the Canadian north often saw sentencing circles as "a quick way out of jail."[94] Another example may be seen in an American case involving two Tlingit men named Adrian Guthrie and Simon Roberts. They assaulted a pizza delivery man named Tim Whittesley with a baseball bat. He suffered a fractured skull and was left deaf and partially blind. Under Washington law, they would each have faced three to five-and-a-half years in jail. Tlingit tribal officials and a Tlingit elder named Rudy James persuaded Judge James Allendoerfer of the Snohomish Superior Court to release the two offenders. The conditions were banishment into a remote wilderness for at least a year and restitution to Whittesley. They would appear before Judge Allendoerfer again after eighteen months to determine whether further punishment would be needed. This resolution instead turned into a part-time camping trip whereby the offenders continued to live in town at their leisure, while little to no progress was made with respect to restitution. Judge Allendoerfer, when he found out what was going on, sentenced them to fifty-five and thirty-one months' imprisonment respectively and held them liable for $35,000 restitution to the victim.[95] Such examples do not reflect the use of restorative justice to place onerous obligations and promote accountability and responsibility but, instead, reflect attempts to abuse restorative idealism and to get off easily.

The incentive to use peacemaking or restorative process to secure the lighter sanction can then present troubling repercussions for crime victims. Lighter sanctions can trivialize harms done to victims, which can, in turn, lead to a sense in a community that causing harm will not lead to any meaningful sanction. Potential offenders know that there is little risk involved. Potential victims, particularly vulnerable people such as women or children, end up in an unsafe environment.[96] Thus, as Silvia Mendes points out, the severity of the sanction cannot be neglected altogether. The sanction still has to be at least significant in order for the other aspects of deterrence – certainty and swiftness – to have any real force. If the sanctions provided for by Aboriginal justice systems are not taken seriously by offenders as signalling the need to reform behaviour and make right by the victim and the community – if they are viewed as getting off easy and devolve to the point that they become insignificant or meaningless for the offender – there may very well be serious concerns for community safety. The Royal Commission on Aboriginal Peoples adds:

> If family violence is addressed without proper concern for the needs of the victims, two dangerous messages are sent. The first is that these offences are not serious. This message puts all who are vulnerable at risk. The second and more immediate message is that the offender has not really done anything wrong. This message gives the offender licence to continue his actions and puts victims in immediate danger.[97]

If Aboriginal processes with restorative emphases do not give sufficient consideration to victim safety, both during discussions and the subsequent resolution, it can compromise not only the victim's right to natural justice but also his or her right to security of the person under section 7. It then becomes crucial to explore how a community court judge can prevent such abuses. Just as with the offender, the judge can insist that at least one person sympathetic to the victim must attend and speak during a process. Chief Justice Robert Yazzie of the Navajo Supreme Court declares: "What, you might say, if the victim is being coerced? That is why we have the victim's relatives attend."[98]

Sometimes even the very presence of the victim during a circle process can be perilous. Donna Coker notes that abusive men have sometimes attacked abused spouses immediately following a Navajo peacemaker session.[99] The nature of domestic assault and sexual assault may be such that the victim wishes to remain in hiding in the interim. What a community court judge can do when dealing with such offences is to allow the victim to provide input to the process through a proxy, even over the objections of the offender and his or her supporters. Coker is indeed adamant that peacemaking processes should not insist resolutely on a victim's attendance if it is too dangerous for her.[100]

What do we do when the process is designed so that the actual discussions take place outside the courtroom? As previously mentioned, the Hollow Water program generated considerable success in the context of pervasive sexual abuse. Ross Gordon Green ascribes these results in part to the program that ensures that support teams were assigned to work with both the offender and the victim. The victim and offender would not be brought together into the restorative process until they were both ready to face each other. As such, it is apparently possible to address even serious power imbalances with intervention prior to the restorative process itself.[101] A community court judge may, for certain offences such as domestic and sexual assault, insist that support teams be provided to both the offender and the victim in the interim until a resolution is worked out.

What remedy is available, though, when the offender and/or supporters use coercion or intimidation against the victim? Adjourning proceedings *sine die* is hardly an adequate remedy because opportunities to address victim safety are left in limbo. One suggestion for a situation in which a community court judge learns that the offender's side has tried to intimidate the victim's side is that the judge can impose terms of resolution, whether such terms involve amending the resolution proposed by the participants or rejecting it outright, and that these terms prioritize the victim's safety over any objections by the offender and his or her supporters. However, this suggestion does not mean that there must be an automatic abandonment of any rehabilitative measures and recourse to incarceration. It is questionable whether automatic recourse to jail promotes victim safety in a meaningful way. Diane Bell relates that Aboriginal women in Australia were concerned about how incarcerating Aboriginal men often resulted in a violent rebound upon themselves.[102]

A restraining order may be a standard term in such situations. A community court judge may be justified in going even further in the right situation. If a community court judge decides that the offender poses a serious threat to the victim and deems that removal is necessary, banishment from the community is an option that is also culturally sensitive. Coker provides a description of how Navajo peacemaking can make creative efforts geared towards the safety of domestic violence victims:

> Peacemaking also provides a forum for the victim's family to intervene on her behalf. For example, in one case an uncle was a co-petitioner with his niece. The uncle expressed concern that his niece's daughters took her husband's side in arguments and that both the father and the daughters verbally and physically abused the mother.
>
> In addition to encouraging family participation, Peacemaking may also provide a mechanism for transferring material resources to the victim, thus lessening her economic and social vulnerability. This could occur in three ways. First, the abuser or his family or both may agree to provide nalyeeh

(reparations) in the form of money, goods, or personal services for the victim. Nalyeeh is a concrete recognition that the harm of battering is real and that responsibility for it extends beyond the individual batterer. In addition, both abuser and victim are likely to be referred to social service providers and to traditional healing ceremonies. The assistance given by agencies and by traditional healers often results in increased community and governmental material support. Finally, the victim's family may overcome past estrangement from the victim and agree to provide her with assistance.

Though it is not clear that extending such assistance to include goods, services, or both is now a common practice in Navajo Peacemaking, such an extension appears congruent with traditional Navajo practices. Assistance of this kind may alter the battered woman's material conditions and decrease her vulnerability to ongoing battering. For example, his family members may agree to such help as loaning a car or providing transportation. Her family members may agree to spend the night with her on a rotating basis. In addition, bank accounts may be changed or split so that she has greater financial independence. The agreement may also include assistance with job training, employment, or childcare. The subsequent reorganization of the financial priorities of the batterer's extended family may serve to emphasize the injustice done to the victim and, at the same time, to decrease the victim's vulnerability to the batterer's control.[103]

If Aboriginal communities adopt the proposal involving community court judges, a community court judge can certainly explore these types of options. A community court judge also need not confine protective terms to only the offender. If other people besides the offender participated in intimidating the victim, the community judge may well consider issuing restraining orders against them as well. This is not intended to be an extensive catalogue. It is meant to show that community court judges can be creative and practicality-oriented when they decide, as a matter of natural justice, that the safety of the victim is to receive the highest priority.

There is no doubt that Acorn and others have made some fairly powerful and persuasive critiques against restorative justice. The question that needs to be asked is whether the problems they have identified are fatal to restorative justice endeavours? I would argue, consistent with my proposals in this chapter, that they provide valuable insights into what can go wrong and what needs to be avoided. The criticisms do not, in my view, reveal fatal flaws for restorative justice. Many of the problems may in fact stem from the time when the parties are left to their own devices, without any form of oversight. It is precisely when there is this lack of oversight that the stronger party can exploit a power differential. I submit that it is entirely possible to prevent the problems that have occurred through a limited form of judicial supervision as well as through other measures in order to ensure equitable participation for the parties.[104] What I have discussed so far are the methods by which a community court judge can enforce natural justice. It remains to be seen how we can expect community judges to hold themselves to standards of fairness when personal connections to the parties themselves may be unavoidable. It is to this subject that we now turn.

A starting point for resolving the issue of personal connections is that common law courts have recognized that it may sometimes be necessary for a judge to hear a case despite partiality or the appearance of bias. The Supreme Court of Canada stated with approval this passage from a textbook: "A person who is subject to disqualification [by reason of bias] at common law may be required to decide the matter if there is no other competent tribunal or if a quorum cannot be formed without him. Here the doctrine of necessity is applied to prevent a failure of justice."[105] The High Court of Australia declares:

> [T]he rule of necessity is, in an appropriate case, applicable to a statutory administrative tribunal, as it is to a court, to prevent a failure of justice or a frustration of statutory provisions. That rule operates to qualify the effect of what would otherwise be actual or ostensible disqualifying bias so as to enable the discharge of public functions in circumstances where, but for its operation, the discharge of those functions would be frustrated with consequent public or private detriment. There are, however, two prima facie qualifications of the rule. First, the rule will not apply in circumstances where its application would involve positive and substantial injustice since it cannot be presumed that the policy of either the legislature or the law is that the rule of necessity should represent an instrument of such injustice. Secondly, when the rule does apply, it applies only to the extent that necessity justifies.[106]

This doctrine has also been recognized by the American Ninth Circuit Court of Appeals[107] and by the Supreme Court of the United States.[108]

This doctrine may be adapted to the particular realities of Aboriginal communities. There is the possibility that in large Aboriginal communities in urban centres, such as Winnipeg and Toronto, community court judges can be assigned to cases in which they will not be personally tied to one or more of the parties. It may be a different story in small rural communities. It could be said that in such communities, if they use a community court system, the doctrine of necessity has ongoing relevance. The doctrine of necessity can be adapted to prevent a constant demand on community court judges to disqualify themselves to avoid the appearance of bias. In other words, community judges do not necessarily have to provide the appearance of fairness and impartiality as long as they actually are being fair and impartial in the performance of their duties.

Can weaker parties trust community judges, left only to their own discretion, to be impartial when they are personally tied to the other party? Rachael Field discusses problems with gender bias in Australian family group conferencing programs.[109] Conference convenors are supposed to be impartial mediators who are present only to ensure that the parties reach a fair resolution. Field asserts that this mandate does not bear out in practice. Convenors can take an active role and drive matters towards a resolution that reflects their own preferences. If a convenor is "a misogynist" or is unimpressed with what he sees as "difficult" behaviour by a female juvenile offender, then that offender may be faced with unfavourable bias during the conference. David Weisbrot is sympathetic to the idea of Aboriginal community courts in Australia but not without measures being taken to ensure natural justice.[110] In his view, appellate review should be available only when there are allegations that the Aboriginal court has denied natural justice to one of the parties.

The suggestion is that there be Aboriginal courts of appeal that are available when community court judges fail to uphold natural justice.[111] Many American Indian tribes have courts of appeal. There is some hesitancy in setting out in detail what these courts would look like, whether there should be one pan-Aboriginal court of appeal, one for every Aboriginal tribe, or various regional courts of appeal. For the most part, the details of how these courts would be constituted would be left to Aboriginal peoples themselves if they choose to go this route. There are, however, two ideals that merit consideration. One ideal is that appellate court judges possess sufficient competency to hold community court judges to natural justice. The Royal Commission on Aboriginal Peoples explains: "Whatever appellate structures are developed, they will have to develop expertise in addressing the unique issues that might arise from the operation of Aboriginal justice systems."[112] The details of this expertise, whether it involves a law degree or other qualifications, would be for Aboriginal peoples to decide. The second ideal is that the appellate court judges would be both Aboriginal and not related to, or personal friends with, anybody in the community from which an appeal rises. This proposal attempts to bring together the best of both worlds. Should natural justice fail at the community court level, an appellate forum not only provides impartiality in fact but also avoids even the appearance of bias. It also insists that the appellate court judges be Aboriginal so that appeals are heard in an Aboriginal forum as opposed to a non-Aboriginal forum.

What is to happen when an appellate court decides that a community court judge has not upheld natural justice? A suggestion that can be made is that appellate courts can provide the same remedies that a community court judge should have. If the process was abused against a marginalized offender, the appellate court can set aside the resolution and order that proceedings be suspended *sine die* until the community justice system proceeds in such a way that fairness is accorded to the offender. If the process is abused against a vulnerable victim, the appellate court can then explore solutions and set out a resolution that prioritizes the victim's safety. Whether or not appeals should be allowed to the Supreme Court of Canada is an issue that will be avoided within this work. For the present, it is enough to suggest that Aboriginal appellate courts can serve a meaningful purpose by ensuring that community court judges discharge their duties to uphold natural justice. Now it is time to explore in some detail a facet of the potential relationship between community and Aboriginal appellate courts.

One idea worth exploring is the requirement that community court judges provide recorded reasons in certain circumstances. The idea behind recorded reasons is that Aboriginal courts of appeal have a basis on which to assess whether community court judges have been impartial in potentially troublesome situations. The Supreme Court of Canada has recently adopted a "functional approach" to situations in which judges are required to provide written reasons for their decisions. Some of the principles of that functional approach are:

1. The delivery of reasoned decisions is inherent in the judge's role. It is part of his or her accountability for the discharge of the responsibilities of the office. In its most general sense, the obligation to provide reasons for a decision is owed to the public at large ...
5. Reasons perform an important function in the appellate process. Where the functional needs are not satisfied, the appellate court may conclude that it is a case of unreasonable verdict, an error of law, or a miscarriage of justice within the scope of s. 686(1)(a) of the *Criminal Code*, depending on the circumstances of the case and the nature and importance of the trial decision being rendered.
6. Reasons acquire particular importance when a trial judge is called upon to address troublesome principles of unsettled law, or to resolve confused and contradictory evidence on a key issue, unless the basis of the trial judge's conclusion is apparent from the record, even without being articulated.
7. Regard will be had to the time constraints and general press of business in the criminal courts. The trial judge is not held to some abstract standard of perfection. It is neither expected nor required that the trial judge's reasons provide the equivalent of a jury's instructions.
8. The trial judge's duty is satisfied by reasons which are sufficient to serve the purpose for which the duty is imposed, i.e., a decision which, having regard to the particular circumstances of the case, is reasonably intelligible to the parties and provides the basis for meaningful appellate review of the correctness of the trial judge's decision.[113]

In *R. v M. (R.E.)*, the Court added that the functional approach of *R. v Sheppard* required that judicial decisions must be sufficient to let the parties know the basis for the decision, to provide for public accountability for judicial decision making, and to allow for effective appellate review.[114] Whether or not the reasons are sufficient to let the parties know requires, in turn, that there be a logical connection between the decision and the basis for the decision.[115]

The idea is that community court judges be required to give recorded reasons under certain circumstances. One circumstance arises when a resolution is proposed to the community court judge, but the judge is personally tied to one of the parties or it is known that one side of the dispute is significantly more powerful than the other. The judge may not have to elaborate reasons for the resolution itself, but he or she would ideally disclose his or her conclusions as to whether the parties have behaved in accordance with natural justice. Suppose that the offence is sexual assault, for example, and that the proposed resolution involves community service, therapy for the offender, and probation, but does not include a term of incarceration. The judge may disclose in reasons that the resolution reflects genuine consensus between the parties by elaborating the fact that a support team was always around the victim in the interim, identifying the members of that support team, and describing the activities used by the support team. The judge may also disclose that he or she inquired of the victim, or the support people, whether the consent was genuine and that the victim or the support people affirmed as much. As another example, a judge may disclose the name of a specific community member who spoke positively of the offender and generally what that member had said about the offender. Reasons may also include an inquiry as to whether the offender's consent to the resolution was genuine.

Another situation arises when a judge is tied to one of the parties and is either called upon to arbitrate during a deadlock or rejects a proposed resolution. Two sets of reasons may then be necessary. The first set discloses either the fact of the deadlock or the reasons for rejecting a proposed resolution. For example, a judge may disclose findings that individuals friendly to the offender tried to harass a victim of domestic violence into going along with a very light resolution for the offender. A second example could be a finding that no one was willing to say anything positive about the offender. The second set of reasons discloses the resolution that the judge imposes and the reasons for it. Using the domestic violence situation again, the judge may explain the terms of a resolution that favours the victim and explain how it is designed to ensure the safety of the victim. As another example, suppose that a judge is invited to break a deadlock. Assume then that the judge decides to use community-based resolutions that emphasize rehabilitation even though the offender had inflicted substantial harm. In addition to disclosing the fact of deadlock, the judge could disclose in reasons why he or she believes the offender is a good candidate for community-based measures.

Canadian authorities prior to *Sheppard* were reluctant to impose on judges a duty to produce written reasons because they had the potential to impose heavy administrative burdens on the court system.[116] One could see a similar concern if a community court system is adopted. Such a system does not need to insist that its judges write out reasons. A system could videotape its proceedings or audio record them so that transcripts are available when required. In these situations, a community court judge could audibly speak out his or her reasons for the decision so that there would be a record for appeal. American tribal court decisions have extolled the production of video recordings or transcripts in order to make a record available to an appeal court.[117]

Objections
Some Aboriginal peoples might object to their own processes being held to common law standards of fairness. I have, at various points, referred to anecdotes or observations provided by Ross that illustrate certain points that I have tried to make. There is, however, at least one of his positions that I emphatically disagree with. He argues that Charter rights may be necessary only to the extent that Western style legal processes and social hierarchies have insinuated themselves into the social fabric of Aboriginal communities. If a return could be made to the past teachings in full force and the social hierarchies resembling Western power structures could be phased out, decision-making power would be dispersed to the community membership at large. There would correspondingly be less need for the rights and protections of the Charter.[118] I have to admit that I find this idea unduly optimistic, to say the least. First of all, it seems to romanticize Aboriginal peoples as being utterly devoid of any proclivity towards hierarchical behaviour, past and present. Human nature, for Aboriginal peoples and non-Aboriginal peoples alike, often motivates many people to act purely out of self-interest. Human nature, coupled with a justice process sans enforceable safeguards, holds out a strong incentive for stronger parties to corrupt the process in pursuit of self-interest at the expense of more vulnerable parties. The observations of Miller, Coker, and others have confirmed this reality with respect to initiatives in which the ostensible purpose was to revive past traditions of justice in order to help the community as a whole.

Contemporary events have often borne out an ongoing need for formal safeguards during peacemaking or restorative processes, whatever particular form these safeguards may take. It is also not to say that we as Aboriginal peoples are more prone to corrupting these kinds of processes. It is rather that the nature of any justice process with a restorative emphasis, whether it is Aboriginal peacemaking or non-Aboriginal programs, necessitates measures to maintain equilibrium between the participants. This has been noted in literature outside of Aboriginal contexts. Berit Albrecht, who did a study on restorative justice programs in Norway and Finland, has emphasized that there is a need for mediators to provide safeguards for processes outside the court system.[119] In one example, a mediator had to step in during one conference when the victim, well aware that the offender was an immigrant and perhaps lacking in knowledge, demanded restitution that vastly exceeded what the courts would have given. Andrew Ashworth has argued that the state should still have a hand in the administration of restorative justice programs in order to ensure that there are safeguards for the fair treatment of offenders.[120] His emphasis was on offenders. Nonetheless, his conclusion can be taken further. If Aboriginal peoples obtain control over their own justice systems, there will be a necessity for safeguards that will ensure fair process for all of the participants, offenders and victims alike. As an Elder told the Human Rights Commission at a conference of First Nations women: "If our communities were perfect, we would not need this protection. But they are not, and we do."[121]

Aboriginal scholars and Aboriginal peoples themselves have touted consensus and the collective good as features of Aboriginal justice. In this light, consider what the application of natural justice is meant to prevent. If a stronger party coerces the other parties into a resolution to its benefit and to the detriment of the weaker parties, does this action reflect genuine consent? If vulnerable victims are compelled to acquiesce in resolutions that do not address their safety, does this move further the collective good? Natural justice can complement rather than detract from Aboriginal approaches to justice as articulated by Aboriginal peoples. Is there truly anything objectionable to the use of adapted standards of natural justice to insist that consensus be genuine in fact? The use of natural justice can also enhance the pursuit of the collective good by ensuring that all victims of crime have their safety addressed, not just those who are tied to powerful elites. Emma LaRocque, for example, states: "All original cultures exercised strict mores and taboos to regulate sexual relations."[122] In other words, the protection of all community members from harm was an objective that resonated in the justice practices of many Aboriginal societies. If contemporary justice processes emphasize only offender re-integration, even at the expense of protecting victims and otherwise vulnerable members of the community, it can be difficult to think of this as a genuine reflection of Aboriginal traditions of justice. Perceived differences between Aboriginal approaches to justice and natural justice may be more imagined than real.

A second objection concerns the idea of a foreign authority structure. It is fundamentally inconsistent with Aboriginal authority structures, ideally housed within the communities themselves, to be overseen by appellate courts that reflect Western authority structures. The presence of appeal courts for Aboriginal societies that do not have such structures may seem problematic. In the end, the proposal for Aboriginal appeal courts is intended only as a last recourse when all else fails. The proposals strive to afford Aboriginal communities every opportunity to use their own laws to resolve disputes at a local level. The idea of making proposed resolutions by the community binding on a community court judge is subject to an important caveat. This caveat is that Aboriginal community court judges hold communities to culturally sensitive standards of natural justice that ensure that consensus is genuine and that they genuinely reflect the collective good of all (for example, including vulnerable victims or marginalized offenders). The proposal also tries to accommodate allowing Aboriginal communities to select their own members as community court judges despite the normal insistence of Western standards of natural justice that judges be free of the appearance of bias. The community court judges do not necessarily have to convey a formal appearance of freedom from bias so long as they actually are impartial in their decisions. Pragmatism suggests, however, that one must account for the possibility that community court judges, left unregulated, may abuse their power to the benefit of parties connected to them. Then, and only then, would Aboriginal appeal courts step in.

Another potential objection is that even if the law has good intentions with respect to fairness and procedure, it can become hollow if it does not provide the intended benefits in the real world. There are in fact many criticisms that question the capacity of restorative justice and Aboriginal initiatives that resemble restorative justice to deliver on their promise. Restorative justice proponents have been able to marshal some statistical evidence in support of their positions. As it turns out, for nearly any study that indicates success, detractors can point to another study that indicates failure. Some studies have suggested that some restorative justice programs have made little to no progress in addressing juvenile criminal recidivism.[123] Carol LaPrairie and Jane Dickson-Gilmore found that among Aboriginal offenders who participated in a sentencing circle in Saskatchewan from 1993 to 2000, 54 percent had reoffended.[124] A recent study by Jacqueline Fitzgerald has found that circle sentencing has had little to no impact at all on Aboriginal criminal recidivism in Australia.[125] LaPrairie and Dickson-Gilmore also emphasize that Aboriginal justice projects have not made a significant impact over the years on Aboriginal over-incarceration.[126] Annalise Acorn assesses Lawrence Sherman and Heather Strang's study as follows:

> However, the evidence about the effectiveness of restorative justice in reducing repeat offending is equivocal. Empirical research on restorative justice and recidivism has found that repeat offending was lower for violent offenders, higher for drunk drivers, and the same for property offenders who

participated in restorative processes in comparison to those who went through the court.[127]

Concerns about the efficacy of restorative approaches are especially pertinent in the context of family violence, an issue that is especially troublesome for Aboriginal communities. The latest statistical estimates are that at least 25 percent of Aboriginal women in Canada have been victims of spousal abuse, a rate that is at least three-and-a-half times greater than the rate experienced by non-Aboriginal women. Aboriginal men are also at greater relative risk for spousal abuse at a rate of 18 percent.[128] Restorative justice has often been lauded in theory as a more constructive alternative for addressing intimate and family violence crimes.[129] There are indications, however, that family violence is a crime that is especially intractable and difficult to deal with, either for the standard justice system or for restorative approaches. Studies by Andrew Fulkerson and Robert C. Davis have concluded that restorative justice initiatives in the United States have failed to address family violence offences with any degree of improvement over the standard justice.[130] Angela Cameron notes that sentencing circles have failed, both on a statistical level and in documented individual cases, to demonstrate improvement in domestic violence cases when it comes to either offender recidivism or realizing safety for abused victims.[131]

Recidivism may be thought of as a crucial challenge for restorative justice since the ability to address crime more effectively relative to the standard justice system is one of its key claims. Nonetheless, other criticisms against restorative justice abound. Leena Kurki and Kay Pranis contend that effects on victims and communities rather than offender recidivism should be emphasized as more important measures of success.[132] LaPrairie and Dickson-Gilmore question the success of the New Zealand family group conferences in this manner:

> First, if victims were present in only about 50 percent of the family group conferences held, and 60 per cent of those victims felt positively about the process, this means that only about one-third of all victims obtained benefits from the conference process. While this is not to be scoffed at, it certainly suggests a much more modest degree of success than popular discourse around the FGC's would tend to associate with these processes.[133]

An evaluation study of the Hollow Water program found that only 28 percent of victims found participation to be a satisfactory experience in contrast to 72 percent of offenders. Only 33 percent of victims felt that they had the support of the broader community. The study also concluded that while the community was supportive of the general principles of the program, very few had either participated in it or had knowledge of its specific operations.[134]

LaPrairie and Dickson-Gilmore also point out that there is a gap in our research as there is no empirical demonstration that restorative justice succeeds in one of its key claims – that it can improve relationships and harmony in the broader community.[135]

Restorative justice idealizes an agreement that harmonizes the interests of the participants, including the victim and the offender. As it turns out, there are plenty of questions surrounding whether such a harmonization can truly occur. At the heart of these questions is the fact that many times the interests of the victim and the offender, and possibly other participants as well, may be so divergent that reaching an agreement may be untenable. Acorn argues that it may be that not every victim has an interest in the conciliatory aspects of restorative justice, particularly when applied to domestic violence. Contriving to continue the relationship between victim and offender, where the offence reflects strained circumstances, may lead only to further hostility, resentment, and even the offender's recidivism. This is particularly so in the context of domestic abuse. Sometimes the victim, for the sake of her own sense of security and peace of mind, may want the relationship to end permanently.[136] Acorn also argues that the denunciatory and retributive aspects of punishment may in themselves be something of worth and value to the victim. She elaborates:

> Retributive justice aspires to bracket the desire for vengeance, to interpose the state between the victim and offender, and even handedly to deal out proportionate allotments of punishment commensurate with the nature of the offence. Thus retribution confines the extent of comeuppance for the offender by claiming a monopoly on violence and insisting that the offender's suffering not extend beyond the token of punishment authorized and delivered by the state. At the same time punishment stands for vengeance and gives official, though circumscribed, acknowledgment and legitimacy to the victim's and community's sense of indignation.[137]

Some programs have indeed been undermined by low victim participation rates, although the particular reasons why are not clearly documented.[138] This reality reveals, at the very least, that not every victim may take an interest in what restorative processes strive for.

The same could be said for offenders. Perhaps not every offender has an interest in accepting responsibility or reforming. As it turns out, available empirical evidence on whether reintegrative shaming can facilitate offender improvement and acceptance of responsibility relative to the standard justice system is equivocal. Some studies have found improvement,[139] while others have found little or no improvement at all.[140] A recent study of a sample of victim-offender conferencing sessions in Canada reveals that offender responses to victim input regarding harm and effects were often defensive, and/or minimized responsibility and the harm caused.[141] Kathleen Daly's evaluation of the South Australia Juvenile Justice Program found that most young offenders apologized to the victim and that 61 percent were truly sorry for what they did.[142] The picture was more complex than that though. A minority of 43 percent found that the victims' story had an effect on them, while the majority said it had little to no effect on them. The same breakdown occurred when they were asked what was important about participating in the conference. A minority of 43 percent stated that repairing the harm caused was important, while the majority were more concerned about avoiding a downfall in reputation and being seen in a more positive light. This number included 27 percent who did not feel sorry about what happened but participated in order to get off easier, 39 percent who said they participated in order to make their families feel better, and a nearly identical percentage who felt pushed into participating.

This debate over whether or not restorative justice is truly capable of fulfilling its stated goals can suggest an entrenched war of statistics and theoretical arguments that cannot be resolved. I would suggest that there is still that potential, although many of the studies I have mentioned suggest we clearly have a long way to go before realizing it fully. There is nonetheless some encouraging evidence, not just with respect to recidivism, but also for victim satisfaction and safety as well. An Australian study that surveyed victim satisfaction with participating in restorative programs found overwhelmingly positive responses, such as having been pleased with the outcome (85 to 91 percent), having experienced any negative consequences afterwards (3 to 10 percent), whether they were willing to do it again (87 to 92 percent), and whether they would recommend it to anyone else (84 to 92 percent).[143] Daly's evaluation of the South Australia Juvenile Justice Project found that 60 percent of victim participants in 1999 indicated that they were fully recovered and that the offence was truly behind them. Fear of the offender dropped from 40 percent prior to participating in the conference to 25 percent after the conference, and even further to 18 percent a year after the conference had taken place.[144] The issue of addressing victim safety and interests is, however, still an unresolved one, just as with the issue of recidivism. It must again be asserted though, notwithstanding Kurki and Pranis's argument, that reducing offender recidivism and addressing victim safety can be intertwined within a community. If crime drops, the community is relatively safer than beforehand, if I may indulge in simple logic. A study that interviewed participants in a conferencing program in Honolulu, Hawaii, found both overwhelming evidence of victim satisfaction (fifty-nine of sixty-two interviewees) and half the recidivism rate of offender participants in comparison to the control group that did not participate.[145]

How then is the question to be resolved when the empirical evidence is equivocal on every front? Why does it work in some instances but not in others? One explanation that readily comes to mind is the issue of financial support and resources. Restorative justice initiatives will be empty shells unless certain programs are available to the community to enable meaningful resolutions. These can include treatment programs, educational programs, job training initiatives, life skills training, and counselling services.[146] Initiatives will require monetary resources for treatment programs, facilities, operational costs, and human resources such as volunteers or paid staff. Restorative justice also places significant demands on human resources.[147] In small Aboriginal communities, finding enough committed individuals to provide qualified staff or a sustained volunteer base can be a challenge. Personnel are needed to run the project itself, which can include monitoring offender progress. In small communities, there may not be as severe a need for justice staff to monitor the offender since the offender may be ever under the watchful eye of his or her peers. The concept of community control may not be as meaningful in urban areas, however, where an offender would enjoy a greater degree of mobility and a less intimate sense of membership in a community than would be the case in a small isolated community. This scenario raises the possibility that an urban Aboriginal community in which an offender lives is less able to follow up and monitor that the offender is complying with his conditions, which may mean that a greater number of justice project staff or probation officers have to assume that role.[148] The result being that location may not rule out the possibility of restorative justice, but that it affects the specifics of its implementation. If the staff, facilities, and programs are there, a restorative justice program has every chance of producing success. Of the first 214 offenders dealt with by the Community Council Program in Toronto, only 13.9 percent had failed to perform their requirements.[149]

On the other hand, a lack of adequate resources to meaningfully support restorative-type initiatives can portend failure. Phillip Stenning and Julian Roberts point out that without adequate resources, restorative resolutions may be set up for failure as Aboriginal offenders find themselves faced with a lack of community supports that can assist with their rehabilitation.[150] The Royal Commission on Aboriginal Peoples has noted that funding for Aboriginal justice initiatives has been dominated by a pilot project mentality, whereby justice initiatives are accorded modest sums and very short time commitments (for example, one to three years). Once the initial time commitment expires, support for the initiative evaporates as budgetary resources are allocated elsewhere, leaving communities unable to pursue any long-term goals with respect to Aboriginal crime and recidivism.[151] LaPrairie and Dickson-Gilmore also argue that lack of stable funding presents risks such as fewer staff to make a project run smoothly and burn-out for those staff and volunteers that a project can employ. This situation, in turn, can endanger the long-term success of any restorative justice project.[152]

How do we know that the varied results from Aboriginal justice projects and their failure to make an appreciable dent in over-incarceration thus far cannot be attributed to Canadian governments' emphasis on piecemeal support and a political culture that sustains offence bifurcation? Until we see real financial, legal, and political commitments to community-based alternatives to incarceration, whether initiated by Canada or driven by Aboriginal communities themselves, the question of whether restorative-type processes can deliver on the promise remains unresolved. In fact, the present legal and political situation in Canada exacerbates the lack of resources available to address the problem. Leonard Mandamin explains that the lack of legally recognized jurisdiction over justice for Aboriginal peoples also means a lack of clout at the negotiation tables and, therefore, a corresponding inability to secure needed funding for initiatives.[153]

If Canada were to make a real legal and political commitment to dealing with the problem or if Canadian courts were willing to interpret section 35(1) rights more broadly so as to provide a "judicial sledgehammer," then the negotiating position of Aboriginal peoples could be strengthened.[154] This strengthened position could then procure significant monetary concessions from Canadian governments so as to make Aboriginal jurisdiction over justice meaningful. An alternative route is for Aboriginal communities to pursue their own economic development, if such opportunities exist. Examples include natural resources such as fisheries and tourist industries. This could, by the way, also lessen Aboriginal reliance upon outside sources of funding, which, in turn, can mean greater legal and political autonomy for Aboriginal communities and less dependence on Canadian funding in the pursuit of justice objectives.[155] If the resources were available to tackle the problems in earnest, whether through negotiated arrangements or through Aboriginal communities having their own economic bases, then perhaps significant progress could be made. Commissions in both Canada and the United Kingdom have urged a reinvestment in community-based alternatives rather than incarceration, with the idea that while it may mean greater short-term spending, the investment could see returns with interest over the long term.[156]

If you have all of the resources in place to fully develop programs, and if all of the legal safeguards to ensure fair process are in place, what then? Will the process just take care of itself and churn out the desired results? Not likely. More is needed than simply throwing more money at the problem. More research will be needed to determine which empirical factors and conditions can contribute to the success or failure of restorative-based projects. Carol LaPrairie writes:

Neither government funders nor communities or project personnel have been dedicated to critical evaluation processes. One consequence is that, despite a profusion of money and initiatives to change and improve the workings of the criminal justice system, a body of information about successful aboriginal interventions is lacking. This is exacerbated by an absence of policies and programs which target aboriginal populations most at risk with the result that there is no clear understanding of effective interventions for these groups ... The approach to funding has primarily been one of reacting to proposals and pressures rather than to systemic research to identify those individuals and communities most at risk, and to the careful evaluation of interventions to determine their risk.[157]

So what is crucial to the empirical success of restorative justice at present, leaving aside for a moment the need for further research? I would contend at this point, and I admit that it is simple hypothesizing on my part, that the ability of any restorative or Aboriginal peacemaking process to produce empirical success is integrally tied to its ability to facilitate a genuine agreement between the participants. Katherine Doolin relates that much of the literature thus far has sought to define and conceptualize restorative justice by an emphasis on procedure.[158] Doolin argues that the desired outcomes of restorative justice should have just as important, if not more important, a role than process in defining restorative justice. Restoration as an outcome is what is important, with process providing the means to get there. What I mean by genuine agreement, and what Doolin emphasizes as being integral aspects of restoration, is a case in which the offender is truly committed and motivated towards making reparation and reforming behaviour, the victim's interests are genuinely accounted for and looked after, and community members are committed to both offender reintegration and looking out for the victim's interests at the same time. I would suggest that if a process cannot facilitate such a genuine agreement, results such as lowered recidivism and victim satisfaction will not easily follow. Daly admits that some of the data in her study were equivocal, but she nonetheless notes: "[W]hen YPs were remorseful and when outcomes were achieved by genuine consensus, they were less likely to re-offend."[159]

A critical case is therefore one in which the interests of the participants are divergent from each other, at least to begin with. If the interests of the participants are widely divergent or if they are unwilling to budge from what they perceive to be their own interests, then the pursuit of harmonizing their interests into a workable agreement is problematic to say the least. Does this mean that the endeavour is futile or miniscule on a practical level, no matter what we do to try to assure legal fairness in restorative processes? Perhaps not. Declan Roche has written a book that focuses on accountability in restorative justice.[160] He found that, aside from the power differentials arising from certain kinds of offences or community power dynamics, the presence of a few strong and assertive individuals in a restorative justice meeting with relatively few participants can dominate the meeting and prove detrimental to the prospect of a genuine and voluntary agreement. Roche argues that there are possible measures to counteract this possibility, such as including a wider circle of participants so that a select few assertive individuals will have a much harder time imposing their will,[161] allowing the attendance of a professional advocate to represent a party who is identified as vulnerable,[162] extensive preparatory work prior to the meeting,[163] and allowing break-out sessions so that some participants may voice matters that they were hesitant to bring forward in front of the larger group.[164] Measures such as these, besides having some potential to help satisfy the legal standards of fairness that I have proposed, can, on a practical level, improve the prospect of a genuine and workable agreement.[165]

A study by Meredith Rossner, based on a video-taped conference that was recorded in London in 2004 (the subject matter being a mugging), indicates other possibilities as well.[166] Rossner argues that it is possible to gauge whether a restorative meeting is making progress from a situation marked by hostility and anxiety towards a situation of agreement and solidarity by observing the interactional dynamics among the participants. Various indicators such as facial expression, eye contact, verbal cues, and non-verbal cues can give signals about the participants' emotions (for example, anger, understanding, empathy), their degree of engagement with the process and with the other participants, and the degree to which they are at a given moment open to joining in an agreement with the other participants. Rossner theorizes that building an interactional rhythm is what is crucial in order for restorative justice to be able to progress from a negative and hostile situation to a positive one of solidarity, thus reaching the desired goal of a restorative resolution. She lists some of the crucial elements of this interactional rhythm:

1. Shared focus through conversational rhythm. Although initially disjointed, over time, participants settle into a turn-taking dynamic marked by a lessening of stutters and silences. They begin to share a common focus and communicate with each other directly.
2. Conversational and power balance. All participants feel empowered to contribute, and no one is dominated. In this conference, Christy talks more than anyone else, but this does not alter the balance of the conference. All participants continue to engage with each other and do not withdraw from the conversation.
3. Turning point. Strong expression of emotions acts as a high point for participants, providing a common focus and drawing them all into the rhythm and the flow of the interaction.
4. Public displays of solidarity. After a rhythm has developed and the interaction has reached a crescendo, participants engage in high-solidarity interactions, such as touching or sustained eye contact.[167]

A possibly fruitful avenue of research is the exploration of how to build interactional rhythm in the setting of an Aboriginal restorative meeting. The reason I suggest this topic is that the cues that Rossner observed in the London conference may not necessarily have the same meaning among Aboriginal persons. A lack of eye contact on the part of an Aboriginal participant, for example, may be explained by a cultural standard that views direct eye contact with other persons as rude and disrespectful rather than signalling a lack of engagement with the process. If subsequent research does reveal how to build interactional rhythm in Aboriginal restorative meetings, such insights can become part of the training of justice personnel who work with Aboriginal justice systems and help facilitate genuine agreements among the parties. The development of such knowledge, by the way, may potentially also address Acorn's concern about how the process can be manipulated by playing to the script. A trained facilitator may be able to observe whether an offender is earnestly moving towards a consensus by observing the offender's cues, apart from the words spoken by the offender.

It is not my intention at this point to engage in exhaustive discussions of the issues raised by Roche and Rossner. What I am trying to convey is that there are practical and logistical possibilities for facilitating the ability of Aboriginal justice processes to produce a genuine agreement, quite apart from any legal principles. Certainly, much of this discussion has turned for the moment to empirical, rather than legal, questions. The point of my legal proposals is simply to make it possible and to help clear away legal obstacles that stand in the way of a fuller realization of Aboriginal approaches to justice. If one side can coerce the other into a lopsided agreement, the initiative becomes hollow and pointless from the outset. The proposal is designed, within limits, to provide legal safeguards that will ensure equitable participation. Once such an initiative is in place, it may well behove Aboriginal communities to explore practical and logistical methods, aside from the law, by which their processes can result in genuine agreement and peacemaking. And as I said earlier, more research in this direction cannot hurt. If legal safeguards (being but one prerequisite), resource support, and effective program design are in place, then perhaps a genuine harmonization of interests can occur. There can then be progress with recidivism, victim safety, and community harmony.

Of course, there is also the possibility that despite the presence of legal safeguards, preparatory work, effective program design, resource support, and anything else that can be tried, the participants just cannot come to a genuine agreement. An individual victim may not want to forgive, may want more compensation than the offender is willing to provide, or may even want retributive vindication. The offender may not be willing to step up and accept genuine responsibility. Supporters for either side may feel intractably antagonistic towards each other. The nature of restorative justice, with its emphasis on voluntary participation, is such that there will always be this possibility. Sometimes, no matter how hard you try, no matter the abundance of good intentions beforehand, a given case will just not be successful. When this happens, you have to fall back on something else. It is only in this instance, or when a breach of natural justice has occurred, that a community court judge should step in.

Another obstacle involves the idea that recorded reasons may be inadequate to ensure that natural justice is upheld since a judge may, through clever wording, use those reasons to obscure the real (biased) basis for the decision. The response to this issue is that the reasons need not be the sole basis for appeal. If a system of video recordings or audio recordings leading to transcripts is available, an Aboriginal appeal court can use them for insight into what has been brought to the community judge's attention as well as the conduct of the community judge beyond the reasons themselves. If only written reasons are available, an Aboriginal appeal court could allow interested parties to present evidence in support of a claim that natural justice was not upheld. There is some hesitancy in making detailed suggestions as to what standards of proof and rules of evidence, if any, Aboriginal appeal courts should use. Such decisions would be for Aboriginal peoples themselves to decide. Two hypothetical examples will be offered to suggest how this could possibly work. Suppose a community judge indicates in written reasons that the victim was not subject to any intimidation, even though both the victim and a support team member have indicated that members of the offender's family have harassed the victim. The ensuing resolution imposes very minimal measures upon the offender. If both the victim and the support team member provide sworn statements or *viva voce* testimony to an Aboriginal appeal court, it could provide a sound basis for appealing the judge's approval of the resolution. Now suppose that a community judge indicates in written reasons that members of the offender's family were present, thereby making consent to a harsh resolution valid. If the offender and members of his or her family provide sworn statements that the family members were excluded from the discussions, there is likewise a sound basis for appeal.

Finally, certain measures, such as support teams, preparatory work, or recruiting a wider circle of participants for the process, can impose onerous burdens in terms of administration, time, and resources. Natural justice in this sense may be unrealistic. Simon Owen argues that one of the reasons that practices in common law sentencing courts, such as plea bargains and brief submissions during sentencing hearings, fall well short of the full discussion that restorative justice idealizes is that the court systems are themselves facing heavy caseloads.[168] This reality induces the court system to reduce the sentencing process to assembly line justice. The troubling implication from this reality is that if restorative justice, with its emphasis on much fuller (and therefore lengthier) discussion, is implemented for a far greater breadth of criminal cases, it would make an even greater demand on time and resources, at least to begin with. There are a couple of possible responses to this issue. One is a backwards reference to my previous discussions: about the need for some fundamental discussions about where we allocate our justice resources, about the extent to which Canada should finance more extensively Aboriginal justice initiatives in the hopes of saving in the long run, and about whether Aboriginal communities can themselves develop their economic bases such that they can independently design their own justice initiatives. Second, the Royal Commission on Aboriginal Peoples argues that Aboriginal peoples' gaining control over criminal justice would not be an overnight affair. There would have to be a transitional phase wherein Aboriginal communities would have to remain in partnership with the standard justice system. As Aboriginal communities become more capable and more accustomed to administering justice, they could then gradually assume full control over justice.[169] The point is that Aboriginal communities should not take on more than they can handle, at least not in the interim. Offences in which the offenders enjoy considerable power over the victims are one context in which an Aboriginal community should not assume responsibility unless they are ready. It can hardly be called justice if victims of domestic violence or sexual assault remain unsafe in their own communities because the justice systems cannot adequately address their concerns. The Peacemaker Court of the Grand Traverse band in Michigan does not use peacemaking for domestic assault precisely because it recognizes the power imbalance involved.[170] In summary, an Aboriginal community should not accept responsibility for certain offences unless it is prepared to devote serious consideration, time, and resources to issues of victim safety.

7
The Trial Phase

The Presumption of Innocence

Canadian Jurisprudence

Situations in which an Aboriginal offender asserts innocence against criminal charges raise interesting issues about conflicts between legal rights and Aboriginal methods of justice. The first such issue is discussed in this chapter. A long cherished tenet of criminal law in common law jurisdictions has been the insistence that the state must prove guilt beyond a reasonable doubt before an accused can be sanctioned. The classic statement of the requirement of proof beyond a reasonable doubt is found in the English case of *Woolmington v Director of Public Prosecutions,* where Viscount Sankey wrote:

> Throughout the web of the English Criminal Law one golden thread is always to be seen, that it is the duty of the prosecution to prove the prisoner's guilt subject to what I have said as to the defence of insanity and subject also to any statutory exception. If, at the end of and on the whole of the case, there is a reasonable doubt, created by the evidence given by either the prosecution or the prisoner, as to whether the prisoner killed the deceased with a malicious intention, the prosecution has not made out the case and the prisoner is entitled to an acquittal.[1]

This "golden thread" is now a constitutional right under section 11(d) of the Charter, which reads:

> Any person charged with an offence has the right:
>
> (d) to be presumed innocent until proven guilty according to law in a fair and public hearing by an independent and impartial tribunal.[2]

Whether a law violates the presumption of innocence depends upon that law's effect on the verdict rendered by the trier of fact. If the law creates the possibility of conviction, despite the trier of fact having a reasonable doubt as to guilt, the right to be presumed innocent is infringed.[3] In the years since 1982, the net for catching laws that *prima facie* violate the presumption of innocence has been cast very wide. Requiring the trier of fact to presume an essential element of the offence – the intent to traffic a narcotic in one's possession, for example – unless the accused proves otherwise on a balance of probabilities violates section 11(d).[4] Requiring the presumption of a collateral fact necessary to lay a charge (the accused was in care and control of a vehicle) as opposed to an essential element (the accused was in an intoxicated state) also violates section 11(d).[5] Requiring the presumption of a relevant fact – for example, that an accused was living off the avails of a prostitute he was regularly in the company of – unless the accused raises evidence to the contrary violates section 11(d).[6] Requiring the accused to prove a defence to a charge on a balance of probabilities – such as insanity, for example – also violates section 11(d).[7]

One could say that the presumption of innocence goes to considerable lengths to tip findings of fact in favour of the accused. Consider this directive from the Supreme Court of Canada on how trial judges are to instruct the jury on the presumption of innocence:

> The trial judge should instruct the jury that: (1) if they believe the evidence of the accused, they must acquit; (2) if they do not believe the testimony of the accused but are left in reasonable doubt by it, they must acquit; (3) even if not left in doubt by the evidence of the accused, they still must ask themselves whether they are convinced beyond a reasonable doubt of the guilt of the accused on the basis of the balance of the evidence which they do accept.[8]

The discussion will now explore how these principles may come into conflict with Aboriginal methods of justice.

The Conflict

Part of the difficulty stems from the fact that criminal trials as we know them had often not been seen among pre-contact Aboriginal societies. The Iroquois did have trials for witchcraft, but these were a notable exception. Even in this case, our knowledge of the details of such trials is rather lacking. The point is that many Aboriginal societies did not find it necessary to establish guilt through a formal adjudicatory process. An Aboriginal society often did not bother with any sort of community intervention unless its members, or a majority of them, were satisfied that an offence had occurred. Once the community at large was satisfied that an offence had occurred, contesting the allegations was often frowned on for it was seen as denying responsibility. Joan Ryan describes Dene practice in the context of theft from a trap:

This offence would be reported to the head man (*k'aowo*) in camp and he would then speak "harsh words" to the person who had stolen the fur. The thief would be asked to acknowledge his theft and to return the fur (or another of equal value) to the person from whom it had been stolen.

If the offender refused to do this, the senior people gathered and confronted him. He was placed in the centre of the circle and people gave him "harsh words" about his inappropriate actions. They demanded he acknowledge his guilt and promise to return the fur. This stressed the importance of restoring harmony within the community, reconciliation with the person he had offended and compensation through replacement of the fur. Once that was done, no further action was taken and no further mention of the offence was made.[9]

Rupert Ross suggests that this prioritization of owning up and taking responsibility may still have contemporary relevance in the Canadian north in this way:

> There are other pressures to plead guilty as well. One comes from the cultural perspective that the proper thing to do is to always acknowledge your misdeeds as quickly as possible, then ask for assistance so that you can both make amends and avoid repeating them in the future. Another comes from the fact that pleading "not guilty" forces others to come forward and speak publicly against you in a hostile or critical manner, a burden that should not be placed on them if at all possible.[10]

The presumption of innocence can potentially interfere with an Aboriginal society's desire to encourage a member to accept responsibility when the society at large is satisfied that the member has committed an offence. The presumption of innocence holds out the prospect of not being subject to any sanction at all and can therefore encourage an offender to "hedge his bets" against the community. It provides an incentive to get out of owning up to the offence before the community and, as a result, can erode the community's desire to promote responsibility and the collective good.

Furthermore, the erosion of this desire can entail a tangible cost to an Aboriginal community. The sentiment behind the presumption of innocence is captured by this timeworn adage: "I would rather see ten guilty men go free than one innocent man go to jail." The idea is that liberal democracies are willing to accept a certain social cost to avoid the state's having too much power to sanction the possibly innocent. Rinat Kitai describes the social cost in this way:

> There is no disputing that the strict standard of proof exacts a high price from society, namely, the cost of the acquittal and release of a considerable

number of offenders and the consequent danger to public safety. The acquittal of an offender violates the rule of law. It causes injury to all actual and potential victims of the deeds of released offenders. The high standard of proof weakens the element of general deterrence amongst the public, thereby exposing the public to the risk of becoming the victims of offenses. The potential offender's knowledge that there are many obstacles to convicting him at trial gives him hope of evading punishment for his actions and thereby decreases the element of personal deterrence. Indeed, the overall objectives of punishment are undermined by the acquittal of guilty offenders. There are those who posit that there is a miscarriage of justice whenever a verdict fails to reflect the factual truth, let alone when a multitude of offenders escape conviction and punishment.[11]

It is not hard to see how these concerns apply to Aboriginal communities trying to deal with crimes committed by their own members. Aboriginal communities are often plagued by any number of social ills expressed through crime such as widespread sexual abuse, domestic abuse, offences committed while intoxicated, drug trafficking, and offences committed by Aboriginal gangs. If a community at large is satisfied that such offences have occurred, would that community be willing to absorb the social cost of sexual molesters, gang members, drug dealers, and alcoholic offenders slipping through the net created by "proof beyond a reasonable doubt" for the sake of avoiding that one innocent man being sanctioned? The presumption of innocence can undermine the capacity of an Aboriginal community to deal with threats to its collective good.

On the other hand, neglecting to hold collective power to prosecute crime to a standard of proof can itself result in grave injustice. Consider the story of Donald Marshall, Jr., a Mi'kmaq man. In 1971, Marshall, while still a teenager, had been walking late at night in Sydney, Nova Scotia, with a Black teenager named Sandy Seale. They came across two white men named Roy Ebsary and Jimmy McNeil. Ebsary, while intoxicated, mistook an attempt at panhandling by the two youths as an attempt to mug him. Ebsary stabbed Seale in the stomach with a knife and then cut Marshall on the arm. Marshall ran away, while Seale subsequently died in hospital.[12] Marshall was sentenced to life imprisonment for murdering Seale.[13] What is relevant to our present discussion is how the investigation and prosecution leading to his conviction was carried out. The officer in charge of the investigation, John McIntyre, was so convinced that Marshall was guilty that he set out to pin the death on Marshall even to the deliberate exclusion of contrary possibilities that he was aware of. For example, MacIntyre was aware of two witnesses, Maynard Chant and John Pratico, who stated seeing two men matching the descriptions of Ebsary and McNeil at the scene but did not see Marshall stab Seale. He coerced and intimidated Chant and Pratico to change their stories into seeing Marshall stab Seale.[14] The Crown prosecutor was aware that these witnesses had given prior inconsistent statements but did not forward them to Marshall's defence lawyers.[15] Defence counsel did not actively seek out these statements despite being aware of them and despite the fact that obtaining witness statements was a standard procedure in their practice. These statements could have been used to challenge the credibility of supposed eyewitnesses to Marshall's stabbing Seale. John Pratico testified that he ran home after seeing Marshall stab Seale. Barbara Floyd, after reading news of this testimony, contacted one of Marshall's lawyers to tell him that Pratico had actually been in a church parking lot after the incident. Floyd was dismissed by the lawyer for being "too late," and this evidence was never followed up.[16]

Marshall was not released from prison until 1982, after the Royal Canadian Mounted Police re-investigated the matter at the initiative of another lawyer acting for Marshall.[17] The Nova Scotia Court of Appeal overturned his conviction in 1983.[18] Marshall was subjected to a presumption of guilt that was not subject to rebuttal throughout the events leading to his conviction, even by his own defence lawyers. Marshall's case illustrates to us that safeguarding against innocent conviction remains necessary. Would Marshall's conviction have been any less of an injustice if the conviction had been handed out by a Mi'kmaq justice system instead of the Canadian justice system? There is evidently a certain tension between safeguarding the presumption of innocence and certain Aboriginal notions of justice. The question becomes how to deal with this tension.

The Proposal
The starting point of the resolution is that a community court is an independent and impartial tribunal for the purposes of section 11(h). The extension of this understanding is that a sanction cannot be visited upon a member of an Aboriginal community unless it has been decided within the community court that his or her actions are such as to warrant community intervention, which amounts to a prohibition against an aggrieved party privately and unilaterally seeking vengeance against an offender. Among the Mi'kmaq, for example, revenge killing and fighting were both legitimate ways to pursue redress against offences. Sometimes disputants would try to resolve their differences by having men from both sides engage in a physical confrontation. An aggrieved party could also declare an intention to seek revenge against an offender (for example, murder). Once this declaration was made, there was no turning back. It had to be seen through to the finish.[19] Leslie Jane MacMillan details how a family feud erupted in a Mi'kmaq community in 1997. A Mi'kmaq man had an affair with somebody else's partner while he was drunk. Several men assaulted him, giving him a life-threatening head injury that required hospital treatment. These men were

apparently themselves subjected to reprisal assaults, with one of them getting both of his legs broken. This assault in turn inspired counter-reprisals. The ultimate result was a cycle of threats and violence that lasted for several years.[20] One may be inclined to dismiss these actions as criminal assaults and lawlessness. A better explanation may be that it was a contemporary expression of Mi'kmaq justice, a contemporary expression of a right to unilaterally and privately seek vengeance against an offending party. What is particularly revealing is that nobody was charged because a code of silence in the community obstructed police investigative efforts.[21]

Prohibiting private vengeance may seem like a paternalistic imposition of an external standard, but consider the potential effects of allowing private vengeance to continue unabated. Is the cycle of violence that manifested in the Mi'kmaq community really a desirable turn of events for any contemporary Aboriginal community? It may be especially dangerous in Aboriginal communities in which some families or factions enjoy greater power relative to others. It may be a recipe for allowing a more powerful family to establish unbridled tyranny over the community. The question then becomes how are facts determined when guilt or innocence becomes a contested issue?

First, the party seeking to establish that an offence has occurred should be required to present the allegations, and the evidence in support of those allegations, before the community court. "The party" does not have to mean a prosecuting lawyer. Aboriginal communities may well decide that their processes do not have to replicate every single feature of Western trial systems. "The party" can include the aggrieved party itself, who may want to present the allegations directly in a manner analogous to that of a civil forum. If Aboriginal communities use police forces (a subject that will be discussed later), the police can present evidence obtained as a result of their investigations. The point, however, is that the process should involve a presentation of the allegations before the community court as well as some evidence in support of these allegations.

Once this threshold has been met, there remains the issue of how to decide whether the commission of an offence is established. As previously mentioned, consensus is often touted as a feature of Aboriginal justice practices. The idea advanced here is that an insistence on consensus can be used as a culturally sensitive safeguard instead of as a formal standard of proof beyond a reasonable doubt. One example of this proposal is seen in the *Code of Offences and Procedures of Justice for the Mohawk Nation at Akwesasne* (*Akwesasne Justice Code*).[22] Article 6, section 1(c) reads: "A conviction of a serious offence is only to be found when all Justices on the Tribunal reach a consensus." Article 6, section 2(c) is a verbatim duplicate of section 1(c) except that "grievous" is substituted for "serious." In the definitions section of the code (Article 8), a tribunal is defined as a hearing consisting of three justice chiefs.

The rule of consensus also applies to minor offences, where mediation and settlement are required. Article 6, section 3 reads:

> A minor offence is heard by two Justice Chiefs. It shall be the duty of the Justice to attempt to mediate the matter until a settlement is reached. If a settlement cannot be reached after all parties are heard, the Justices will reach a consensus and then pronounce the findings.

The idea embodied in these provisions can readily be adapted to the proposals involving community court judges. If an accused contests the allegations, conviction will require the unanimous consent of a panel of more than one community court judge. However, the possible uses of consensus are not necessarily limited to community court judges.

The jury as we know it may not have had an equivalent among even those Aboriginal societies that used trials. Despite this fact, Christopher Gora suggests that the jury system can be adapted to act as a bridge between the Canadian justice system and Aboriginal cultural traditions.[23] Standard jury selection procedures emphasize the thorough randomness of the process such that non-Aboriginal jurors from outside an Aboriginal community are likely to sit on a jury for the trial of an Aboriginal accused.[24] The failure of the existing jury system to be representative of Aboriginal communities was highlighted when a judge presiding over a murder trial in Thunder Bay, Ontario, adjourned the case because he concluded that there were not enough prospective Aboriginal jurors in the jury pool. This case has prompted the appointment of former Supreme Court of Canada Justice Frank Iacobucci to investigate the current jury selection process as well as the question of including members of First Nation communities in the jury rolls.[25] With Aboriginal control over justice, there is the potential to have jurors drawn exclusively from the community to decide whether an offence has occurred.[26] This possibility can comport roughly with the historical observation that the community at large had to be satisfied that an offence occurred before community intervention was merited. The structure of the court itself can also be adapted to reflect cultural mores. Gora explains:

> The organization of the courtroom is quite different from that of the traditional council. Certainly, there is a wide variety in traditional layouts, but some consistent themes emerge. For instance, when the disposition of an offender is being considered, he or she is the one who must face the victim, the elders, and the rest of the community. There is an element of public shaming at work, a process of reckoning and atonement that seeks to restore harmony. In the common law courtroom, however, it is the judge, as representative of the interests of all of the people, who faces the audience. The

accused sits with his or her back turned to the community, and the victim is not accorded a particular position in the process. This foreign atmosphere can be alienating for the victim as well as for the members of the community and is not conducive to the goal of consensus decision-making that is fostered in customary situations ...

A possible reform would be to recognize "native gathering ergonomics" and foster a more relevant environment by modifying the seating arrangement in the courtroom. Thus, for example, the accused and the Crown would sit facing the judge who would be surrounded by the audience. In this way, an atmosphere of collective input is created, a symbolic union of judge and community, similar to the way in which the elders sitting at the council table were surrounded by other members of the community. The jury could still be seated to one side in order to have a clear view of the proceedings. And the victim, seated in the audience, would, in effect, be mingled with and surrounded by her/his neighbours. There could even be some accommodation made when she/he has to testify. Another possibility is the traditional circular arrangement where all parties – judge, jury, accused, victim and community members – are bound together in a way that promotes the aboriginal customary spirit of reconciliation and reintegration.[27]

The idea then is that a jury comprised of community members, its structure culturally adapted, must reach consensus in order to decide that an offence has occurred. It represents a culturally sensitive safeguard.

The obvious danger that Gora identifies is that power structures in Aboriginal communities can plague this sort of trial process just as much as restorative processes.[28] If all of the jury members are tied to powerful elites, then they can assert consensus against a marginalized accused despite a preponderance of evidence speaking to innocence. If both the accused and some of the jury members are tied to powerful elites, those jury members can prevent consensus despite a preponderance of evidence supporting conviction. In *R. v Fatt,* the Crown successfully applied for a change of venue for a murder trial away from the accused's Dene community because there was evidence that the community favoured the accused over the victim.[29] In *R. v K.I.,* the victim was a teenaged girl who had been sexually assaulted.[30] She and the accused were related both to each other and to most of the other community members. The victim was pressured by several members to withdraw the charges and was frequently criticized for making the allegations to begin with. The Crown obtained a change of venue on the basis that trying the accused in the same district as his community risked mental harm to the victim as well as not providing the victim with the opportunity to give honest testimony free from intimidation. The idea of a jury drawn from the community itself and the idea of requiring consensus have the potential to comport roughly with the theme of the community itself being satisfied that an offence has occurred. If power relations pose too great a threat to the integrity of such a structure, however, it may well behoove an Aboriginal community to go with consensus by a panel of community court judges instead. This alternative may be more successful since an Aboriginal appeal court would ideally have access to the records of the proceedings as well as the judges' reasons should an injustice occur. In summary, these proposals are an attempt to be culturally sensitive by incorporating a celebrated theme of Aboriginal justice – consensus – into the fact-finding process and to produce a meaningful safeguard against having the fact-finding process determined solely by the unfettered discretion of one individual.

Objections

The first objection involves the idea that even if there is a safeguard that is different from proof beyond a reasonable doubt, it can still encourage accuseds to enter not guilty pleas and avoid responsibility. One can respond to this issue in two different ways. The first is that Donald Marshall's story illustrates the dangers involved with not allowing an accused to assert innocence. Defendants in Aboriginal communities, like anybody else accused of committing a crime, should somehow be allowed to assert *bona fide* defences to the allegations. The second response is that there is still plenty of room to persuade an accused to accept responsibility outside of the courtroom process itself. Recall the fact that Elders in Aboriginal societies often exercised gentle persuasive authority rather than coercive authority. Nothing should really stop an accused from willingly accepting responsibility under such persuasion. Ross describes an example of this scenario:

> I recall, for instance, a young man charged with smuggling liquor into his dry reserve community. His lawyer urged him to plead "not guilty," because the search methods by which the alcohol was found were in breach of his rights under the Charter of Rights and Freedoms. After a month-long adjournment, the young man came back to court, without a lawyer and entered a plea of "guilty" instead. He explained that he had consulted with the elders who had spoken of their wish that the community be alcohol-free for the health of all. Because of that, he told us he had chosen not to "use the whiteman's law to go against the wishes of the elders," even though he knew he could have.[31]

I have opposed Ross's view regarding whether or not some application of the Charter is necessary. I agree with the anecdote he provides in that it suggests there is still room for persuasion and willing acceptance of responsibility, short of coercion, even when the Charter may be in some way applicable. It is quite another matter for me to say that it will not be necessary to have some form of safeguard in place. Taking such a position to its logical extreme seems to carry with it a dangerous and fallacious assumption that power abuses will never occur. Having rights protections in place does not necessarily mean that they have to be invoked by Aboriginal defendants whenever they are potentially applicable. However, they should be there as an option and whenever coercion or power abuse enters the picture. There is still another objection, but one that stems from opposing concerns.

Another possible contention is that not holding Aboriginal processes to proof beyond a reasonable doubt increases the risk of convicting the innocent. One must also be cognizant that in Aboriginal communities, as in mainstream Canadian society, the possibility of false or flawed accusations is a danger. Even if all of the community members or every panel member of community court judges reach a consensus that the accused is guilty, those members or judges may be adding their voices to consensus despite having a reasonable doubt. There are two replies to this objection. The first is the fact that even if the insistence for consensus does increase the risk, that in and of itself is not necessarily offensive to Charter standards. The tests for justifying Charter infringements under section 1 from *R. v Oakes* have frequently been called upon to justify lowering the standard of proof to the balance of probabilities or even placing the onus of proof on the accused.[32] The Supreme Court of Canada has often made a distinction between laws that resolve competing interests or protect vulnerable groups and laws that pit the state as a singular antagonist against the accused.[33] The former deserve a greater degree of deference. The latter deserve greater scrutiny under the Charter. An example of where protecting a vulnerable group has resulted in greater tolerance for a violation of the presumption of innocence is *R. v Downey*.[34] The accused was charged with living off of the avails of another person's prostitution, contrary to section 212(1)(j) of the *Criminal Code*.[35] At issue was section 212(3), which provides that evidence that a person is habitually in the company of a prostitute is proof of living off the avails of prostitution, in the absence of evidence to the contrary. This presumption was challenged as a violation of the right to be presumed innocent. The Supreme Court of Canada agreed that it created the possibility of conviction despite the existence of a reasonable doubt.[36] The majority found that the violation was justified under section 1. Justice Peter Cory applied the rational connection test as follows:

> In order to be valid the measures taken must be carefully designed to respond to the objective. Yet the proportionality test can and must vary with the circumstances. Parliament is limited in the options which it has at hand to meet or address the problem. Rigid and inflexible standards should not be imposed on legislators attempting to resolve a difficult and intransigent

problem. Here, Parliament has sought, by the presumption, to focus on those circumstances in which maintaining close ties to prostitutes gives rise to a reasonable inference of living on the avails of prostitutes. This is not an unreasonable inference for Parliament to legislatively presume, as it cannot be denied that there is often a connection between maintaining close ties to prostitutes and living on the avails of prostitution.[37]

The Court held that requiring an accused to raise evidence to the contrary to defeat a presumption of an essential element of the offence was justified for the sake of protecting women as a vulnerable group.

Another exception applies when the facts are presumed because of considerable repercussions for the administration of justice. An example is *R. v Chaulk*, where the Court held that requiring the accused to prove insanity on the balance of probabilities was justified since requiring the Crown to prove sanity beyond a reasonable doubt would have tremendous repercussions for the administration of justice, such as the costs of always having to hire expert witnesses to prove sanity and the resulting time delays and case backlogs.[38]

Courts are also often willing to relax the standard of proof for regulatory offences. In *R. v Wholesale Travel Group Inc.*, a majority of the Court held that requiring an accused to prove due diligence on the balance of probabilities as a defence to a regulatory offence was justified under section 1.[39] Justice Cory went so far as to say that the impugned law did not violate the presumption of innocence. His conclusion was based upon a contextual approach to Charter rights. Charter rights mean different things in different contexts. The presumption of innocence has a certain meaning in the context of "true criminal offences" and a different one in the context of "regulatory offences." To treat the presumption of innocence differently when it came to regulatory offences depended upon two justifications. His first justification was the licensing justification. When a person (individual or corporate) engages in a regulated activity, that person consents to accepting responsibility towards the public as well as the consequences for the public that may flow from engaging in that activity. The second justification was the vulnerability justification. Requiring the accused to prove due diligence was necessary for the sake of protecting society, especially its vulnerable members.[40]

In summary, Supreme Court of Canada jurisprudence on section 11(d) has frequently shown deference to legislation that has enacted *prima facie* violations of the presumption of innocence. The Court has recognized in its analyses under section 1 that constant insistence upon proof beyond a reasonable doubt can entail considerable social costs. One could of course suggest that the threshold for regulatory offences was lowered because the sanctions typically involve fines instead of incarceration. What is interesting to note is that in *Downey* and *Chaulk* the Court was still willing to lower the threshold when imprisonment was a distinct possibility (for example, for living off the avails of prostitution) on the basis of rationales such as easing the administration of justice and protecting vulnerable groups in society.[41] It is therefore reasonable to accommodate Aboriginal approaches to justice with a similar rationale. Certain crimes threaten the collective well-being of Aboriginal societies, such as gang activity, offences tied to substance abuse, drug trafficking, and sexual and domestic abuse of vulnerable members. The use of consensus need not be strictly held to proof beyond a reasonable doubt in recognition that it may comport roughly with Aboriginal notions of justice and that proof beyond a reasonable doubt may result in harmful social costs to Aboriginal communities. There is also a second and perhaps even better response to this objection.

The second response is that consensus, even if it is not held to proof beyond a reasonable doubt, can still provide a meaningful safeguard against convicting the innocent. Gora notes that in Northwest Territories, Crown prosecutors, defence lawyers, and members of Aboriginal communities alike have been under a perception that local juries tended to acquit more often than did judges in judge-alone trials.[42] The juries in these cases did of course receive instructions from the judge concerning proof beyond a reasonable doubt during these trials. Gora hints, however, that more than this judicial direction may be involved: "Defence counsel, on the other hand, were more apt to believe that the verdicts might in fact be appropriate given such factors as the jury's more intimate knowledge of the circumstances, including the motive of the complainant, or their reasonable doubt as to the facts and so on."[43] If consensus becomes the defining feature of deciding whether an offence has occurred, we may not actually know for certain whether it will lower the threshold in practice. For all we know, it may result in more convictions or fewer convictions depending on a number of factors, including the particular facts that come before community juries or community court judge panels, and the community's knowledge of the events in question. Consensus may not necessarily result in a higher or lower threshold. It is simply different from proof beyond a reasonable doubt. It ideally provides a culturally sensitive, but still meaningful, safeguard against sanctioning the innocent. This issue, however, is not the only problem that arises when an accused asserts innocence, as we will see in the next discussion on the accused's right to adversarial procedure during a trial.

Adversarial Trials

Canadian Jurisprudence
In *R. v Swain*, Chief Justice Antonio Lamer said: "The principles of fundamental justice contemplate an accusatorial and adversarial system of criminal

justice which is founded on respect for the autonomy and dignity of the person. These principles require that an accused person have the right to control his or her own defence."[44] There is also a facet of adversarial justice that is especially worth noting, namely the right to cross-examine the witnesses against the accused. Justices Cory, Iacobucci, and André Bastarache had this to say in *R. v Rose:* "[T]he right to make full answer and defence has links with the right to full disclosure and the right to engage in a full cross-examination of Crown witnesses, and is concerned with the right to respond, in a very direct and particularized form, to the Crown's evidence."[45] In *R. v Osolin,* Justice Cory also had this to say:

> It is of essential importance in determining whether a witness is credible. Even with the most honest witness, cross-examination can provide the means to explore the frailties of testimony. For example, it can demonstrate a witness's weakness of sight or hearing. It can establish that the existing weather conditions may have limited the ability of a witness to observe, or that medication taken by the witness would have distorted vision or hearing.[46]

There are other facets of adversarial procedure that are enshrined as Charter rights, such as the right to disclose the Crown's case, the right to a closing address, and so on. It is, however, the bare requirement of adversarial procedure and the right to cross-examine that are particularly problematic for Aboriginal approaches to justice, as we will now see.

The Conflict

Recall that restorative processes are designed to promote relationship reparation and community harmony. The mere presence of adversarial procedures is seen as a threat to this pursuit. Ross argues that the use of adversarial processes in Aboriginal communities can create problems:

> [W]estern law puts people through adversarial processes, necessarily *adding* to the feelings of antagonism between them. Traditional teachings, not surprisingly, suggest that antagonistic feelings within relationships are in fact the *cause* of antagonistic acts. Traditional law thus requires that justice processes must be structured to *reduce,* rather than escalate, that antagonism.[47]

The right to cross-examine also presents potential difficulties. Cross-examination in common law courtrooms is often very confrontational. Consider the following questions from a sample cross-examination relating to shoplifting:

> It was during this time that you saw Mr. Andrews put the bottle in his bag correct?

It is also correct that after putting the bottle in the bag, Mr. Andrews remained in the eye care area for a time?

During that time he continued to look at various items?

Now after leaving the eye care area he did not directly leave the store did he?

He went to the cashier?

And as far as you know he never purchased any items?

Then there was actually no need for him to go to the cashier?

In fact he spoke with the cashier for a time?

You never spoke with the cashier about what he talked to her about?

After speaking with the cashier Mr. Andrews then left the store?

Now the bottle of eye solution found in his bag is large isn't it?

And when Mr. Andrews emptied his bag in the office, the bag was open at that time?

So after Mr. Andrews put the bottle in his bag, he never closed it?

There were also other items in the bag?

Specifically there were a number of books weren't there?

When you stopped him outside the store he was co-operative?

He never tried to run away did he?

In fact, he never baulked at all about going with you to the store office?

Once the bag was emptied, Sir, did he not say, "I forgot all about that bottle in my bag as I was looking for my eye solution?"

In fact, whilst in the office he continued to protest his innocence, didn't he?

Your store policy is simply if a person leaves the store without paying for an item the police are called, right?

Prosecute all shoplifters?

And that, Sir, is why we are here today?[48]

The questions are not obviously rude, but they are still confrontational in that they constantly question the witness' understanding and representations of the events. Not only can the tone of the questions themselves be confrontational, but some of the grounds upon which a witness can be cross-examined can also amount to personal attacks. Witnesses other than the accused can be confronted with evidence of bad character.[49] The accused can be confronted with evidence of bad character if the accused asserts his or her good character during the examination-in-chief.[50] Other grounds include bias (for example, improper or tainted motive to testify against one of the parties),[51] interest (for example, standing to benefit materially or emotionally from the outcome of the proceeding),[52] and corruption (for example, deliberate fabrication or attempting to suborn such lies from another witness).[53]

Many Aboriginal societies have ethical standards of personal interaction that prohibit them from saying "hostile, critical, implicitly angry things about someone in their presence."[54] A cross-examination can invite an Aboriginal witness to speak negatively of somebody present during the process. Some of the recognized grounds for cross-examination can by their very nature also involve questions that direct negative commentary towards the witness. Cross-examination can be problematic for many Aboriginal societies in that it invites the commission of cultural *faux pas*. A Hopi witness once expressed indignation towards the cross-examination tactics of a non-Hopi lawyer: "He hasn't sat up there once, and had any kind of devious answer to anything. In fact, he – if I had to say that he was badgered by Mr. Keith. 'Answer me! Yes or no! Yes or no!' Hopi way, we don't practice like that. Not even in the kiva, and you men know that."[55] John Borrows also explains:

> While presenting evidence in an adversarial setting is a harrowing experience for most people, it can be especially troubling for Elders from certain groups, for whom such treatment is tantamount to discrediting their reputation and standing in the community. Apart from the tremendous strain placed on the individual enduring this experience, the process represents a major challenge to the culture more generally. To directly challenge or question Elders about what they know about the world, and how they know it, "strains the legal and constitutional structure" of many Aboriginal communities. To treat Elders in this way is a substantial breach of one of the central protocols within many Aboriginal nations, a fundamental violation of the legal order somewhat akin to requiring judges to comment on their decision after it is written. To subject Elders to intensive questioning demonstrates an ignorance and contempt for the knowledge they have preserved, and a disrespect and disdain for the structures of the culture they represent. Yet such behaviour is mandated by the Canadian legal system.[56]

Justices of the Federal Court of Canada have recently recognized the problems that Borrows describes when it comes to Elders participating as witnesses in Aboriginal rights litigation. The justices have also met with members of the

Indigenous Bar Association to discuss non-adversarial and more culturally appropriate methods of obtaining oral history evidence from Elders. Their suggestions include using a circle approach until the Elders and other circle participants (for example, academic experts) have reached a consensus on what is the correct history and holding "on-site" hearings away from the courtrooms and within the Aboriginal communities.[57]

These discussions have occurred in the context of Elders giving oral history evidence that is relevant to Aboriginal rights litigation under section 35. However, it is easy to anticipate similar concerns during a criminal trial in an Aboriginal community. If an Elder is a material witness to what happened, cross-examining on mistaken observation, character, motives behind the testimony, or suggestions of fabrication can become very disrespectful towards the Elder. It could amount to an especially serious cultural taboo. The commission of cultural *faux pas* during cross-examinations can also raise problems that are multi-layered. Ross points out that subjecting Aboriginal women and children who have been victimized by domestic or sexual abuse to an aggressive cross-examination can also amount to a second victimization inside the courtroom.[58] Judy Atkinson adds:

> Recently, a number of underage girls testified in a criminal trial to their alleged long-term sexual abuse at the hands of a senior community policeman. The policeman was defended by the Aboriginal and Islander Legal Services. In court the girls were subjected to the usual discriminatory, degrading cross-examination, which aims to prove that the accused is the victim and that the girls were the abusers. If this experience has done nothing else, it has shown these young women and their mothers that it is futile to seek help or protection from the western criminal justice system.[59]

Western styles of cross-examination can not only violate cultural taboo but also violate taboo in an especially serious manner by inflicting emotional or even psychological harm on already vulnerable victims. How can this kind of conflict be addressed?

The Proposal

One possible solution is to keep adversarial trials as a distinctly separate process from those processes that resemble restorative justice. There remains a problem in that some Aboriginal societies may want to collapse fact-finding and restorative processes together into the same process. An example of this preference is provided by the *Akwesasne Justice Code*. Anyone participating in a trial of a serious offence may present evidence to the tribunal of justices hearing the case (Article 6, section 5). Justice chiefs are also encouraged to consider all affected interests in the community in reaching a decision.

Article 6, sections 5(e) and 5(h) state that the justice chiefs shall ask the accused, the accuser, and the witnesses to explain what happened and what they think would be a just and equitable solution to the matter. Implicit in this request is the possibility that the justice chiefs can ask questions of anyone who presents evidence. Indeed, a grand tribunal of justices that hears an appeal from a trial may ask any party involved to provide an oral statement (Article 6, section 8). The *Akwesasne Justice Code*'s processes do involve ascertaining the truth of what happened but with a more inquisitorial emphasis. Restorative objectives and fact finding are collapsed into the same process.

A possible solution is to limit the scope of fully adversarial trials to more limited circumstances. The idea is that restorative processes can still be used in situations in which it is clear that the accused performed a criminal act, but one in which the reasons why remain unclear. Ross describes one such scenario:

> As a separate issue, it should be noted that many of the charges in the North occur when the accused is so intoxicated that he or she claims no memory of the event. At present, offenders must choose either to plead guilty on the basis of police summaries or to call for a full-blown trial so they can hear from the witnesses directly. If they choose a trial, their plea of "not guilty" really just means "I don't know." That all-or-nothing scenario could be avoided through a more informal pre-trial process, where witnesses relate what took place either directly to the accused (though perhaps in a less adversarial manner) or indirectly, to a group whose word and judgment the accused accepts.[60]

Another scenario could be that the accused performed the deed but has had a troubled life and/or performed the act in an extremely emotional state. The facts of *R. v Gladue* are worth noting. The accused killed her common law husband because she became enraged both by his being with another woman and by his verbal taunts. The victim had also physically abused her in 1994. While her trial was pending, she was undergoing counselling for alcohol and drug abuse.[61]

Acting in self-defence can be a complete defence to charges such as assault or murder under the *Criminal Code*.[62] As radical as it may sound, it is conceivable that even self-defence cases could be excluded from fully adversarial trials. Even if the accused had to defend him or herself from harm, the community may want to know why this necessity arose to begin with and how to deal with it. The incident itself may have occurred due to a family feud, and, therefore, it signals to the community that there are relationships in need of repair. The fact that the accused had to act in self-defence would ideally lessen the sanctions, if any, that would have to be faced personally.

In the meantime, the restorative process would provide the community with an opportunity to ascertain why the incident occurred and how to resolve community tensions. The point is that for cases in which the accused apparently did something causing harm, Aboriginal communities need not insist on the "all-or-nothing" proposition that comes with adversarial trials.

There are, however, situations in which it may be appropriate to insist on an adjudicatory process (more details on this later). These situations would involve an issue as to whether the accused had even performed an act meriting community intervention to begin with. One example may be a case where only circumstantial evidence is provided against the accused. Another situation may involve eyewitness testimony under circumstances where its reliability is open to question (for example, the identification occurred in circumstances of poor lighting or the witness is short-sighted).

The remaining issue is that even where trials are used, there remain problems with the use of cross-examination. The Royal Commission on Aboriginal Peoples argues that it may still be necessary to allow an accused to vigorously challenge prosecution evidence in order to establish *bona fide* defences.[63] Its suggestion for realizing this proposal is to structure cross-examination questions in a culturally sensitive format. The commission offers this description:

> The practice of making a point not by simply asserting it but by presenting a narrative, perhaps drawn from another time and place, to illustrate the point or lesson, has deep roots in Aboriginal societies. Aboriginal counsel might well develop a style of questioning witnesses that draws on this narrative tradition. Narratives might be drawn from the extensive repertoire of "Trickster" stories so common among Aboriginal peoples in Canada.[64]

Using this approach, the sample cross-examination taken from the *Advocacy Primer* could be reworded in the following way:

> The Trickster, as a figure of legend, often conveyed many qualities? Some of them often contradictory, yes?
>
> The Trickster could show great wisdom and foresight, but he could also show absent-mindedness. Correct? He was also often disposed towards friendly conversation with those around him, yes?
>
> Suppose the Trickster comes into a lodge of several brothers as a visitor. He sees several medicine pouches, furs, and various works of art that capture his interest. One medicine pouch in particular catches his fancy. He is well aware that the brothers will require payment in order for him to receive the pouch. He has brought beads to compensate the brothers. He places the pouch inside his satchel so that he can admire the other belongings that he sees in the lodge. One of the brothers is close by. The Trickster, feeling a

spirit of warmth and friendliness at that time, begins to converse with that brother. The Trickster has his attention absorbed by the words of friendship that he shares with the brother. When the conversation concludes, he walks out of the lodge with the pouch still in his satchel. Is it possible that on this occasion the Trickster was forgetful?

Could this story of the Trickster finish as follows? One of the other brothers kept close watch on the Trickster. This particular brother was charged with keeping watch over the goods of the lodge, and did his duties as best he could. He honestly believed that the Trickster was up to no good. The brother did not realize that the Trickster had beads for the brothers, but had forgotten to give them to the brothers. When the Trickster is confronted, the Trickster realizes that he has been forgetful and explains himself. The Trickster even shows the beads that he has brought for the brothers to show his good faith.[65]

This story is made up, but it does show how culturally sensitive modes of cross-examination can work. It does not have to be limited to cross-examination. Examinations-in-chief can also be presented in narrative form to avoid saying hostile or angry things about somebody. The Queensland Criminal Justice Commission has recommended the use of narrative format for examinations-in-chief of Aboriginal witnesses.[66] I can take this idea further and suggest that, even in the limited instances in which the fact of the act's having been committed will be in dispute, eliciting testimony from an Aboriginal witness need not adhere slavishly to the examination-in-chief followed by the cross-examination format that is followed in common law systems. It may actually be desirable to structure fact finding with a decidedly more inquisitorial emphasis, with some allowances for "adversarial" challenges to allegations, in order have the process fit more easily with Aboriginal perspectives. I will elaborate further on this point in the remainder of this chapter.

Objection
The key objection to this concept is that it invites the imposition of sanctions or obligations on an accused in situations in which the accused is normally entitled to a "not guilty" verdict. Why should an accused face any consequences if he was too intoxicated to form intent? Why should an accused face any consequences if he had to act in self-defence? Kent Roach points out that determining what is criminal conduct is a highly subjective and normative exercise.[67] The question of what conduct warrants state intervention changes from society to society and from time to time within the same society. Canada itself has demonstrated this varied perspective. Under Canadian common law, intoxication is a defence to offences with a specific intent, an intention to produce consequences beyond the action

itself. An example would be assault with the intent to resist arrest. Intoxication is not a defence to offences with general intent, such as simple assault.[68] In *R. v Daviault*, the Supreme Court of Canada ruled that the Charter required that intoxication be a defence to general intent offences when that intoxication produces a state akin to automatism.[69] Parliament responded to this decision with section 33.1 of the *Criminal Code*, which reads:

33.1

(1) It is not a defence to an offence referred to in subsection (3) that the accused, by reason of self-induced intoxication, lacked the general intent or the voluntariness required to commit the offence, where the accused departed markedly from the standard of care as described in subsection (2).

(2) For the purposes of this section, a person departs markedly from the standard of reasonable care generally recognized in Canadian society and is thereby criminally at fault where the person, while in a state of self-induced intoxication that renders the person unaware of, or incapable of consciously controlling, their behaviour, voluntarily or involuntarily interferes or threatens to interfere with the bodily integrity of another person.

(3) This section applies in respect of an offence under this Act or any other Act of Parliament that includes as an element an assault or any other interference or threat of interference by a person with the bodily integrity of another person.

One could suggest that section 33.1 reflects increased recognition that there is something blameworthy in self-induced intoxication that leads to harm relative to the previous state of the law. In addition, Western societies had in the past frequently criminalized certain forms of sexual behaviour such as pre-marital sexual relations and homosexuality, but they no longer do so. If Canadian society can alter the standards of acceptable behaviour, whether through increased or decreased criminalization, why can Aboriginal societies not enjoy the same privilege as well? Roach's point about subjectivity and normativity becomes apparent in this discussion.[70]

Aboriginal societies need not blindly accept the "all-or-nothing" proposition that comes with adversarial trials. Ideally, whatever sanctions or obligations are involved would be accepted willingly by an offender as part of the process of reaching consensus. An example of this idea can be found in an anecdote that does not arise from within any Aboriginal culture but is still particularly illustrative. Mas Oyama, a famous karate master, stood up for a young girl who was being harassed by a man. The man pulled out a knife and attempted to stab Oyama. Oyama delivered a punch to the man's head with such force that it killed him. Japanese courts decided that Oyama acted in self-defence. Oyama, however, was still personally overcome with guilt over the man's death. He went to the farm where the man's widow and child resided. He worked for the wife on her farm until she was satisfied that he was remorseful.[71] The lesson for us in this case is that even in situations that qualify for defences recognized under Western law, there can still be room for Aboriginal peacemaking to operate. Is there anything that truly precludes an Aboriginal accused from willingly accepting certain sanctions or obligations during restorative processes? Ideally, the sanctions or obligations faced by the accused would often be lessened in recognition of the circumstances, particularly if the accused has sympathetic parties who are there to participate in the process. Susan Olson and Albert Dzur add: "Rather than relying on procedural justice to achieve a black-and-white determination of legal guilt, restorative justice aspires to substantive justice and recognizes that it may often be gray."[72] It can also be imagined that the process can decide that no sanctions or obligations are required for the accused personally, while focusing on other aspects of the conflict (a family feud, for example). Of course, the only caveat to this recognition is that community court judges must ensure that the processes adhere to natural justice and that they themselves are, in turn, held to standards of impartiality by the appellate courts.

Getting to the Truth

This subject merits a section unto itself since it is a potential objection to the proposals directed towards both the presumption of innocence and adversarial modes of justice. The objection is that no matter how much you try to make any sort of criminal justice process fair, or imbue it with legitimacy, there remains the prospect of injustice, which hangs like a spectre, either through someone innocent getting convicted or someone guilty getting off scot-free. The prospect stems from the possibility that the process, no matter how fair you try to make it for everyone, will not flush out the truth of what happened and that a verdict will be based on mistaken conclusions. Mistaken conclusions can arise because of a gap between the perceived credibility of evidence led during a trial and the degree to which the evidence accurately reflects the truth of what actually happened.

This phenomenon can cut both ways. For example, it is well known that wrongful convictions have at times been based on mistaken eyewitness identification evidence. Eyewitness identification evidence can at times have enormous perceived credibility for either a judge or a jury because the eyewitness projects confidence, sincerity, and honesty. This perceived credibility can be out of proportion to the accuracy of that honest belief about identity.[73] The work of Deborah Connolly and Heather Price reveals that child abuse crimes may still prove immensely difficult to prosecute because of lingering assumptions about child witness credibility. Child abuse may often occur repeatedly for a victim. Testimony about repeated events, however, will not project the same level of confidence as testimony describing a unique event. Testimony about repeated events is also susceptible to differences and inconsistencies of details when describing one event compared to another. The younger the child is, the less credibility the child will be given. All of these factors will negatively impact a child's credibility as a witness in the courtroom. Controlled experiments whereby children are asked to observe events and then subsequently report on them have found that reports are often very accurate, despite the lack of confidence in reporting, the younger ages, and inconsistencies in comparing one event to the next.[74] Therefore, the gap between perceived credibility and factual accuracy can hinder a meritorious prosecution for a crime that has occurred.

In fact, one can detect a certain recognition of this gap, even a resignation to it, within the Canadian legal system. Don Stuart, Ronald Delisle, and David Tanovich argue that the truth-seeking function of adversarial court systems is in some respects compromised because it also has to address other matters:

> Besides searching for a different truth than the scientist, our methods are also circumscribed by other considerations, which require our fact-finding to be done in a way which is acceptable to the parties and to society. Our courts provide a forum for the purpose of resolving disputes between parties which may themselves have been unable to resolve in any other way ... Resolution of conflict now must be done in a way which ensures social tranquility generally, and which is also acceptable to the individual parties. The parties should be able to leave the court feeling that they have had their say, that their case has been presented in the best possible light, and that they have been judged by an impartial trier.[75]

Justice Edson Haines, formerly of the Ontario High Court, once proclaimed: "Truth may only be incidental."[76] The goal of the legal system is not so much to determine definitively the factual truth but, rather, to settle a dispute with a "legal truth." This idea was implicit when the Ontario Court of Appeal denied the appeal of William Mullins-Johnson, who wanted a verdict of innocence instead of not guilty. Mullins-Johnson was wrongfully convicted for the sexual assault and murder by strangulation of his then four-year-old niece, owing mostly to the biased and incompetent work of now disgraced Ontario forensic pathologist, Dr. Charles Smith.[77] Mullins-Johnson was thus not content with a not-guilty verdict, which went no further than to say that the state had merely failed to satisfy the standard of proof beyond a reasonable doubt. He wanted factual vindication, a positive affirmation of his innocence. The Court denied this request, in part with an emphasis that "the criminal trial is not a vehicle for declarations of factual innocence."[78]

My proposals thus far, I must admit, fall into the same kind of trap. They are about producing an Aboriginal, or even quasi-Aboriginal, version of a "legal truth," a conclusion that is arrived at by a process that accords, at least to some degree, with Aboriginal perspectives on resolving disputes. And this version is indeed subject to similar criticisms. If the safeguard inherent in requiring consensus results in an offender who actually committed the crime getting off because a panel of judges or an Aboriginal jury have doubts based on their own notions of what makes evidence credible, can this decision undermine the good of the community since guilty offenders walk free? The reverse may also be true. If consensus results in sanctioning somebody who turns out to be factually innocent (that is, never did the deed), an injustice results.

The resignation to settling for "legal truth" may certainly be open to criticism. Richard Lippke, for example, takes issue with the adage that watching ten guilty men go free is preferable to watching one innocent man going to jail.[79] The presumption of innocence should not amount to an institutional preference to let the guilty go free rather than convicting the possibly innocent. It should instead seek a balance between the risk to the public of letting the guilty go free and the risk of subjecting an innocent person to a miscarriage of justice. In other words, a criminal justice system must strive to maximize its effectiveness in sorting out the guilty from the factually innocent.

An endeavour for some researchers – legal psychologists, in particular – is to determine whether the gap between accuracy and perceived credibility can be bridged. If this gap can be bridged, can this endeavour address Lippke's concerns and maximize the efficacy with which a justice system can sort out the factually guilty from the factually innocent? Can it dissolve altogether a tension between crime (social) control and due process during the trial stage by ensuring that only those who are truly guilty of crimes be subjected to sanction? Much of the research in pursuit of this goal has focused on how to facilitate the effective examination of child witnesses and/or the testimony of sexual assault complainants.[80] The research often emphasizes using expert witness testimony to provide the trier of fact with information that can be used to assess lay witness credibility. This sort of measure has often met with resistance from common law legal systems for fear that it is tantamount to usurping the proper role of the trier of fact and effectively handing over decision-making power to the experts.[81]

If Aboriginal peoples gain control over their own justice systems, they do not need to adhere to common law rules of evidence or, for that matter, to the common law practice of examination-in-chief followed by cross-examination. Aboriginal legal systems may want to pursue their own methods of bridging the gap between accuracy and perceived credibility so they can effectively sort out the guilty from those who will not warrant sanctioning. Unfortunately, there is a lack of research with this kind of focus concerning Aboriginal peoples specifically. There is some Australian research, particularly by Diana Eades, that focuses on factors that negatively affect Aboriginal witness credibility before common law courts, such as different cultural methods of communication, linguistic differences in how Aboriginal persons use English, or vulnerability to suggestion during cross-examination.[82]

Martine B. Powell has done some research on how to conduct forensic interviews with a view towards obtaining an honest and accurate account of past events from an Australian Aboriginal person who may be a material witness to what happened.[83] The first step is to acquire sufficient background information about the interviewee, including both personal circumstances and cultural background, with a view towards fleshing out how best to structure and conduct a forensic interview. For example, some Aboriginal peoples in Australia have a belief that a deceased person should not be named out loud, nor his photograph viewed, nor any of her possessions used by anyone else, for at least six months. If this information is acquired beforehand, it can merit a decision to postpone an interview until such a period has elapsed.[84] Linguistic differences between how a non-Aboriginal person and how an Aboriginal person use English may need to be researched. For example, among the Torres Strait Creole, the word "kill" may mean to hurt or maim and not necessarily to cause death.[85] As another example, direct questioning may be considered "intrusive and discourteous" in some Aboriginal cultures. Aboriginal persons may also take longer to respond to requests for information in comparison with non-Aboriginal persons.[86] It may therefore be more appropriate to politely share some information about the events in question and then allow a period of silence, as an implicit invitation to the interviewee to share information about the events in return.[87]

Once the background information is obtained, it is then used to plan out the logistics and conduct of the interview itself. The goal of making this plan is to facilitate meaningful rapport with the interviewee, thereby increasing the chances of a truthful and accurate recounting of events. Some of the factors that Powell lists as having the potential to facilitate rapport include whether the room's logistics help the interviewee be at ease (that is, the right temperature, whether the room is spacious enough), whether the interviewee will feel more at ease with fewer people in proximity, whether it is necessary to avoid direct eye contact with the interviewee, and whether it would be good to allow the interviewee to have a support person of his or her own choice present during the interview.[88]

Diana Eades suggests an alternative, using the circle method of discussion also as a method of fact determination. She suggests that the circle method can avoid some of the limitations of examination questions, which often deliberately limit what the witness can refer to. Witnesses would be encouraged to speak freely on whatever they wish, including matters that may not meet common law standards of relevancy and materiality, which may limit evidence to what can actually prove the commission of the act itself. Eades admits that such an idea may be untenable in a trial context, if current rules surrounding the presumption of innocence and the right to cross-examination remain in place.[89] It is, however, precisely this kind of fact-finding process that the *Akwesasne Justice Code* envisioned for determining the truth of allegations against someone accused of a crime.

If the little research that is available suggests that Aboriginal witnesses may render more truthful and accurate accounts of what happened in settings that differ markedly from the direct examination format of common law systems, with preferences for private interviews or "circle talking," there is an important implication that must be considered. This implication may be that fact-finding processes may need to be pulled away from adversarial structures and pointed in a decidedly more inquisitorial direction. One alternative is to have every witness tell his or her story in a private forensic interview conducted by an appropriate professional who has adequately researched the necessary background information and can prepare the interview in order to facilitate effective rapport with the interviewee. Another alternative is to use a more public circle-talking method of determining facts. There may be other alternatives as well. Indeed, all of these ideas highlight a need for research specifically for Canadian Aboriginal peoples in order to determine how best to facilitate truthful and accurate recounting of events.

This suggestion may certainly be controversial, and, on its own, it may not account for situations in which witnesses may be telling their stories in optimal conditions, but in which the accused disagrees with what the witnesses are saying. One of the key points behind adversarial criminal process is to allow the accused to challenge evidence that supports conviction. Powell is well aware of this possibility. She suggests that a way of overcoming potential bias on the part of an interviewer is to require the interviewer to present several alternative hypotheses or scenarios to the interviewee, along with an implicit invitation to comment on these alternative hypotheses.[90] Let us take this idea a little further. Imagine that a witness describes events that make out a crime on the part of the accused. An advocate (issues involving the right to counsel will be discussed more fully in the next chapter), in consultation with the accused, can then provide the interviewer with alternative hypotheses or scenarios, perhaps in narrative format, to present to the witness. The interviewer would be obliged to record all responses and report them back, before either an Aboriginal jury or a judge panel. If a circle format is used, the advocate can present the alternative hypotheses, again perhaps in narrative format, as a subject to be considered next during the circle process. This process is what I meant when I suggested that "trials" could be pulled in a more inquisitorial direction but with some allowance for "adversarial challenges" to the allegations. I may for the time being have to remain content with putting forward the proposals as facilitating an Aboriginal version of a "legal truth," at least until more research is done on this issue in Canada.

8
The Investigative Stage

Right against Unreasonable Search and Seizure

Canadian Jurisprudence

Section 8 of the Canadian Charter of Rights and Freedoms reads: "Everyone has the right to be secure against unreasonable search and seizure."[1] An important preliminary issue is "what does section 8 protect?" The Supreme Court of Canada has consistently maintained that the right against unreasonable search and seizure protects a person's reasonable expectations of privacy. In *R. v Edwards*, the Court listed a number of factors to be considered in assessing whether a person has a reasonable expectation of privacy for the purposes of section 8:

1. presence at the time of the search;
2. possession or control of the property or place searched;
3. ownership of the property or place;
4. historical use of the property or item;
5. ability to regulate access;
6. existence of a subjective expectation of privacy; and
7. objective reasonableness of that expectation.[2]

The list is non-exhaustive. The reasonableness of the expectation is to be assessed on the totality of the circumstances.[3]

A search and seizure must usually must be permitted by prior and written authorization (a warrant) provided by someone impartial and capable of acting in a judicial capacity that is considered reasonable.[4] The authorization must be based upon reasonable and probable grounds that the evidence, items, or persons to be searched or seized will be found at the location in question.[5] Reasonable grounds cannot be based on an intuitive hunch on the part of the investigating officer, no matter how accurate it proves afterwards. Reasonable grounds must be based on information, provided either by the officers' own objective observations or by informants, available prior to applying for a warrant. The fact that evidence is discovered after the search cannot afterwards justify an unconstitutional search.[6] An investigative authority cannot provide itself with its own written authorization, since the authority cannot be deemed impartial or capable of acting in a judicial capacity in such circumstances. The search must also be carried out in a reasonable manner (that is, not in an abusive fashion).[7]

Warrantless searches are *prima facie* unreasonable. However, this presumption of unreasonableness can be overcome by proof of factors that support the reasonableness of the search or seizure.[8] Canadian jurisprudence recognizes exceptions whereby warrantless searches can be deemed reasonable. An accused can consent to the search so long as the investigative authorities inform the accused of his or her constitutional right not to consent and of the consequences of consent (that is, the evidence may be used against him).[9] Circumstances of necessity or urgency can justify a warrantless search where police would not be able to obtain the evidence if they took the time and effort to obtain a warrant. However, exigent circumstances do not create a blanket exception but, instead, are assessed, along with all of the other circumstances, on a case-by-case basis.[10] Furthermore, investigative authorities can seize items in plain view.[11] The police must, however, have properly stayed within their constitutional limits prior to getting a plain view. In other words, they cannot conduct what was initially an unconstitutional search as a pretext towards getting a plain view of incriminating evidence in order to justify the initial search after the fact.[12]

Searches incidental to arrest can also be justified without a warrant. Such searches must be pursuant to a valid objective, such as assuring the safety of arresting officers, removing objects that the accused may use to escape, and procuring evidence of a crime for which the accused has already been charged.[13] In *R. v Golden,* the Supreme Court of Canada recognized that a strip search was "inherently humiliating and degrading" to the detainee.[14] The Court nonetheless held that a warrantless strip search could be permissible when it was justifiably incidental to the arrest and pursuant to any of the valid objectives. The mere possibility of finding weapons or evidence is not enough to justify a strip search, as a frisk search will usually be sufficient to fulfil either valid objective. It is when a frisk search has revealed either weapons or evidence, thus suggesting that a more intrusive search may be necessary, or the particular circumstances of a case provide reasonable and probable grounds to believe that the usual frisk search may not be sufficient, that the police can go further and proceed with a strip search. The strip search must usually be conducted at the police station and in privacy, unless there are sufficiently exigent circumstances that justify an immediate strip search.[15]

Glen Luther describes the fundamental purpose of section 8: "Sections 8 and 9 are first and foremost, limitations on police power."[16] This purpose is viewed as being critical to preserving liberty in Canada and preventing the emergence of a police state. For example, in *R. v Storrey,* Justice Peter Cory stated:

> Section 450(1) (now 495(1)) makes it clear that the police were required to have reasonable and probable grounds that the appellant had committed the offences of aggravated assault before they could arrest him. Without such an important protection, even the most democratic society could all too easily fall prey to the abuses and excesses of a police state.[17]

In *R. v Stillman,* the police seized scalp hairs and buccal swabs from the accused even though he refused to give his consent. The Court came down strongly on this action:

> It serves as a powerful reminder of the powers of the police and how frighteningly broad they would be in a police state. If there is not respect for the dignity of the individual and the integrity of the body, then it is but a short step to justifying the exercise of any physical force by police if it is undertaken with the aim of solving crimes. No doubt the rack and other stock in trade of the torturer operated to quickly and efficiently obtain evidence for a conviction. Yet repugnance for such acts and a sense of a need for fairness in criminal proceedings did away with those evil practices. There must always be a reasonable control over police actions if a civilized and democratic society is to be maintained.[18]

A more recent statement is provided in *R. v Mentuck:* "A fundamental belief pervades our political and legal system that the police should remain under civilian control and supervision by our democratically elected officials; our country is not a police state."[19]

The Conflict

One might think offhand that police forces as we think of them have no basis in the Aboriginal past and that there may not be any conflict between Aboriginal methods of justice and the right against unreasonable search and seizure. William Newell states that when the Grand Council of the Iroquois met for a witchcraft trial, the nation took matters in hand by bringing the offender to justice.[20] Douglas George-Kanentiio also states that responsibility for obtaining satisfaction for the victim of a crime rested with the family or the clan of the victim.[21] This responsibility may entail investigative activity to discover who performed the deed. On the other hand, Arthur C. Parker writes: "There were no houses for punishment, no police. The standard of behavior was enforced by means of ostracism and by social persecution."[22] No society, however, Aboriginal societies included, has ever been able to fully escape the need to investigate wrongdoing and to employ some measure of force to preserve order. It seems clear that Aboriginal peoples in their daily lives were usually involved in activities other than enforcing the law and investigating crimes. Cultural and subsistence activities come readily to mind. Yet they may have been willing to act as enforcers and investigators as and when the occasion demanded it. What would not have been a part of pre-contact Aboriginal practice is a formal, professional, and centralized police agency that enforces the law and actively investigates crime on a full-time basis. This conclusion may be strengthened by the observation that private justice was occasionally exercised by some Aboriginal societies before contact.[23] One of the key goals behind modern police forces is to prevent the exercise of private justice.

If this particular form of policing does not resonate with pre-contact practices, it has not stopped many Aboriginal communities from establishing their own police forces staffed by their own community members. As an example, the Royal Canadian Mounted Police has entered into community police service agreements with Aboriginal communities in British Columbia, Prince Edward Island, Saskatchewan, and Yukon. Other bands, including the Siksika in Alberta, have entered into tripartite agreements with federal and provincial governments.[24] Akwesasne has its own Mohawk police service.[25] Even when Aboriginal communities use modern police services, the officers often use approaches that resonate with traditional values. Aboriginal police officers have often used methods analogous to those of community enforcement. Robert Depew writes:

Native policing may be observed to operate in the context of reciprocal constraints that are derived from a variety of social relationships and, therefore, is shaped and directed by the interests of the wider community. The obvious theoretical implication here is that non-urban, traditional native communities are structured in such a way that community responses to crime and deviance are likely to take precedence over those of a formal, centralized police agency, at least in certain circumstances.[26]

A survey of police officers working in Aboriginal communities, conducted by Chris Murphy and Don Clairmont, found a recurrent theme in many of the responses.[27] Officers often found that they had to develop a more informal style of police work to be effective. This style included giving breaks for minor offences, getting to know everybody in the community, encouraging people to settle disputes outside of the justice system, and involving community agencies in problems that arose. Murphy and Clairmont were unsure whether this reflected practicality on the part of the officers or whether it was produced by the traditional values of the community.

Previous discussions have made clear that there are certain types of crime that pose serious threats to contemporary Aboriginal communities. Offences brought about by substance abuse and drug trafficking are two examples. Aboriginal gang activity can also pose a very significant threat. It can be readily imagined that Aboriginal communities may look upon police forces as an expedient way to deal with these and other threats to their collective well-being. Police forces can actively investigate such crimes and deal with threats to public safety as they occur. In fact, one can anticipate that police methods will not always have a conciliatory approach and, instead, be quite forceful. In the Mohawk community of Kanesetake, newly elected grand chief John Gabriel fired the incumbent police chief Tracy Coon for being "soft on crime." The criminal element in question was Mohawk gangsters tied to the Hell's Angels, who were reportedly conducting marijuana production and cigarette bootlegging operations in the community. Gabriel then brought in Aboriginal police officers from outside the reserve with a view towards cracking down on these operations. The response was swift. On 12 January 2004, Gabriel's house was burned to the ground. The gang members barricaded the newly hired police chief and over forty officers inside their own detachment for over thirty-six hours.[28] The crisis ended when Quebec's public security minister, Jacques Chagnon, brokered a deal that allowed for the release of the barricaded officers and the appointment of Mohawk peacekeepers from nearby Kahnawake as the interim police force.[29] This scenario illustrates both the potential threat posed to an Aboriginal community by gang activity and the possible need for law enforcement to deal with such a threat, possibly in a forceful fashion (for example, SORT team tactics). As another example, an Aboriginal community may decide that it wants to ban the consumption of drugs and alcohol and prevent the importation of such substances. Therefore, the community may want to empower its police force to detect and investigate such activities.

In summary, certain types of crime threaten the collective well-being of contemporary Aboriginal communities. Modern police forces may not reflect pre-contact Aboriginal practices. Aboriginal communities may, however, desire to use them as an expedient means of dealing with threats to their collective well-being. The conflict arises in that section 8 limits the powers of police to investigate crime and thereby take action against certain activities that threaten the collective well-being of Aboriginal communities. The question becomes how to address such a conflict.

The Proposal
The starting part of the resolution is that Aboriginal police officers must apply for a warrant before a community court judge, based on reasonable and probable cause, before a search can be conducted. However, this procedure is only a starting point. There are other contours in the Supreme

Court of Canada's jurisprudence on section 8 that commend themselves very well to a suitable way to address the conflict. In addition to the afore-mentioned exceptions that allow for warrantless searches, the tests for reasonable expectation of privacy as applied by the Court through several cases has produced a variety of results. A warrantless search of a private residence will usually attract a high degree of scrutiny.[30] A recurring theme in Canadian criminal law is that the law is to protect the bodily integrity of individual persons. For example, a person who commits assault cannot claim victim consent as a defence when the victim has suffered serious bodily harm.[31] A person also has the right to express, either by words or by a course of conduct, a lack of consent to sexual contact that requires the other person to desist from further efforts at sexual contact.[32] Likewise, investigative searches that intrude upon the bodily integrity of a person, such as strip searches and taking blood samples, will invite a high degree of Charter scrutiny, albeit subject to the rules in *Golden*.[33] However, a lower expectation of privacy has been found in other contexts. People will have a lower expectation of privacy during a border crossing or at airport terminals.[34] This lower threshold makes it constitutionally permissible for customs officers to search any person entering or leaving Canada on the basis of reasonable grounds that the person is carrying contraband, and they may do so without a warrant.[35] The Court has also found there is no reasonable expectation of privacy in materials deposited in the garbage for public collection.[36] A lower expectation of privacy also applies to students when school authorities conduct searches and seizures. School authorities or police need only reasonable grounds that a crime is occurring, or has occurred, within a school setting. It is a lower threshold than reasonable *and* probable grounds.[37]

The *Edwards* criterion for determining reasonable expectations of privacy requires a court to look at the totality of the circumstances. The previous discussion makes it clear that this consideration can result in lowering the level of protection under section 8. The *Edwards* criteria therefore provide workable mechanisms for incorporating Aboriginal perspectives into the analysis. Aboriginal cultural viewpoints can speak to the criteria of subjective expectation of privacy, objective reasonableness of the expectation, and the totality of the circumstances, which can result, where an Aboriginal community's traditions and contemporary needs become relevant, in modifying the requirements of a valid search under section 8. An example of how this analysis can work is provided by the Hopi tribal court. In *Hopi Tribe v Kahe*, Kahe had not been seen by his neighbours for more than a day. One of his neighbours, feeling concern, asked the Hopi police to look for him. The police complied with this request and found him. Upon finding him, the police then asked for his licence and conducted a search of his vehicle. They found alcohol, which was illegal, leading to his subsequent conviction. The Hopi court found that the initial search for Kahe was justified as a welfare check. The subsequent demands for a licence and vehicle search were not.[38] In holding that the initial search was justified, the court held that standards for justifying that searches were to be determined by "customary and traditional ways of the Hopi people. Because of the extended family system, Hopi people look out for and take care of each other. It is Hopi to be concerned about the welfare of your family and neighbors and to make sure that they are okay."[39]

On the surface, this justification may not sound like a big deal since the subsequent search of the vehicle itself was not permissible. Consider, however, the possibilities if Aboriginal communities in Canada adopt a similar analysis based on concerns for the well-being of all. If such an initial check ends up exposing evidence of a crime within plain view, Aboriginal police then have a legitimate basis for seizing that evidence and then searching the location in question. Now suppose that police receive calls out of concern for a battered spouse or somebody who is being sexually abused. Traditional concerns for the well-being of all can justify the police in making an initial entry into the residence to ensure the safety of the victim. Questions asked of the victim or other residents upon initial entry, evidence in plain view, or any information or observations that are readily apparent to the officers without actually making a search, could be used to apply to a community court judge for a warrant to search the residence. There are other exceptions as well.

It is well known that Aboriginal notions of property are often different from those of Western society, the former having a greater emphasis on the collective good. Suppose that a clan leader, an Elder, or a person of similar traditional authority gives consent to a police officer to conduct a search and seizure in relation to the accused's residence or belongings. If an Aboriginal accused accepts the leader's authority as a matter of traditional belief, an argument could be made that the accused has a lower expectation of privacy. A sample clause in an Aboriginal Charter of rights could read in this way: "When a peace officer has reasonable grounds to believe that a person has committed an offence, that peace officer may search that person's residence without warrant provided that consent has been given by a recognized Elder of that person's clan."

When the Supreme Court of Canada has applied the *Edwards* criteria, its analyses of whether there exist reasonable expectations of privacy also include analyses of whether a refusal to lower the threshold of permissible searches entails an unacceptable social cost. In *R. v Simmons*, Chief Justice Brian Dickson wrote:

> I accept the proposition advanced by the Crown that the degree of personal privacy reasonably expected at customs is lower than in most other situations. People do not expect to be able to cross international borders free

from scrutiny. It is commonly accepted that sovereign states have the right to control both who and what enters their boundaries. For the general welfare of the nation the state is expected to perform this role. Without the ability to establish that all persons who seek to cross its borders and their goods are legally entitled to enter the country, the state would be precluded from performing this crucially important function.[40]

In *R. v M. (M.R.)*, we also read:

A reasonable expectation of privacy, however, may be diminished in some circumstances. It is lower for a student attending school then it would be in other circumstances because students know that teachers and school authorities are responsible for providing a safe school environment and maintaining order and discipline in the school.[41]

Aboriginal perspectives on reasonable expectations of privacy, coupled with threats to community well-being, can operate in a similar fashion to lower the threshold for permissible searches. One example is where an Aboriginal community considers it necessary to prohibit the consumption or importation of alcohol and drugs, due to a crime endemic brought on by substance abuse. Tammy Landau relates that Aboriginal communities in northern Ontario have often looked to police services to stop the inflow of alcohol where they perceive other community agencies to be unable to tackle the problem.[42] In *R. v Hatchard*, the Big Trout Lake First Nation in northwestern Ontario had passed a bylaw under the *Indian Act* authorizing a constable to conduct a search of any person or piece of luggage for intoxicating substances.[43] This bylaw was developed in addition to a system of community patrols in an effort to stop the importation of alcohol that was fuelling endemic alcoholism in the community. The bylaw was constitutionally challenged after First Nations officers acted on a tip that the accused was returning to the community with drugs for trafficking and seized those drugs during a warrantless search as there was no resident justice of the peace who could issue a warrant under the *Criminal Code*.[44] Justice Erwin Stach noted: "The search was part of the collective effort of a remote Aboriginal community to remove from its midst the social destructiveness of intoxicants and admission of the real evidence obtained in the search will not bring the administration of justice into disrepute."[45] The Royal Commission on Aboriginal Peoples states:

If a court were to find that such actions did contravene the Charter, the problems that would be created are apparent. Attempts by a community to control activities it regards as detrimental to its overall health would be seriously impaired if it were required to conform to a balancing of individual and collective rights that did not take into account that community's culture, traditions and needs.[46]

A clause in an Aboriginal Charter of rights could read: "When the government of our community declares that drugs, alcohol, and other prohibited substances present a serious threat to the well-being of our community, a peace officer may, without warrant, conduct a search of a person and his or her personal effects on the basis of reasonable belief that the person is in possession of drugs, alcohol, or another prohibited substance." The words "reasonable belief" still set a threshold on the validity of the search and seizure and so avoid giving community peace officers a complete *carte blanche* to search as and whenever they please. In other words, there still has to be at least some basis of information to found this belief.

One could expect that Aboriginal communities may want the threshold similarly reduced when gang activity poses a serious threat. A clause in an Aboriginal Charter of rights could read: "When a peace officer believes on reasonable grounds that a member of the community is engaged in criminal activity for the benefit of a criminal association, the peace officer may detain and question that person, and may search that person without warrant." Note that I did not expressly include strip searches in this hypothetical clause. I personally believe, and I admit this is simply my own preference, that a warrantless strip search should not occur unless it is truly necessary according to the criteria set out in *R. v Golden*.[47] The threshold for searching locations of gang activity, and not gang members themselves, can also be lowered. Another sample clause could read: "A peace officer may apply before a community court judge for a warrant authorizing a search of a private residence or any other site within the community on the basis of the peace officer's having a reasonable belief that the site is being used to carry out criminal activity for the benefit of a criminal association." In summary, the *Edwards* tests afford a workable mechanism to incorporate Aboriginal perspectives and lower the protection of section 8 in appropriate contexts.

Objection
An objection that can be raised is that a collection of exceptions whereby the threshold is reduced to below reasonable and probable grounds, or where warrantless searches are justified, can in effect lead to the creation of police states inside of Aboriginal communities. The exceptions all combine to give police forces inordinate power to subject individual members of Aboriginal communities to searches. There are three ways to respond to this issue. One is that Aboriginal cultural perspectives on what an individual can reasonably expect to be kept private from other members of the community, assuming they still have modern currency, may differ significantly from

liberal Western notions of individual privacy. The exceptions described in this chapter may simply describe the outcome of an objective application of the *Edwards* tests. Aboriginal peoples, assuming they still adhere to cultural values and understandings, may themselves not have an issue with lowered expectations of privacy. Second, there may be a social cost involved with a constant insistence on search warrants issued on reasonable and probable grounds. This social cost can stem from threats to the collective well-being of Aboriginal communities through certain types of offences such as offences brought on by substance abuse and gang activity. Recall that the collective good was often a cherished principle of Aboriginal societies. Aboriginal communities may themselves desire to adjust the level of protection in order to deal with threats to their well-being. Third, the level of protection remains meaningful. Even where warrantless searches are authorized or where the threshold is reduced from "reasonable and probable grounds" to, say, "reasonable belief," it does not mean that the officers have a complete *carte blanche* to search where and whenever they please. There must still be some information to justify the search. Furthermore, an idea that will be developed is that the Aboriginal police officers will have to justify searches before a community court judge. This concept will be considered in more detail when the exclusion of evidence as a remedy is dealt with at the end of Chapter 9.

Right to Silence

Canadian Jurisprudence
Although there does not exist a "right to silence" provision in the Charter, the Supreme Court of Canada has recognized that the principles of fundamental justice under section 7 protect a general right against self-incrimination. At the core of the right is allowing an accused to decide whether to provide self-incriminating evidence to authorities or, more broadly speaking, whether to say anything at all to authorities.[48] The accused must be detained by state authorities before the right to silence becomes operative. The test for whether there is detention is set out by the Court in *R. v Grant:*

1 Detention under ss. 9 and 10 of the Charter refers to a suspension of the individual's liberty interest by a significant physical or psychological restraint. Psychological detention is established either where the individual has a legal obligation to comply with the restrictive request or demand, or a reasonable person would conclude by reason of the state conduct that he or she had no choice but to comply.

2 In cases where there is no physical restraint or legal obligation, it may not be clear whether a person has been detained. To determine whether

the reasonable person in the individual's circumstances would conclude that he or she had been deprived by the state of the liberty of choice, the court may consider, *inter alia*, the following factors:

(a) The circumstances giving rise to the encounter as they would reasonably be perceived by the individual: whether the police were providing general assistance; maintaining general order; making general inquiries regarding a particular occurrence; or singling out the individual for focused investigation.

(b) The nature of the police conduct, including the language used; the use of physical contact; the place where the interaction occurred; the presence of others; and the duration of the encounter.

(c) The particular characteristics or circumstances of the individual where relevant, including age; physical stature; minority status; level of sophistication.[49]

Upon detention, the right to silence has many facets within the criminal process. It includes a right not to be compelled to testify at trial[50] and a right to remain silent during pre-trial investigations by authorities.[51] If authorities in disguise are used to garner self-incriminating statements, they are prohibited from actively eliciting evidence. They can wait and passively receive the evidence.[52] There is also the right not to have the trier of fact (jury) invited to make an adverse inference on the basis of not testifying.[53] If an accused is compelled to testify at a public inquiry, he or she has the right not to have his testimony read into evidence at his or her trial. He or she can also apply for the exclusion of evidence derived from the testimony (for example, real evidence) if it could not have been found or if its significance could not have been appreciated but for the testimony.[54] An accused can be excused altogether from testifying at a public inquiry if it can be established that it would cause undue prejudice at a subsequent criminal trial.[55]

As with section 8, an important concern underlying the right to silence is to prevent the emergence of a police state. At the core of the right is the desire to prevent a state authority, at virtually every stage of the criminal proceedings, from coercing or tricking an accused into self-incrimination. In *R. v S. (R.J.)*, the Court quoted with approval this passage from *Thomson Newspapers Ltd. v Canada (Director of Investigation and Research, Restorative Trade Practices Commission)*: "The state must have some justification for interfering with the individual and cannot rely on the individual to produce the justification out of his own mouth. Were it otherwise, our justice system would be on a slippery slope towards the creation of a police state."[56] In *R. v Hebert*, the Court explained: "The state has the power to intrude on the individual's physical freedom by detaining him or her. The individual cannot walk away. This physical intrusion on the individual's mental liberty in turn may enable the state to infringe the individual's mental liberty by techniques made possible by its superior resources and power."[57] And later it stated: "The scope of the right to silence must be defined broadly enough to preserve for the detained person the right to choose whether to speak to the authorities or to remain silent, notwithstanding the fact that he or she is in the superior power of the state."[58]

Concerns about preventing the emergence of a police state extend to the trial stage as well. Unlike the general right to silence under section 7, there is a specific provision for a right not to testify at trial, section 11(c), which reads: "Any person charged with an offence has the right ... not to be compelled to be a witness in proceedings against that person in respect of the offence." In *R. v Amway of Canada Ltd.*, the Court said that the underlying purpose of section 11(c) is to prevent the prosecution from compelling the accused to supply evidence from his or her own mouth.[59] As with confessions obtained by coercion or by trickery before trials, the Court also sees compelled testimony as a dangerous road towards a police state. Chief Justice Lamer made this statement in *Hebert:*

> The privilege against self-incrimination, like the confessions rule, is rooted in an abhorrence of the interrogation practised by the old ecclesiastical courts and the Star Chamber and the notion which grew out of that abhorrence that the citizen involved in the criminal process must be given procedural protections against the overwhelming power of the state.[60]

In summary, the Court has made some strong statements about how the right to silence is necessary to prevent the creation of a police state.

The Conflict

The right to silence has the potential for conflict with Aboriginal truth-speaking traditions. An illustrative example of this potential conflict comes from the American experience. The *Indian Civil Rights Act* was the product of investigations conducted by the Subcommittee on Constitutional Rights of the Senate Committee on the Judiciary.[61] The chair of the subcommittee, Senator Sam Ervin, decided to investigate the degree of constitutional protection afforded to American Indians.[62] John S. Boyden voiced this objection to the right against self-incrimination on behalf of the Ute and Hopi tribes:

> The defendants' standard of integrity in many Indian courts is much higher than in the State and Federal Courts of the United States. When requested to enter a plea to a charge the Indian defendant, standing before respected tribal judicial leaders, with complete candor usually discloses the facts. With mutual honesty and through the dictates of experience, the Indian judge often takes a statement of innocence at face value, discharging the

defendant who has indeed, according to tribal custom, been placed in jeopardy. The same Indian defendants in off-reservation courts soon learn to play the game of "white man's justice," guilty persons entering pleas of not guilty merely to throw the burden of proof upon the prosecution. From their viewpoint, it is not an elevating experience. We are indeed fearful that the decisions of Federal and State Courts, in light of non-Indian experience, interpreting "testifying against oneself" would stultify an honorable Indian experience.[63]

The reason for objecting to the right against self-incrimination was that it was in conflict with truth-speaking traditions. The truth-speaking tradition was itself considered a meaningful safeguard since the word of an accused was often taken at face value. Hopi and Ute delegates shared an apprehension that accuseds would "hide" behind a right against self-incrimination, try to evade responsibility, and force the burden of proof on the prosecution. The Charter's right against self-incrimination may present similar difficulties if Aboriginal societies in Canada also have truth-speaking traditions.

There is also another context worth considering. The Iroquois, and likely other societies as well, were willing to sanction deception as to one's involvement with an offence. Jonathan Rudin and Dan Russell describe a scenario in which three Mohawk youths were charged with various offences:

On Wednesday evening, February 17, 1988, after a drinking bout, Ryan Deer, Dean Horne and a young person under 18, drove to a variety store on the reserve, stole some newspapers and used them to start two fires at abandoned buildings. Later that evening, Deer was apprehended by the Reserve's police force – the Peace Keepers – and taken to the Quebec Provincial Police Detachment in Longeuil where he was questioned about the fires. *Deer denied having anything to do with the events and subsequently accused the police of attempting to "frame" him for the fires. His accomplices similarly denied their involvement in the affair.* After a police investigation into the matter, the three were charged with arson on March 18th.

Well before the criminal charges were laid however, Deer, Horne and the young offender had second thoughts about their actions. The three admitted their guilt to the Reserve's War Chief and asked that they be judged according to the laws of the Longhouse. After receiving the consent of the victims of the offences, the offenders and their parents to submit to its jurisdiction, the Longhouse convened on February 22nd.

The Longhouse was convened by appointing members of the Mohawk Nation to sit in consultation in the Longhouse, to hear the facts of the case and determine how it should be resolved. After deliberations lasting a number of days the Longhouse decreed: "Based on the evidence given to us and the statements of guilt of the offenders we find that in conjunction with arson, four other offences were committed; stealing of newspapers, deception, substance abuse and driving while intoxicated."

Punishment for the offences was dispensed in the following manner (the offences are presented in the order they appeared in the Longhouse judgment):

Theft of newspapers: The three individuals had to apologize to the store owners and pay back twice the cost of the goods stolen.

Alcohol Abuse: As alcohol abuse was a community wide problem, alcohol evaluation programs and workshops were to be established and a professional engaged to help all members of the community who wished to help. The three offenders were required to attend an alcohol evaluation workshop and follow any program designed by the evaluator.

Deception: The three offenders had to make a public apology to the people of the Longhouse for having lied to them with respect to their involvement in the offences. The offenders were also given their first warning according to the custom and practice of the three warning system.

Driving While Intoxicated: The three were forbidden to drive an automobile on the Reserve from sundown to sunrise for one year unless accompanied by a parent or adult appointed for that purpose by the War Chief.

Arson: The three had to apologize to the individuals whose property was damaged and pay full compensation for the damages.[64]

Silence before Aboriginal police authorities could conceivably be construed as deceit or not telling the truth, hypothetically speaking. To administer punishment for lying to the police, or refusing to speak to them, could potentially conflict with the accused's right to silence under s. 7.

The Proposal

Pre-Trial Right to Silence

A theme that is occasionally found in the Court's jurisprudence on legal rights is that the principles of fundamental justice mean different things in different contexts. In *R. v. Lyons,* the Court decided that the accused was not constitutionally entitled to have his dangerous offender hearing heard before a jury.[65] Justice Frank Iacobucci wrote:

It is clear that, at a minimum, the requirements of fundamental justice embrace the requirements of procedural fairness. It is also clear that the requirements of fundamental justice are not immutable; rather, they vary according to the context in which they are invoked. Thus, certain procedural protections might be constitutionally mandated in one context but not in another.

Suffice it to say, however, that a jury determination is not mandated in the present context. The offender has already been found guilty of an offence in a trial at which he had the option of invoking his right to a jury. Moreover, the procedure to which he was subjected, subsequent to the finding of guilty does not impact on his liberty to the same extent as that initial determination.[66]

Likewise, in *R. v Swain,* the common law rule allowing the Crown to adduce evidence of the accused's insanity was altered into a general prohibition against that practice.[67] The reasoning was that it compromised the accused's ability to control his defence and, in turn, violated his right to liberty unless proven guilty. However, once a guilty verdict has been entered, the Crown may then adduce evidence of insanity. There is no longer a danger to the accused's right to control his or her own defence.[68]

One can discern a rough correlation between the nature of the proceedings and the requirements of fundamental justice. Where the accused's guilt or innocence remains an unsettled issue, especially when matters are still at the police investigative stage, the requirements of fundamental justice tend to be more stringent. Where the accused has been found guilty, the requirements tend to become more relaxed. The proposal is that when the police are in the process of investigating a crime – when the requirements of fundamental justice should be stricter – a suspect is protected by the right to silence. An Aboriginal accused may elect not to speak to Aboriginal police officers investigating his or her suspected involvement with a crime. This concept ideally satisfies section 7 principles that value the right to silence as a safeguard against the emergence of a police state. It may be an appropriate balance to suspend the operation of a truth-speaking tradition until matters proceed to ascertaining guilt or innocence in an adjudicative setting, while allowing a right to silence to remain in force during the investigative stage.

However, assume that an Aboriginal society in the past required those alleged to have committed transgressions to speak for themselves as part of a truth-speaking tradition. Now assume that the society wants to revive a truth-speaking tradition. A significant issue becomes whether an Aboriginal accused should be able to assert a right to silence when there is a trial. A suggestion for resolving this issue is to utilize a modified case-to-meet rule that requires the prosecution to establish a *prima facie* case against an accused – to tender enough evidence that, if it is believed, could justify convicting the accused – before the prosecution can call upon the defence to present its case. Once this *prima facie* case is established, the accused is then required to speak on his or her behalf. This proposal reflects a compromise. It can encourage Aboriginal defendants to be forthright during fact-determination proceedings in compliance with a truth-speaking tradition. It can discourage contesting allegations save where the accused truly wishes to assert his or her innocence. It also operates as a gatekeeper. The requirement of a *prima facie* case would ideally prevent subjecting Aboriginal persons to criminal proceedings on the basis of spurious or unfounded accusations. Even so, there remains one more issue to address.

The Canadian justice system does criminalize lying under certain circumstances. Obstruction of justice is an offence under section 139(2) of the *Criminal Code* and is punishable by a term of imprisonment not exceeding ten years. Even after the advent of the Charter, there have been prosecutions for obstructing justice when an accused has lied to a police officer in the course of a pre-trial investigation.[69] Justice Cory explains:

> It is true that a witness has no legal obligation to assist the police in their investigation ... Yet once a witness does speak to the police in the course of their investigations, they must not mislead the investigating authorities by making statements that are false. The right to say nothing cannot protect a witness from the consequences of deliberately making a false statement.[70]

There is also perjury, a crime that is punishable to a maximum of fourteen years under section 131 of the *Criminal Code*.

As previously mentioned, Aboriginal societies often did attach sanction to deceit. The Iroquois tradition of banishment after lying three times is one example. There is a way to accommodate such traditions. During police investigations, an Aboriginal accused has a right to silence. If that right is violated, the accused then has a right to apply for exclusion of evidence under section 24(2) or other remedies under the general remedial provision of the Charter, section 24(1). However, if an Aboriginal accused voluntarily makes a statement with the intention to mislead authorities, then sanctioning deceit should be permissible. It is important to note that saying nothing at all is not obstruction of justice, but a voluntary statement intended to mislead authorities is. In summary, Aboriginal societies can sanction deceit where an accused says something with the intention to mislead in circumstances analogous to the obstruction of justice or perjury.

Objections

The idea of compelled testimony may not sit well with Western civil libertarians since it in effect subjects an Aboriginal accused to an inquisitorial mode of justice. One of the points behind a genuine application of constitutional balancing though is to encourage Western jurists to think outside their own box. Furthermore, this suggestion of a modified case-to-meet rule may not be as offensive to Western standards of rights protection as it appears at first blush. Chief Justice Lamer, although dealing with the context of drawing adverse inferences against an accused who would not take the stand, stated:

> Once ... the Crown discharges its obligation to present a prima facie case, such that it cannot be non-suited by a motion for a directed verdict of acquittal, the accused can be expected to respond ... and failure to do so may serve as the basis for drawing adverse inferences ... [Once] there is a "case to meet" which, if believed, would result in conviction, the accused can no longer remain a passive participant in the prosecutorial process and becomes – in a broad sense – compellable. That is, the accused must answer the case against him or her, or face the possibility of conviction.[71]

This position has since been abandoned in *R. v Noble*.[72] Nonetheless, the comment does illustrate that disagreements and changes of course over the scope of the right to silence can occur even among Western jurists. It also suggests that creative solutions can be explored as a part of constitutional balancing and in pursuit of culturally sensitive interpretations of legal rights. In the end, the proposed solution still provides a meaningful safeguard. It prevents subjecting an accused to spurious or unfounded accusations if there is insufficient evidence to support them. Once a *prima facie* case is made, the truth-speaking tradition becomes operative. Within this context, the accused can benefit still from another safeguard. A panel of community court judges, or a culturally adapted jury panel, must reach consensus that the accused committed the act.

The second possible objection comes from the other direction and suggests that even the modified case-to-meet rule goes too far in limiting truth-speaking traditions. It is easy to emphasize that pre-contact Aboriginal societies did not have the equivalent of modern police services and, therefore, Aboriginal police officers of today would not be persons of cultural or spiritual authority who would be owed cultural truth-speaking duties. This line of thinking, however, falls into a trap in that it may fail to account for diversity among Aboriginal societies. Consider this example of an investigation carried out by the Cheyenne:

> Somebody found an aborted fetus in the vicinity of the camp. The discovery was made known to the Council. They believed that the fetus was that of a Cheyenne, but nothing was known about it. The soldier chiefs were consulted, and by them a plan of investigation was produced. The two head chiefs of a soldier society convened their group, while the society announcer was sent out to broadcast the order of the soldiers for all women to assemble in public. When it was seen that all were at hand, the women were ordered to expose

their breasts for inspection. The soldier chiefs looked closely at each one to note lactation enlargements of the breast as a sign of recent pregnancy. One girl showed symptoms, and she was charged with the crime, judged guilty, and banished from the tribe until after the Arrows had been renewed.[73]

From this example, one may suggest that at least some Aboriginal societies imbued certain individuals with cultural or moral authority such that they were owed truth-speaking duties by those suspected of crime when matters were still at an investigative stage. It can be readily imagined that contemporary Aboriginal communities may desire that individuals with cultural, moral, or spiritual authority serve as police officers. An Aboriginal community may also want suspects to observe a truth-speaking duty to such officers. Indeed, it must be noted that the longhouse council that was described earlier attached a warning as a consequence for lying to police.

There are two replies to such an objection. First, one must consider the power that modern-day police officers can wield. Police officers are typically armed with firearms and a baton. When police make an arrest, they often make a frisk search with the point of relieving the suspect of any weapons that he or she may be carrying. This frisk search does fulfil the legitimate expectation of ensuring the officers' own safety. However, it also has the effect of ensuring that the police officers secure the monopoly on deadly force relative to the suspect. The police at that point may then bring the suspect into their detachment for interrogation. The suspect may then be isolated in a cell or subjected to interrogation alone in a room with more than one officer. The suspect is typically unarmed and alone in a building filled with officers armed with weapons. The potential for coercion and intimidation in such a setting is considerable. Prudence suggests that some checks must still be placed on the inordinate amount of power that the police would enjoy in such situations, notwithstanding any Aboriginal truth-speaking traditions and their possible contemporary adaptations. Insisting on the right to silence at the investigative stage serves the practical purpose of avoiding police states in Aboriginal communities.

Second, the obstacles that face the contemporary revival of truth-speaking traditions must be borne in mind. Western democracies typically insist on the right to silence during both the investigative and trial stages of the criminal process. To accommodate truth-speaking traditions once a case to meet has been established would be a considerable concession to Aboriginal communities in the face of civil libertarian insistences on the right to silence. In the end, Aboriginal communities, if they value truth-speaking traditions, stand to gain. The case-to-meet rule ideally provides a check against both the emergence of a police state and the subjection of an Aboriginal individual to spurious or unfounded accusations. Once this case to meet is established, truth-speaking traditions are then operative.

Right to Counsel

Canadian Jurisprudence

Section 10(b) of the Charter reads:

> Everyone has the right on arrest or detention
>
> (b) to retain and instruct counsel without delay and to be informed of that right.

As with the right to silence, a prerequisite to the right to counsel is that the accused must be detained. Once there is detention, the police are under an obligation to inform the accused of his right to counsel. This obligation is known as the informational component of the right to counsel, for which there are several rules:

1. A detainee must also be informed of access to Legal Aid, where the detainee meets the prescribed financial criteria.[74]
2. A detainee must be informed of access to duty counsel, who will provide free, immediate, and temporary legal advice, provided such services exist in the jurisdiction. If a toll-free number for duty counsel exists, it must be provided.[75]
3. The information provided must be timely, comprehensive, and comprehensible.[76]
4. There is no constitutional requirement to determine whether the detainee understands his or her rights, unless that detainee provides positive indications that he or she does not.[77]
5. There is a fundamental relationship between the right to counsel and the right to be informed of the reasons for arrest or detention under section 10(a). If there has been a fundamental or discrete change in the purpose of the investigation, one involving an unrelated or more serious offence, the detainee must again be informed of the right to counsel.[78]
6. If an accused initially expresses a desire to consult counsel but indicates a change of mind, police must inform him of his right to counsel again.[79]

Once the informational component has been satisfied, the implementation component of the right is triggered. Police must provide the detainee with a reasonable opportunity to exercise his right to counsel. There are also a number of rules for the implementation component as follows:

1. The obligation to provide a reasonable opportunity does not arise until the detainee expresses a desire to exercise his right in response to the informational component.[80]

2. Until the reasonable opportunity has been provided, police may not continue to question or otherwise elicit incriminating evidence from the detainee. They must hold off.[81]

3. The police, however, may question or elicit evidence from the accused without the reasonable opportunity where there exist exigent circumstances. Mere evidentiary or investigative expediency does not amount to exigent circumstances.[82]

4. Jurisdictions are not required to implement a duty counsel system. Where none exists though, the meaning of a reasonable opportunity to consult counsel will be affected. The police may be required to wait until the next day to continue their investigations.[83]

5. If an accused is not reasonably diligent about exercising his right to counsel, the police duty to hold off until a reasonable opportunity is provided is suspended.[84]

6. A detainee must be provided the opportunity to consult counsel in privacy, whether or not the detainee expresses a desire for privacy.[85]

7. A detainee may waive his right to counsel, though the standard is high. The waiver must be clear and unequivocal, free and voluntary, and made with full knowledge of the rights being surrendered.[86]

8. There is no rule under section 10(b) that mandates that defence counsel be present with the accused during the police interrogation. The emphasis is on whether the accused was adequately informed of the right to counsel and had a reasonable opportunity to consult with counsel. This rule is subject, however, to circumstances where the accused should be allowed another opportunity to consult with counsel, such as whether the accused is facing a new jeopardy since consulting with counsel or whether the information previously provided by police was deficient.[87]

David Tanovich argues that the right to counsel is a particularly important right since it is by representation by counsel that other Charter rights are enforced.[88] Alan Young also explains:

As "champion" of the interests of the accused, defence lawyers bear the burden of ensuring that their client's constitutional rights have been respected by police, prosecutors and judges. Therefore, in the absence of some institutional mechanism for supervisory, quality control over the process, the implementation of constitutional rights is contingent upon the competency of counsel.[89]

This relationship between the right to counsel and other constitutional rights also resonates in the Supreme Court of Canada's treatment of section 10(b). In *R. v Manninen*, the decision reads: "The purpose of the right to counsel is to allow the detainee not only to be informed of his rights and obligations under the law but, equally if not more important, to obtain advice as to how to exercise those rights."[90] The Court reiterated this comment almost verbatim in *R. v Ross*.[91] The Court has also recognized that the role of lawyers as defenders of civil liberties is an important justification for allowing the legal profession to establish self-governing bodies (law societies). In *Pearlman v Manitoba Law Society Judicial Committee,* the Court quoted with approval this passage from the *Report of the Professional Organization Committee (Ministry of the Attorney General of Ontario):*

> Stress was rightly laid on the high value that free societies have placed historically on an independent judiciary, free of political interference and influence on its decisions, and an independent bar, free to represent citizens without fear or favor in the protection of individual rights and civil liberties against incursions from any source, including the state.[92]

We will now consider how these principles may conflict with Aboriginal approaches to justice.

The Conflict

The concept of a spokesperson or an advocate was not necessarily alien to all Aboriginal societies. As previously mentioned, the Navajo Supreme Court declared that a spokesperson speaking on behalf of somebody accused of committing an infraction was a concept that had existed in Navajo traditional law. One must account, however, for diversity in Aboriginal societies. It is conceivable, even likely, that other Aboriginal societies may in past times have preferred an "accused" to speak directly for himself or herself. What this possibility may translate into, should present-day Aboriginal societies gain control over justice, is a preference not to include spokespersons or advocates in contemporary processes. The *Code of Offences and Procedures of Justice for the Mohawk Nation at Akwesasne,* for example, makes absolutely no mention of any right to counsel.[93] Insisting on a right to counsel may conflict with the desire of Aboriginal communities to structure their justice systems in such a way as to not include advocates.

Even if past Aboriginal societies did include spokespersons in their processes, there may still be problems. The principles on the right to counsel that were described clearly suggest that the right to counsel involves a lawyer who is called to one of the provincial bars. Admission to a bar typically requires obtaining a Bachelors in Law or a Juris Doctor degree in one of Canada's accredited law schools,[94] completion of a term of legal clerkship under the supervision of a lawyer with enough experience (for example, four years of practice),[95] and a training course that tests a candidate's knowledge of provincial laws and practice skills.[96] Even if Aboriginal societies are open to the use of advocates or spokespersons in their processes, they may not necessarily want to insist on such exacting qualifications. An Aboriginal society, for example, may be content with good character or the reputation of an advocate participating in their process.

These are not the only problems though. Another problem stems from the expected role of a lawyer. All provincial law societies require that lawyers advocate for the best interests of their clients, subject to other ethical standards such as not knowingly misleading the court and treating opposing parties and lawyers with respect.[97] These standards can create problems where an Aboriginal society aspires to deal with crime through restorative processes. Larry Chartrand argues that a lawyer's duty of advocacy does not fit well with Aboriginal sentencing circles.[98] This duty of advocacy typically requires pursuing the lightest sanction possible under the law during a sentencing hearing. A sentencing circle involves members of an Aboriginal community at large speaking to the judge and influencing the decision. This process can involve a number of different opinions on what the best resolution would be and would not necessarily reflect what the defence lawyer would pursue. Furthermore, sentencing circles are designed to give Aboriginal communities at least some measure of control over the process. A defence lawyer advocating a position on behalf of the client can threaten the transformative potential of the process and devalue the community's role. A defence lawyer challenging the credibility of participants in a sentencing circle can likewise undermine the process.

Yvonne Boyer describes two specific examples of how a defence lawyer's functions can prove incompatible with Aboriginal community-based approaches to justice. The first example is where a lawyer's advice not only undermined the goals behind a sentencing circle but may also have backfired on the offender:

> The defense counsel, police, prosecutor, victim, offender, and community supporters were present. Training sessions had been held, and the judge, prosecutor, and police had been briefed on how the circle works. The defense counsel had not been available to take calls, so the first time he appeared was at the circle itself.
>
> The circle went as planned, yet there was a major component absent, namely, a feeling of "truthfulness" within the circle. A consensus was reached, and the judge passed the offender recommendations, which were very harsh. The victim and the offender were related, and the offense arose from a longstanding family feud that resulted in serious charges. There was no victim-offender reconciliation.
>
> In the "debriefing" following the circle, however, it came to light that the defense counsel had forbidden the offender to say anything. This simple point corrupted the whole circle process, and the community was

left to pick up the pieces, trying to salvage the positive points of the circle experience.[99]

The second example demonstrates how a lawyer's insistence on remuneration can present difficulties:

A few days ago, the justice coordinator in one of the Saskatoon Tribal Council communities asked me to help set up a sentencing circle in the fall. This particular community is advanced in their justice initiatives but realized the problems that lay ahead. The justice committee requested permission to handle the circle without the judge, defense counsel, prosecutor, and the police. It is unlikely that their request will be granted because of the severity of the offense. The defense counsel is a prominent criminal lawyer and has expressed to the justice committee that he wants the circle over with as quickly as possible, since "his time is money." In desperation, the community has asked me to speak to this individual to try to help him understand the circle process. I doubt that I can change this person's attitude, and the circle will once again be dishonored.[100]

Boyer is ultimately of the opinion that lawyers should not have a role in Aboriginal community-based justice.[101]

Paul Jonathan Saguil presents a rather more optimistic view.[102] He is of the view that Aboriginal legal traditions have the potential to mould lawyer ethics and practice in beneficial directions. Aboriginal legal traditions, if applied in a dispute, may sometimes, but not always, lead to a different result than would have ensued if common law or civil law had been applied to the same dispute. This viewpoint, however, is not the critical point of Saguil's thesis. His key idea is that Aboriginal legal traditions have the potential to expand a lawyer's ethical duties and practices beyond a narrow focus on advocating a single client's cause and pursuing with full vigour a favourable verdict for the client in an adversarial forum. One of his ideas involves a lawyer's duty to avoid taking client advocacy to the point of causing harmful actions to others or actions that would bring discredit to a community member, the client, or the lawyer.[103] Another idea is what he calls "community lawyering." A lawyer, in seeking a resolution for the client, should also consider to some degree the interests of the other party and other community members. Saguil makes a point of saying that such action does not involve the lawyer's sacrificing the client's interests for the sake of the community. His point is that the duty of advocacy is tempered to some degree. The interests of the other parties, and other community members, should enter the equation at least to some degree when the lawyer is pursuing an equitable and satisfactory resolution on behalf of the client. The question now becomes how to deal with these difficulties. Whose approach to this question is to be preferred?

The Proposal

In this section, we again can draw upon *R. v Lyons* for the theme that Charter rights can be structured according to different contexts and different stages of the criminal process. A suggestion can be made with reference to the right to counsel at the investigative stage. The context of police investigation and interrogation attracts a higher degree of protection *vis-à-vis* the right to counsel. Therefore, in keeping with Tanovich's rationale, the right to counsel as a guardian of an accused's rights is operative. Even so, there is room to adopt a culturally sensitive perspective. The suggestion is that "right to counsel" need not necessarily mean a licensed attorney or member of the bar. An Australian court developed this idea in *R. v Anunga*.[104] In this case, the court articulated a number of guidelines for the interrogation of Aboriginal suspects, which have since become known as the *Anunga* rules. One of the guidelines is that an Aboriginal suspect should have a "prisoner's friend" with him during a police interrogation. The person would not necessarily be a lawyer but, rather, someone in whom the suspect will have confidence and who will make him or her feel supported. Aboriginal communities in Canada may well consider the incorporation of a similar concept if and when they design their own Charters. The prisoner's friend need not necessarily be an attorney, but he or she should perhaps possess knowledge of the traditional laws of the suspect's community, and basic knowledge of legal rights under the local Charter.

The *Anunga* rules have been the subject of favourable comment in the Canadian context. The report of the justice inquiry in Manitoba,[105] the Alberta *Justice on Trial* report,[106] and the Law Reform Commission of Canada's report on Aboriginal peoples and justice[107] have all recommended that Canadian police abide by the *Anunga* guidelines when it comes to Aboriginal suspects. The existence of organizations such as Native Counselling Services of Alberta[108] and Aboriginal Legal Services of Toronto[109] reflect implementations of *Anunga* in Canada. Development of the *Anunga* concept provides Aboriginal communities with a way to accommodate a Charter right to counsel during the investigative stage but in a culturally sensitive manner.

Previous discussions in this chapter have suggested that in some circumstances processes for disputing factual allegations may remain important. Such a context may likewise attract a high degree of protection *vis-à-vis* the right to counsel. This issue may seem especially problematic since the expectation in Canada is that a member of the bar is usually necessary to advocate a criminal accused's cause during a trial. Most provincial standards of ethics require that an accused's advocate have bar membership where an indictable offence or the prospect of imprisonment is involved. Consider also section 802.1 of the *Criminal Code,* which reads:

> Despite subsections 800(2) and 802(2), a defendant may not appear or examine or cross-examine witnesses by agent if he or she is liable, on summary conviction, to imprisonment for a term of more than six months, unless the defendant is a corporation or the agent is authorized to do so under a program approved by the lieutenant governor in council of the province.

Programs approved by the lieutenant governor typically accommodate articling students as a path to admission to the bar.

The American experience is again instructive. Tribal court systems frequently rely on tribal advocates, who are community members admitted to practice without any educational or examination requirements. The Navajo, Rosebud Sioux, and Pine Sioux have apparently gone so far as to administer their own tribal bar examinations.[110] The *Red Cliff Band of Lake Superior Chippewas Tribal Law and Constitution* allows lay advocates to practise before a tribal court upon passing a bar exam that tests knowledge of Indian law and the local tribal code.[111] Perhaps this concept could be adopted in Canada. At a minimum, Aboriginal processes could rely upon community members as advocates. Aboriginal communities could have their own admission requirements separate from the provincial bar admission requirements, which could include being of good character, being learned in customary law, having legal rights under the community's own Charter, and so on. As previously mentioned, it was suggested that cross-examination (or the presentation of alternative scenarios through an interviewer as discussed in Chapter 7) could be structured in narrative format to avoid committing cultural *faux pas*. If lay advocates are used during factual adjudication, they could be required to adhere to such a concept, similar to the ethical standards that bind lawyers in provincial bars.

There remains the question of an advocate's involvement during restorative processes. At this point, one can assume that an accused has done something that merits community involvement. As such, and in accordance with *Lyons*, one can suggest that the context speaks to lower standards of rights protection. One could also suggest that Tanovich's concerns about the importance of counsel as a guardian of other Charter rights are no longer quite as acute in this context. It is not to say that a right to counsel needs to be abandoned altogether, but the advocate's role can be modified to accommodate restorative processes. Chartrand provides a suggestion for how the lawyer's (or advocate's) duty of advocacy could be tempered by cultural considerations. Insofar as an Aboriginal community utilizes a restorative process, the idea is that the lawyer ceases to be an advocate but, instead, more of a resource person.[112] Chartrand is not clear what this role involves. Perhaps the lawyer limits his role to instructing the participants in unclear areas of law, pointing out resources that can be used to facilitate community-based resolutions, or suggesting options that can be used as conditions of a sentence.

Suppose that an Aboriginal community not only uses processes that resemble restorative justice but also allows the option for adversarial processes when the accused wishes to plead not guilty. The advocate can be required to discuss the availability of community-based options with the client. The advocate must also discuss the risks involved with participating in the process: that it waives rights to contest the allegations, that it could involve substantial sanctions and restrictions on the client's liberty, and that the advocate would no longer be, in substance, an advocate within that process. So long as the client is advised of the risks, the advocate will have discharged his or her modified duties to the accused.

It does not mean, however, that a representative's role has to be completely void of any elements of advocacy during a restorative process. The advocate can remain a guardian of an accused's rights to natural justice. He or she can, for example, inquire as to whether there are any community members who are willing to speak positively on behalf of the accused and submit to the other participants that such persons should be present. So long as the accused enjoys the benefits of natural justice, the advocate can "sit back" and let the participants craft their own resolution. The advocate, however, is also in place to observe whether or not the accused is being accorded natural justice. If the advocate is of the opinion that a breach of natural justice occurred to the detriment of the accused and it was not addressed adequately by the community court judge, the advocate is then in an excellent position to assist the accused with an appeal.[113]

Objections

This objection is similar to the one made concerning community court judges. Obliging aspiring lawyers to obtain a law degree and pass bar examinations assures the public that the legal profession can provide competent services. The objection is that not imposing similar requirements on Aboriginal advocates does not seem to insist on a very high standard of competency. The replies are similar to the ones made concerning community court judges. First, one of the premises behind this work is the idea that Aboriginal communities should enjoy as much autonomy as possible when it comes to justice. Why should Aboriginal communities, assuming they are open to the idea of advocates for Aboriginal defendants, not be able to set their own qualification standards?

Second, given the nature of law and the processes that one can expect to be developed by an autonomous Aboriginal community, for which the methods of application and learning are often fundamentally different, is it really necessary to insist on Western approaches to legal education and training? Law degrees and bar examinations are more understandable if an articling student wants to become a general practitioner who can offer services in civil litigation, real estate planning, corporate structuring, and so on. Consider, however, whether we need to be so particular when it comes to advocating within Aboriginal justice processes as envisioned by the proposals that have been made in this chapter. At the investigative stage, an advocate acting as a "prisoner's friend" may very well require knowledge of the local Aboriginal Charter of rights. Instruction on the local Charter could be a requirement of admitting a lay advocate to speak before a community court. During restorative processes, the proposal envisions the advocate reducing his or her role to a resource person and to a guardian of natural justice rights and appellate advocate when necessary. During factual adjudication, there may be a demand for certain skills such as assessing evidence, cross-examination (perhaps in narrative style), or the presentation of alternative scenarios if my suggestions for determining facts through private interviews or circle discussion are adopted. An Aboriginal community may be well advised to provide training in such skills as part of the process of admitting lay advocates to speak before community courts. Given these ideas for the role of lay advocates, it should be for Aboriginal communities to decide what particular qualifications may be required.

The second objection comes from the opposite direction. Insisting on the presence of advocates, even if not full-fledged lawyers, amounts to an external imposition of Western notions of justice and an infusion of adversarial influences. My disagreement with Yvonne Boyer, who would prefer a complete exclusion of lawyers from Aboriginal processes, should be obvious.[114] There are a number of ways to respond to this issue. The previous discussion on search and seizure expounded the idea that while Aboriginal societies are willing to use modern professional police forces to realize the collective good, they may not entirely resonate with what we know about pre-contact Aboriginal justice practices. This recognition indicates that Aboriginal communities sometimes willingly depart from the past when it is expedient to do so. Furthermore, police forces still present the danger of police states if left with unfettered power. Taking these factors into consideration, it does not seem entirely offensive to various Aboriginal notions of justice to insist on a right to a prisoner's friend during the investigative stage. During Aboriginal processes that parallel restorative justice, the role of an advocate is purposefully diminished. The advocate is to sit back, act as a resource person, and allow the participants to craft their own resolutions. The role of the community and its members is given maximum room to operate. Acting as a true advocate is limited to when it is necessary to safeguard the accused's rights to natural justice. In this respect, I do not find myself in complete agreement with Saguil either, since my view is that the role of advocates should be significantly limited, at least during certain points of the process.

It is conceded that where "trials" are concerned, this proposal does involve lay advocates either being able to cross-examine in narrative format or to present some form of adversarial challenge through alternative scenarios to the evidence in support of sanctioning. It must be borne in mind, however, that the previous proposals make a considerable concession to Aboriginal restorative processes by allowing them to operate in situations in which Western law would assert that the accused is entitled to a full defence. Factual adjudication is confined to situations in which the accused denies committing the act itself, and even then I have suggested that trials can be pulled in inquisitorial directions that make some allowance for adversarial challenges. The disruptive effect of a right to counsel is minimized by confining "true lawyering" to denials of the act itself, advocating natural justice rights and appellate advocacy. There is also still plenty of room for incorporating Saguil's suggestions within this framework. For example, it may be an advocate's role to suggest alternative hypotheses to be put to witnesses, either during private interviews or circle deliberations, in order to present a different view of the facts in a way that does not discredit either the advocate or the client and is also respectful of other parties and community members.

Lastly, I wish to stress that I (and also Chartrand implicitly) am not more right than either Boyer or Saguil. I am simply expressing my own opinion of the matter, for reasons I have described, and tentatively putting out an alternative proposal. It is for each Aboriginal community to decide for itself what its needs are and how to deal with these matters. An Aboriginal community may very well decide it wants no place for advocates in its justice system (although I think taking it that far poses a danger of inviting some form of legal intervention, as I have previously emphasized). Another Aboriginal community may very well prefer Saguil's ideas, with ethical standards of practice that include his notions of avoiding discredit in conduct and "community lawyering" and that do not provide any limitation on when an advocate can participate in Aboriginal processes. It is now time to consider legal rights that involve potential final resolutions.

9
The Final Resolution

Cruel and Unusual Punishment

Jurisprudence

Section 12 of the Canadian Charter of Rights and Freedoms reads: "Everyone has the right not to be subjected to any cruel and unusual treatment or punishment."[1] Much of the Supreme Court of Canada's jurisprudence on this section involves the proportionality of prison terms in relation to the nature of the offence committed. A full discussion of those authorities will not be provided here.[2] The discussion will focus instead on execution and corporal punishment, which may still be of contemporary relevance to Aboriginal communities.

Canada has in the past used the death penalty for murder. Such usage was challenged under the *Canadian Bill of Rights* on the basis that it violated the bill's right against cruel and unusual punishment in *R. v Miller and Cockriell*.[3] Chief Justice Bora Laskin, on behalf of a Supreme Court of Canada majority, upheld the *Criminal Code*'s death penalty provisions on the basis that only the method of execution was subject to review under the right against cruel and unusual punishment under the *Canadian Bill of Rights*.[4] In the post-Charter context in *United States v Burns,* the Court was called upon to decide whether extraditing a person to an American state jurisdiction, without assurances that the death penalty would not be sought, violated that person's rights under the Charter.[5] The Court held that such an extradition did violate the Charter. This decision was actually based upon section 7, which held that extradition without assurances violated rights to life, liberty, and security of the person because execution was a potential consequence of that extradition.[6] Section 12 did not directly determine the outcome.[7] The court, however, did provide an *obiter* that indicated that execution would be prohibited by section 12:

It is, however, incontestable that capital punishment, whether or not it violates s. 12 of the Charter, and whether or not it could be upheld under s. 1, engages the underlying values of the prohibition against cruel and unusual punishment. It is final. It is irreversible. Its imposition has been described as arbitrary. Its deterrent value has been doubted. Its implementation necessarily causes psychological and physical suffering. It has been rejected by the Canadian Parliament for offences committed within Canada. Its potential imposition in this case is thus a factor that weighs against extradition without assurances.[8]

The Court further noted that Canada has a history of wrongful convictions for murder, including Donald Marshall, David Milgaard, Guy Paul Morin, Thomas Sophonow, and Gregory Parsons. The latter four individuals were exonerated by DNA evidence.[9] The Court noted the personal unavailability of any meaningful redress to the wrongfully executed:

In all of these cases, had capital punishment been imposed, there would have been no one to whom an apology and compensation *could* be paid in respect of the miscarriage of justice (apart, possibly, from surviving family members), and no way in which Canadian society with the benefit of hindsight could have justified to itself the deprivation of human life in violation of the principles of fundamental justice.[10]

It is therefore safe to say that the Court understands both section 7 and section 12 as prohibiting execution.

When Western states inflict capital punishment, it is done with more than one hope in mind. One hope is that others will be deterred by the prospect of death as a consequence of committing any offence (for example, murder) in the select category of offences for which capital punishment is assessed. Another hope is to inflict retribution for, and, at the same time, express public indignation over, the crime committed by the offender.[11] Canadian law, cognizant of the finality of the sanction once it is carried out, has taken the stance that its potential costs exceed its potential benefits. Michael Cousins suggests that Aboriginal views of capital punishment may often have been quite different. Iroquois vengeance was also meant to put matters right between the killer and the victim in the life to come. The concern for harmonizing relationships and making right by past wrongs was not just an earthly endeavour but also a spiritual one that anticipated setting good foundations for the afterlife.[12] Be that as it may, Canadian law has made it clear that capital punishment is not a constitutionally acceptable sanction.

The Supreme Court of Canada also understands section 12 as prohibiting the infliction of corporal punishment. In *R. v Smith*, Justice Antonio Lamer stated:

> Finally, I should add that some punishments or treatments will always be grossly disproportionate and will always outrage our standards of decency: for example, the infliction of corporal punishment, such as the lash, irrespective of the number of lashes imposed, or, to give examples of treatment, the lobotomisation of certain dangerous offenders or the castration of sexual offenders.[13]

This principle has since been affirmed in *Kindler v Canada (Minister of Justice)* and in *Suresh v Canada (Minister of Citizenship and Immigration)*.[14]

The Conflict

In Chapter 2, a number of distinctly punitive sanctions among pre-contact Aboriginal societies were described, such as public whipping and execution. One could suggest that such sanctions are relics of a bygone age and that Aboriginal justice, as presently envisioned, has been stripped of its harsher elements but retains its more benign and holistic elements. Michael Jackson surmises that it does not appear that a right to corporal punishment has been asserted in any contemporary context in Canada.[15] One can ask whether this lack of assertion reflects a lack of opportunity or whether Aboriginal communities would be willing to carry out such sanctions in more clandestine circumstances.

Consider the case of *Thomas v Norris*.[16] David Thomas was Coast Salish by ancestry, though he did not identify with Coast Salish culture. He was nabbed by several members of the Coast Salish, including Elders, and was forced to participate in a spirit dancing ritual. He was confined to a longhouse for approximately four days. During this period, he was subjected to several treatments including deprivation of food but not water, being dunked underwater, being whipped with cedar branches, and being lifted up several times while the others dug their fingers into his sides and bit him. This ritual was initiated at the request of the plaintiff's wife, who hoped that it would cure his alcoholism and improve their marriage. He ended up in the hospital since his pre-existing ulcer was worsened. He sued his assailants for assault, battery, and false imprisonment. The idea of healing, dealing with the root causes of misbehaviour, and forward-looking correction could be attributed to the men who nabbed Norris. However, the resemblance to restorative justice seems to end there. One can just as easily suggest that there are elements of corporal punishment present in the form of whipping, dunking, hoisting, finger digging, and biting. What is really telling, though, is that members of the Coast Salish community unilaterally exercised collective power against an individual against his will. They unilaterally subjected him to some pretty significant physical measures. Depending on the perspective, it has the appearance not of harmonious restorative justice but, rather, of an imposed corporal sanction in pursuit of a collective good.

Thomas may not represent an isolated instance either. Marianne Edwards and Clifford Sam died during participation in spirit dancing rites. These deaths had nothing to do with forced reform. Both individuals had volunteered for participation. In Edwards' case, it was with the hope of overcoming significant health problems such as kidney failure.[17] Apparently, at least eight people have died under similar circumstances since the 1970s.[18] There is at the very least suspicion that David Thomas has not been the only individual subjected to the ritual with the idea of forced reformation. One news article states:

Outside critics – and even some within the First Nations – are asking whether the closed ceremony fits the modern age. It often begins with a kidnapping, followed by days of forced fasting and other rigours designed to produce a trance, such as the ritual winter purification that preceded Edwards's collapse.

"We have to adapt. We have to make changes to accommodate the modern society in which we live when there are chances that there will be tragic accidents," said Doug Kelly, one of the chiefs of the 54 bands of Coast Salish who practise the Spirit Dance ...

Supporters see the dance as a way to continue their traditions and increasingly as a remedy for the modern evils of alcoholism, drug abuse and poor health. But the deaths, Kelly concedes, have created "a backlash of fear among people who wonder 'What the hell those damned Indians are up to'" ...

Some people seek that spiritual turning point voluntarily, but others are forced into it. They are grabbed by men with black-painted faces and carried to the longhouse at the behest of other dancers or family members who feel the person needs reform.[19]

Details of this particular use of the ritual remain foggy, not least because the ritual itself is thought of as a secret that is exclusive to the Coast Salish societies and is not to be casually exposed to outsiders. Thomas relates that he was afterwards subjected to beating, threats, and shunning until he was obliged to move away from the Coast Salish community.[20] This scenario can suggest that the community did not appreciate the fact that he had exposed the ritual, that they had approved of the use of the ritual that he was subjected to, or both.

This discussion has thus far centred on the Coast Salish spirit dance ritual. Other Aboriginal societies, however, have used corporal sanctions such as whipping or flogging in the past. Present-day use of corporal punishment may offer a certain utility to contemporary Aboriginal societies, if they choose to avail themselves of such. Corporal punishment may offer traditional alternatives to incarceration. The idea is of a sanction that can provide deterrence and denunciation, but without the long-term negative effects associated with imprisonment. The pain of corporal punishment is "short but sharp," but it also does not expose an offender to the hardening effects, criminal culture, and lifestyle of prisons. Corporal sanctions can also provide a supplement to restorative resolutions. This idea can be clarified by elaborating upon a certain context. Writers such as Emma Larocque and Sherene Razack have raised serious concerns about emphasizing only healing and rehabilitation in addressing offences such as sexual assault.[21] It can jeopardize victim safety by trivializing the harm done to the victim and by signalling to potential offenders that consequences following harmful conduct will be minimal. Suppose now that a community has to deal with sexual assault. The community decides not to use imprisonment but, instead, emphasizes offender rehabilitation through programs that include sexual offender counselling. The community, however, may decide not to stop there. If that community's ancestors had used corporal punishment in the past, it can have a contemporary role. The community may wish to assess corporal punishment to the offender in addition to the rehabilitative program. It may be the community's way to accord satisfaction to the victim, to express to the victim that her safety is being taken seriously, and to express indignation at the harm caused. It can also announce to the community at large that sexual predation will not be tolerated. No Aboriginal group in Canada has so far openly asserted the use of execution. In any event, whether it is corporal punishment or execution, the conflict is fairly obvious. Both are expressly prohibited by the Supreme Court of Canada's interpretations of section 12.

The Proposal

This conflict seems particularly difficult to resolve since express prohibitions are involved. The discussion will begin with execution. The position that I would like to argue is that a prohibition against execution under section 12 should remain in place. It is admittedly a very subjective and arbitrary conclusion on my part, but it is well worth considering the Supreme Court of Canada's commentary on the consequences of erroneously assessed death penalties. If an Aboriginal community executes one of its individuals for something that member never did in the first place, what can that community possibly do to make right by that member? Aboriginal traditions may contemplate reparation to the executed member's relations, of course, and may often engage spiritual concerns aside from deterrence or denunciation. Even so, the consequence of executing an innocent individual is irreversible for that individual in the event that it was given out in error. If capital punishment is precluded in a contemporary Aboriginal justice system, should the same be extended to non-lethal corporal punishment? On this issue, Australian jurisprudence provides some insight.

R. v Joseph Murray Jungarai involved domestic homicide. The accused was initially denied bail, but he successfully appealed. Chief Justice William Forster of the Northern Territory Supreme Court granted the appeal and bail in recognition that the accused was planning on consenting to a traditional punishment of having a spear wound scored upon his leg and then getting banished into the bush for a fixed period of time. Forster noted that the punishment amounted to retribution and payback within an Aboriginal understanding and was necessary to diffuse potential reprisal from the victim's family.[22] During sentencing, however, Justice James Muirhead imposed a sentence of six years and six months with a period of parole ineligibility lasting two years and six months. He rejected defence counsel's submission for a suspended sentence of imprisonment (meaning probation subject to good behaviour). He did acknowledge that the accused was subjected to traditional punishment by being beaten unconscious. However, he felt that not imposing imprisonment would have sent a message that the law did not apply to the Aborigines.[23] The sentence was upheld on appeal by the Federal Court.[24]

Australian courts have also allowed Aboriginal use of corporal punishment to act as a mitigating factor to reduce the sentences handed out to the Aboriginal offenders. In *R. v Jadurin,* the Federal Court heard an appeal against a sentence of four years after the accused had fatally injured his wife after beating her with a pipe.[25] The court had ultimately dismissed the appeal on the basis that four years was deemed a very lenient sentence for the crime in question. However, the court did provide this explanation:

> In the context of Aboriginal customary or tribal law questions will arise as to the likelihood of punishment by an offender's own community and the nature and extent of that punishment. It is sometimes said that a court should not be seen to be giving its sanction to forms of punishment, particularly the infliction of physical harm, which it does not recognise itself. But to acknowledge that some form of retribution may be exacted by an offender's own community is not to sanction that retribution. It is to recognise certain facts which exist only by reason of that offender's membership of a particular group. That is not to say that in a particular case questions will not arise as to the extent to which the court should have regard to such facts or as to the evidence that should be presented if it is to be asked to take those facts into account.[26]

In *R. v Minor,* Justice Dean Mildren indicated that payback is a relevant sentencing consideration because it is part of "all material facts, including those facts which exist only by reason of the offender's membership of an ethnic or other group. So much is essential to the even administration of criminal justice."[27] Justice Mildren also noted that it had been a long-standing practice in the Northern Territory to recognize tribal law when it came to sentencing tribal members.[28] In *R. v Mamarika,* the Australian Federal Court of Appeal was willing to use a probationary suspended sentence with conditions even for a murder case, in recognition that the accused had previously been subjected to severe payback.[29]

There are additional rationales for such decisions as well. As with the bail cases, there is also recognition that accommodating traditional sanctions is necessary to prevent community tensions from getting out of hand. John Chesterman indicates that in one case the Northern Territory Supreme Court took into consideration the fact that an Aboriginal man who had caused the death of another community member received payback in the form of being speared twice in the leg and been beaten on the head several times, and it sentenced him, as a result, to eighteen months' imprisonment. The court did not condone the practice of payback but took it into account nonetheless in recognition that it "proved to be important in avoiding further conflict."[30] Another rationale is that such a decision avoids excessive punishment, with concerns similar to the right against double jeopardy. The Australian Law Reform Commission notes:

> [T]here is an inevitability about Aboriginal customary processes taking their course regardless of what the courts might do. Thus a physical "punishment" may be imposed on an offender without any account being given to what the courts have done or might do. Although in practice it appears that some balancing of punishments is done within both systems. Within Aboriginal communities account will usually be taken of the fact that the courts have imposed, or are likely to impose, a penalty.[31]

Australian courts have not so much embraced the use of corporal sanctions among Aboriginal communities but have tolerated it out of a sense of pragmatism. There is recognition that payback is a culturally meaningful sanction that, coupled with standard prison terms for statutory offences, can impose an excessive burden on Aboriginal offenders. There is also recognition that payback can diffuse hostilities in the communities. These insights suggest to us that there is room for compromise where section 12's prohibition against cruel and unusual punishment is concerned.

A frequent theme of the Supreme Court of Canada's interpretation of Charter rights in the criminal process is that they can be waived. Waiver of a legal right "is dependent upon it being clear and unequivocal that the person is waiving the procedural safeguard and is doing so with full knowledge of the rights the procedure was enacted to protect and of the effect the waiver will have on those rights in the process."[32] The idea is that an Aboriginal community can assess a corporal sanction if an offender genuinely consents to it, free of coercion or intimidation. The doctrine of waiver is adapted to allow an Aboriginal offender to waive his or her right not to be subjected to a punishment prohibited by judicial interpretation of section 12. It represents a compromise. It accommodates traditional sanctions against an express prohibition. It also does not allow Aboriginal communities to subject their own members to such punishments against their will.

Note that a key point of a waiver is an awareness of the consequences test. There may be concern that corporal punishment can lead to severe injuries in the form of permanent scarring or fractured bones. Therefore, the offender should have a right to be informed of the potential outcome of a corporal sanction. In this case, an Aboriginal advocate may also have a role to play. An advocate could perhaps acquire information about the potential medical consequences of a corporal sanction for the offender. The offender is then free to make an informed decision.

Objections

Recall that Justice Lamer interpreted section 12 as prohibiting the use of corporal punishment since it grossly offends society's sense of decency. This notion stems from the Supreme Court of Canada attaching value to the sanctity of the human body such that directly inflicting physical pain is deemed to be cruel and degrading.[33] Recall as another example that a full cavity search is an especially serious violation of an individual's rights under section 8. The objection is that inflicting corporal punishment under any circumstances is inherently cruel and degrading towards the subject and should never be allowed.

However, this consideration, in turn, raises other questions. Whose sense of decency does the use of corporal punishment offend? Which society finds the use of corporal punishment so offensive? Punishments are, whatever form they take, designed to inflict pain upon the offender. Retributive rationales of punishment seek to inflict pain in proportion to either the moral blameworthiness of the offender or the pain caused by the offender. Utilitarian rationales call upon pain with the purpose of discouraging crime. Carrying out the sanction after conviction communicates to the offender that the pain is a direct consequence of the offender's actions, with the promise of more should misbehaviour occur again. This promise of pain is also made to society at large, letting everyone know what they can expect if they follow the offender's example. It is open to question whether incarcerating offenders is any less cruel and degrading in its effects. Geoffrey Scarre provides this commentary:

Many people think it admissible for a court to sentence an offender to ten months in prison but not to ten strokes of the birch. Why? It can certainly be argued that a penalty which is swiftly over – though still a deterrent and an effective provoker of thought owing to its power over the imagination – is really more humane, less cruel, than a drawn-out sentence of imprisonment. Putting an offender behind bars for months or years may give him time to reflect upon his acts but it seriously interferes with the course of his life and flouts his autonomy for the duration; it may also induce boredom, frustration, depression, claustrophobic feelings and a sense of helplessness. (It also causes unmerited hardship for family members or others who depend on him for income, services or companionship: a drawback absent in the case of corporal punishment). Although an offender sentenced to a corporal penalty may feel fear and anxiety before the punishment, this can be minimized by ensuring that the administration of justice is swift. In any case, many prisons are themselves fear-inducing places in which inter-inmate violence is common and a spirit of *sauve qui peut* prevails. Sending someone to jail means subjecting him to a substantial risk of physical and mental abuse. Setting aside prejudice and political correctness, it is far from evident that incarceration is the "civilised" alternative to a sharp but brief physical chastisement, after which the subject can spend the night in his own bed.[34]

What is cruel and degrading is in the eye of the beholder. The view taken by one individual may indeed be subject to cultural subjectivity. Present-day Western legal systems may not be willing to use corporal punishment due to the perception that corporal punishment is cruel and degrading to the subject. Consider a contemporary Aboriginal society in Canada whose ancestors had used corporal punishment. Add to this scenario the fact that many Aboriginal people go to prison with the promise of becoming hardened by the experience of incarceration, being subjected to violence and abuse while in prison, and being exposed to the gangland cultures that exist within prisons. An Aboriginal community may therefore find that corporal punishment will often be a preferable, and less cruel, way of resolving criminal conflicts than incarceration. An Aboriginal community should be allowed to make use of corporal punishment, subject to the offenders' willingly undergoing it.

It must, however, be conceded that this idea may be untenable within Canada, at least for the time being. International human rights law on judicial corporal punishment does not allow for an exception based on voluntary consent (more on this later). International law also relies on the political will to try and enforce it. Recent indications are that international opinion may be squarely against the practice, at least to such a degree that any nation states that still use it may find themselves stigmatized. Amnesty International and women rights groups have protested Malaysia's use of

corporal punishment for offences such as adultery and immigration offences.[35] In fact, public outrage and the media spotlight recently convinced
a Malaysian court to commute a sentence of corporal punishment that was
to be carried out on a woman who was convicted of drinking beer in public.[36]
In another recent example, the sentence of public lashing for journalist
Lubna Hussein over wearing loose trousers in violation of Sudan's public
indecency laws has triggered public outcry both internationally and within
Sudan itself.[37] It is admittedly difficult to foresee either Canadian politicians
or Canadian judicial authority accommodating this proposal in the near
future, even allowing for the insistence on voluntary consent.

Even so, there remains the genuinely valid question of whether incarceration is truly more humane or civilized than judicial corporal punishment. There is no shortage of studies indicating that inter-inmate violence
is prevalent and commonplace in prison systems.[38] One study has also
suggested that violent conditions in prison will significantly increase inmate
suicides.[39] A Canadian study confirmed that Canadian males incarcerated
in prison suffer death by homicide and suicide at far greater rates than
Canadian males who are not incarcerated.[40] The argument could certainly
be put forward that incarceration in the aggregate very often does far more
to expose an offender to physical harm, and even to violent death, than a
brief instance of corporal punishment. Of course, one could say that the
violence that occurs in prisons is unfortunate and something that is not
sanctioned by official policy. Thus, it is quite another matter to explicitly
and directly assess physical harm as an objective of penal policy. I would
have to respond to this assertion by saying that such an argument is a little
too convenient. On the one hand, we say that we are too humane to subject
someone to a brief instance of corporal punishment, but we are perfectly
willing to send someone to prison knowing full well that the person is going
to be subjected to abuse and violence, perhaps even to such an extent that
it will exceed any instance of corporal punishment. The latter is acceptable
because it is not officially sanctioned, even though we know for a certainty
that it will happen. Such rhetorical justification seems rather hollow. It is
also hard to contest that, far from deterring incarcerated offenders against
future misbehaviour, incarceration typically succeeds only in making inmates
more entrenched in criminal lifestyles. The extensive use of imprisonment
is just not working. We need to search for alternatives, not just for restorative
or community-based approaches but also for alternatives where the restorative alternatives may be deemed inappropriate or unrealistic. The motivation
for discussing corporal punishment is the desire to try and spur discussion
and a much-needed search for alternatives. This position has also been
modulated by an insistence on offender consent to corporal punishment.
Making the choice available to the offender is, however, also a source of
objection.

The idea of requiring an offender's consent can be problematic in more than one way. The Australian cases that were mentioned earlier imply that the offenders subjected themselves willingly to payback. It is unclear whether these Aboriginal communities enjoyed a prerogative to unilaterally inflict payback absent consent. It is clear that for some Aboriginal cultures, authorities could require corporal punishment without an offender's consent. An adulterous Iroquois woman could be subject to public flogging with or without her consent. A Senpoil or Nespelem headman could order whipping with or without the offender's consent. The problem then becomes one of inconsistency with Aboriginal traditional understandings of when corporal punishment can be assessed. It can amount to an external imposition of a standard of consent. There is a second problem as well. If Aboriginal communities desire to use corporal punishment as a deterrent sanction, a great deal of this deterrent value is lost if potential offenders know that they can simply veto the application of corporal punishment when they are called to task.

There are two ways to respond to these objections. One is premised on the idea of "take what you can get." Aboriginal peoples are faced with a policy that insists on the full application of the Charter for any accommodations of Aboriginal governance. Included within this insistence is an express prohibition against any corporal punishment. Aboriginal peoples would not only be faced with this policy but also with the international standards of human rights. Article 7 of the *International Covenant on Civil and Political Rights* reads: "No one shall be subjected to torture or to cruel, inhuman or degrading treatment or punishment. In particular, no one shall be subjected without his free consent to medical or scientific experimentation."[41] This article has been interpreted as including a prohibition against judicial corporal punishment. In *Osbourne v Jamaica,* the complainant was convicted in a Jamaican court of illegal possession of a firearm, robbery with aggravation, and wounding with intent. He was sentenced to fifteen years imprisonment along with hard labour and ten strokes of a tamarind birch stick.[42] The United Nations Human Rights Committee declared that the use of tamarind birch strokes violated Article 7's prohibition against "cruel, inhuman or degrading treatment or punishment."[43] The European Court of Human Rights has also declared that judicial corporal punishment violates the covenant.[44] To negotiate any room at all for the use of corporal punishment in the face of such authorities would necessarily require Aboriginal communities to make a concession. In this context, the concession takes the form of allowing the use of corporal punishment subject to the free and informed consent of the offender. It presents itself as a compromise in accordance with the concept of constitutional balancing and ideally avoids inspiring a total prohibition under both section 12 and international law.

The second reply is that an offender's decision may, in the context of contemporary Aboriginal practices, involve more than the desire to escape the physical pain involved. Restorative justice purports to inspire contrition and responsibility in the offender. The victim and other community members also have the opportunity to describe how the offender's actions have affected them. The offender is forced to face up to the consequences, which can lead to contrition, remorse, and an acceptance of responsibility. It can produce a genuine desire for reformation and making right by those who have been affected. This dynamic ideally provides a stronger assurance that the accused will complete any rehabilitative measures that are agreed upon.[45]

The concept typically involves resolutions such as counselling and community service. It does not involve corporal punishment and may not seem directly applicable. Consider, however, what is involved. Victims, and those supportive of the victims, are able to communicate directly to the offender how the offender's behaviour has affected them. Where serious consequences are involved, such as those stemming from sexual assault, for example, the process can be quite discomfiting for the offender, to say the least. Theoretically, the process of victim and community confrontation contemplated by restorative justice can inspire contrition in the offender and, in turn, encourage an increased willingness to accept corporal punishment as a way of making amends. Such an assertion is admittedly highly speculative since such an endeavour has yet to be put to the test within Canada, all the more so because the evidence on whether restorative processes can promote offender remorse and acceptance of responsibility is itself equivocal. It is not an unreasonable assertion though. Consider that in some of the Australian cases, the offender sometimes made a bail application with the very point of submitting to payback in order to smooth over community relations.

There are additional elements involved with Aboriginal justice that vary from the Western models of restorative justice (for example, victim-offender mediation), which can encourage a willingness to accept corporal punishment. Suppose that Elders are present during an Aboriginal justice process. These Elders may communicate cultural values regarding the offence, its consequences, and expectations regarding the making of amends. These Elders may also decide to encourage corporal punishment as a route to reintegration and making right by those affected. What is to stop an offender from allowing himself to be willingly persuaded to accept the admonitions of the Elders? Justice in some Aboriginal societies also has a distinctly clan or familial aspect. Fear of bringing shame upon one's own clan has often been an effective deterrent against misbehaviour. Assume that clan structures remain relevant to a contemporary Aboriginal society. What is to stop the clan leaders or Elders from persuading an offender to willingly accept corporal punishment as a way of excising the shame involved?

This recourse may seem to approach the borders set by the previous discussions concerning natural justice. The idea being that consent may not be genuine if an offender accepts under the pressure brought upon him or her by a chorus of voices urging acceptance. It can be suggested that the dividing line be marked by the difference between persuasion and coercion. If admonitions from the Elders, clan leaders, or other participants in the process depend on persuasion, rather on coercion or intimidation, then consent to corporal punishment can be constitutionally valid.

There remains the question of satisfaction to the victim or others affected by the crime, assuming that corporal punishment is intended to fulfil such a goal. Such persons may feel cheated if an offender insists on "digging in his heels." Keep in mind that the proposals for natural justice are meant to even the playing field for all concerned. If the victim and supporters are unable to procure assent to corporal punishment from the offender, they can then push for alternative modes of satisfaction. These alternatives could include periods of banishment, onerous terms of community service, and the provision of labour or material reparation to the victim and others affected by the crime. Theoretically, an offender may be more willing to agree to alternatives, even onerous alternatives, in the realization that corporal punishment is a legitimate expectation on the part of the victim and others affected. All of the people concerned should ideally participate in a setting of genuine equality, and likely play give and take, until a satisfactory resolution is reached.

Another objection is that consent can be superficial in some situations. One situation that stands out in particular is that in which community authorities, or the victim and his or her supporters, push hard for satisfaction for the wrongs committed by the offender. They can take a hard line that insists that if the offender is not willing to undergo corporal punishment then incarceration will be the only available alternative. If the offender is fearful of going to prison, it may seem like a tacit form of coercion into accepting corporal punishment that renders the Charter standard of waiver hollow.

A response to this argument can perhaps be found in social contract theory. The concept of a social contract is that members of a civil society enter into an understanding with the governing authority. Government fulfils its end of the social contract by using its powers to preserve order and to realize the common good. Citizens fulfil their end of the social contract by subjecting themselves to the legal and political authority of the government in order to realize the benefits of governance, order, and civil rights.[46] Social contract theory has also been used as a justification for punishing crime. Governing authority is given the mandate to protect the collective good. Government fulfils this mandate by punishing those who commit crimes that threaten the common good. To be a member of civil society is to implicitly accept responsibility for upholding the obligations that come along with it. This acceptance, in turn, means an implicit acceptance of the consequences for failing to live up to contractual obligations, such as punishment for committing a crime.[47]

Social contract theory has typically been written with reference to Western political structures such as constitutional monarchies and republics. It is nonetheless useful to view past Aboriginal societies as having worked out their own social contracts. Members of the society agree to live by customary law, by spiritual values, and to fulfil certain obligations to the collective. The society as a collective could, when appropriate, investigate allegations of wrongdoing, try to further negotiated resolutions, or enforce a sanction. Now imagine that Aboriginal societies regain criminal justice jurisdiction. This goal could mark the resumption of a social contract between the Aboriginal community and its individual members. Now consider the tie between the social contract and punishment. When an individual community member makes a choice to engage in actions that abdicate his or her responsibilities under the social contract, that marks implicit acceptance of punishment by the collective. The greater an individual's harmful behaviour departs from what is expected under the social contract, the more limited that individual's options will be in terms of what the collective can mete out. When an Aboriginal individual commits an action that he or she knows is detrimental to the community of which he or she is a member, such action is implicitly an acceptance of collective sanction. An Aboriginal individual should on some level be aware ahead of time that the greater the departure from community standards, the fewer options that will be available when collective intervention becomes necessary. Some Aboriginal societies may very well decide that for certain kinds of offences, behaviours, and situations, only two options at most will be available.

Exclusion of Evidence

Canadian Jurisprudence
The efficacy of a law depends upon the availability of remedies as a means of redressing transgressions of that law. Charter rights are no exception. In criminal law, the most important remedial provision under the Charter is section 24(2), which reads: .

> Where ... a court concludes that evidence was obtained in a manner that infringed or denied any rights or freedoms guaranteed by this Charter, the evidence shall be excluded if it is established that, having regard to all the circumstances, the admission of it in proceedings would bring the administration of justice into disrepute.

A prerequisite to the application of section 24(2) is that the evidence must be obtained in a manner that infringed a Charter right. The Supreme Court of Canada rejected causation as the determining factor. If there is temporal proximity between the Charter violation and the obtaining of the evidence, section 24(2) applies.[48] However, the concept of causation has not been entirely discarded. If the connection between the Charter violation and the evidence is found to be remote, it may be concluded that the evidence was not obtained in a manner that violated the Charter.[49]

The first case to set out the tests for excluding evidence was *R. v Collins*.[50] The analysis in *Collins* began with a consideration of the words "would bring the administration of justice into disrepute." One possibility for interpreting this provision was to ascertain the views of the community through opinion polls.[51] This approach was rejected in *Collins*. The Supreme Court of Canada's reasons included the dangers of leaving the determination of constitutional standards to an uninformed public and the public's lack of sympathy for an accused's rights until he or she becomes an accused.[52] The Court articulated this standard instead: "Would the admission of the evidence bring the administration of justice into disrepute in the eyes of the reasonable man, dispassionate and fully appraised of the circumstances of the case." By "dispassionate," the Court meant unaffected by strong feelings in the community at the time of trial.[53]

Collins also set out three sets of factors to be considered in determining whether the admission of evidence would bring the administration of justice into disrepute:

1. Factors involving the fairness of the accused's trial.
2. Factors involving the seriousness of the Charter breach. A serious breach supports exclusion. A less serious breach may support admission of the evidence.
3. Disrepute brought to the administration of justice by the exclusion of evidence, potentially a mitigating factor against exclusion.[54]

Of the three sets of factors, the first set had by far assumed the greatest importance. Trial fairness involves a distinction between conscripted evidence and non-conscripted evidence. Evidence is conscripted if the accused has been compelled or tricked into participating in its production.[55] If real evidence (for example, the handgun with the accused's fingerprints) was obtained by information conscripted from the accused in violation of the Charter, the real evidence would also be deemed conscripted.[56] There is an exception though. If the real evidence would (not could) have been found without the information conscripted from the accused, it would not affect the fairness of the trial.[57] If it is determined that admission of evidence would render the trial unfair, it would generally be excluded without consideration of the other two sets of factors.[58]

This framework was recently abandoned in favour of a less rigid and more discretionary approach. In *R. v Grant,* which was released in July 2009, the Supreme Court of Canada articulated a new approach that assesses (1) the seriousness of the Charter breach and (2) the impact of the violation on the accused's Charter-protected interests against (3) society's interest in adjudication on the merits.[59]

Much of the jurisprudence on seriousness of the Charter breach that was developed while the *Collins* tests were still in force remain applicable under the new *Grant* framework. The seriousness of the Charter breach will often turn on whether the state authorities can be said to have acted in good faith, or in bad faith, given their knowledge, or lack thereof, of acceptable standards under the Charter. A finding of good faith requires that the state authorities have an honest and reasonable belief that they are acting in compliance with the Charter.[60] Good faith has therefore been found in cases where authorities acted in good faith reliance on laws, the constitutionality of which was unsettled or unclear, that were ultimately struck down.[61] There will not be a finding of good faith where the Supreme Court of Canada, or courts within local provincial jurisdiction, have clearly settled the applicable limits under the Charter. For state authorities to violate the Charter in ignorance of established and settled Charter standards will increase the seriousness of the Charter violation.[62] More serious still will be those instances when the state authorities wilfully and knowingly violated the Charter standards, leading to an unequivocal finding of bad faith.[63] "Extenuating circumstances, such as the need to prevent the disappearance of evidence, may attenuate" the seriousness of a Charter violation.[64]

The Court describes the second criterion for evaluating whether the admission of evidence would bring the administration of justice into disrepute in these terms:

This inquiry focuses on the seriousness of the impact of the Charter breach on the Charter-protected interests of the accused. It calls for an evaluation of the extent to which the breach actually undermined the interests protected by the right infringed. The impact of a Charter breach may range from fleeting and technical to profoundly intrusive. The more serious the impact on the accused's protected interests, the greater the risk that the admission of evidence may signal to the public that Charter rights, however high-sounding, are of little actual avail to the citizen, breeding public cynicism and bringing the administration of justice into disrepute.[65]

The Court goes on to discuss how various kinds of evidence would be treated under this test. Self-incriminatory statements obtained by state authorities will represent a high degree of impact on Charter-protected interests and, thus, will be presumptively admissible.[66] If the statement is obtained by a technical violation, or where the accused would likely have provided the statement even if no violation had occurred, the impact of the Charter-protected statements may be considerably lessened.[67] Bodily evidence, such as a DNA sample, is assessed by the degree to which the investigative technique intrudes upon an accused's bodily integrity. A full strip search will represent a greater intrusion on bodily integrity and, therefore, heighten the impact on Charter-protected interests. Taking a breath sample or a hair sample, by comparison, is less intrusive and will result in a lesser impact on Charter-protected interests.[68] Non-bodily physical evidence is assessed on a similar scale. For example, physical evidence obtained by a strip search or a cavity search will represent a higher impact on Charter-protected interests.[69] The concept of discoverability retains relevance for assessing derivative evidence – evidence that was obtained as a result of a statement by the accused. The more likely that state authorities would have discovered the evidence without the statement, the less impact the rights violation will have on the accused's Charter-protected interests. The reverse is also true. The more likely that state authorities could not have obtained the derivative evidence but for the statement, the greater the impact the rights violation will have on the accused's Charter-protected interests.[70]

The third prong of the new framework – society's interest in meritorious adjudication – is the one that speaks in favour of admitting the evidence as opposed to excluding it. The exclusion of reliable evidence will more strongly engage the societal interest in meritorious adjudication and increase the likelihood that excluding the evidence will bring the administration of justice into disrepute, in comparison to the exclusion of evidence that is unreliable.[71] If the evidence is crucial to the Crown's case, it will more strongly engage the societal interest in meritorious adjudication.[72] The Court states that the new framework is more discretionary and flexible in comparison to the old *Collins* tests and that it is not meant to be reduced to "mathematical precision."[73]

The Conflict

At the risk of generalization, it may be said that Aboriginal justice practices have emphasized hearing everything from anyone who had something relevant to say. For example, under the *Code of Offences and Procedures of Justice for the Mohawk Nation at Akwesasne (Akwesasne Justice Code)*, anyone can present evidence before a convening of the justice chiefs.[74] Where an accused asserts innocence, Article 6, section 5, reads:

> C. The accuser states the facts surrounding the offense, and presents all physical evidence to the Tribunal of Justices.

D. Any and all other witnesses state the facts and present any physical evidence they have.

F. The accused states the facts and presents physical evidence on his behalf.

G. The Accused may have witnesses state facts and present evidence on his behalf as well as witnesses who will attest to his character.

The very concept of excluding evidence pertinent to the criminal act itself in order to protect the individual against collective power would certainly be alien to Aboriginal traditions, even if one accounts for diversity. Contemporary adaptations of Aboriginal justice processes would likely be inclusive enough to include the testimony of Aboriginal police officers, who are also subject to the terms of section 24(2). There is potential conflict between an Aboriginal emphasis on "hearing everything" and an Aboriginal accused's right to apply for the exclusion of evidence. Imagine the possibilities if an Aboriginal accused applies for exclusion of evidence by considering the following scenario:

> Mr. X is a member of an Aboriginal community. After a series of negotiations with federal and provincial governments, that Aboriginal community has established a separate criminal justice based on its traditional practices. On the way home, Mr. X stops his car after a police car signals him to pull over. Two Aboriginal police officers, both from his community, exit their vehicle and approach Mr. X. They ask him to take a roadside test. He accedes to their request. Another police vehicle with a roadside screening device arrives within 10 minutes. He takes the test, which indicates that he is over the legal limit. The police then inform him of his right to counsel by reading from a standard card. They then arrest Mr. X and drive him to their police detachment. The police then show Mr. X to a phone room. They leave him by himself in the room. Mr. X then picks up the phone, but then places it back on the receiver. He comes out and tells the police officers, "I don't need a lawyer. I just want to get this over with." The police officers then take a breath sample from him.

The police did everything right up until the end. Under section 254(2) of the *Criminal Code,* a police officer may make a demand for a roadside screening test on a reasonable suspicion that the detainee has alcohol in his body while in care or control of a motor vehicle and without informing the accused of his right to counsel.[75] The roadside test must be administered "forthwith" after the demand is made. The Supreme Court of Canada held this rule to be a reasonable limit on the right to counsel. Once the roadside test is failed and the police want to take a breathalyzer test that would be admissible in evidence against the accused, they must then inform the accused of his right to counsel.[76] They must not attempt to elicit incriminating evidence from the accused until he has been given a reasonable opportunity to exercise his right to counsel.[77] The accused must be allowed to exercise his right to counsel in privacy, whether or not he expresses a wish for privacy.[78] In the earlier scenario, the police's mistake was that once Mr. X indicated that he did not wish to exercise his right to a lawyer they were required to inform him again of his right to counsel.[79]

The absence of this requirement would enable Mr. X to apply to a "court of competent jurisdiction" under section 24(2) to exclude the breath sample from evidence.[80] Under the old *Collins* framework, the breath sample would be classified as conscriptive evidence. It would affect the fairness of the accused's trial and would likely be subject to exclusion. There may be cause for concern even under the new *Grant* tests. The argument can be made that when an accused indicates that he does not wish to exercise the right to counsel, it is by now a clear and established guideline that the police must again inform the accused of the right to counsel. The failure of the police to do so may not reflect bad faith or egregious conduct, but it still represents a serious Charter breach because the guideline is clear and long established. Failing to do so may warrant exclusion of the evidence, notwithstanding how important the breath sample may be to meritorious adjudication. In fact, a court decision has recently excluded a breath sample on precisely this rationale and in a very similar fact scenario.[81]

This kind of situation could be problematic where Aboriginal justice traditions are concerned. If the breath sample is excluded, it means that Mr. X will not be subject to any process at all. A system based on Aboriginal traditions may not necessarily want to imprison Mr. X but, rather, to attempt to discover the underlying causes of his alcoholism and deal with those causes as part of a healing process. This system will not be able to do so if Mr. X successfully applies to have the breath sample excluded. Such a result may be harder to countenance due to the fact that the police did not intentionally violate Mr. X's rights. They made a slip at the end.

The reasonable person standard in section 24(2) can also be problematic in that it carries with it a certain cultural assumption that is often, but not always, found in Western democracies. This assumption is that excluding questionably obtained evidence of a crime, even if it is otherwise reliable evidence, is an acceptable cost to pay to avoid allowing the state to have too much power. The reasonable person standard is also uniform in that it is not subject to the vagaries of public opinion or to be varied to the personal characteristics or beliefs of each member of a community who is apprised of the circumstances of a case. Here again the issue of cultural subjectivity becomes relevant. Is this reasonable person standard appropriate for traditional Aboriginal approaches to justice? Consider the following quote from Kathy Brock:

To the extent that section 24(2) in any way prevents or inhibits the straightforward prosecutions of mandated criminal law if it is reflexively and unthinkingly applied and evidence is excluded bringing the administration of justice into disrepute, this section has the potential to cause the delegitimation of criminal justice and weaken moral strictures.[82]

Section 24(2) can become problematic for the legitimacy of Aboriginal justice systems. In a sense, the new *Grant* tests display some common ground with Aboriginal perspectives by recognizing the importance of adjudication on the merits of ascertaining the truth of what happened. *Grant,* however, recognizes that even where evidence is vital to adjudication on the merits it can still be excluded if it is necessary for the judiciary to dissociate itself from serious Charter breaches or breaches that have a significant impact on Charter-protected interests. It is this concept, namely the exclusion of relevant evidence as a means to limit state power, that is alien to traditional processes. It could be fairly stated that the exclusion of evidence, in the eyes of a reasonable Aboriginal person, at least one of traditional belief, would invariably "bring the administration of justice into disrepute." A reason for this result is that if evidence is excluded it could lead to the accused not being subject to any process at all. In a system that emphasizes healing and the restoration of community harmony, such a result may be very hard to countenance.

Another cause for concern is the reflexive nature of the tests, both past and present, for excluding evidence. Under the *Collins* tests, the exclusion of evidence is vital to preserving the fairness of an accused's trial. If an accused's trial is rendered unfair, the evidence will generally be excluded without reference to the other sets of factors. This tendency has inspired a fair share of criticism in academic circles. Steven Penney states with reference to the conscripted versus non-conscripted distinction: "In the context of section 24(2) determinations, this newly formulated conception of the right to silence has become a kind of 'superright.'"[83] Jamie Cameron, with partial reference to *Dagenais v Canadian Broadcasting Corporation,* asserts: "Moreover ... the Court held that the right to a fair trial must prevail when the competing interests cannot be accomplished."[84] Jennifer Koshan argues: "Despite the promise of the *Dagenais* case, a model of conflicting rights appears to be entrenched in the courts with the balance perpetually tipped in favour of the accused."[85] The *Collins* tests show that the Court had convinced itself that excluding conscripted evidence is vital to preserving the fairness of trials.

The *Grant* tests may have made significant departures from the old *Collins* framework, but there may still be concerns, at least from Aboriginal perspectives, that they too are a recipe for the reflexive exclusion of evidence. Since the *Grant* tests have been handed out, distinct trends have been noticeable in their application in lower Canadian courts. The third criterion – society's interest in adjudication on the merits – is the criterion that speaks for the admission of evidence notwithstanding the Charter violation. The over-whelming trend that has emerged, however, is that a court is usually only willing to use this criterion, even when the evidence is reliable and/or vital to the Crown's case, when it is confident that the Charter violation is neither serious nor has had a significant impact on Charter-protected interests.[86] Courts have since *Grant* been willing to routinely exclude evidence found to have had a significant impact on Charter-protected interests, such as self-incriminatory statements[87] and intrusions on a private home.[88] Evidence has also been routinely excluded on a finding that the Charter breach was serious. What is particularly revealing is that while some cases have involved a finding of bad faith or egregious conduct on the part of state officials,[89] many others have not. These cases rested instead on findings of carelessness or negligence in the failure to adhere to Charter standards that were clear and settled. Exclusion followed even when the evidence was reliable and/ or vital to the Crown's case.[90] There is occasionally a reported case that runs against this grain, but such instances are rare in comparison to the distinctly noticeable trend that has emerged.[91]

It is apparent that notwithstanding the departure from the old *Collins* framework, the new *Grant* tests are themselves a recipe for reflexive exclu-sion of evidence. So long as the violation is deemed to be serious or has had a significant impact on Charter-protected interests, the societal interest in meritorious adjudication rarely, if ever, operates to justify the admission of the evidence. Perhaps this tendency represents an appropriate balance for mainstream Canadian society. The question that is being asked is whether Aboriginal perspectives, which often place primacy on ascertaining the truth of what happened, would view this policy as an appropriate balance. A legit-imate answer, at least for some Aboriginal societies that want to adopt past justice methods for contemporary use, may be "no."

If the tests for excluding evidence as articulated by the Supreme Court of Canada are applied rigidly and mechanically whenever Aboriginal defend-ants make section 24(2) applications against their own justice systems, one can expect a social cost to follow. Law and sociology professors at Pepper-dine University in California engaged in an extensive study to assess the empirical effects of American jurisprudence, which usually (but not always) requires the exclusion of evidence if it is obtained in the course of violating the accused's constitutional rights. The study included past studies and a survey of over 450 law enforcement officials in California.[92] They made a number of findings regarding the effects of the exclusionary rule. There are two that are particularly relevant to our discussion. One finding is the sub-stantial loss of convictions and prosecutions to the suppression of evidence hearings and the increased use of plea bargains in anticipation of suppression hearings.[93] The second finding is increased criminal recidivism.[94] Another study performed in Emory University in California also concluded that crime rates underwent a sustained increase as a consequence of American exclusionary rules.[95]

Reflexively excluding evidence if it is found to be obtained by a violation that is either serious or has had a significant impact on Charter-protected interests could be of concern to Canadian society in general. It may be especially problematic from an Aboriginal perspective. At this point, it may be helpful to elaborate on the significance of the Pepperdine and Emory studies. Deterrence theory, as previously mentioned, has the three components of certainty, swiftness, and severity. Severity, even conceding Sylvia Mendes' point that a sanction must still at least be significant, is often thought to be the weak link in deterrence theory.[96] It is certainty with swiftness that may have real deterrent value, although even then this deterrent value may not be realized in some social contexts. This is the danger that a rigorous enforcement of constitutional legal rights, backed by a powerful remedy in the form of excluding evidence, presents from a social control perspective. The routine exclusion of evidence following a constitutional violation can undermine the certainty and swiftness with which a sanction can be meted out. The Pepperdine and Emory studies perhaps suggest that crime rates will rise when it becomes common knowledge that the availability of the exclusion remedy will reduce the probability that a sanction will become certain and swift. The exclusion of evidence may therefore present a social cost to Aboriginal communities that they may not be willing to accept. Of course, the certainty and swiftness package may be problematic for some kinds of crimes that often plague Aboriginal communities, such as substance abuse, sexual abuse, domestic violence, and gang activity. However, reducing the probability that anything will happen across the board after the commission of any crime in Aboriginal communities cannot be helpful either. One may speculate that such a development could exacerbate the social problems faced by Aboriginal communities. The use of section 24(2) threatens to impair the ability of Aboriginal communities to deal with crime by their own members by offering Aboriginal accuseds the prospect of not being subject to any process at all. This concern may be especially acute given the nature of the Supreme Court of Canada's tests under section 24(2), which often result in excluding evidence whenever the Charter violation is serious or has had a significant impact on Charter-protected interests.

The Proposal
Rupert Ross and David Cayley suggest a possible solution, a partnership (Ross) or separation (Cayley) of adversarial and restorative processes.[97] Section 24(2) could continue to operate in a separate trial process while

remaining inapplicable in the restorative process. There remains a problem. In pre-colonial times, Aboriginal justice tended to collapse "determination of guilt" and restorative processes together. This is true of the *Akwesasne Justice Code*. The code does allow an accused to plead guilty or not guilty. Yet even when a matter goes to trial on a not guilty plea, Article 6, section 5, reads in part:

> E. The Tribunal of Justices asks the accuser and witnesses in turn, what each thinks would be a just and equitable solution or end to the matter.
> H. The Tribunal of Justices ask the accused and each of his witnesses in turn what they think would be a just and equitable solution or end to the matter.

The imposition of section 24(2) upon such a process could be especially problematic. As a result, a search for alternatives may be in order.

It is interesting to note that most common law jurisdictions, excluding the United States, have until recently tended to include evidence obtained by questionable police methods so long as it is relevant to the case being heard. English common law, for example, would only allow the exclusion of relevant, though questionably obtained, evidence in very exceptional circumstances. It was not until the 1950s that English authorities even began to consider the question of excluding such evidence. Although cases such as *Kuruma v The Queen* and *R. v Sang* created a new discretion to exclude confessions (but not evidence obtained by searches) if they affected the fairness of a trial, it was apparent that the discretion would only be exercised in very exceptional circumstances.[98] Before the advent of the Charter, the Supreme Court of Canada explicitly rejected the idea that a trial judge may exclude relevant evidence on the basis that it may be unfair to the accused or that its admission would bring the administration of justice into disrepute.[99]

An alternative approach is constructed by J.A.E. Pottow. His idea is that section 24(1), the general remedial provision of the Charter, can be used alongside section 24(2). It provides a more flexible approach to remedying Charter violations. Excluding evidence could be reserved for the most serious of violations, such as extracting a confession by torture. For less serious violations, section 24(1) can provide a flexible range of remedies, such as costs against the prosecution, monetary awards or damages, or a reduction of sentencing.[100] Of course, Aboriginal communities need not restrict themselves to Pottow's suggestions. In drafting their own Charters, Aboriginal communities can design their own range of remedies and specify which violations they should apply to. Remedies available under section 24(1) can run nearly the whole spectrum so as to accommodate the circumstances of

The Final Resolution 207

each individual case. For first or trivial instances, a verbal warning may be appropriate. For more serious or repeat instances, fines could be levied. For very serious instances or very repetitive occurrences, sanctions such as suspension, payment of damages (for example, the accused was also physically harmed), or even dismissal can be used.

It is not to say that evidence need never be excluded. Aboriginal communities may well decide for themselves that exclusion may be in order when the evidence has been obtained in such a manner as to make it unreliable. An Australian case provides an illustrative example of this kind of decision. In *R. v Williams and Orrs,* five Aboriginal youths were charged with rape. Their verbal comprehension levels were estimated to be that of boys aged seven to eleven years. The Queensland Supreme Court excluded confessions that were obtained by police interrogations. Justice John Dowsett stated:

> A child, especially an Aboriginal child, should be told that he has a choice to remain silent otherwise it is difficult to see how a court can ever be satisfied that he has freely chosen to speak. If he is to be told, he must be told in a way which he will understand. If care is not taken to explain the matter to him and his comprehension tested to ensure that the advice has assimilated, one may just as well speak to him in Greek ... The absence of a meaningful warning coupled with his (the accused child) being taken to the police station and questioned are, I consider, sufficient external circumstances to create a *prima facie* case of lack of voluntariness.
>
> It would have been a simple matter to ask (the accused child) to explain to the police, after consulting (in) private with (the JP), his understanding of his right to silence, but no attempt was made to do this.
>
> I cannot be satisfied that the perfunctory warning (the accused child) received, not tested for impact privately by (the JP), was sufficient to negative the oppression of the situation in which he was placed. I doubt that any 14 year old boy could be expected to cope with such a gross attack on his freedom, let alone one with only a limited ability to communicate verbally. Again, the confession must be excluded.[101]

This commentary is made in the context of the common law rule of confessions, which involves voluntariness and reliability. It does, however, provide a possible example of a situation in which an Aboriginal community may wish to exclude evidence. Another example may be where police beat a confession out of an Aboriginal suspect. The idea is that Aboriginal communities can, if they so choose, exclude evidence in circumstances in which exclusion does not hamper an Aboriginal emphasis on ascertaining the truth of what has occurred. This proposal, however, is not immune to objections.

Objections

Steven Penney describes potential problems with Pottow's approach:

> Even if alternatives to exclusion could be implemented without political initiative (for example, by substituting non-exclusionary section 24(1) remedies for exclusion under section 24(2)), no alternative is likely to be superior to exclusion in optimizing the balance between deterrence and truth-seeking. Non-exclusionary remedies are very likely to generate either too little or too much deterrence. To avoid under-deterrence, alternative remedies must impact police interests severely enough to influence their future conduct. Most Charter violations would warrant only modest compensatory damages. Few victims would find it worthwhile to incur the costs required to obtain these awards. As a result, police would likely consider damage awards a minor cost of doing business. In theory, this problem can be overcome by the use of such mechanisms as class actions, administrative hearings, and non-compensatory remedies (such as punitive damages, statutory liquidated damages, and injunctions). But such initiatives would require significant legislative or judicial innovation, and it is not clear that they would be financially, administratively, or politically feasible.[102]

The use of section 24(2) to enforce legal rights under the Charter relies upon the accused making an application for the exclusion of evidence. Imagine now if an Aboriginal Charter limits the circumstances under which the exclusion of evidence is available as a remedy. It can be readily imagined that if an Aboriginal accused can only look forward to a verbal warning, or a minor compensatory award, with every prospect of the evidence being admitted and justifying sanction against the accused, there would be a lack of incentive to even bother with an application under an Aboriginal Charter of rights. Police may not be particularly dissuaded against unconstitutional practices in the knowledge that remedies may not be particularly onerous for them and with every prospect of the evidence being admitted regardless. This possibility can become even more acute if Aboriginal defendants simply do not even bother with making applications.

There is a way to deal with this situation. A previous proposal involved having an Aboriginal community establish a *prima facie* case before an accused can face sanctions. This request likely involves a hearing similar to a preliminary inquiry prior to any other procedures that a community may desire, such as healing circles. The idea is that during this same hearing, a community court judge can require the community to establish the fact that the evidence against the accused has been procured in a manner consistent with the local Aboriginal Charter of rights. During this meeting, the community court judge can elicit what happened from the investigative authorities as well as from the accused. Once everyone has been heard from, a community court judge can then decide whether a rights violation has occurred and, if so, what the appropriate remedy would be. This concept envisions an inquisitorial mode of justice as a means of overseeing whether there is compliance with the local Charter of rights. An accused's participation could be obligatory, but there is nothing to stop an accused from actively seeking a remedy during such a process either. If an accused has been coerced into a confession by police, the accused may well feel inclined to seek an exclusion of the confession during the hearing. This idea is not entirely without foundation in Canadian common or civil law either. Whenever the Crown seeks to lead a confession into evidence, a trial judge is required to hold a *voir dire* in order to ascertain whether the confession meets the common law rules regarding voluntariness.[103] The Supreme Court of Canada has also noted that while the defence has the legal burden of proof to show that the state obtained evidence in an unconstitutional manner, the state will sometimes have a practical onus to demonstrate otherwise since it often possesses superior knowledge of the events in question.[104]

There is the obvious problem in that requiring this sort of hearing in every single case can pose considerable administrative difficulties for Aboriginal justice systems, with the resulting threat of greater resource demands, greater time demands, and a mounting backlog of matters that need to be resolved. There is a way to deal with this result as well. Just as a waiver is available for many Charter rights as well as for modified Aboriginal legal rights that have been proposed previously, a waiver can also apply in this instance. It is certainly conceivable that an Aboriginal accused may have absolutely no desire to contest accusations at all. If an Aboriginal accused expresses a desire to waive the preliminary hearing, a community court judge can inquire of the accused whether there is an awareness that the right to hold the community to a *prima facie* case is being waived and whether there is an awareness that the right to have an inquiry as to whether any other rights violations have occurred is being waived as well. It could also be made clear to the accused that the benefits from a hearing could be lost, including compensatory damages, excluding evidence, dismissal of proceedings for lack of evidence, and disciplinary action against police officers. An Aboriginal accused would ideally have the benefit of advice from a community advocate as well. However, the idea of using inquisitorial methods of justice to oversee respect for Aboriginal legal rights is itself a source of objection.

This proposal involves collapsing together the judicial function of remedying a violation of legal rights and those functions associated with a police disciplinary commission. The objection is that section 24(2) is a remedial provision, meant to personally correct for an accused a violation of his or her constitutional rights. Combining this provision with police disciplinary measures misconstrues the nature of section 24(2). Jack Watson argues that the use of the word "remedy" has a certain connotation in the context of section 24 as a whole.[105] It is meant to be restorative to a person who has had his constitutional rights violated and not be turned into something that becomes randomly punitive of the public. Pottow provides a counter to Watson's argument: "As currently interpreted, exclusion is an all-or-nothing remedy, in two ways: first, it is the *only* remedy available in the evidentiary realm, and second, it is an *indivisible,* heavy-handed remedy that can easily overshoot the constitutional wrong."[106] Pottow's comment requires some qualification. Section 24(2) is not the only available constitutional remedy for excluding evidence. Under section 11(d), the right to a fair trial and to be presumed innocent, evidence that has not been obtained in a manner that infringes the Charter can be excluded if it would render the trial unfair.[107] Section 24(1) provides a discretion to exclude evidence that would violate an accused's right to a fair trial.[108] In addition, the *Collins* test for exclusion under section 24(2) was not quite as heavy-handed or indivisible as Pottow suggests. In *R. v Burlingham,* and while the *Collins* tests were still in force, Justice Frank Iacobucci provided this caution against interpreting section 24(2) too rigidly: "Thus, to the extent that this Court decides to set down such a rule in regard to 'trial fairness,' I believe that it should take care not to define that concept so broadly as to allow the 'trial fairness' tail to wag the section 24(2) dog."[109] *R. v Harper* is an example of a case in which confessional evidence was not excluded.[110] Both before and after the investigating police officers fulfilled the informational component of the right to counsel, the accused provided confessional statements with very little initiative on the part of the officers. The Court concluded that the accused would have confessed even if his right to counsel had not been violated. To admit the evidence would not have brought the administration of justice into disrepute.[111]

Pottow's criticism that exclusion can produce effects out of proportion to the constitutional violation is valid nonetheless. Under the old *Collins* tests, exclusion of conscripted evidence was almost always sure to follow without considering the other sets of factors. Under the new *Grant* tests, exclusion of evidence is an apparent probability upon a finding that the Charter violation is serious or that there has been a significant impact on the accused's Charter-protected interests, even when the evidence is reliable and/or vital to the prosecution's case, such as in the engagement of societal interests in adjudication on the merits. Some American legislators have seemingly agreed with Pottow as well. In 1995, the American Senate passed the *Violent Crime Control and Law Enforcement Act of 1995.*[112] The bill sought to abrogate the rule of excluding evidence, to remove the immunity of police officers from civil liability, and to award tort damages against the United States for violation of Fourth Amendment rights. The bill did not, however, pass through the House of Representatives.[113] The fact that excluding evidence can produce effects out of proportion to the constitutional wrong is possibly more acute in the context of Aboriginal approaches to justice. It may therefore be more appropriate to allow Aboriginal communities to use section 24(1) as an alternative base of remedy if they so choose.

This aspect of the proposal, however, also flies in the face of Supreme Court of Canada jurisprudence. In *Burlingham*, the Court stated explicitly that section 24(2) is not to be used as a source of police discipline.[114] This reasoning should not be a real impediment to using section 24(1) for a number of reasons. One is that on a practical level section 24(2) is all about obliging authorities to conform to the *Charter*. The police must perform certain obligations when they have detained an accused or else the evidence that they obtain may be excluded. This is an aspect of excluding evidence that American jurisprudence explicitly recognizes. In *United States v Calandra*, the Supreme Court of the United States went so far as to reject excluding evidence as a personal remedy of the accused and, instead, emphasized that excluding evidence was designed exclusively to deter police misconduct.[115] Another reason is that there is recognition that section 24(1) can be used as a penalty and a civil remedy in instances of state malfeasance. In *Mackin v New Brunswick (Minister of Finance)*, Justice Charles Gonthier stated: "In theory, a plaintiff could seek compensatory and punitive damages by way of 'appropriate and just' remedy under section 24(1) of the *Charter*."[116] In *R. v 974649 Ontario Inc.*, the Supreme Court of Canada upheld an appellate court's decision that a justice of the peace had jurisdiction under section 24(1) to award legal costs against the Crown for violating the right to disclosure.[117] In *Vancouver (City) v. Ward*, the Court upheld an award of damages as a section 24(1) remedy against the Vancouver police department after they had detained a man and subjected him to a strip search without reasonable cause.[118] Another reason is that the exclusion of evidence can have drastic consequences for Aboriginal processes such that it could hardly be deemed a constitutional balance in any meaningful way. Section 24(1) provides an alternative source of remedies so that Aboriginal perspectives on justice are accommodated to some degree, while still obliging investigative authorities to respect Charter values.

10
Conclusion

Much of these discussions have proceeded on an assumption that Aboriginal peoples want to adapt past methods of justice for contemporary use. This does not account for the very real possibility of competing visions of justice within Aboriginal communities. It cannot be assumed that every member of an Aboriginal community is traditional in terms of justice ideology. Aboriginal people today interact with a different world than the one that existed before contact with Europeans. Studies by Carol LaPrairie have indicated that Aboriginal communities are often divided over issues such as the acceptance of traditional or contemporary values, individualism versus collectivism, and traditional spirituality versus other religions such as Christianity and new age spirituality.[1] An Aboriginal community, or at least the majority of its members, would not necessarily want a justice system that reflects traditional values. The system would not be in keeping with their more "contemporary values" and therefore would be illegitimate. One of Bruce Miller's criticisms against the South Vancouver Island Justice Education Project was that it was a top-down affair that failed to ascertain contemporary justice ideologies among the broad membership of the Coast Salish community, some of whom did not consider themselves to be traditional.[2]

The proposed *Code of Offences and Procedures of Justice for the Mohawk Nation at Akwesasne* may itself have instigated intense conflict over justice ideology.[3] Douglas George-Kanentiio suggests that Mohawk smugglers who trade contraband across the Canadian and American border have felt threatened by the prospect of a unified justice system and police force in all Mohawk communities and, therefore, have worked against the adoption of the code. However, he is unclear as to who they have worked with and what methods they have used to block the code.[4] Another problem could be that Mohawk communities are often divided into factions. Some consider themselves modernists or progressives. Part of their agenda is the continued existence of elected councils and, for some, the discontinuance of the longhouse councils. Then there are the traditionalists, who believe in the revival of traditional forms of governance.[5] E. Jane Dickson-Gilmore argues that this dichotomy is overly simple since even within each side there are further variations of ideology and objectives.[6] Nonetheless, she still acknowledges that a rough progressive and traditional division exists within Mohawk communities.[7] The council may have refused to adopt the proposed code to prevent traditional forms of governance from gaining ground, although there is no way of knowing this for sure.

As Bruce Miller indicates, a fundamental prerequisite to any meaningful exercise of self-determination in the area of criminal justice is for an Aboriginal community to be able to agree at large on a cohesive vision of justice.[8] This prerequisite means that extensive and inclusive consultations at the community level are necessary before any efforts at reinvigorating traditional justice are made. These consultations would necessarily have to gauge the possible presence of competing justice ideologies. If there are multiple and conflicting justice ideologies, then negotiations would be necessary to try and produce a vision of justice that is at least to some degree acceptable to the community at large.

One potential drawback to this idea is that the end result is a compromise that may not be fully satisfactory for anyone concerned. As a hypothetical example, a possible compromise is that the justice system will by and large resemble the Canadian justice system, simply allowing for diversion programs for those that want to utilize traditional approaches. For traditionalist members of the community, this possibility could simply amount to the same kind of minimalist accommodation that can be expected from the Canadian state. A second plausible drawback is that ideological divisions in an Aboriginal community may be so sharp and intense that any meaningful effort to exercise self-determination will grind to a halt before it can even start. That is to say that no community vision of justice can ever be realized because the intensity of community divisions makes even the process of negotiation and compromise a futile exercise. Perhaps this scenario is precisely what manifested among the Coast Salish and the Akwesasne Mohawk. There is also no mistaking that the challenges involved with this kind of situation are considerable.

However, it is not impossible. One could suggest that in this day and age trying to view matters through a traditionalist-modern dichotomy fails to capture the full complexities involved with Aboriginal peoples' having to adapt to a changed world. Cultural affiliation and identity are not sum-zero propositions. Joyce Green provides this critique of Taiaiake Alfred's nationalist model:

> Alfred's model is also silent on the difficulties posed by hybridity. It does not address the problems that LaRocque raises, of both the syncretic nature

of cultures (which makes absolute characteristics problematic) and of the many contingent choices individuals make in their cultural selections.[9]

Many Aboriginal peoples, by necessity of living in a changed world, will represent varying degrees of syncretism and hybridity in their cultural identities and practices. It may at once be a source of division or a source of relative unity and compromise. It is altogether possible that there may be enough common ground in some Aboriginal communities to provide a foundation for a cohesive vision of justice. I will admit that I am speaking in hypothetical terms, but it is important to stress that real life situations are likely a good deal more complex than what the presented cultural dichotomies may convey.

Before an Aboriginal community can make any serious demand for self-determination over criminal justice, or engage in any meaningful fashion with any potential conflicts between the Canadian Charter of Rights and Freedoms and past methods of justice, it must first sort out for itself what it (and its members at large) want out of justice.[10] Chances are, some communities may very well find themselves unable to resolve divisions over justice ideology in a way that has broad-based support. However, if other communities do become resolved on adapting past methods of justice to address contemporary needs, and assuming that they actually do obtain substantive jurisdiction over criminal justice, the issue of the Charter's potential application is a critical one towards which they will have to turn their efforts.

What happens if and when Aboriginal individuals assert their legal rights under the Charter against Aboriginal justice systems? This possibility engages the well-known tension between individual liberty and the pursuit of the collective good. Emphasizing Charter rights can involve the external imposition of Western liberal values that undermine Aboriginal visions of justice that emphasize furthering the collective good and protecting this collective good against harmful criminal activities. If Aboriginal justice systems do not make any allowance for due process safeguards, that lack can lead to abuses of collective power against Aboriginal individuals. Examples include innocent individuals being subjected to undeserved punishment, stronger parties coercing weaker parties into lopsided resolutions, and the use of police forces to intimidate community members. The tension is not an easy one to resolve, but it is one that Aboriginal communities must address if they want to advance their visions of justice in contemporary settings in any meaningful way. The key point behind this work is to break ground and provide springboards for these kinds of discussions.

An approach that can commend itself to Aboriginal peoples is the Royal Commission on Aboriginal Peoples' concept of the culturally sensitive interpretation of legal rights.[11] The idea is that the legal rights of the Charter are reinterpreted so as to provide greater room for the operation of Aboriginal methods of justice and yet still provide meaningful safeguards against the abuse of collective power in Aboriginal communities. Canadian constitutional law provides a workable mechanism for realizing this pursuit. The *R. v Oakes* tests for constitutional justification, as refined by *Dagenais v Canadian Broadcasting Corporation*, suggest that when constitutional rights come into conflict (for example, Aboriginal rights to criminal jurisdiction versus legal rights), then each must be accommodated as much as possible in a non-hierarchical approach.[12] This process can imply a blending of older Aboriginal teachings and newer Canadian legal principles. In the chapters of this book, I have provided a detailed look at how this exercise can unfold. The chapters construct proposals for addressing the tension in the context of nine different Charter rights: the right to be heard by an independent tribunal, the right to natural justice, the right to be presumed innocent until proven guilty beyond a reasonable doubt, the right to contest guilt through adversarial procedures, the right against unreasonable search and seizure, the right to silence, the right to counsel, the right against cruel and unusual punishment, and the right to have evidence obtained in the course of violating constitutional rights excluded.

The right to be heard by an independent tribunal presents a number of difficulties. Canadian and Aboriginal legal traditions each emphasize different criteria for vesting persons with authority to hear and resolve criminal conflicts. Canadian modes of judicial authority have certain coercive aspects to them, while Aboriginal modes of authority often, but not always, have relied on spiritual teaching and persuasion by comparison. The solution that I have presented is to establish community court judges who would be protected by the three features of judicial independence: security of tenure, security of remuneration, and security of administration. Aboriginal communities could otherwise set their own qualifications for community court judges. The role of community judges is to ensure that the parties to a conflict behave fairly towards each other. So long as this fairness is ensured, a community court judge has to adopt the consensus of the parties.

The right to natural justice presents difficulties on account of the doctrine that a judicial authority not be personally connected to any party to the proceedings. The practical effect of this doctrine may be the perpetual disqualification of community court judges, given the often closely-knit nature of smaller Aboriginal communities. There is, however, a real need for fairness in criminal proceedings in Aboriginal communities since power dynamics and relationships can be abused to the severe disadvantage of either Aboriginal accuseds or victims. The resolution that is proposed is based on a generous understanding of the doctrine of necessity that can shield community court judges from being perpetually disqualified from hearing disputes. So long as community court judges are actually being fair in the discharge of their duties, natural justice will not be violated. If the parties have any concerns about a community court judge's fairness, Aboriginal courts of appeal and the requisition of recorded reasons also provide possible safeguards.

The right to be presumed innocent can present difficulties for Aboriginal teachings that have encouraged offenders to accept responsibility for their actions instead of hedging their bets through a not guilty plea. It can also involve social costs for Aboriginal communities when factually guilty offenders exploit the high burden of proof to get off without having to face any sanction. This action can frustrate community efforts at exercising crime control over certain activities that threaten Aboriginal communities, such as substance abuse, intergenerational sexual abuse, and gang activity. At the same time, the presumption of innocence does serve the real point of preventing the undeserved conviction of the innocent. The solution presented in this book is to use consensus, either by a panel of community court judges or community members, instead of a formal burden of proof beyond a reasonable doubt. Consensus has some basis in Aboriginal tradition and, ideally, also provides a meaningful safeguard against conviction of the innocent.

The right to use adversarial procedures to contest allegations of misconduct also presents problems. Adversarial procedures are thought to encourage competition and hostility, whereas Aboriginal processes are designed to promote harmony and healing relationships. Cross-examining witnesses in confrontational or hostile fashion also presents the risk of committing cultural *faux pas*. The solution presented in this book is to limit truly adversarial trials to situations in which there is the question of whether the accused has committed any wrongful act and to not include situations in which it is apparent the accused has done something harmful but the reasons why remain unclear. Another possible approach is to restructure cross-examination in a narrative format that resembles traditional storytelling to avoid committing cultural *faux pas*. Another approach allows that even during the limited instances in which fact determination becomes necessary there is not necessarily a need to adhere strictly to the common law format of examination-in-chief followed by cross-examination. The process can be pulled in inquisitorial directions designed to sort out those who need to be sanctioned from those who do not, while allowing for some form of adversarial challenge to the evidence in support of allegations.

The right to search and seizure is designed to prevent the police from having too much power to intrude upon what citizens may reasonably regard as their own private affairs. Modern and professional police services may not have had an equivalent in past Aboriginal practices, but contemporary

Aboriginal communities may still want to use them as expedient vehicles for preserving the collective good against harmful criminal activities. Canadian jurisprudence on reasonable expectations of privacy provides a workable mechanism for bringing Aboriginal perspectives into the analysis. Aboriginal philosophies of property holding or the collective good may in appropriate circumstances result in lower expectations of privacy and, therefore, justify either warrantless searches where peace officers have a reasonable basis for their suspicions or the authorization of warrants on a lower threshold (for example, reasonable belief) than reasonable and probable grounds.

The right to silence has the potential for conflict with Aboriginal truth-speaking traditions. Part of the solution presented in this book is to allow the right to silence to remain operative while matters are still at an investigative stage in order to prevent the possibility of a police state. The accused could not be compelled to speak to investigative authorities. However, if the accused voluntarily chooses to mislead authorities in circumstances resembling the obstruction of justice, traditional sanctions for deception could become applicable. The other part is to require the accusers to provide a bona fide case-to-meet against the accused. If this requirement is fulfilled, the truth-speaking tradition becomes operative and the accused must say his or her side of the story. This insistence provides some room for truth-speaking traditions but still provides a meaningful safeguard against spurious or unfounded accusations.

The right to counsel also presents certain difficulties. Some Aboriginal societies did have the concept of a spokesperson for an accused, but others did not. For the latter, the right to counsel may represent an external imposition. The lawyers' duty of advocacy can also present difficulties for Aboriginal processes with a restorative emphasis since the best interests of the client and the interests of the Aboriginal community are not necessarily harmonious to begin with. One possible approach is to adapt the Australian concept of the prisoner's friend, a person who, while not necessarily a member of the bar, can nonetheless look out for an accused's rights when matters are still at an investigative stage. Another approach is to allow for advocates before community courts, though they do not necessarily have to have membership in provincial bars. Their roles can be modified during restorative processes so that they become more resource persons than true advocates. Nonetheless, an advocate can remain vigilant about an accused's rights to natural justice during restorative processes and can assist an accused with an appeal should the accused's rights to natural justice be violated.

Aboriginal corporal sanctions may have contemporary relevance in that they are short and sharp punishments that can provide deterrence and retribution and yet avoid the hardening effects associated with prison life.

Corporal sanctions are, however, expressly prohibited under jurisprudence on the right against cruel and unusual punishment. A solution presented in this text is to allow an accused to waive this right and voluntarily undergo corporal punishment, so long as he or she is properly apprised of the risks. The writer is of the opinion that the prohibition against execution should remain in place since someone who is wrongfully executed would have no possible redress.

The right to have unconstitutionally obtained evidence excluded is problematic in more than one way. The whole concept of excluding relevant evidence as a method of checking state power would be alien to any Aboriginal notions of justice, which frequently emphasized ascertaining the truth of what happened. This concept potentially raises problems of cultural illegitimacy. The court's jurisprudence on section 24(2) may be a recipe for reflexive exclusion of evidence when it is found to have stemmed from a serious Charter violation or to have had a significant impact on Charter-protected interests, even when the evidence is reliable and crucial to substantiating the allegations. This proposal can also entail social costs to Aboriginal communities as factually guilty Aboriginal accuseds get off without any sanction. The solution presented here is to limit the exclusion of evidence to the most serious cases, those in which it could be said that the evidence was itself unreliable. For other instances, the preference is to rely upon section 24(1), the general remedial provision of the Charter, as an alternative source of remedy.

These proposals are not intended to be the only possible culturally sensitive interpretations of legal rights. It is anticipated and recommended that Aboriginal communities pursue their own culturally sensitive interpretations of legal rights that best reflect their local needs and particular cultural values. At this point, there may still be lingering concerns about how any of this can be considered truly Aboriginal. A fair question is whether this is how Aboriginal peoples would do things, if we assume non-Aboriginal Canadians had suddenly disappeared or had packed up and gone elsewhere, leaving Aboriginal peoples to start over with a clean slate. A plausible answer is certainly no, since by its very nature the culturally sensitive interpretation of legal rights unfolds to some degree by reference to what Canadian law finds acceptable. It can also be suggested that it would amount to mere Indigenization, merely staffing a version of the Canadian system with Aboriginal staff members, with perhaps some cultural practices sprinkled in. Leslie Jane MacMillan criticizes Indigenization as inadequate.[13] One reason she gives is that it is inadequate for addressing ongoing social problems since it involves token concessions by a justice system that is fundamentally tied to colonialism and assimilation. Her other reason is that Indigenization can exacerbate community conflicts over whether past customary laws should be adapted for contemporary use.

Be that as it may, the truth of the matter is that the presence of the Canadian state is a reality that has to be lived with, and adapted to, like it or not. Dwayne Trevor MacDonald, while contrasting the visions of Taiaiake Alfred and Dale Turner, provides this insight:

> But, then again, contradiction also reflects the complexity of being indigenous in Canada today. The emphasis on legal and political definitions of Indianness coupled with the intense social and cultural ramifications of the Imaginary Indian has created a situation in which the people, still reeling from the devastating effects of colonization, yearn for an authentic understanding of who they are and what it might mean. However, in advocating for the resurgence of an Onkwehonwe path, Taiaiake suggests that we can somehow free ourselves of colonial realities just by acting in authentic ways. The truth is that most indigenous societies are so deeply marked by colonialism that the possibility of living day to day outside of those structures is illusionary [sic]. This does not discount the vital and ongoing work of ceremonial and spiritual leaders who have spurred the revitalization of language and culture in their communities. However, most of these same leaders realize that a commitment to live according to the ethical and spiritual principles of their people must be accompanied by a willingness to adjust those beliefs to the demands of living today. Rather than striving toward some form of unattainable authenticity, we should instead be concerning ourselves with the ways in which indigenous cultural and spiritual principles can provide guidance on how to engage and teach the dominant society about balance, justice, peace and living well on the land. After all, as one Blackfoot elder advised, our teepees are all held down by the same peg now.[14]

As a matter of practicality, the culturally sensitive interpretation of legal rights still represents a relatively better means of securing space for Aboriginal visions of justice than the unilateral imposition of the Charter. Much of what I have developed as tentative proposals may, to some, appear as Indigenization. If Indigenization is defined as simply staffing the standard system with Aboriginal persons and sprinkling a few cultural practices here and there, I would argue that what I have proposed amounts to something more. The reason that some of the proposals that have been made in this book (judges, advocates, and courts) resemble features of common law legal systems – and may therefore invite criticisms that they amount to mere Indigenization – is that they reflect a real need to prevent power abuses in contemporary Aboriginal communities, as such abuses have been well documented. In today's world, every society needs to be concerned with the need to prevent abuses connected with collective powers of criminalization and punishment, Aboriginal and non-Aboriginal alike. Much of what I explore here may reflect an adjustment to the demands of living today.

The proposals advanced in this book do amount to something more than Indigenization, however, because they involve some fairly fundamental shifts in institutional structure, decision-making power, and practices. The idea of limiting judges' roles to situations in which power abuses may require intervention, removing the judicial veto when the participants have crafted their own resolution, substantially enlarging the potential role for Aboriginal customary law, limiting the scope of trials, possibly reviving the use of corporal punishment, and pulling the processes of "trials" in decidedly more inquisitorial directions must all surely be thought of as something substantially different than a mere replication of the Canadian justice system. Indeed, if I may call upon this thesis as a barometer, much of what I suggest here would inspire rather heated criticisms from Canadian jurists and civil libertarians for departing too far from Canadian legal standards.

Lastly, I suggest that to adhere to thinking that "if it has any degree of resemblance to Western justice systems it must be Indigenization and therefore must be rejected" may be overly dogmatic. It seems to ascribe to the "illusory" belief that we can simply choose to "live day by day" outside the society and structures that surround us. If taken to its extreme, such an insistence can impede a pragmatic search for initiatives and solutions that could be workable in present circumstances. Authors such as Scott Clark and Harry Blagg, while not framing their arguments in precisely the same way as I have, emphasize that greater community empowerment where Aboriginal laws are used is desirable.[15] Nonetheless, they also argue that as a matter of practicality, some degree of intersection with the standard justice system remains necessary. For example, some form of resourcing and management support may be required to get the initiatives started and to help Aboriginal communities take back control over justice at their own pace. It may sound defeatist to some, but, at the end of the day, there is such a thing as making the best of the situation you find yourself in instead of yearning for a likely (in the near future at least) unattainable ideal.

Of course, this premise does not address MacMillan's valid point, that anything I suggest may not necessarily suffice to diffuse community conflicts over visions of justice. I must again stress that it is for communities themselves to tackle issues such as the potential application of the Charter and the role of past law and justice practices in contemporary circumstances. It may sound like an easy cop out on my part and a dodging of MacMillan's point. However, I have been adamant all along that my suggestions are precisely that – suggestions that are tentatively offered to stimulate some much needed discussion of the issues. For me to suggest that communities, irrespective of their circumstances, needs, and membership, whether it includes Christians and/or traditionalists, have to accept what I propose as the one and only way of doing things would only represent a slide into a kind of academic paternalism, notwithstanding my Cree heritage. Some communities may be unable to resolve internal conflicts over visions of justice, some may like my proposals, some may want to vary them, some may reject them completely. All of these are valid choices that communities have a right to make for themselves, although I would personally find the prospect of irreconcilable internal conflict unfortunate. I must add, however, the caveat that rejecting any proposal I make to the extent that the Charter has no application whatsoever to Aboriginal justice, and without any workable alternatives for preventing power abuses, may represent a self-determinative choice, just not a well-advised one. My taking this position is not because I personally think the Charter should have some role to play (which I do) but, rather, because to go this route would likely lead to certain difficulties, such as power abuses and community conflicts over justice and power dynamics.

An alternative idea that has been touted, albeit infrequently, is that Aboriginal legal orders have their own methods of preventing abuses of collective power against individual members.[16] The idea certainly has its appeal. The problem is that there is a relative paucity of descriptions or literature that conveys the details of such methods or how they can work in contemporary social settings. There may be several reasons for this paucity. An obvious one could be the disruptive effects of colonialism. Another one is that so much literature in the field of Aboriginal justice focuses on parallels to restorative justice and sentencing initiatives. So very little of the literature focuses on determining the truth of allegations when the issue of factual guilt is unresolved or on potential conflicts between individual legal rights and the collective emphasis in many Aboriginal justice methods. As an aside, the reason I appear to "rely" on Rupert Ross (with whom I disagree on certain issues) at several points is that he is one of the few authors who has ever offered concrete observations when it comes to specific ramifications of applying the Charter in Aboriginal contexts.[17] Another reason for this paucity may be an understandable reluctance on the part of Aboriginal communities themselves to articulate to outsiders the precise contents of their customary laws. In 1992, John Borrows, a law professor of Anishinabe descent, DeLloyd Guth, now a colleague of mine who is settling into retirement from Robson Hall, and Alfred Scow, who was the first Aboriginal judge of British Columbia and a member of the Kwicksutaineukn First Nation, joined together in an effort at primary research. They travelled to meet with the Kwakiutl people of Kingcombe Inlet and the Okanagan people of Upper Nicola, in an effort to learn about Aboriginal customary law on a grant from the attorney general of British Columbia. All three men were warmly greeted by the First Nations people at a social level. They hit an insurmountable wall of polite reticence when they were ready with their questions in order to ascertain the contents

222 Aboriginal Justice and the Charter

of customary law. The First Nations people in question were reluctant to reveal the details of their customary laws for representation to the outside world.

If Aboriginal peoples want to use methods of preventing power abuses that have a basis in their cultural past, with no reference to Canadian rights standards, there is perhaps an onus on Aboriginal peoples themselves to communicate what those methods are and how they can work meaningfully in contemporary social settings where inequities of wealth and political power are pervasive. Reticence, while understandable, may perhaps not be such a good thing when the issue of reviving customary law for contemporary use is often itself a divisive issue among Aboriginal peoples, as is the issue of what role the Charter should have or should not have in Aboriginal governance. There was one thing that the Aboriginal women of Kingcombe Inlet and Upper Nicola were not at all reticent about. They made it clear to Borrows, Guth, and Scow that they wanted the Charter to continue to apply to Aboriginal governance, as a source of legal protection for themselves and their children.[18] If traditionalists in Aboriginal communities want to revive past laws and practices for contemporary use, there will by necessity have to be a dialogue with other members of the community who may be fearful of what will happen if there is no possibility of redress under the Charter.

There is another concern. There may indeed be aspects of Aboriginal customary law that act as checks and balances on the abuse of collective power. The contemporary interpretations of Navajo legal concepts and the willingness to take an accused man at his word as part of a truth-speaking tradition are examples of these limitations. Such limitations may not be true of all Aboriginal customary laws though. If past customary law is recoverable, there is also the possibility that not all of those laws are necessarily conducive to realizing a workable balance to the tension between the collective good and individual freedom in contemporary communities. Some customary laws, hypothetically speaking, may become tools of tyranny and power abuse if Aboriginal elites draw upon them as justifications for abusing their power based on the "collective good." Bruce Miller warns that "traditional law" is itself a resource that can be tapped into during struggles for political power in Aboriginal communities.[19] The concern here is that community factions may engage in selective and editorial representations of tradition to justify their pursuit and exercise of power. The recovery of customary law as an alternative method of reaching a balance between the collective good and individual freedom that has no reference to the Charter will not itself be without challenges and dangers of which Aboriginal communities would have to be mindful. Perhaps, and I am suggesting this idea very tentatively, it may be necessary to have some degree of formal protection in place, even if they resemble Canadian legal practices to some degree, in order to mitigate against this possibility.

The proposals that are offered in this book, besides being designed to maximize the room for community law to operate while leaving in place formal safeguards as fail-safes only after power abuses occur, are at the end of the day simply meant to get the ball rolling. If Aboriginal communities can recover their own customary laws and adapt those laws in a way that reaches a balance that is acceptable to the communities on their own terms, this would be a perfectly legitimate direction for the ball to roll in.

Notes

Foreword

1 Royal Commission on Aboriginal Peoples, *Bridging the Cultural Divide: A Report on Aboriginal People and Criminal Justice in Canada* (Ottawa: Minister of Supply and Services Canada, 1996).
2 *Constitution Act, 1982*, being Schedule B to the *Canada Act 1982*, (U.K.), 1982, c. 11.
3 *Canadian Charter of Rights and Freedoms*, Part 1 of the *Constitution Act, 1982*, being Schedule B to the *Canada Act 1982* (U.K.), 1982, c. 11.
4 *R. v Oakes*, [1986] 1 S.C.R. 103. *Dagenais v Canadian Broadcasting Corporation*, [1994] 3 S.C.R. 835 at 889.
5 Karl Llewellyn and Edward Adamson, *The Cheyenne Way: Conflict and Case Law in Primitive Jurisprudence* (Norman: University of Oklahoma Press, 1941).
6 Taiaiake Alfred, *Peace, Power, Righteousness* (London, UK: Oxford University Press, 2008); Thomas Flanagan, *First Nations, Second Thoughts* (Montreal and Kingston: McGill-Queen's University Press, 2000).

Chapter 1: Introduction

1 *Canadian Charter of Rights and Freedoms*, Part I of the *Constitution Act, 1982*, being Schedule B to the *Canada Act 1982*, (U.K.), 1982, c. 11.
2 Betty Ellen Unterberger, "Self-Determination" in Alexander Deconde (ed.), *American Encyclopedia of Foreign Policy* (2nd ed.) (New York: Schribner, 2002) 461 at 461.
3 *International Covenant on Economic, Social and Cultural Rights*, 16 December 1966, UN General Assembly Resolution 2200(XXI), Art. 1(1), 993 U.N.T.S. 3 (entered into force 3 January 1976).
4 *Declaration of the Rights of Indigenous Peoples*, UN General Assembly, 7 September 2007, Doc. A/61/L.67.
5 Taiaiake Alfred, *Peace, Power, Righteousness* (London, UK: Oxford University Press, 2008), and Jeff Corntassel, "Indigenous Governance amidst the Forced Federalism Era" (2009) 19:1 Kan. J.L. & Pub. Pol'y 47. Please note that both Alfred and Corntassel are members of the Indigenous Governance Program at the University of Victoria. Using the term "Indigenous" instead of "Aboriginal" is important to both scholars because, they argue, the former properly reflects the ideal of full nationhood while the latter implies submission to the colonial order. I do not intend offence by referring to either of them as Aboriginal. My intention is simply to maintain consistent terminology throughout the book.
6 Alan Cairns, *Citizens Plus: Aboriginal Peoples and the Canadian State* (Vancouver: UBC Press, 2000); Thomas Flanagan, *First Nations, Second Thoughts* (Montreal and Kingston: McGill-Queen's University Press, 2000).
7 Dale Turner, *This Is Not a Peace Pipe: Towards a Critical Indigenous Philosophy* (Toronto: University of Toronto Press, 2006); John Borrows, *Recovering Canada: The Resurgence of Indigenous Law* (Toronto: University of Toronto Press, 2002).

8   See, for example, Mary Ellen Turpel-Lafond and Patricia Monture-Angus, "Aboriginal Peoples and Canadian Criminal Law: Rethinking Justice," Special Edition on Aboriginal Justice (1992) 26 U.B.C. L. Rev. 239.

9   Michael Jackson, "Locking Up Natives in Canada" (1988-89) 23 U.B.C. L. Rev. 215; Carol LaPrairie, "Aboriginal Over-Representation in the Criminal Justice System: A Tale of Nine Cities" (2002) 44:2 Can. J. Crim. 181; Howard Sapers, *Annual Report of the Office of the Correctional Investigator 2005-2006* (Ottawa: Minister of Public Safety, 2006).

10 Samuel Perreault, *The Incarceration of Aboriginal People in Adult Correctional Services* (Ottawa: Statistics Canada, 2009) at 20.

11 *Ibid.* at 21.

12 *Aboriginal Peoples in Canada in 2006: Inuit, Metis, and First Nations, 2006 Census* (Ottawa: Statistics Canada, 2006) at 9.

13 Mary Ellen Turpel-Lafond, "Aboriginal Peoples and the Canadian Charter: Interpretive Monopolies, Cultural Differences" (1989-90) Can. H.R. Y.B. 2 at 41.

14 Royal Commission on Aboriginal Peoples, *Bridging the Cultural Divide: A Report on Aboriginal People and Criminal Justice in Canada* (Ottawa: Minister of Supply and Services Canada, 1996).

Chapter 2: Indigenous Aspirations for Justice

1   *R. v Wigglesworth*, [1987] 2 S.C.R. 541.

2   Mirko Bagaric and John Morss, "International Sentencing Law: In Search of a Justification and a Coherent Framework" (2006) 6:2 Int'l Crim. L. Rev. 191; Kevin M. Carlsmith, "The Roles of Retribution and Utility in Determining Punishment" (2006) 42:4 Journal of Experimental Social Psychology 437; Richard A. Bierschbach and Alex Stein, "Deterrence, Retributivism, and the Law of Evidence" (2007) 93:6 Va. L. Rev. 173; Kevin M. Carlsmith, "On Justifying Punishment: The Discrepancy between Words and Actions" (2008) 21:2 Social Justice Research 119; Matthew Haist, "Deterrence in a 'Sea of Just Deserts': Are Utilitarian Goals Achievable in a World of 'Limiting Retributivism'?" (2009) 99:3 J. Crim. L. & Criminology 789.

3   Theodore Blumoff, "Justifying Punishment" (2001) 14 C.J.L.S 161.

4   *Criminal Code*, R.S.C. 1985, c. C-46.

5   See, for example, Carol Hedderman, *Building on Sand: Why Expanding the Prison Estate Is Not the Way to "Secure the Future,"* Briefing 7 (Leicester, UK: Centre for Crime and Justice Studies, 2008); Sonja Snackens and Crystal Beyens, "Sentencing and Prison Overcrowding" (1994) 2:1 Eur. J. Crim. Pol'y & Research 84.

6   Geoffrey C. Hazard and Dana C. Remus, "Advocacy Revalued" (2011) 159:3 U. Penn. L. Rev. 751; Gerald Walpin, "America's Adversarial and Jury Systems: More Likely to Do Justice" (2003) 26:1 Harv. J.L. & Pub. Pol'y 176; Simon Brinott and Henry Mares, "The History and Theory of the Adversarial and Inquisitorial Systems of Law" (2004) 16:3 Legaldate 1 at 1-2.

7   Nils Christie, "Conflicts as a Property" (1977) 17:1 Brit. J. Crim. 1; Meredith Gibbs, "Using Restorative Justice to Resolve Historical Injustices of Indigenous Peoples" (2009) 12:1 Contemporary Justice Rev. 45.

8   Randy Barnett, "Restitution: A New Paradigm of Criminal Justice" (1977) 87 Ethics 279; Ralph Henman and Grazia Mannozzi, "Victim Participation and Sentencing in England and Italy: A Legal and Policy Analysis" (2003) 11:3 Eur. J. Crime, Crim. L. & Crim. J. 278; Albert Dzur and Susan Olson, "The Value of Community Participation in Restorative Justice" (2004) 35:1 J. Social Philosophy 91; Stephanos Bibas, "Transparency and Participation in Criminal Procedure" (2006) 81:3 N.Y.U. L. Rev. 911; Jonathan Doak, "Victims' Rights in Criminal Trials: Prospects for Rehabiliation" (2005) 32:2 J.L. & Soc'y 294.

9   Margarita Zernova, *Restorative Justice: Ideals and Realities* (Hampshire, UK: Ashgate Publishing, 2007) at 42-43; Marian Liebmann, *Restorative Justice: How It Works* (London: Jessica Kingsley Publishers, 2007) at 26. Dzur and Olson, *supra* note 8; Susan Sarnoff, "Restoring Justice to the Community: A Realistic Goal?" (2001) 65:1 Federal Probation 3.

10 Michael Coyle, "Traditional Indian Justice in Ontario: A Role for the Present?" (1986) 24 Osgoode Hall L.J. 605 at 618-24.

11 *Ibid.*

12 Robert Yazzie, "The Navajo Response to Crime," in Wanda D. McCaslin (ed.), *Justice as Healing: Indigenous Ways* (St. Paul, MN: Living Justice Press, 2005) 121.
13 Joan Ryan, *Doing Things the Right Way* (Calgary: University of Calgary Press, Arctic Institute of North America, 1995) at 33.
14 These societies lived in what is now Washington State. Brad Asher, *Beyond the Reservation: Indians, Settlers, and the Law in Washington Territory, 1853-1889* (Norman: University of Oklahoma Press, 1999) at 25-26.
15 Leslie Jane MacMillan, *Koqqwaja'ltimk: Mi'kmaq Legal Consciousness* (Ph.D. dissertation, Department of Anthropology, University of British Columbia, 2002) at 74.
16 Bruce Miller, *The Problem of Justice: Tradition and Law in the Coast Salish World* (Lincoln, NB: University of Nebraska Press, 2001) at 63-64.
17 Coyle, *supra* note 10 at 620-21.
18 Zenon Szablowinski, "Punitive Justice and Restorative Justice as Social Reconciliation" (2008) 49:3 Heythrop Journal 18; Gordon Bazemore, "Young People, Trouble and Crime: Restorative Justice as a Normative Theory of Informal Social Control and Social Support" (2001) 33:2 Youth and Society 199.
19 John Braithwaite and Stephen Mugford, "Conditions of Successful Reintegration Ceremonies: Dealing with Juvenile Offenders" (1994) 34 Brit. J. Crim 139. See also Nathan Harris, "Reintegrative Shame, Shaming, and Criminal Justice" (2006) 62:2 J. Social Issues 327; Nathan Harris, Lode Walgrave, and John Braithwaite, "Emotional Dynamics in Restorative Conferences" (2004) 8:2 Theor. Crim. 191.
20 Zernova, *supra* note 9 at 65-70; Liebmann, *supra* note 9 at 27; Loren Walker and Leslie A. Hayashi, "Pono Kaulike: A Hawaii Criminal Court Provides Restorative Justice Practices for Healing Relationships" (2007) 71:3 Federal Probation 18. Note that Tony Ward and Robyn Langland emphasize that restorative justice and offender rehabilitation are distinct concepts. There are some common goals and overlap, but restorative justice has objectives above and beyond those concerning an individual offender. See Tony Ward and Robyn Langlands, "Repairing the Rupture: Restorative Justice and the Rehabilitation of Offenders" (2009) 14:3 Aggression and Violent Behavior 205.
21 Jo-Anne Fiske and Betty Patrick, *Cis Dideen Kat: The Way of the Lake Babine Nation* (Vancouver: UBC Press, 2000) at 97-101.
22 David Cornwell, *Criminal Punishment and Restorative Justice: Past, Present and Future* (Winchester, UK: Waterside Press, 2006) at 61.
23 Frank D. Williams and Marilyn P. McShane, *Criminological Theory* (3rd edition) (Englewood Cliffs, NJ: Prentice Hall, 1999) at 16-18.
24 Raymond Paternoster, "How Much Do We Really Know about Criminal Deterrence" (2010) 100:3 J. Crim. L. & Criminology 765; Charles Tittle, Ekaterina Botchkovar, and Alena Antonaccio, "Criminal Contemplation, National Context and Deterrence" (2011) 27:2 J. Qualitative Criminology 225.
25 Michael L. Radelet and Traci L. Lacock, "Do Executions Lower Homicide Rates: The Views of Leading Criminologists" (2009) 99:2 J. Crim. L. & Criminology 489; Gary Kleck et al. "The Missing Link in General Deterrence Research" (2005) 43:3 Criminology 623.
26 Avinashi Singh Bati and Alex R. Piquero, "Estimating the Impact of Incarceration on Subsequent Offending Trajectories: Deterrent, Crimogenic, or Null Effect?" (2008) 98:1 Criminology 207; George Bridges and James A. Stone, "Effects of Criminal Punishment on Perceived Threat of Punishment: Toward an Understanding of Specific Deterrence" (1986) 23:3 J. Research in Crime & Delinquency 207; David Weisburd, Elin Waring, and Ellen Chayet, "Specific Deterrence in a Sample of Offenders Convicted of White Collar Crimes" (1995) 33:4 Criminology 587.
27 Justice E.D. Bayda, "The Theory and Practice of Sentencing: Are They on the Same Wavelength?" (1996) 60 Sask. L. Rev. 317; Shawn D. Bushway and Peter Reuter, "Deterrence, Economics, and the Context of Drug Markets" (2011) 10:1 Criminology & Pub. Pol'y 183; Thomas Baker and Alex R. Piquero, "Assessing the Perceived Benefits–Criminal Offending Relationship" (2010) 38:5 J. Crim. Justice 981.
28 Fiske and Patrick, *supra* note 21 at 193; Bradley R.E. Wright et al., "Does the Perceived Risk of Crime Deter Criminally Prone Individuals: Rational Choice, Self-Control and Crime"

(2004) 41:2 J. Research in Crime & Delinquency 180; Stephen W. Baron and Leslie W. Kennedy "Deterrence and Homeless Male Youths" (1998) 40:1 Can. J. Crim. 27; Daniel S. Nagin and Raymond Paternoster, "Personal Capital and Social Control: The Deterrence Implications of a Theory of Individual Differences in Criminal Offending" (1994) 32:4 Criminology 581.

29 Kimberly N. Varna and Anthony Doob, "Deterring Economic Crimes: The Case of Tax Evasion" (1998) 40:2 Can. J. Crim. 165.

30 Baker and Piquero, *supra* note 27.

31 Daniel O'Connel et al., "Decide Your Time: Testing Deterrence Theory's Certainty and Celerity Effects on Substance-Abusing Probationers" (2011) 39:3 J. Crim. Justice 261; John S. Goldkamp, "Optimistic Deterrence Theorizing" (2011) 10:1 Criminology & Pub. Pol'y 115; Cheryl Maxson, Kristy Matsuda, and Karen Hennigan, "'Deterrability' among Gang and Non-Gang Juvenile Offenders: Are Gang Members More (or Less) Deterrable Than Other Juvenile Offenders?" (2011) 57:4 Crime & Delinquency 516; Jonathan Shepherd, "Criminal Deterrence as a Public Health Strategy" (2001) 358:9294 Lancet 1717; Daniel Nagin and Greg Pogarsky, "Integrating Celerity, Impulsivity, and Extralegal Sanction Threats into a Model of Deterrence: Theory and Evidence" (2001) 39:4 Criminology 865.

32 Silvia Mendes, "Certainty, Severity, and Their Relative Deterrent Effects: Questioning the Role of Risk in Criminal Deterrence Theory" (2004) 32:1 Pol'y Studies J. 59.

33 Monica Barratt, "Cannabis Law Reform in Western Australia: An Opportunity to Test Theories of Marginal Deterrence and Legitimacy" (2005) 25:4 Drug & Alcohol Rev. 321.

34 Greg Pogarsky, Kim KiDeuk, and Ray Paternoster, "Perceptual Change in the National Youth Survey: Lessons for Deterrence Theory and Offender Decision-Making" (2005) 22:1 Justice Q. 1.

35 Douglas Marlowe et al., "Perceived Deterrence and Outcomes in Drug Courts" (2005) 23:2 Behav. Sci. & L. 183.

36 Greg Pogarsky, Alex Piquero, and Ray Paternoster, "Modeling Change in Perceptions about Sanction Threats: The Neglected Linkage in Deterrence Theory" (2004) 20:4 J. Quantitative Criminology 343; Shelly Keith Matthews and Robert Agnew, "Extending Deterrence Theory" (2008) 45:2 J. Research in Crime & Delinquency 91.

37 D. Alex Heckert and Edward Gondolf, "The Effect of Perceptions of Sanctions on Batterer Program Outcomes" (2000) 37:4 J. Research in Crime & Delinquency 369.

38 David Cayley, *The Expanding Prison: The Crisis in Crime and Punishment and the Search for Alternatives* (Toronto: House of Anansi Press, 1998) at 101-22.

39 Jose Cid, "Is Imprisonment Crimogenic? A Comparative Study of Imprisonment Rates between Prison and Suspended Sentence Sanctions" (2009) 6:6 Eur. J. Criminology 459.

40 Cassia Spohn, "The Deterrent Effect of Imprisonment and Offenders' Stake in Conformity" (2007) 18:1 Crim. Justice Pol'y 31.

41 Stuart A. Kinner and M.J. Milloy, "Collateral Consequences of an Ever Expanding Prison System" (2011) 183:5 C.M.A.J. 632 at 632.

42 Rupert Ross, *Returning to the Teachings: Exploring Aboriginal Justice* (Toronto: Penguin Books Canada, 1996) at 74.

43 *R. v Gingell* (1996), 50 C.R. (4th) 326 (Y. Terr. Ct.) at 342-43.

44 Mark Carter, "Of Fairness and Faulkner," Colloquy on "Empty Promises: Parliament, the Supreme Court, and the Sentencing of Aboriginal Offenders" (2002) 65 Sask. L. Rev. 63 at 65.

45 Robert DeFina and Lance Hannon, "For Incapacitation, There Is No Time Like the Present: The Lagged Effects of Prisoner Re-entry on Property and Violent Crime Rates" (2010) 39:6 Social Science Research 1004.

46 Fiske and Patrick, *supra* note 21 at 41.

47 George W. Knox, *The Problem of Gangs and Security Threat Groups in American Prisons Today: Recent Research Findings from the 2004 Prison Gang Survey* (Peotone, IL: National Gang Crime Research Center, 2004).

48 Jana Grekul and Patti Laboucane-Benson, "Aboriginal Gangs and Their (Dis)placement: Contextualizing Recruitment, Membership and Status" (2008) 50:1 Can. J. Crim. Justice 59; Mark Totten, "Aboriginal Youth and Violent Gang Involvement in Canada: Quality Prevention Strategies" (2009) 3 I.P.C. Rev. 135.

49 Criminal Intelligence Service of Canada, *2003 Annual Report on Organized Crime in Canada* (Ottawa: Criminal Intelligence Service Canada, 2003) at 5.
50 Totten, *supra* note 48 at 136.
51 *Ibid.* at 143.
52 Franklin E. Zimring and David T. Johnson, "Public Opinion and the Governance of Punishment in Democratic Political Systems" (2006) 605:1 Ann. Am. Acad. Pol. & Soc. Sci. 265; Julian V. Roberts and Loretta J. Stalans, *Public Opinion, Crime and Criminal Justice* (Boulder, CO: Westview Press, 2006).
53 Cayley, *supra* note 38 at 32-35.
54 *Ibid.* at 23-26; See also Marie Gottschalk, "The World's Warden: Crime, Politics and Punishment in the United States" (2008) 55:4 Dissent 58; Kevin B. Smith, "The Politics of Punishment: Evaluating Political Explanations of Incarceration Rates" (2004) 66:3 J. Politics 925.
55 *Ibid.* at 3 and 98. See also David Garland, *The Culture of Control: Crime and Social Order in Contemporary Society* (Oxford: Oxford University Press, 2001).
56 Bayda, *supra* note 27 at 326.
57 Cindy Sousa et al., "Longitudinal Study on the Effects of Child Abuse and Childrens' Exposure to Domestic Violence, Parent-Child Attachments, and Antisocial Behavior in Adolescence" (2011) 12:2 Asia Pacific J. Anthropology 146; Emily Salisbury, Kris Henning, and Robert Holdford, "Fathering by Partner-Abusive Men: Attitudes on Children's Exposure to Interparental Conflict and Risk Factors for Child Abuse" (2009) 14:3 Child Maltreatment 232; Carolyn A. Smith, Timothy O. Ireland, and Terrence B. Thornberry, "Adolescent Maltreatment and Its Impact on Young Antisocial Behavior" (2005) 29:10 Child Abuse & Neglect 1099; Richard A. Van Dorn and James Herbert Williams, "Correlates Associated with Escalation of Delinquent Behavior in Incarcerated Youths" (2003) 48:4 Social Work 523.
58 Jennifer Wareham, Denise Paquette Boots, and Jorge M. Chavez, "A Test of Social Learning and Intergenerational Transmission among Batterers" (2009) 37:2 J. Crim. Justice 163; Patrick Lussier, David P. Farrington, and Terrie E. Moffitt "The Abusive Man? A Forty-Year Propsective Longtitudinal Study of the Development Antecedents of Intimate Partner Violence" (2009) 47:3 Criminology 741.
59 Amy R. Murrell, Karen A. Christoff, and Chris R. Henning, "Characteristics of Domestic Violence Offenders: Associations with Childhood Exposure to Violence" (2007) 22 J. Family Violence 523.
60 Dannia Sutherland, Cecilia E. Casaneuva, and Heather Ringeisen, "Young Adult Incomes and Mental Health Problems among Transition Age Youth Investigated for Maltreatment during Adolescence" (2009) 31:9 Child & Youth Services Rev. 947; Katerina Maniadaki and Efthymios Kakouros, "Social and Mental Health Profiles of Young Male Offenders in Detention in Greece" (2008) 18 Crim. Behavior & Mental Health 207.
61 Some of the most recent ones include Marc Hooghe et al., "Unemployment, Inequality, Poverty and Crime: Spatial Distribution Patterns of Criminal Acts in Belgium, 2001-06" (2011) 51:1 Brit. J. Crim. 1; Kaaryn Gustafson, "The Criminalization of Poverty" (2009) 99:3 J. Crim. L. & Criminology 643; Ricardo Sabates, "Educational Attainment and Juvenile Crime: Area-Level Evidence Using Three Cohorts of Young People" (2008) 48 Brit. J. Crim. 395; Scott Atkins, "Racial Segregation, Concentrated Disadvantage, and Violent Crime" (2009) 7 J. Ethnicity in Crim. Justice 30; Patricia F. Case, "The Relationship of Race and Criminal Behavior: Challenging Cultural Explanations for a Structural Problem" (2008) 34 Critical Sociology 213.
62 Some of the most recent studies on this include David E. Eitle, Stewart J. D'Alessio, and Lisa Stolzenberg, "Economic Segregation, Race, and Homicide" (2006) 87:3 Social Sci. Q. 638; Jessenia M. Pizarro and Jean Marie McGloin, "Explaining Gang Homicides in Newark, New Jersey: Collective Behavior or Social Disorganization?" (2006) 34:2 J. Crim. Justice 195; William Alex Pridemore, "A Methodological Addition to the Cross-National Empirical Literature on Social Structure and Homicide: A First Test of the Povery-Homicide Thesis" (2008) 46:1 Criminology 133.
63 Richard Spano, Joshua D. Frielich, and John Bolland, "Gang Membership, Gun Carrying, and Employment: Applying Routine Activities Theory to Explain Violent Victimization among Inner City, Minority Youth Living in Extreme Poverty" (2008) 25:2 Justice Q. 381.

64 Sabates, *supra* note 61.
65 James S. Vacca, "Crime Can Be Prevented If Schools Teach Juvenile Offenders to Read" (2008) 30:9 Children & Youth Services Rev. 1055.
66 Shelby A.D. Moore, "Understanding the Connection between Domestic Violence, Crime, and Poverty: How Welfare Reform May Keep Battered Women from Leaving Abusive Relationships" (2003) 12 Texas J. Women & Law 451; Diane M. Purvin, "Weaving a Tangled Safety Net: The Intergenerational Legacy of Domestic Violence and Poverty" (2003) 9 Violence against Women 1263.
67 Steve Sussman et al., "Prediction of Violence Perpetration among High-Risk Youth" (2004) 28:2 Am. J. Health Behavior 134.
68 Emma Barrett, Katherine A. Mills, and Maree Teeson, "Hurt People Who Hurt People: Violence amongst Individuals with Comorbid Substance Abuse Disorder and Post-Traumatic Stress Disorder" (2011) 36:7 Addictive Behaviors 721.
69 Elizabeth Reed et al., "Experiences of Racial Discrimination and Relation to Violence Perpetration and Gang Involvement among a Sample of Urban African American Men" (2010) 12:3 J. Immigrant & Minority Health 319; Preeti Chauhan, N. Dickon Reppucci, and Eric N. Turkmeier, "Racial Differences in the Associations of Neighbourhood Disadvantage, Exposure to Violence, and Criminal Recidivism among Female Juvenile Offenders" (2009) 27:4 Behav. Sci. & L. 351.
70 Carter Hay et al., "The Impact of Community Disadvantage on the Relationship between the Family and Crime" (2006) 43 Juvenile Crime & Delinquency 326.
71 Preeti Chauhan and N. Dickson Reppucci, "The Impact of Neighbourhood Disadvantage and Exposure to Violence on Self-Report of Antisocial Behavior among Girls in the Juvenile Justice System" (2009) 38 J. Youth & Adolescence 401; Richard Spano, Craig Rivera, and John Bolland, "The Impact of Timing of Exposure to Violence on Violent Behavior in a High Poverty Sample of Inner City African American Youth" (2006) 35 J. Youth & Adolescence 681.
72 Alison Ritters and Jennifer Chalmers, "The Relationship between Economic Conditions and Substance Abuse and Harms" (2011) 30:1 Drug & Alcohol Rev. 1.
73 Although Canada did not fight wars against its Aboriginal peoples as often as the United States, they did use military subjugation on occasion. A particularly notorious example was the defeat of the Rebellion of 1885 involving Métis and Cree groups. See Olive Patricia Dickason, *A Concise History of Canada's First Nations* (Don Mills, ON: Oxford University Press, 2006) at 234-47; J.R. Miller, *Skyscrapers Hide the Heavens: A History of Indian-White Relations in Canada* (Toronto: University of Toronto Press, 2000) at 202-11.
74 For a historical overview of the numbered treaties in the western provinces, see Miller, *supra* note 73 at 216-24; Dickason, *supra* note 73 at 173-87.
75 Miller, *supra* note 73 at 260-63; Dickason, *supra* note 73 at 184, 224.
76 Miller, *supra* note 73 at 135-36, 340-41; Dickason, *supra* note 73 at 227-29.
77 Dawn Smith, Colleen Varcoe, and Nancy Edwards, "Turning around the Intergenerational Impact of Residential Schools on Aboriginal People: Implications for Health Policy and Practice" (2005) 37:4 Can. J. Nursing Research 38.
78 Joan Kendall, "Circles of Disadvantage: Aboriginal Poverty and Underdevelopment in Canada" (2001) 31:1-2 Am. Rev. Can. Stud. 43.
79 Annie K. Yessine and James Bonta, "The Offending Trajectories of Youthful Aboriginal Offenders" (2009) 51:4 Can. J. Crim. 435.
80 James Waldram, *The Way of the Pipe* (Peterborough, ON: Broadview Press, 1997) at 44.
81 Denis C. Bracken, Lawrence Deane, and Larry Morrissette, "Desistance and Social Marginalization: The Case of Canadian Aboriginal Offenders" (2009) 13:1 Theoretical Criminology 61.
82 Barry Stuart, *Building Community Justice Partnerships: Community Peacemaking Circles* (Ottawa: Department of Justice, Canada, 1997) at 8 and 13; Ross, *supra* note 42 at 44-51.
83 Daniel Kwochka, "Aboriginal Injustice: Making Room for a Restorative Paradigm" (1996) 60 Saskatchewan L. Rev. 153 at 159. See also Moana Jackson, *The Maori and the Criminal Justice System, He Whaipaanga Hou: A New Perspective*, Part 2 (Auckland, New Zealand: New Zealand Department of Justice, 1988) at 36-44; Juan Tauri and Allison Morris, "Re-forming Justice: The Potential of Maori Processes" (1997) 30:2 Austl. Crim. & N.Z. J. 149.

84   There is significant literature, both in Aboriginal and non-Aboriginal contexts, that stresses the healing function of restorative justice for offenders, victims, and other participants. See, for example, Jarem Sawatsky, *The Ethic of Traditional Communities and the Spirit of Healing Justice: Studies from Hollow Water, the Iona Community, and Plum Village* (Philadelphia, PA: Jessica Kingsley Publishers, 2009); Douglas E. Knoll and Linda Harvey, "Restorative Mediation: The Application of Restorative Justice Practice and Philosophy to Clergy Sexual Abuse Cases" (2008) 17:3-4 J. Child Sexual Abuse 377; Barbara Gray and Pat Lauderdale, "The Great Circle of Justice: North American Indigenous and Contemporary Justice Programs" (2007) 10:2 Contemporary Justice Rev. 215; Philip Lane, "Mapping the Healing Journey: First Nations Research Project on Healing in Canadian Aboriginal Communities" in Wanda D. McCaslin (ed.) *Justice as Healing: Indigenous Ways* (St. Paul, MN: Living Justice Press, 2005) 369; Suzanne Goren, "Healing the Victim, the Young Offender, and the Community via Restorative Justice: An International Perspective" (2001) 22 Issues in Mental Health Nursing 137.

85   Mark S. Umbreit, Robert B. Coates, and Betty Vos, "Restorative Justice Dialogue: A Multi-Dimensional, Evidence-Based Practice Theory" (2007) 10:1 Contemporary Justice Rev. 23; John S. Ryals, Jr., "Restorative Justice: New Horizons in Juvenile Offender Counseling" (2004) J. Addictions & Offender Counseling 18.

86   Cayley, *supra* note 38 at 219-20. See also Daniel Johnson, "From Destruction to Reconciliation: The Potential of Restorative Justice" (2004) 23:1-2 J. Religion & Spirituality in Social Work 83; Mark S. Umbreit, Robert B. Coates, and Betty Vos, "Restorative Justice Circles: An Exploratory Study" (2003) 6:3 Contemporary Justice Rev. 265.

87   Heather Strang, *Repair or Revenge? Victims and Restorative Justice* (Oxford: Clarendon Press, 2002); Katherine van Wormer, "Restorative Justice: A Model for Personal and Societal Empowerment" (2004) 23:4 J. Religion & Spirituality in Social Work 103.

88   Ross, *supra* note 42 at 20.

89   *Ibid.* at 202.

90   Cayley, *supra* note 38 at 219.

91   *Ibid.* at 219-20 and 290; Jennifer Kitty, "Gendering Violence, Remorse, and the Role of Restorative Justice: Deconstructing Public Perceptions of Kelly Ellard and Warren Glotawski" (2010) 13:2 Contemporary Justice Rev. 155; Leonard Dagny, "When Offenders and Victims Sit Down and Talk" (2010) 20:9 C.Q. Researcher 206.

92   Ross, *supra* note 42 at 263 and 265-66.

93   Barbara Gray-Kanatiiosh and Pat Lauderdale, "The Web of Justice: Restorative Justice Has Presented Only Part of the Story" (2006) 21:1 Wicazo Sa Rev. 29 at 32; Richard Gosse, "Charting the Course for Aboriginal Justice Reform through Aboriginal Self-Government" in Richard Gosse, James Youngblood Henderson, and Roger Carter (eds.), *Continuing Poundmaker and Riel's Quest: Presentations Made at a Conference on Aboriginal Peoples and Justice* (Saskatoon: Purich Publishing, 1994) 1; A.C. Hamilton and C.M. Sinclair, *Report of the Inquiry into the Administration of Justice and Aboriginal People* (Winnipeg: Government of Manitoba, Public Inquiry into the Administration of Justice and Aboriginal People, 1991) at 22. See also Robert Porter, "Strengthening Tribal Sovereignty through Peacemaking: How the Anglo-American Legal Tradition Destroys Indigenous Societies" (1996-97) 28 Colum. H.R.L. Rev. 235 at 278-80.

94   William Nugent et al., "Participation in Victim-Offender Mediation and Reoffense: Successful Replication?" (2001) 11:1 Research on Social Work Practice 5.

95   Kimberly de Beus and Nancy Rodriguez, "Restorative Justice Practice: An Examination of Program Completion and Recidivism" (2007) 35:3 J. Crim. Justice 337.

96   Lawrence Sherman, Heather Strang, and Daniel Woods, *Recidivism Patterns in the Canberra Reintegrative Shaming Experiments* (Canberra, Australia: Reintegrative Shaming Experiments, 2000) [unpublished].

97   Jeff Latimer, Craig Dowden, and Danielle Muise, *The Effectiveness of Restorative Justice Programs: A Meta-Analysis* (Ottawa: Department of Justice, Research and Statistics Division, 2001); Lawrence Sherman and Heather Strang, *Restorative Justice: The Evidence* (London: Smith Institute, 2009); William Bradshaw, David Roseborough, and Mark S. Umbreit, "The Effect of Victim-Offender Mediation on Juvenile Offender Recidivism: A Meta-Analysis" (2006) 24:1 Conflict Resolution Q. 87.

98 Tanya Rugge, James Bonta, and Suzanne Wallace-Capretta, *Evaluation of the Collaborative Justice Project: A Restorative Justice Program for Serious Crime, 2002-2005* (Ottawa: Public Safety and Emergency Preparedness Canada, 2005).

99 Kathleen Daly, "Restorative Justice and Sexual Offences: An Archival Study of Court and Conference Cases" (2006) 46 Brit. J. Crim. 334.

100 Alan R. Clough, Kylie Kim San Lee, and Katherine M. Conigrave, "Promising Performance of a Juvenile Justice Diversion Programme in Remote Aboriginal Communities, Northern Territories, Australia" (2008) 27 Drug & Alcohol Rev. 433.

101 Ross, *supra* note 42 at 36.

102 J. Couture et al., *A Cost-Benefit Analysis of Hollow Water's Community Holistic Circle Healing Process* (Ottawa: Ministry of the Solicitor General, 2001).

103 Ira Bansen, "Doing the Crime and Doing the Time," *CBC Reality Check Team* (5 January 2006).

104 Prison Justice Day Committee, *Behind Bars in Canada: The Costs of Incarceration* (Vancouver: Prison Justice Day Committee, 2008).

105 Rob White, "Community Corrections in Criminal Justice" (2004) 16:1 Current Issues in Criminal Justice 42 at 47.

106 "Bill Doesn't Reflect Crime Rate Drop," *Kitchener-Waterloo Record* (26 July 2010) at A6.

107 Judge F.M.W. McElrea, "Restorative Justice: The New Zealand Youth Court – A Model for Development in Other Courts?" (1994) 4 J. Judicial Administration 36 at 53.

108 Mandeep K. Dhami and Penny Joy, "Challenges to Establishing Volunteer-Run, Community-Based Restorative Justice Programs" (2007) 10:1 Contemporary Justice Rev. 9 at 19.

109 *Ibid.* at 19.

110 Mary Ellen Turpel-Lafond and Patricia Monture-Angus, "Aboriginal Peoples and Canadian Criminal Law: Rethinking Justice," Special Edition on Aboriginal Justice (1992) 26 U.B.C. L. Rev. 239 at 248.

111 Coyle, *supra* note 10 at 616 for the Iroquois, and 624 for the Cree and Anishinabe. For the Dene and Inuit, refer to Margaret Carswell, "Social Controls among the Native Peoples of the Northwest Territories in the Pre-Contact Period" (1984) 22 Alta. L. Rev. 303 at 307.

112 Ryan, *supra* note 13 at 57-58.

113 Karl Llewellyn and Edward Adamson, *The Cheyenne Way: Conflict and Case Law in Primitive Jurisprudence* (Norman, OK: University of Oklahoma Press, 1941) at 132-68.

114 Coyle, *supra* note 10 at 619-20 and 622.

115 Kathleen Du Vaal, "Cross-Cultural Crime and Osage Justice in the Western Mississipi Valley, 1700-1826" (2007) 54:4 Ethnohistory 697.

116 *Ibid.* at 618-19.

117 *Ibid.* at 618.

118 Kalervo Oberg, "Crime and Punishment in Tlingit Society" (1934) 36:2 Am. Anthropologist 145.

119 Llewellyn and Adamson, *supra* note 113 at 123.

120 *Ibid.* at 168-172.

121 W.J. Hoffman, "Curious Aboriginal Customs" (1879) 13:1 American Naturalist 6.

122 Asher, *supra* note 14 at 26-27.

123 *Ibid.* at 29.

124 Steve M. Karr, "Now We Have Forgotten the Old Indian Law: Choctaw Culture and the Evolution of Corporal Punishment" (1998-99) 23 Am. Indian L. Rev. 409.

125 Ryan, *supra* note 13 at 33.

126 Coyle, *supra* note 10 at 624; For the Stó:lo, public shaming before the village also had a deterrent emphasis, see Miller, *supra* note 73 at 152.

127 Michael Cousins, "Aboriginal Justice: A Haudenosaunee Approach" in Wanda D. McCaslin (ed.), *Justice as Healing: Indigenous Ways* (St. Paul, MA: Living Justice Press, 2005) 141 at 150-51.

128 Australian Law Reform Commission, *The Recognition of Aboriginal Customary Laws*, Report no. 31, vol. 2 (Canberra, Australia: Australian Government Publishing Service, 1986) at 27-28.

129 *Canadian Charter of Rights and Freedoms,* Part 1 of the *Constitution Act, 1982,* being Schedule B to the *Canada Act 1982* (U.K.), 1982, c. 11.

130　Christopher Bennett, *The Apology Ritual* (Cambridge: Cambridge University Press, 2008).
131　Kathleen Daly, "Revisiting the Relationship between Retributive and Restorative Justice" in Heather Strang and John Braithwaite (eds.), *Restorative Justice: Philosophy to Practice* (Dartmouth, UK: Ashgate, 2000) 33; Declan Roche, *Accountability in Restorative Justice* (Oxford: Oxford University Press, 2003) at 174-77; Mark Lokanan, "An Open Model for Restorative Justice: Is There Room for Punishment?" (2009) 12:3 Contemporary Justice Rev. 289; Kent Roach, "Changing Punishment at the Turn of the Century: Restorative Justice on the Rise" (2000) 42 Can. J. Crim. 239; Dena M. Gromet and John M. Darley, "Punishment and Beyond: Achieving Justice through the Satisfaction of Multiple Goals" (2009) 43:1 L. & Soc'y Rev. 1.
132　*Ibid.* at 35 and 40.
133　Ross D. London, "The Restoration of Trust: Bringing Restorative Justice from the Margins to the Mainstream" (2003) 16:3 Criminal Justice Studies 175; Sherman and Strang, *supra* note 97 at 82-83.
134　Roach, *supra* note 131 at 271.
135　Kwochka, *supra* note 83 at 184. Ian Edwards notes that restorative justice programs often have different and varying degrees of emphasis on victim participation. See Ian Edwards, "Victim Participation in Sentencing: The Problems of Incoherence" (2001) 40:1 How. L.J. 39.
136　Ross Gordon Green, "Aboriginal Community Sentencing and Mediation: Within and Without the Circle" (1997) 24 Man. L.J. 77 at 94-95.
137　Daly, *supra* note 131 at 48; John Braithwaite, "In Search of Restorative Jurisprudence" in Lode Walgrave, *Restorative Justice and the Law* (Devon, UK: Willan, 2002) 150; Ross, *supra* note 42 at 229.
138　Judge Heino Lilles, "Tribal Justice: A New Beginning" (Paper delivered to a conference entitled Achieving Justice: Today and Tomorrow, Whitehorse, Yukon, 3-7 September 1991) at 11-12 [unpublished].
139　Correctional Service Canada, http://www.csc-scc.gc.ca/text/pblct/rht-drt/05-eng.shtml.
140　John Huntsman, cited in Tim Poor, "Singapore Caning Brings Outpouring of Agreement Here," *Washington Post* (10 April 1994) at 1A.
141　*Ibid.*

Chapter 3: The Current Situation in Canada
1　*Indian Act*, S.C. 1985, c. I-5.
2　*Criminal Code*, R.S.C. 1985, c. C-46.
3　*R. v Gladue*, [1999] 1 S.C.R. 688 at para. 58-65.
4　*Ibid.* at para. 64.
5　*Ibid.* at para. 74.
6　*Ibid.* at para. 67.
7　*Ibid.* at para. 69.
8　*Ibid.* at para. 83-84.
9　*R. v Wells*, [2000] 1 S.C.R. 207 at para. 27-28, 44-50.
10　Robin J. Wilson, Bria Huculak, and Andrew McWhinnie, "Restorative Justice Innovations in Canada" (2002) 20 Behav. Sci. & L. 363.
11　Barry Stuart, *Building Community Justice Partnerships: Community Peacemaking Circles* (Ottawa: Department of Justice, Canada, 1997).
12　Canada, Aboriginal Corrections Policy Unit, *The Four Circles of Hollow Water*, Aboriginal Peoples Collection (Ottawa: Ministry of the Solicitor General, 1997).
13　Anne Harrison, Muriel Meric, and Alan Dickson, *Justice and Healing at Sheshatshit and Davis Inlet* (Ottawa: Peace Brigades International, 1995).
14　*R. v Morin* (1995), 134 Sask. R. 120 (C.A.).
15　*Ibid.* at para. 9.
16　For examples, see *R. v Morris* (2004), B.C.A.C. 235 [*Morris*]; *R. v H.R.* (1997), 205 A.R. 226 (Prov. Ct.); and *R. v Desnomie* (2005), Sask. R. (C.A.).
17　Note that this is often, but not always, the case. There are examples of programs where once a matter is diverted the offender remains accountable only to members of the Aboriginal community, while the Crown has no further role. See, for example, Ted Palys and Winona

Victor, "'Getting to a Better Place': Qwi:Qwelstom, the Sto:lo, and Self-Determination" in Law Commission of Canada (ed.), *Indigenous Legal Traditions* (Vancouver: UBC Press, 2007) 12.

18 *Aboriginal Justice Strategy Summative Evaluation: Final Report* (Ottawa: Department of Canada, Evaluation Division, 2007).

19 Karen Whannock, *Aboriginal Courts in Canada* (Vancouver: Scow Institute, 2008) at 12-14.

20 Karen Whannock, "A Tale of Two Courts: The New Westminister First Nations Court and the Colville Tribal Court" (2011) 44 U.B.C. L. Rev. 99.

21 *Research Framework for a Review of Community Justice in Yukon: Community Justice – Peacemaker Diversion Project* (Whitehorse, YT: Department of Justice, 2003).

22 *Ibid.* at 21.

23 Gladue (Aboriginal Persons) Court, online: Aboriginal Legal Services of Toronto, http://www.aboriginallegal.ca/gladue.php.

24 Aboriginal Legal Services of Toronto's Community Council Program, online: Aboriginal Legal Services of Toronto, http://aboriginallegal.ca/docs/outline.htm.

25 Norma Large, "Healing Justice: The Tsuu T'ina First Nation's Peacemaker Court Throws Out Punitive Justice and Restores the Ancient Tradition of ... Talking," *Alberta Views* (May/June 2001) 20; Marian E. Bryant, "Tsuu T'ina First Nations: Peacemaker Justice System," *Law Now* (February/March 2002) 14. Since Mandamin's appointment to the Federal Court in 2007, there has not been any public announcement for a judge to replace him.

26 *Criminal Code, supra* note 2 at s. 743.1.

27 Carole LaPrairie, *Examining Aboriginal Corrections in Canada* (Ottawa: Aboriginal Corrections, Ministry of the Solicitor General, 1996) at 80-83.

28 *Corrections and Conditional Release Act,* S.C. 1992, c. 20.

29 Howard Sapers, *Annual Report of the Office of the Correctional Investigator 2005-2006* (Ottawa: Minister of Public Safety, 2006) at 84-85.

30 *Ibid.* at 83.

31 John Howard Society of Alberta, *Halfway House: Executive Summary* (Edmonton: John Howard Society of Alberta, 2001).

32 LaPrairie, *supra* note 27 at 85-86.

33 Ross Gordon Green, "Aboriginal Community Sentencing and Mediation: Within and Without the Circle" (1997) 24 Man. L.J. 77 at 119-20. For two examples, see *Morris, supra* note 16; *R. v Cappo,* [2005] S.J. no. 720 (C.A.).

34 *Constitution Act, 1982,* being Schedule B to the *Canada Act 1982,* (U.K.), 1982, c. 11.

35 *R. v Van der Peet,* [1996] 2 S.C.R. 507 at para. 53 [*Van der Peet*].

36 *Ibid.* at paras. 46, 52, and 69.

37 *R. v Pamajewon,* [1996] 2 S.C.R. 821 at para. 27 [*Pamajewon*].

38 *Ibid.* at para. 69.

39 *R. v Sappier; R. v Gray,* [2006] 2 S.C.R. 686 at para. 26 [*Sappier*].

40 *Ibid.* at para. 60-61.

41 *R. v Powley,* [2003] 2 S.C.R. 207.

42 *Ibid.* at para. 55.

43 *Ibid.* at para. 73.

44 *Ibid.* at para. 49.

45 *Ibid.* at para. 62.

46 *Ibid.* at para. 71. Lamer C.J.C. quoted the Oxford dictionary for the meaning of distinctive.

47 *Van der Peet, supra* note 35 at para. 46.

48 *Sappier, supra* note 39 at para. 40.

49 *Ibid.* at para. 41.

50 *Ibid.* at para. 45.

51 *Ibid.* at para. 64.

52 *R. v Sparrow,* [1990] 1 S.C.R. 1075 at 1091-93 [*Sparrow*].

53 *Mitchell v Canada (Minister of National Revenue),* [2001] 1 S.C.R. 911 at para. 63; *Pamajewon, supra* note 37.

54   Russell Lawrence Barsh and Sákéj Henderson, "The Supreme Court's *Van der Peet* Trilogy: Naïve Imperialism and Ropes of Sand" (1997) 42 McGill L.J. 993 at 1000-1.
55   *Canadian Charter of Rights and Freedoms,* Part 1 of the *Constitution Act, 1982,* being Schedule B to the *Canada Act 1982* (U.K.), 1982, c. 11.
56   *Sparrow, supra* note 52 at 1109.
57   *Ibid.* at 1112.
58   *R. v Gladstone,* [1996] 2 S.C.R. 723 at para. 43 [*Gladstone*].
59   *Sparrow, supra* note 52 at 1112.
60   *Ibid.* at 1113.
61   *Gladstone, supra* note 58 at para. 72.
62   *Ibid.* at para. 75.
63   *Delgamuukw v British Columbia,* [1997] 3 S.C.R. 1010 at para. 165 [*Delgamuukw*].
64   *Guerin v The Queen,* [1984] 2 S.C.R. 335.
65   In *Guerin, supra* note 64 at 365, 375-76, the fiduciary obligation arose in the context of negotiating a lease of reserve land on behalf of the band.
66   *Sparrow, supra* note 52 at 1114.
67   *Ibid.* at 1119.
68   Matthias R.J. Leonardy, *First Nations Criminal Jurisdiction in Canada* (Saskatoon: Native Law Centre, University of Saskatchewan, 1998) at 184-85.
69   *R. v Sioui,*[1990] 3 C.N.L.R. 127 at 152 [*Sioui*].
70   *Ibid.* at 135.
71   *R. v Simon,* [1985] 2 S.C.R. 387 at 402 [*Simon*].
72   *Sioui, supra* note 69 at 134. *R. v Horseman,* [1990] 3 C.N.L.R. 95 at 102 (S.C.C.) [*Horseman*].
73   *Jones v Meehan,* 175 U.S. 1 (1899); cited in *R. v Nowegijick,* [1983] 1 S.C.R. 29 and in *R. v Simon, supra* note 71 at 402.
74   *Simon, supra* note 71 at 402.
75   *Ibid.* at 403.
76   *R. v Badger,* [1996] 1 S.C.R. 771 at para. 45 [*Badger*].
77   Bruce H. Wildsmith, "Treaty Responsibilities: A Co-Relational Model," Special Edition on Aboriginal Justice (1992) U.B.C. L. Rev. 324 at 330-31.
78   *Horseman, supra* note 72 at 117.
79   *Sioui, supra* note 69 at 147.
80   *R. v Horse,* [1988] 1 S.C.R. 187 at 206.
81   Wildsmith, *supra* note 77 at 333-35; For a similar argument, see John Borrows, "Tracking Trajectories: Aboriginal Governance as an Aboriginal Right" (2005) 38 U.B.C. L. Rev. 285.
82   Wabanaki Compact, 1725, Article 6, in a letter, with enclosures, of Lt. Governor Dummer of New England to Duke of Newcastle, Secretary of States, Calendar of State Papers, Colonial Series (America and West Indies), vol. 35 (8 January 1726), UK Public Records Office, Colonial Office Papers, Series 5/898 at 173-74.
83   Sákéj Henderson, "Constitutional Powers and Treaty Rights" (2000) Sask. L. Rev. 719 at 723.
84   Gordon Christie, "Justifying Principles of Treaty Interpretation" (2000) 26 Queen's L.J. 143.
85   *R. v Marshall,* [1999] 3 S.C.R. 456 at para. 14 [*Marshall (no. 1)*].
86   *Ibid.* at para. 59.
87   Christie, *supra* note 84 at 186.
88   *Badger, supra* note 76 at para. 54.
89   *Ibid.* at para. 55.
90   John Borrows, "Domesticating Doctrines: Aboriginal Peoples after the Royal Commission" (2001) McGill L.J. 615 at 631-32.
91   *Badger, supra* note 76 at para. 74-82. Cory J. reasoned that as both inherent and treaty rights are included in section 35, a common approach to legislative infringement should be used for both types of rights.
92   Henderson, *supra* note 83 at 746-47.
93   *R. v Marshall,* [1999] 3 S.C.R. 533 at para. 37 [*Marshall (no. 2)*].
94   *Ibid.* at para. 39.
95   Henderson, *supra* note 83 at 743.
96   Borrows, *supra* note 90 at 624.

97 *Nisga'a Final Agreement* (Ottawa: Library of Parliament, 1999), Chapter 11, 165-79.
98 *Ibid.* at Chapter 12, s. 128.
99 *Act Relating to Self-Government for the Sechelt Indian Band,* S.C. 1986, c. 27.
100 *Tsawwassen First Nation Final Agreement Act,* Bill 40, 3rd Session, 38th Parliament, 2007, ss. 133-36.
101 *R. v Taylor and Williams* (1981), 34 O.R. (2d) 360 (C.A.).
102 Leonardy, *supra* note 68 at 113.
103 *Sparrow, supra* note 52 at 1003.
104 *Delgamuukw, supra* note 63 at para. 141.
105 *Haida Nation v British Columbia (Minister of Forests),* [2004] 3 S.C.R. 511 at paras. 20 and 25.
106 *Ibid.* at para. 17.
107 John Borrows, *Recovering Canada: The Resurgence of Indigenous Law* (Toronto: University of Toronto Press, 2002); Patricia Monture-Angus, *Journeying Forward: Dreaming First Nations' Independence* (Halifax: Fernwood Publishing, 1999); Gordon Christie, "A Colonial Reading of Recent Jurisprudence: *Sparrow, Delgamuukw,* and *Haida Nation*" (2005) 23 Windsor Y.B. Access Just. 17; Leena Heinamaki, "Inherent Rights of Aboriginal Peoples in Canada: Reflections of the Debate in National and International Law" (2006) 8 Int'l Community L. Rev. 155; Michael Asch and Patrick Macklem, "Aboriginal Rights and Canadian Sovereignty: An Essay on *R. v Sparrow*" (1991) 29:2 Alta. L. Rev. 517; D'arcy Vermette, "Colonialism and the Suppression of Aboriginal Voice" (2008-09) 40 Ottawa L. Rev. 225.
108 Catherine Bell, "New Directions in the Law of Indigenous Rights" (1998) 77 Can. Bar Rev. 36 at 65-66.
109 Quoted in Cristin Smitz, "SCC Wrong Forum for Native Land Claims: Bastarache" *Lawyers Weekly* (19 January 2001) 20:34.
110 *Delgamuukw, supra* note 63 at para. 207.
111 Bell, *supra* note 108 at 66; Jonathan Rudin, "One Step Forward, Two Steps Back: The Political and Institutional Dynamics behind the Supreme Court of Canada's Decisions in *R. v. Sparrow, R. v. Van der peet,* and *Delgamuukw*" (1998) 13 J.L. & Soc. Pol'y 67 at 85.
112 Examples include Law Reform Commission of Canada, *Studies on Diversion,* Working paper no. 7 (Ottawa: Law Reform Commission, 1975) at 23-24; Standing Committee on Justice and Solicitor General, House of Commons, *Report of the Standing Committee on Justice and Solicitor General on Its Review of Sentencing, Conditional Release and Related Aspects of Corrections, Taking Responsibility* (Ottawa: Solicitor General, 1988) at 75; Law Reform Commission of Australia, *The Recognition of Aboriginal Customary Laws,* Report no. 31, vol. 1 (Canberra, Australia: Australian Government Publishing Service, 1986) at 7.
113 Evelyn Zellerer and Chris Cunneen, "Restorative Justice, Indigenous Justice, and Human Rights" in Gordon Bezemore and Mara Schiff (eds.), *Restorative Community Justice: Repairing Harm and Transforming Communities* (Ottawa: Anderson Publishing, 2001) 245 at 253.
114 David Garland, *The Culture of Control: Crime and Social Order in Contemporary Society* (Oxford: Oxford University Press, 2001) at 142-43.
115 Andrew Ashworth and M. Hough in "Sentencing and the Climate of Opinion" (1996) Crim. L. Rev. 761 at 780-81.
116 Alberta Currie et al., *The 2007 National Justice Survey: Tackling Crime and Public Confidence* (Ottawa: Department of Justice Canada, 2007). See also Karin Stein, *Public Perception of Crime and Justice in Canada: A Review of Opinion Polls* (Ottawa: Department of Justice Canada, 2001).
117 David Paciocco, *Getting Away with Murder: The Canadian Criminal Justice System* (Toronto: Irwin Law, 1999) at 19-21.
118 *Ibid.* at 21.
119 "Cotler to Table Bills Inspired by Cadman," *Vancouver Sun* (28 September 2005) A1.
120 Jonathan Fowlie, "Liberals to Ramp Up War on Meth," *Vancouver Sun* (12 December 2005) A1.
121 "Harper Government's Abolition of Early Parole Act Receives Royal Assent: Criminals Convicted of White Collar Crimes Will No Longer Be Released from Prison after Serving Only One-Sixth of Their Sentence," *Marketwire* (24 March 2011).
122 Steven Chase, "Conservative Majority Would Hustle Crime Bills into Law All at Once: Harper Vows to Enact Omnibus Legislation within 100 Days of Taking Office," *Globe and Mail* (7 April 2011).

123 Julian V. Roberts and Loretta J. Stalans, "Restorative Sentencing: Exploring the Views of the Public" (2004) 17:3 Social Justice Research 315.

124 For a similar argument with regard to Australia, see Russell Hogg, "Penality and Modes of Regulating Indigenous Peoples in Australia" (2001) 3:3 Punishment & Society 355. A great deal of American literature makes similar arguments with respect to "tough on crime" and "war on drugs" policies as applied to Blacks and Latinos. For a couple of examples, see, for example, Paul Butler, "One Hundred Years of Race and Crime" (2010) 100:3 J. Criminal L. & Criminology 1043; Deborah Small, "The War on Drugs Is a War on Racial Justice" (2001) 68:3 Social Research 896; Garland, *supra* note 114 at 132.

125 Chris Andersen, "Governing Aboriginal Justice in Canada: Constructing Responsible Individuals and Communities through 'Tradition'" (1999) 31 Crime, Law and Social Change 303.

126 "Systemic Racism," *Ottawa Citizen* (1 May 1999) B5. In a subsequent editorial, the *Ottawa Citizen* demanded that "Parliament should repeal differential sentencing." "Badly Formed Sentences," *Ottawa Citizen* (5 April 2001) A14; "Sorry's Not Enough," *National Post* (28 June 1999) A19; "Crime, Time and Race," editorial, *Globe and Mail* (16 January 1999) D6; "Aboriginals Deserve Equal, Not Special, Treatment: Overplaying the Race Card Is in No One's Interest," *Globe and Mail* (29 April 1999) A12; Linda Williamson, "Different Strokes for Different Folks: This Is Social Engineering Disguised as Justice for All," *Toronto Star* (30 April 1999) 17; "A Messy Prescription for Native Offenders," *Globe and Mail* (12 August 2002) A12; Tanis Fiss, "Special Treatment Can't Right Wrongs to Aboriginals," *Guelph Mercury* (9 January 2004) A9.

127 Rachel Dioso and Anthony Doob, "An Analysis of Public Support for Special Consideration of Aboriginal Offenders at Sentencing" (2001) 43:3 Can. J. Crim. 405 at 409.

128 "Dad Guilty in Freezing Deaths to Be Sentenced: Saskatchewan Man's Punishment to Be Determined by Aboriginal Sentencing Circle" *Edmonton Sun* (8 January 2009) 7.

129 Chris Purdy, "Healing Won't Happen in Jail: Life of Spiritual Guidance Needed, Say Elders, but a Judge Will Get the Final Say," *Globe and Mail* (14 February 2009) A8.

130 Tim Cook, "Grieving Grandmother Calls for Change: Saskatchewan Reserve Where Young Sisters Froze to Death Needs Alcohol Ban, Counseling, She Says," *Globe and Mail* (4 February 2008) A7.

131 Purdy, *supra* note 129.

132 "Father of Two Girls Who Froze to Death Needs Treatment, Not Jail, Judge Hears," *CBC News* (13 February 2009).

133 Mindelle Jacobs, "Don't Impair Justice," *Ottawa Sun* (9 December 2008) 15. See also Rosie DiManno, "Jail Only Just Term in Freezing Deaths," *Toronto Star* (9 January 2009) A2; Lysiane Gagnon, "A Telling Take on Yellow Quill," *Globe and Mail* (22 June 2009) A15; Alex Kinsella, "Punishment Deserved," *Waterloo Region Accord* (20 February 2009) A8.

134 John Mohan, "Own Up and Bring Our Sanity Back," *Portage Daily Graphic* (15 April 2009) 4.

135 "Letters to the Editor Column," *Winnipeg Sun* (20 January 2009) 8.

136 Jennifer Graham, "Father of Frozen Girls Jailed, Judge Hands Man Prison Term Despite Sentencing Circle Decision," *Calgary Sun* (7 March 2009) 7.

137 Judge Morgan noted that because the offence can merit a term of life imprisonment, it, in turn, reflects the fact that the offence is a very serious one. See *R. v Pauchay*, [2009] 2 C.N.L.R. 314 (Sask. P.C.).

Chapter 4: Addressing the Tension

1 *Canadian Charter of Rights and Freedoms,* Part 1 of the *Constitution Act, 1982,* being Schedule B to the *Canada Act 1982* (U.K.), 1982, c. 11.

2 Pakel Mekka, "Collective Agents and Moral Responsibility" (2007) 38:3 J. Social Philosophy 456.

3 See, for example, C.B. McPherson, *The Political Theory of Possessive Individualism* (Oxford: Clarendon Press, 1962); John Locke, *Second Treatise of Government*, edited by Peter Laslett (Cambridge: Cambridge University Press, 1960).

4 Loren Lomasky, "Classical Liberalism and Civil Society" in Simone Chambers and Will Kymlicka (eds.), *Alternative Conceptions of Civil Society* (Princeton, NJ: Princeton University Press, 2002) 50 at 55.

5 Joan Ryan, *Doing Things the Right Way* (Calgary: University of Calgary Press, Arctic Institute of North America, 1995) at 33-34.
6 Gordon Christie, "Law, Theory, and Aboriginal Peoples" (2003) 2 Indigenous L.J. 67.
7 Quoted in Reuben G. Thwaites (ed.), *The Jesuit Relations and Allied Documents*, volume 43 (Cleveland, OH: Burrows Brothers, 1897) at 271.
8 Jo-Anne Fiske and Betty Patrick, *Cis Dideen Kat: The Way of the Lake Babine Nation* (Vancouver: UBC Press, 2000) at 60-61.
9 Steven Wall, "Collective Rights and Individual Autonomy" (2007) 117 Ethics 234 at 240-41.
10 Christie, *supra* note 6.
11 Mary Ellen Turpel-Lafond, "Aboriginal Peoples and the Canadian Charter: Interpretive Monopolies, Cultural Differences" (1989) Can. H.R. Y.B. 2 at 41.
12 Roger Gibbins, "Citizenship, Political, and Intergovernmental Problems with Indian Self-Government" in J. Rick Ponting (ed.), *Arduous Journey: Canadian Indians and Decolonization* (Toronto: McClelland and Stewart, 1986) 369 at 374-75.
13 Bruce G. Miller, "The Individual, the Collective, and the Tribal Code" (1997) 21:1 Am. Indian Culture & Research Journal 185; Robert B. Porter, "Strengthening Tribal Sovereignty through Peacemaking: How the Anglo-American Legal Tradition Destroys Indigenous Societies" (1996-7) 28 Colum. H.R.L. Rev. 235.
14 *Indian Act*, S.C. 1985, c. I-5.
15 Candis McLean, "A Spoon-Fed Mentality" (2002) 29:15 Newsmagazine 8.
16 Kevin Steel, "No Love for Indian Democracy" (1998) 25:36 Alberta Report 9.
17 *R. v Hunter* (1997), 52 Alta. L.R. (3d) 359 (Prov. Ct.).
18 *Ibid.* at 362-65. See also John Reilly, *A Judge's Struggle for Justice in a First Nations Community* (Calgary: Rocky Mountain Books, 2010); For other allegations of corruption, see Candis McLean, "Twenty-Dollar Bribes" (2002) 29:4 Newsmagazine 14; Paul Barnsley, "Author Reveals SIGA 'Mistakes'" (2001) 18:8 Windspeaker 3; Shafer Parker, Jr., "Self-Government or Gangsterism?" (1996) 23:27 Alberta Report 27; Robert Shepherd and Russell Diablo, "A Government-First Nations Dialogue on Accountability: Re-establishing Understanding on the Basics of a Complex Relationship" (2005) 15:2 Native Studies Rev. 61 at 62.
19 *Hunter, supra* note 17 at 363-65.
20 Herbert Packer, *The Limits of the Criminal Sanction* (Stanford, CA: Stanford University Press, 1968) at 153.
21 *Ibid.* at 158.
22 *Ibid.* at 62-70.
23 *Ibid.* at 158-60.
24 *Ibid.* at 164-65.
25 *Ibid.* at 165-66.
26 Sascha Domink-Bachmann, "Control Order Post-911 and Human Rights in the United Kingdom, Australia, and Canada: A Kafkaesque Dilemma?" (2010) 15:2 Deakin L. Rev. 131; Alan Fowler and Kasturi Sen, "Embedding the War on Terror: State and Civil Society Relations" (2010) 41:1 Development and Change 1; Christopher B. Banks, "Security and Freedom after September 11" (2010-11) 13:1 Public Integrity 5; Lucia Zedner, "Securing Liberty in the Face of Terror: Reflections from Criminal Justice" (2005) 32:4 J.L. & Soc'y 507.
27 For recent examples, see Arne F. Soldwedel, "Testing Japan's Convictions: The Lay Judge System and the Rights of Criminal Defendants" (2008) 41:5 Vand. J. Transnat'l. L. 1417; Hannah Quirk, "Identifying Miscarriages of Justice: Why Innocence in the UK Is Not the Answer" (2007) 70:5 Modern L. Rev. 759; W. James Annexstad, "The Detention and Prosecution of Insurgents and Other Non-Traditional Combatants: A Look at the Task Force 134 Process and the Future of Detainee Prosecutions" (2007) 410 Army L. 72.
28 Kent Roach, "Criminology: Four Models of the Criminal Process" (1999) 89 J. Crim. L. & Criminology 671 at 711.
29 *Ibid.* at 711.
30 Kathleen Daly, "Restorative Justice and Sexual Offences: An Archival Study of Court and Conference Cases" (2006) 46 Brit. J. Crim. 334.

31 Perhaps "social control" is a better term to use here than "crime control." Some literature argues that when restorative justice fulfils its objectives, it enhances social control of society, just not in quite the same way as the standard criminal justice system. See Barbara D. Warner, Elizabeth Back, and Mary L. Ohmer, "Linking Informal Social Control and Restorative Justice: Moving Social Disorganization Theory beyond Community Policing" (2010) 13:4 Contemporary Justice Rev. 355; Johannes Wheeldon, "Finding Common Ground: Restorative Justice and Its Theoretical Construction(s)" (2009) 12:1 Contemporary Justice Rev. 91; Gordon Bazemore, "Young People, Trouble, and Crime: Restorative Justice as a Normative Theory of Informal Social Control and Support" (2001) 33:2 Youth & Society 199.

32 Jonathan Rudin and Dan Russell, *Native Alternative Dispute Resolution Systems: The Canadian Future in Light of the American Past* (Mississauga, ON: Ontario Native Council on Justice, 1993) at 51.

33 Royal Commission on Aboriginal Peoples, *Bridging the Cultural Divide: A Report on Aboriginal People and Criminal Justice in Canada* (Ottawa: Minister of Supply and Services Canada, 1996) at 268. For a similar argument, see Thomas Isaac, "Canadian Charter of Rights and Freedoms: The Challenge of the Individual and Collective Rights of Aboriginal People" (2002) 21 Windsor Y.B. Access Just. 431 at 448.

34 "Saskatchewan's First Aboriginal Police Force Faces Questions of Conduct," *First Nations Drum* (September 2007) 23.

35 Douglas George-Kanentiio, *Iroquois Culture and Commentary* (Santa Fe, NM: Clear Light Publishers, 2000) at 23-25 and 98-99.

36 Note that I am not using the terms "different economics" and "different technologies" as synonymous with "advancement" or "progress." I am simply trying to make the point that the world is now much changed and that this situation presents challenges for making past teachings adaptable to contemporary circumstances.

37 Porter, *supra* note 13 at 78-79.

38 "How Flexible Should the Law Be against Criminal Corporate Executives?" 52:4 Beijing Rev. 46; Wolfgang Hetzer, "Corruption as Business Practice? Corporate Criminal Liability in the European Union" (2007) 15:3-4 Eur. J. Crime, Crim. L. & Crim. Justice 383.

39 José De Córdoba and David Luhnow, "Mexican Officials Allege Drug Cartel Infiltrated Attorney General's Office," *Wall Street Journal* (eastern edition) (28 October 2008) A8.

40 Serguei Cheloukhine and Joseph King, "Corruption Networks as a Sphere of Investment Activities in Modern Russia" (2007) 40:1 Communist & Post-Communist Studies 107.

41 "Trying Times for Taiwan's Judiciary," *Global Agenda* (31 January 2009) 10; "Blame the Judges" 49:16 Africa Confidential (1 August 2008) 6; "Berlusconi Fiddles, Italy Burns" 388: 5859 Economist (19 July 2008) 59.

42 Diane E. David, "Law Enforcement in Mexico City: Not Yet under Control" (2003) 37:2 N.A.C.L.A. Report on the Americas 17; Bohdan Harasymiw, "Policing, Democratization and Political Leadership in Postcommunist Ukraine" (2003) 36:2 Can. J. Pol. Sci. 319.

43 Lydia Polgreen, "Nigeria Reassigns Corruption Fighter, Motive Is Hazy," *New York Times* (29 December 2007) 3.

44 Theodore P. Gerber and Sarah E. Mendelson, "Public Experiences of Police Violence and Corruption in Contemporary Russia: A Case of Predatory Policing?" (2008) 42:1 L. & Soc'y Rev. 1; Mark Ungar, "Contested Battlefields: Policing in Caracas and La Paz" (2003) 37:2 N.A.C.L.A. Report on the Americas 30.

45 Patricia Monture-Angus, *Journeying Forward: Dreaming First Nations' Independence* (Halifax: Fernwood Publishing, 1999) at 35-36; Taiaiake Alfred, *Peace, Power, Righteousness* (London, UK: Oxford University Press, 2008).

Chapter 5: Realizing the Culturally Sensitive Interpretation of Legal Rights

1 *Constitution Act, 1982,* being Schedule B to the *Canada Act 1982* (U.K.), 1982, c. 11.

2 *Reference re Section 94(2) of the Motor Vehicle Act, B.C.,* [1985] 2 S.C.R. 486 at 503 [*Motor Vehicle Reference*].

3 *Canadian Charter of Rights and Freedoms,* Part 1 of the *Constitution Act, 1982,* being Schedule B to the *Canada Act 1982* (U.K.), 1982, c. 11.

4 Douglas Sanders, "The Rights of Aboriginal Peoples of Canada" (1983) 61 Can. Bar. Rev. 314 at 332; Kent McNeil, "The Constitutional Rights of the Aboriginal Peoples of Canada" (1982) 4 Sup. Ct. L. Rev. 255 at 262; Peter Hogg, *Constitutional Law of Canada* (2nd edition) (Toronto: Carswell, 1985) at 556, 564; William F. Petney, *The Aboriginal Rights Provisions in the Constitution Act, 1982* (Ottawa: University of Ottawa Press, 1987) at 109; Bruce Wildsmith, *Aboriginal Peoples and Section 25 of the Canadian Charter of Rights and Freedoms* (Saskatoon: Native Law Centre, University of Saskatchewan, 1988) at 11-12.
5 Petney, *supra* note 4 at 109; Norman Zlotkin, *Unfinished Business: Aboriginal Peoples and the 1983 Constitutional Conference*, Discussion Paper no. 15 (Kingston, ON: Institute of Intergovernmental Relations, Queen's University, 1983) at 46; See also Kenneth Lysyk, "The Rights and Freedoms of the Aboriginal Peoples of Canada (Sections 25, 35, and 37)" in W. Tarnopolsky and G.A. Beaudoin (eds.), *The Canadian Charter of Rights and Freedoms: Commentary* (Toronto: Carswell, 1982) 470 at 471-72.
6 *R. v Nicholas and Bear*, [1989] 2 C.N.L.R. 131 (N.B.Q.B.); *Steinhauer v The Queen*, [1985] 3 C.N.L.R. 187 (Alta. Q.B.); *Augustine and Augustine v The Queen; Barlow v The Queen*, [1987] 1 C.N.L.R. 20 at 44 (N.B.C.A.).
7 Peter Hogg and Mary Ellen Turpel-Lafond, "Implementing Aboriginal Self-Government: Constitutional and Jurisdictional Issues" (1997) 74 Can. Bar. Rev. 187 at 214-15.
8 Brian Slattery, "First Nations and the Constitution: A Question of Trust" (1992) 71 Can. Bar. Rev. 261 at 286.
9 Royal Commission on Aboriginal Peoples, *Restructuring the Relationship*, volume 2, part 1, chapter 3, "Governance" (Ottawa: Royal Commission on Aboriginal Peoples, 1993) at 229.
10 Jonathan Rudin and Dan Russell, *Native Alternative Dispute Resolution Systems: The Canadian Future in Light of the American Past* (Mississauga, ON: Ontario Native Council on Justice, 1993) at 47.
11 Thomas Isaac, "Canadian Charter of Rights and Freedoms: The Challenge of the Individual and Collective Rights of Aboriginal People" (2002) 21 Windsor Y.B. Access Just. 431. For similar arguments, see also Timothy Dickson, "Section 25 and Intercultural Judgment" (2003) 61 U.T. Fac. L. Rev. 141; and Jane M. Arbour, "The Protection of Aboriginal Rights within a Human Rights Regime: In Search of an Analytical Framework for Section 25 of the Canadian Charter of Rights and Freedoms" (2003) 21 Sup. Ct. L. Rev. (2d) 3.
12 Kent McNeil, "Aboriginal Governments and the *Canadian Charter of Rights and Freedoms*" (1996) 34:1 Osgoode Hall L.J. 61 at 74.
13 Wildsmith, *supra* note 4 at 23.
14 *Ibid.* at 50-52.
15 Kerry Wilkins, "But We Need the Eggs: The Royal Commission, the Charter of Rights and the Inherent Right of Aboriginal Self-Government" (1999) 49 U.T.L.J. 53 at 113.
16 *Motor Vehicle Reference*, *supra* note 2 at 504-9. Canada, Special Joint Committee of the Senate and House of Commons on the Constitution, *Proceedings and Evidence of the Special Joint Committee of the Senate and of the House of Commons on the Constitution* (Ottawa: Queen's Printer, 1981).
17 Wilkins, *supra* note 15 at 115.
18 *Reference re Bill 30, An Act to Amend the Education Act (Ontario)*, [1987] 1 S.C.R. 1148 at 1197.
19 *Adler v The Queen in Right of Ontario*, [1996] 3 S.C.R. 609 at 643.
20 Wilkins, *supra* note 15 at 116-17.
21 Gordon Christie, "Aboriginal Citizenship: Sections 35, 25 and 15 of Canada's *Constitution Act, 1982*" (2003) 7:4 Citizenship Studies 481 at 488-89.
22 *Campbell v British Columbia (A.G.)*, [2000] 8 W.W.R. 600 (B.C.S.C.) at 605.
23 *Ibid.* at 632-33.
24 Quoted in Joan Bryden, "Limit Native Government, Former Chief Justice Warns," *Kitchener-Waterloo Record* (16 March 1992) A1.
25 Royal Commission on Aboriginal Peoples, *Bridging the Cultural Divide: A Report on Aboriginal People and Criminal Justice in Canada* (Ottawa: Minister of Supply and Services Canada, 1996) at 467-68.
26 *R. v Kapp*, [2008] 2 S.C.R. 483.
27 *Ibid.* at paras. 64-65.

28   *Ibid.* at para. 103.
29   *Ibid.* at paras. 97, 99, and 109.
30   *Ibid.* at para. 65.
31   *R. v Big M Drug Mart Ltd.*, [1985] 1 S.C.R. 295 at 322.
32   *R. v Oakes*, [1986] 1 S.C.R. 103 at 138-39.
33   *Dagenais v Canadian Broadcasting Corporation*, [1994] 3 S.C.R. 835 at 889.
34   Peter Hogg, *Canadian Constitutional Law* (5th edition) (Toronto: Carswell, 2007) at 60.
35   *Ibid.* at 877.
36   *Ibid.* at 878.
37   *R. v Keegstra*, [1990] 3 S.C.R. 697.
38   Department of Indian Affairs and Northern Development, *The Government of Canada's Approach to Implementation of the Inherent and the Negotiation of Aboriginal Self-Government* (Ottawa: Minister of Public Works and Government Services Canada, 1995).
39   *Nisga'a Final Agreement* (Ottawa: Library of Parliament, 1999), chapter 2, article 9.
40   *Sechelt Agreement-in-Principle* (Vancouver: Library of the Legislature of British Columbia, 1999), s. 1.4.2.
41   *Tsawwassen Final Agreement* (Vancouver: Government of British Columbia, 2006), chapter 2, s. 11.
42   *Canadian Human Rights Act*, R.S.C. 1985, c. H-6.
43   Canada Human Rights Commission, *Still a Matter of Rights: A Special Report of the Canadian Human Rights Commission on the Repeal of Section 67 of the Canadian Human Rights Act* (Ottawa: Minister of Public Works and Government Services, 2008).
44   *Ibid.* at 4.
45   *Ibid.* at 5-6.
46   *Ibid.* at 13. For a further discussion, see Bradford W. Morse, Robert Groves, and D'Arcy Vermette, *Balancing Individual and Collective Rights: Implementation of Section 1.2 of the Canadian Human Rights Act* (Ottawa: Canadian Human Rights Commission, 2008).
47   *Ibid.* at 13.
48   *Ibid.* at 4-6.
49   Mary Ellen Turpel-Lafond, "Aboriginal Peoples and the Canadian Charter: Interpretive Monopolies, Cultural Differences" (1989) Can. H.R. Y.B. 2 at 41-42; Patricia Monture-Angus, *Journeying Forward: Dreaming First Nations' Independence* (Halifax: Fernwood Publishing, 1999) at 144-52.
50   For a discussion of this idea, see Royal Commission on Aboriginal Peoples, *supra* note 25 at 227-32.
51   Frank Pommerscheim, *Braid of Feathers: American Indian Law and Contemporary Tribal Life* (Berkeley, CA: University of California Press, 1995) at 58, 61-136.
52   *Major Crimes Act*, 18 U.S.C. s. 1153; *Indian Civil Rights Act*, 25 U.S.C. s. 1301-3.
53   *Pommerscheim, supra* note 51 at 99; See also Mark J. Wolff, "Spirituality, Culture and Tradition: An Introduction to the Role of Tribal Courts and Councils in Reclaiming Native American Heritage and Sovereignty" (1994-95) 7 St. Thomas L. Rev 761.
54   Justin B. Richland, "'What Are You Going to Do with the Village's Knowledge?' Talking Tradition, Talking Law in Hopi Tribal Court" (2005) 39 L. & Soc'y Rev. 235.
55   James Zion, "Taking Justice Back: American Indian Perspectives," quoted in the Royal Commission on Aboriginal Peoples, *Aboriginal Peoples and the Justice System: Report of the National Round Table on Aboriginal Justice Issues* (Ottawa: Supply and Services, 1993) 309 at 311.
56   Larry Nesper, "Negotiating Jurisprudence in Tribal Court and the Emergence of a Tribal State: The Lac Du Flambeau Ojibwe" (2007) 48:5 Current Anthropology 675.
57   Mark D. Rosen, "Multiple Authoritative Interpreters of Quasi-Constitutional Federal Law: Of Tribal Courts and the *Indian Civil Rights Act*" (2000) 69 Fordham L. Rev. 479 at 483.
58   Raymond D. Austin, *Navajo Courts and Navajo Common Law: A Tradition of Tribal Self-Governance* (Minneapolis, MN: University of Minnesota Press, 2009) at 109-28.
59   Navajo Nation Bill of Rights, N.N.C. s. 1 et seq. (2005); *Indian Civil Rights Act, supra* note 52.
60   Royal Commission on Aboriginal Peoples, *supra* note 25 at 278-79.
61   *Ibid.* at 266-67.

Chapter 6: The Sentencing Process

1 *Canadian Charter of Rights and Freedoms,* Part 1 of the *Constitution Act, 1982,* being Schedule B to the *Canada Act 1982* (U.K.), 1982, c. 11.
2 *R. v Valente,* [1985] 2 S.C.R. 673 [*Valente*].
3 *Reference re Rumeration of the Judges of the Provincial Court of Prince Edward Island; Reference re Independence and Impartiality of Judges of the Provincial Court of Prince Edward Island; R. v Campbell; R. v Ekmecic; R. v Wickman; Manitoba Provincial Judges Assn. v Manitoba (Minister of Justice),* [1997] 3 S.C.R. 3 [*Remuneration Reference*].
4 *Mackin v New Brunswick; Rice v New Brunswick,* [2002] 1 S.C.R. 405 at para. 125.
5 Rupert Ross, *Returning to the Teachings: Exploring Aboriginal Justice* (Toronto: Penguin Books Canada, 1996) at 205-8.
6 Philmer Bluehouse and James Zion, "Hozhooji Naat'aanii: The Navajo Justice and Harmony Ceremony" (1993) 10:4 Mediation Q. 328 at 328-29.
7 Michael Coyle, "Traditional Indian Justice in Ontario: A Role for the Present?" (1986) 24 Osgoode Hall L.J. 605 at 622-24.
8 Douglas George-Kanentiio, *Iroquois Culture and Commentary* (Santa Fe, NM: Clear Light Publishers, 2000) at 70-72.
9 *Ibid.* at 53-56.
10 *Ibid.* at 122. Donald S. Lutz "The Iroquois Confederation Constitution: An Analysis" (1998) 28:2 Publius: The Journal of Federalism 99 at 110-12.
11 George-Kanentiio, *supra* note 8 at 95-97.
12 Lewis Morgan, *League of the Iroquois,* ed. Herbert M. Lloyd, volume 1 (New York: Dodd, Mead, and Company, 1901) at 47-51.
13 *Constitution Act, 1867,* (U.K.), 30 and 31 Victoria, c. 3.
14 *Indian Act,* S.C. 1985, c. I-5.
15 See, for example, Ontario Judicial Appointments Advisory Committee, *Policies and Process* (Toronto: Ontario Courts, 2005) at 3.
16 Mary Ellen Turpel-Lafond and Patricia Monture-Angus, "Aboriginal Peoples and Canadian Criminal Law: Rethinking Justice," Special Edition on Aboriginal Justice (1992) U.B.C. L. Rev. 239 at 246.
17 Jo-Anne Fiske and Betty Patrick, *Cis Dideen Kat: The Way of the Lake Babine Nation* (Vancouver: UBC Press, 2000) at 50-54, 86-91.
18 Ontario Judicial Appointments Advisory Committee, *supra* note 15 at 3-4.
19 *Ibid.* at 9.
20 Royal Commission on Aboriginal Peoples, *Bridging the Cultural Divide: A Report on Aboriginal People and Criminal Justice in Canada* (Ottawa: Minister of Supply and Services Canada, 1996) at 231.
21 Rupert Ross, *Returning to the Teachings: Exploring Aboriginal Justice* (Toronto: Penguin Books Canada, 1996) at 223.
22 Turpel-Lafond and Monture-Angus, *supra* note 16 at 246.
23 Coyle, *supra* note 7 at 623-24.
24 Michael Jackson, "In Search of the Pathways to Justice: Alternative Dispute Resolution in Aboriginal Communities" (1992) *U.B.C. L. Rev.,* Special Edition on Aboriginal Justice 147 at 207-8.
25 Patricia Monture-Angus, *Journeying Forward: Dreaming First Nations' Independence* (Halifax: Fernwood Publishing, 1999) at 141; Sherene Razack, *Looking White People in the Eye: Gender, Race, and Culture in Courtrooms and Classrooms* (Toronto: University of Toronto Press, 1998) at 56-68; Taiaiake Alfred, *Peace, Power, Righteousness* (London, UK: Oxford University Press, 2008) at 54-58, 138-44.
26 Monture-Angus, *supra* note 25 at 14 and 141-45; Ross, *supra* note 21 at 205-10.
27 "Nunavut Unveils 'Prudent' $1.3B Budget," *CBC News* (8 March 2010).
28 See, for example, the *Absente Shawnee Tribe of Oklahoma Tribal Code* (circa 1999), s. 102.
29 *Blackfeet Tribal Code* (circa 1999), s. 2; *Chitimaca Comprehensive Codes of Justice* (last amended 15 April 2003), s. 303; *Stockbridge-Munsee Tribal Code,* ch. 1, s. 1.6(M); *Law and Order Code of the Fort McDowell Yavapai Community, Arizona,* adopted by Resolution no. 90-30, subsequently amended (includes amendments dated 2000 and the caveat that the candidate must complete any additional training required by the tribal council), s. 1-18.

242 Notes to pages 88-94

30 *Ely Shoshone Tribal Law and Order Code* (last revised 2000), ch. 1-2, s. 01.

31 *Hopi Indian Tribe Law and Order Code*, ch. 3, s. 1.3.4.

32 *Ibid.*, ch. 3, s. 1.3.3.

33 *Oglala Sioux Tribe: Law and Order Code*, ch. 1, s. 2-4.

34 *R. v Mills*, [1986] 1 S.C.R. 863 at 955-56 and 958-59.

35 *Ibid.* at 956.

36 *Code of Offences and Procedures of Justice for the Mohawk Nation at Akwesasne*, Draft no. 10 (the draft was provided by Martha LaFrance of the Akwesasne Justice Department) [*Akwesasne Justice Code*].

37 Jonathan Rudin and Dan Russell, *Native Alternative Dispute Resolution Systems: The Canadian Future in Light of the American Past* (Mississauga, ON: Ontario Native Council on Justice, 1993) at 49-50.

38 *Ibid.* at 55.

39 Jayne Wallingford, "The Role of Tradition in the Navajo Judiciary: Reemergence and Revival" (1994) 19 Okla. City U.L. Rev. 141.

40 Barry Stuart, *Building Community Justice Partnerships: Community Peacemaking Circles* (Ottawa: Department of Justice, Canada, 1997) at 81, 86.

41 Simon Owen, "A Crack in Everything: Restorative Possibilities of Plea-Based Sentencing Courts" (2011) 48 Alta. L. Rev. 847; Kathleen Daly, "Revisiting the Relationship between Retributive and Restorative Justice," in Heather Strang and John Braithwaite (eds.), *Restorative Justice: Philosophy to Practice* (Dartmouth, UK: Ashgate, 2000) 33.

42 Owen, *supra* note 41 at 871-86.

43 George Zdenkowski, "Customary Punishment and Pragmatism: Some Unresolved Dilemmas" (1993) Indigenous Law Bulletin 33.

44 J.R. Miller, *Skyscrapers Hide the Heavens: A History of Indian-White Relations in Canada* (Toronto: University of Toronto Press, 2000) at 5.

45 *Ibid.* at 55-56.

46 Roger Keesing, *Custom and Confrontation: The Kwaio Struggle for Cultural Autonomy* (Chicago: University of Chicago Press, 1992) at 13. See also Sarah Holcombe, "The Arrogance of Ethnography: Managing Anthropological Research Knowledge" (2010) 2 Australian Aboriginal Stud. 22.

47 Mary Ellen Turpel-Lafond, "Aboriginal Peoples and the Canadian Charter: Interpretive Monopolies, Cultural Differences" (1989) Can. H.R. Y.B. 2 at 30.

48 Linda Tuwihai Smith, *Decolonizing Methodologies: Research and Indigenous Peoples* (New York: Zed Books, 1999). For similar arguments, see Leanne R. Simpson, "Anticolonial Strategies for the Recovery and Maintenance of Indigenous Knowledge" (2004) 28:3-4 Am. Indian Q. 373; Celia Haig-Brown, "Continuing Collaborative Knowledge Production: Knowing When, Where, How, and Why" (2001) 22:1 J. Intercultural Stud. 19.

49 Besse Mainville, "Traditional Native Culture and Spirituality: A Way of Life That Governs Us" (2010) 8:1 Indigenous L.J. 1.

50 Leonard Tsuji, "Loss of Cree Traditional Ecological Knowledge in the Western James Bay Region of Northern Ontario, Canada: A Case Study of the Sharp-Tailed Grouse, *Tympanachus phasianellus phasianellus*" (1996) 26:2 Can. J. Native Stud. 283; Kathleen Orge, "Cultural Knowledge under Siege" (May 2004) Ontario Birchbark 8.

51 Georgina Earring-Chosa, "Loss of a Language: Forgotten through Time" (2009) 29:1 Tribal College J. 44; Brian Lin, "Preserving Native Languages" (2005) 8:10 Raven's Eye 6; John Hunt Peacock, Jr., "Lamenting Language Loss at the Modern Language Association" (2006) 30:1-2 Am. Indian Q. 138; Leanne Hinton, "Language Loss and Revitalization in California: Overview" (1998) 32 Int'l J. Sociology of Language 132; Clifton Pve, "Language Loss among the Chilcotin" (1992) 93 Int'l J. Sociology of Language 75.

52 Carol LaPriarie, " Aboriginal Crime and Justice: Explaining the Present, Exploring the Future" (1992) 34 Can. J. Crim. 281 at 287.

53 Harald Finkler, "Community Participation in Socio-Legal Control: The Northern Context" (1992) 34 Can. J. Crim. 503.

54 Pat Sekaqualptewa, "Evolving the Hopi Common Law" (2000) 9 Kan. J.L. & Pub. Pol'y 761; For her follow-up study in which she describes some examples of newer customs that emerged

in Hopi common law, see Pat Sekaqualptewa, "Key Concepts in the Finding, Definition, and Consideration of Custom Law in Tribal Lawmaking" (2007-08) 32:2 Am. Indian L. Rev. 319.

55 Sekaqualptewa, "Evolving the Hopi Common Law," *supra* note 54 at 777.
56 Sákéj Hendersen "Indigenous Legal Consciousness" (2002) 1 Indigenous L.J. 1 at 26.
57 J.E.S. Fawcett, *The Application of the European Convention on Human Rights* (Oxford: Clarendon Press, 1969) at 156, quoted in *Valente, supra* note 2 at 686.
58 *Ethical Principles for Judges* (Ottawa: Canadian Judicial Council of Canada, 1998) at 29.
59 *Reference re Section 94(2) of the Motor Vehicle Act, B.C.,* [1985] 2 S.C.R. 486 at 512-13.
60 Royal Commission on Aboriginal Peoples, *supra* note 20 at 275.
61 Michel G. Herman, "The Dangers of ADR: A Three-Tiered System of Justice" (1989-90) 3 J. Contemporary Legal Issues 117; Michael Coyle, "Defending the Weak and Fighting Unfairness: Can Mediators Respond to the Challenge?" (1998) 36 Osgoode Hall L.J. 625; Ilan G. Gewurz, "(Re)Designing Mediation to Address the Nuances of Power Imbalance" (2001) 19:2 Conflict Resolution Q. 135; Terenia Urban Gill, "A Framework for Understanding and Using ADR" (1996-97) 71 Tul. L. Rev. 1313.
62 Quoted in David Cayley, *The Expanding Prison: The Crisis in Crime and Punishment and the Search for Alternatives* (Toronto: House of Anansi Press, 1998) at 206 (the quote is Cayley's description of Crnkovich's views in his words).
63 *Ibid.* at 207.
64 *Akwesasne Justice Code, supra* note 36, Article 6, section 9.
65 Royal Commission on Aboriginal Peoples, *supra* note 20 at 277.
66 Interview with Donald McKay, Jr. (13 December 1994), Cumberland House, Saskatchewan. Cited in Ross Gordon Green, "Aboriginal Community Sentencing and Mediation: Within and Without the Circle" (1997) 24 Man. L.J. 77 at 105.
67 Ross, *supra* note 21 at 207.
68 Elizabeth E. Joh, "Custom, Tribal Court Practice, and Popular Justice" (2000-01) 25 Am. Indian L. Rev 117 at 123.
69 Fiske and Patrick, *supra* note 17 at 50 and 100.
70 Quoted in Green, *supra* note 66 at 113.
71 *Ibid.* at 114.
72 *Colville Tribal Law and Order Code,* 7 N.T.C. section 606.
73 *Boos v Yazzie,* No. A-CV-35-90 (Navajo, 24 September 1990), paras. 31-32.
74 Interview by Ross Gordon Green over the telephone with Judge Claude Fafard (16 December 1994). Cited in Green, *supra* note 66 at 111-12.
75 *Ibid.* at 112.
76 *R. v Lyons,* [1987] 2 S.C.R. 307 at para. 26.
77 *R. v Mills,* [1999] 3 S.C.R. 668. *Criminal Code,* R.S.C. 1985, c. 46.
78 *Dagenais v Canadian Broadcasting Corporation,* [1994] 3 S.C.R. 835.
79 *Ibid.* at paras. 76 and 89.
80 Allison Morris and Loraine Gelsthorpe, "Re-visioning Men's Violence against Female Partners" (2000) 39:4 How. L.J. 412; Jonathan Rudin and Kent Roach, "Broken Promises: A Response to Stenning and Roberts' Colloquy on 'Empty Promises: Parliament, the Supreme Court, and the Sentencing of Aboriginal Offenders'" (2002) 65:1 Sask. L. Rev. 1 at 30-31.
81 Julie Stubbs, "Domestic Violence and Women's Safety: Feminist Challenges to Restorative Justice" in Heather Strang and John Braithwaite (eds.), *Restorative Justice and Family Violence* (Cambridge: Cambridge University Press, 2002); Quince C. Hopkins, Mary Koss, and Karen Bachar, "Applying Restorative Justice to Ongoing Intimate Violence: Problems and Possibilities" (2004) 23:1 St. Louis U. Pub. L. Rev. 289; Angela Cameron, "Stopping the Violence: Canadian Feminist Debates on Restorative Justice and Intimate Violence" (2006) 10:1 Theor. Criminology 49.
82 Annalise Acorn, *Compulsory Compassion: A Critique of Restorative Justice* (Vancouver: UBC Press, 2004) at 74.
83 *Ibid.* at 150-58.
84 *Ibid.* at 75-76.

85   Emma Cunliffe and Angela Cameron, "Writing the Circle: Judicially Convened Sentencing Circles and the Textual Organization of Criminal Justice" (2007) 19:1 C.J.W.L. 1.
86   Anne McGillivray and Brenda Comaskey, *Black Eyes All of the Time: Intimate Violence, Aboriginal Women, and the Justice System* (Toronto: University of Toronto Press, 1999) at 116.
87   Razack, *supra* note 25 at 77-78.
88   *Ibid.* at 66.
89   Chassidy Pachula et al., "Using Traditional Spirituality to Reduce Domestic Violence within Aboriginal Communities" (2010) 16:1 J. Alternative & Complementary Medicine 89.
90   Bruce G. Miller, *The Problem of Justice: Tradition and Law in the Coast Salish World* (Lincoln: University of Nebraska Press, 2001) at 198-99.
91   Dean Pritchard, "Perv Elder Spared Jail" *Winnipeg Sun* (28 July 2010) 3.
92   Theresa Nahanee, "Dancing with a Gorilla: Aboriginal Women, Justice, and the *Charter*" in Royal Commission on Aboriginal Peoples, *Aboriginal Peoples and the Justice System: Report on the Round Table on Aboriginal Justice Issues* (Ottawa: Minister of Supply and Services, 1993) 359.
93   Acorn, *supra* note 82 at 56-60.
94   Quoted in Cayley, *supra* note 62 at 206.
95   William C. Bradford, "Reclaiming Indigenous Autonomy on the Path to Peaceful Coexistence: The Theory, Practice, and Limitations of Tribal Peacemaking in Indian Dispute Resolution" (2000) Notre Dame L. Rev. 551 at 590-96.
96   Razack, *supra* note 25; McGillivray and Comaskey, *supra* note 86; Pauktuutit Inuit Women's Association, *Setting Standards First: Community-Based Justice and Corrections in Inuit Canada* (Ottawa: Pauktuutit, 1995); Kelly MacDonald, *Literature Review: Implications of Restorative Justice in Cases of Violence against Aboriginal Women and Children* (Vancouver: Aboriginal Women's Network, 2001).
97   Royal Commission on Aboriginal Peoples, *supra* note 20 at 269.
98   Robert Yazzie, "The Navajo Response to Crime" in Wanda D. McCaslin (ed.) *Justice as Healing: Indigenous Ways* (St. Paul, MN: Living Justice Press, 2005) 121 at 131.
99   Donna Coker, "Enhancing Autonomy for Battered Women" (1999) 47 U.C.L.A. L. Rev. 1 at 82.
100   *Ibid.* at 82-83.
101   Green, *supra* note 66 at 94-95. See also Stuart, *supra* note 40 at 45-47.
102   Diane Bell, "Aboriginal Women and the Recognition of Customary Law in Australia" in Bradford W. Morse and Gordon R. Woodman (eds.), *Indigenous Law and the State* (Dordrecht, the Netherlands: Foris Publications, 1988) 297 at 304.
103   Coker, *supra* note 99 at 45-46.
104   I have taken this kind of position before. See David Milward, "Making the Circle Stronger: An Effort to Buttress Aboriginal Use of Restorative Justice in Canada against Recent Criticisms" (2008) 4:3 Int'l J. Punishment & Sentencing 124.
105   Stanley A. de Smith, Lord Woolf, and Jeffrey Jowell, *Judicial Review of Administrative Action* (5th edition) (London: Sweet and Maxwell, 1995) at 544; quoted in *Reference re Remuneration of Judges of the Provincial Court of Prince Edward Island; Reference re Independence and Impartiality of Judges of the Provincial Court of Prince Edward Island; R. v Campbell; R. v Ekmecic; R. v Wickman; Manitoba Provincial Judges Assn. v Manitoba (Minister of Justice)*, [1998] 1 S.C.R. 3 at para. 6 [*Remuneration Reference (no. 2)*].
106   *Laws v Australian Broadcasting Tribunal* (1990), 93 A.L.R. 435 at 454.
107   *Malone v City of Poway*, 746 F2d 1375, 1376 (9th Cir 1982).
108   *United States v Will*, 449 US 200, 213-14 (1980); *Evans v Gore*, 253 US 245, 247-48 (1920).
109   Rachael Field, "Victim-Offender Conferencing: Issues of Power Imbalance for Women Juvenile Participants" (2004) 11:1 Murdoch U.E.J.L. at para. 37.
110   David Weisbrot, "Comment on the ALRC Discussion Paper: *Customary Law*" (1981) 1:1 Aboriginal Law Bulletin 3.
111   Declane Roche considers the availability of external judicial review as a necessary means of ensuring fairness between the parties that use restorative processes. Declane Roche, *Accountability in Restorative Justice* (Oxford: Oxford University Press, 2003) at 208-12 and 216-21.
112   Royal Commission on Aboriginal Peoples, *supra* note 20 at 279.

113 *R. v Sheppard*, [2002] 1 S.C.R. 869 at para. 55.
114 *R. v M. (R.E.)*, [2008] 3 S.C.R. 3 at para. 25. *Sheppard, supra* note 113.
115 *R. v M. (R.E.), supra* note 114 at para. 35.
116 *R. v MacDonald*, [1977] 2 S.C.R. 665; *R. v Burns*, [1994] 1 S.C.R. 656; *R. v Barrett*, [1995] 1 S.C.R. 752.
117 *Crow Tribe of Indians v Bull Tail*, 2000 Crow 8 (Crow, 12 October 2000); *Fort Peck Assiniboine and Sioux v Howard*, No. 057 (Fort Peck, 11/38/1988); *Thompson v Yazzie*, no. SC-CV-21-06 (Navajo, 14 July 2006); *St. Peter v Colville Confederated Tribes*, 2 CCAR 2 (Colville Confederated, 28 September 1993).
118 Ross, *supra* note 21 at 205-6. For a very similar argument, see Alfred, *supra* note 25 at 95.
119 Berit Albrecht, "Multicultural Challenges for Restorative Justice: Mediators' Experiences from Norway and Finland" (2010) 11:1 J. Scandinavian Stud. Criminology & Crime Prevention 3 at 15.
120 Andrew Ashworth, "Responsibilities, Rights and Restorative Justice" (2002) 43:3 Brit. J. Criminology 578; See also Katherine Doolin, "But What Does It Mean: Seeking Definitional Clarity in Restorative Justice" (2007) 71:5 J. Crim. L. 427 at 430.
121 Canada Human Rights Commission, *Still a Matter of Rights: A Special Report of the Canadian Human Rights Commission on the Repeal of Section 67 of the Canadian Human Rights Act* (Ottawa: Minister of Public Works and Government Services, 2008) at 6.
122 Emma LaRocque, "Re-examining Culturally Appropriate Models in Criminal Justice Applications" in Michael Asch (ed.), *Aboriginal and Treaty Rights in Canada: Essays on Law, Equality, and Respect for Difference* (Vancouver: UBC Press, 1997) 75 at 84.
123 Hennessey Hayes, "Assessing Reoffending in Restorative Justice Conferences" (2005) 38:1 Aust. Crim. & N.Z. J. 77; Mike Niemeyer and David Schicor, "A Preliminary Study of a Large Victim/Offender Reconciliation Program" (1996) 60 Federal Probation 30; Mark S. Umbreit, *Victim Meets Offender: The Impact of Restorative Justice and Mediation* (Monsey, NY: Willow Tree Press, 1994); Sudipto Roy, "Two Types of Juvenile Restitution Programs in Two Midwestern Counties: A Comparative Study" (1993) 57 Federal Probation 48.
124 Carol LaPrairie and E. Jane Dickson-Gilmore, *Will the Circle Be Unbroken? Aboriginal Communities, Restorative Justice, and the Challenges of Conflict and Change* (Toronto: University of Toronto Press, 2005) at 218.
125 Jacqueline Fitzgerald, "Does Circle Sentencing Reduce Aboriginal Offending?" (2008) 115 Contemporary Issues in Crime & Justice 1.
126 *Ibid.* at 208-12.
127 Acorn, *supra* note 82 at 61. Lawrence Sherman and Heather Strang, *Restorative Justice: The Evidence* (London: Smith Institute, 2009).
128 Jodi-Anne Brzozowski, Andrea Taylor Butts, and Sara Johnson, *Victimization and Offending among the Aboriginal Population in Canada* (Ottawa: Canadian Centre for Justice Statistics, 2006) at 6.
129 Peggy Grauwiler and Linda G. Mills, "Moving beyond the Criminal Justice Paradigm: A Radical Restorative Justice Approach to Intimate Abuse" (2004) 31:1 J. Sociology & Welfare 49; Robert J. Hampton et al., "Evaluating Domestic Violence Interventions for Black Women" (2008) 16:3 J. Aggression, Maltreatment, & Trauma 330; Katherine van Wormer, "Restorative Justice as Social Justice for Victims of Gendered Violence: A Standpoint Feminist Perspective" (2009) 54:2 Social Work 107.
130 Andrew Fulkerson, "The Use of Victim Impact Panels in Domestic Violence Cases: A Restorative Justice Approach" (2001) 4:3-4 Contemporary Justice Rev. 355; Robert C. Davis, "Brooklyn Mediation Field Test" (2009) 5:1 J. Experimental Criminology 25.
131 Angela Cameron, "Sentencing Circles and Intimate Violence: A Feminist Perspective" (2006) 18:2 C.J.W.L. 479.
132 Leena Kurki and Kay Pranis, *Restorative Justice as Direct Democracy and Community Building* (St. Paul, MN: Minnesota Department of Corrections, Community and Juvenile Services Division, 2000).
133 LaPrairie and Dickson-Gilmore, *supra* note 124 at 195.
134 Therese Lajeunesse, *Evaluation of the Hollow Water Community Holistic Circle Healing Project* (Ottawa: Solicitor General of Canada, 1996).

135   LaPrairie and Dickson-Gilmore, *supra* note 124 at 209-10.

136   Acorn, *supra* note 82 at 99-119.

137   *Ibid.* at 53.

138   Ros Burnett and Catherine Appleton, *Joined-Up Youth Justice: Tackling Youth Crime in Partnership* (Lyme Regis, United Kingdom: Russell Publishing, 2004); Adam Crawford and Tim Newburn, *Youth Offending and Restorative Justice: Implementing Reform in Youth Justice* (Devon, United Kingdom: Willan Publishing, 2003); David Karp, Gordon Bazemore, and J.D. Chesire, "The Role and Attitudes of Restorative Board Members: A Case Study of Volunteers in Community Justice" (2004) 50:4 Crime & Delinquency 487; Christina Stahlkopf, "Restorative Justice, Rhetoric or Reality? Conferencing with Young Offenders" 12:3 Contemporary Justice Rev. 231.

139   Avery Calhoun and William Pelech, "Responding to Young People Responsible for Harm: A Comparative Study of Restorative and Conventional Approaches" (2010) 13:3 Contemporary Justice Rev. 287; Barton Poulson, "A Third Voice: A Review of Empirical Research on the Psychological Outcomes of Restorative Justice" (2003) Utah L. Rev. 167.

140   Ibolya Losoncz and Graham Tyson, "Parental Shaming and Adolescent Delinquency" (2007) 40:2 Aust. Crim. & N.Z. J. 161; Kimberly J. Cook, "Doing Difference and Accountability in Restorative Justice Conferences" (2006) 10:1 Theoretical Criminology 107.

141   Scott J. Kenney and Don Clairmont, "Using the Victim as Both Sword and Shield" (2009) 38:3 J. Contemporary Ethnography 279.

142   Kathleen Daly, "Mind the Gap: Restorative Justice in Theory and Practice" in Andrew Von Hirsch, Julian V. Roberts, and Anthony Bottoms (eds.), *Restorative Justice and Criminal Justice: Competing or Reconcilable Paradigms?* (Oxford: Hart Publishing, 2003) 219 at 224.

143   Heather Strang et al., "Victim Evaluations of Face-to-Face Restorative Justice Conferences: A Quasi-Experimental Analysis" (2006) 62:2 J. Social Issues 281 at 301.

144   Daly, *supra* note 142 at 230.

145   Loren Walker and Leslie A. Hayashi, "Pono Kaulike: A Hawaii Criminal Court Provides Restorative Justice Practices for Healing Relationships" (2007) 71:3 Federal Probation 18.

146   Carol LaPrairie, "Community Justice or Just Communities? Aboriginal Communities in Search of Justice" (1995) Can. J. Crim. 521; Stuart, *supra* note 40 at 117-19; See also Karen A. Souza and Mandeep K. Dhami, "A Study of Volunteers in Community-Based Restorative Justice Programs" (2008) 50:1 Can. J. Crim. 31.

147   Patricia Hughes and Mary Jane Mossman "Re-Thinking Access to Criminal Justice in Canada: A Critical Review of Needs and Responses" (2002) 13 Windsor Rev. Legal Soc. Issues 1 at 118.

148   Green, *supra* note 66 at 116-117.

149   Royal Commission on Aboriginal Peoples, *supra* note 20 at 153.

150   Phillip Stenning and Julian V. Robert, "The Sentencing of Aboriginal Offenders in Canada: A Rejoinder," Colloquy on 'Empty Promises: Parliament, the Supreme Court, and the Sentencing of Aboriginal Offenders'" (2002) 65:1 Sask. L. Rev. 75 at 88.

151   Royal Commission on Aboriginal Peoples, *supra* note 20 at 294-302. See also Barbara Tomporowski, *Exploring Restorative Justice in Saskatchewan* (MA thesis, Department of Social Studies, University of Regina, 2004); Evelyn Zellerer and Chris Cunneen, "Restorative Justice, Indigenous Justice, and Human Rights" in Gordon Bezemore and Mara Schiff (eds.), *Restorative Community Justice: Repairing Harm and Transforming Communities* (Ottawa: Anderson Publishing, 2001) 245 at 255.

152   LaPrairie and Dickson-Gilmore, *supra* note 124 at 198.

153   Leonard Mandamin, "Aboriginal Justice Systems" in Royal Commission on Aboriginal Peoples, *Aboriginal Peoples and the Justice System, Report of the National Round Table on Aboriginal Justice Issues* (Ottawa: Supply and Services, 1993) at 298-99.

154   Catherine Bell, "New Directions in the Law of Indigenous Rights" (1998) 77 Can. Bar Rev. 36 at 66.

155   For discussions of this theme, see Royal Commission on Aboriginal Peoples, *Restructuring the Relationship*, volume 2, part 2 (Ottawa: Royal Commission on Aboriginal Peoples, 1993) at 775-1014; Kate Spilda Contreras, "Cultivating New Opportunities: Tribal Government Gaming on the Pechunga Reservations" (2006) 50:3 American Behavioral Scientist 315.

156 *Aboriginal Peoples and Criminal Justice: Equality, Respect and the Search for Justice*, Report no. 34 (Ottawa: Law Reform Commission of Canada, 1991); *Cutting Crime: The Case for Justice Re-Investment* (London, United Kingdom: House of Commons Justice Committee, 2009). For academic discussions that suggest that the concept of justice reinvestment is relatively underexplored and underdeveloped and that therefore caution is still needed, see Chris Fox, Kevin Alberton, and Frank Wharburton, "Justice Reinvestment: Can It Deliver More for Less?" (2011) 50:2 How. J. Crim. Just. 119; and Shadd Maruna, "Lessons for Justice Reinvestment from Restorative Justice and the Justice Model Experience" (2011) 10:3 Criminology & Public Pol'y 661.
157 Carol LaPrairie, "The Impact of Aboriginal Justice Research on Policy: A Marginal Past and an Even More Uncertain Future" (1999) Can. J. Crim. 249 at 256-57.
158 Doolin, *supra* note 120.
159 Daly, *supra* note 142 at 231.
160 Roche, *supra* note 111 at 83-84.
161 *Ibid.* at 87-88.
162 *Ibid.* at 91-92.
163 *Ibid.* at 92-93, 169-70.
164 *Ibid.* at 93-94.
165 *Ibid.*
166 Meredith Rossner, "Emotions and Interaction Ritual: A Micro Analysis of Restorative Justice" (2011) 51 British J. Criminology 95.
167 *Ibid.* at 116.
168 Owen, *supra* note 41 at 860-61, 888.
169 Royal Commission on Aboriginal Peoples, *supra* note 20 at 175-76.
170 Nancy A. Costello, "Walking Together in a Good Way: Indian Peacemaker Courts in Michigan" (1999) 76 U. Det. Mercy L. Rev 875 at 884, n 66.

Chapter 7: The Trial Phase
1 *Woolmington v Director of Public Prosecutions*, [1935] A.C. 462 (H.L.) [*Woolmington*].
2 *Canadian Charter of Rights and Freedoms*, Part I of the *Constitution Act, 1982*, being Schedule B to the *Canada Act 1982*, (U.K.), c. 11.
3 *R. v Oakes*, [1986] 1 S.C.R. 103 [*Oakes*]; *R. v Chaulk*, [1990] 3 S.C.R. 1303 [*Chaulk*].
4 *Woolmington*, *supra* note 1; *Oakes*, *supra* note 3 at 132-35.
5 *R. v Whyte*, [1988] 2 S.C.R. 3.
6 *R. v Downey*, [1992] 2 S.C.R. 10 [*Downey*].
7 *Chaulk*, *supra* note 3 at 1328-35.
8 *R. v W.D. [D.W.]*, [1991] 1 S.C.R. 742.
9 Joan Ryan, *Doing Things the Right Way* (Calgary: University of Calgary Press, Arctic Institute of North America, 1995) at 33-34.
10 Rupert Ross, *Returning to the Teachings: Exploring Aboriginal Justice* (Toronto: Penguin Books Canada, 1996) at 209.
11 Rinat Kitai, "Protecting the Guilty" (2003) 6 Buff. Crim. L.R. 1163 at 1166.
12 *Royal Commission on the Donald Marshall, Jr., Prosecution* (Halifax: Province of Nova Scotia, 1989) at 19-26.
13 *Ibid.* at 15.
14 *Ibid.* at 39-67.
15 *Ibid.* at 71-72.
16 *Ibid.* at 72-77.
17 For the re-investigation, see *ibid.* at 91-109. For the years spent in prison and release on bail in anticipation of his conviction being overturned, see *ibid.* at 109-11.
18 *Ibid.* at 117.
19 Leslie Jane MacMillan, "Koqqwaja'ltimk: Mi'kmaq Legal Consciousness" (Doctoral dissertation, Department of Anthropology, University of British Columbia, 2002) at 71-74.
20 *Ibid.* at 347-51.
21 *Ibid.* at 347.
22 *Code of Offences and Procedures of Justice for the Mohawk Nation at Akwesasne*, Draft no. 10.

23   Christopher Gora, "Jury Trials in the Small Communities of the Northwest Territories" (1993) Windsor Y.B. Access Just. 156.

24   *Charter* challenges by Aboriginal accuseds to this reality have uniformly been unsuccessful. For challenges that attempted to have the jury panel drawn from the district in which the accused resided instead of where the offence was committed, see *R. v Bear* (1993), 90 Man. R. (2d) 286 (Q.B.); and *R. v F.A.* (1993), 30 C.R. (4th) 333 (Ont. Ct. of Justice (Gen. Div.)). For unsuccessful attempts to have the jury drawn exclusively from the smaller Aboriginal community in which the accused resided instead of the larger judicial district, see *R. v Nepoose* (1985), 85 Alta. L.R. (2d) 18 (Q.B.); and *R. v Yooya*, [1995] 2 W.W.R. 135 (Sask. Q.B.). For similar challenges coupled with applications to change venue to the accused's community itself, see *R. v Redhead* (1995), 42 C.R. (4th) 252; and *R. v West* (1992), Docket no. Prince George 21151 (B.C.S.C.).

25   "Native Representation on Juries to Be Reviewed," *Hamilton Spectator* (12 August 2011) A8.

26   Gora, *supra* note 23 at 178-79, suggests something similar, though his commentary is better understood as jurors being drawn for juries constituted under the *Criminal Code,* R.S.C. 1985, c. 46.

27   Gora, *supra* note 23 at 177.

28   *Ibid.* at 180.

29   *R. v Fatt,* (1986) 54 C.R. (3d) 281 (N.W.T.S.C.).

30   *R. v K.I.,* [1990] N.W.T.R. 388 (S.C.).

31   Ross, *supra* note 10 at 209-10.

32   *Oakes, supra* note 3.

33   *Irwin Toy Ltd. v Quebec (A.G.),* [1989] 1 S.C.R. 927; *R. v Keegstra,* [1990] 3 S.C.R. 697.

34   *Downey, supra* note 6.

35   *Criminal Code, supra* note 26.

36   *Downey, supra* note 6 at 34.

37   *Ibid.* at 36-37.

38   *Chaulk, supra* note 3 at 1337.

39   *R. v Wholesale Travel Group Inc.,* [1991] 3 S.C.R. 154 at 204 (Lamer C.J.C. and Sopinka J.); at 209-10 (La Forest J.).

40   *Ibid.* at 224-34.

41   The Court in *Downey* was considering section 195(1) (now section 212(1)) of the *Criminal Code,* which makes living off the avails of prostitution an indictable offence with a maximum punishment of ten years imprisonment.

42   Gora, *supra* note 23 at 172. Gora notes that statistics of these matters are not kept in the Northwest Territories but that it was simply a commonly shared perception among the various participants (at n. 87).

43   *Ibid.*

44   *R. v Swain,* [1991] 1 S.C.R. 933 at 936.

45   *R. v Rose,* [1998] 3 S.C.R. 262 at 319.

46   *R. v Osolin,* [1993] 2 S.C.R. 313 at 663.

47   Ross, *supra* note 10 at 271.

48   Lee Stuesser, *An Advocacy Primer* (2nd edition) (Scarborough, ON: Thomson Carswell, 2005) at 168-69.

49   *R. v Bell* (1930), 53 C.C.C. 80 (Alta. C.A.); *R. v Cullen* (1989), 52 C.C.C. (3d) 459 (Ont. C.A.). Cross-examining co-accuseds on bad character is also legitimate. See *R. v Leon-Uzarraga* (1998), 123 C.C.C. (3d) 291 (B.C.C.A.); *R. v Kendall* (1987), 57 C.R. (3d) 249 (Ont. C.A.); *R. v Pollock* (2004), 23 C.R. (6th) 98 (Ont. C.A.); *R. v Atkins* (2002), 5 C.R. (6th) 400 (Ont. C.A.).

50   *R. v McNamara (No. 1)* (1981), 56 C.C.C. (2d) 193 (Ont. C.A.); *R. v McFadden* (1981), 28 C.R. (3d) 33 (B.C.C.A.); *R. v Vanezis* (2006), 43 C.R. (6th) 116 (Ont. C.A.); *R. v P. (N.A.)* (2002), 8 C.R. (6th) 186 (Ont. C.A.).

51   *R. v McDonald,* [1960] S.C.R. 186; *R. v S. (A.)* (2002), 165 C.C.C. (3d) 426 (Ont. C.A.).

52   *R. v Teneycke* (1996), 108 C.C. (3d) 53 (B.C.C.A.); *R. v Bencardino* (1973), 24 C.R.N.S. 173 (Ont. C.A.); *R. v Stevenson* (1971), 5 C.C.C. (2d) 415 (Ont. C.A.).

53 *R. v P. (P.N.)* (1993), 81 C.C.C. (3d) 525 (Nfld. C.A.); *R. v Demeter* (1975), 25 C.C.C. (2d) 417 (Ont. C.A.).
54 Royal Commission on Aboriginal Peoples, *Bridging the Cultural Divide: A Report on Aboriginal People and Criminal Justice in Canada* (Ottawa: Minister of Supply and Services Canada, 1996) at 207.
55 Justin B. Richland, "'What Are You Going to Do with the Village's Knowledge?' Talking Tradition, Talking Law in Hopi Tribal Court" (2005) 39 L. & Soc'y Rev. 235 at 249.
56 John Borrows, *Recovering Canada: The Resurgence of Indigenous Law* (Toronto: University of Toronto Press, 2002) at 91-92.
57 Federal Court, Indigenous Bar, Aboriginal Law Bar Liaison Meeting, 25 October 2007 (9:00 a.m. – 4:30 p.m.), Victoria, British Columbia, online: http://cas-ncr-nter03.cas-satj.gc.ca/fct-cf/pdf/Aboriginal%20Bar%2025-10-2007%20ENG.pdf; Federal Court, Indigenous Bar, Aboriginal Law Bar Liaison Meeting, 8 March 2007 (9:00 a.m. – 5:00 p.m.), Winnipeg, Manitoba, online: http://cas-ncr-nter03.cas-satj.gc.ca/fct-cf/pdf/Aboriginal%20Law%20Bar%2008_03_2007_ENG.pdf.
58 Ross, *supra* note 10 at 202-3.
59 Judy Atkinson, "Violence against Aboriginal Women: Reconstitution of Community Law – The Way Forward" (1990) 2:46 Indigenous Law Bulletin 6.
60 Ross, *supra* note 10 at 245-46.
61 *R. v Gladue,* [1999] 1 S.C.R. 688 at 695-98.
62 *Criminal Code, supra* note 26 at sections 34 and 35.
63 Royal Commission on Aboriginal Peoples, *supra* note 54 at 207.
64 *Ibid.* at 207-8.
65 Stuesser, *supra* note 48.
66 *Aboriginal Witnesses in Queensland's Criminal Courts* (Brisbane, Australia: Queensland Criminal Justice Commission, Goprint, 1996) at 91.
67 Kent Roach, "Changing Punishment at the Turn of the Century: Restorative Justice on the Rise" (2000) 42 Can. J. Crim. 239 at 259-60.
68 *R. v Lemky,* [1996] 1 S.C.R. 757.
69 *R. v Daviault,* [1994] 3 S.C.R. 63.
70 Roach, *supra* note 67.
71 Michael Lorden, *Mas Oyama: The Legend, The Legacy* (Burbank, CA: Unique Publications, 2000) at 9-10.
72 Susan Olson and Albert Dzur, "The Practice of Restorative Justice: Reconstructing Professional Roles in Restorative Justice Programs" (2003) Utah L. Rev. 57 at 64.
73 See *R. v Hanemaayer* (2008), 234 C.C.C. (3d) 3 (Ont. C.A.); Lauren O'Neill Shermer, Karen C. Rose, and Ashley Hoffman, "Perceptions and Credibility: Understanding the Nuances of Eyewitness Testimony" (2011) 27:2 J. Contemporary Criminal Justice 183.
74 Deborah Connolly et al., "Perceptions and Predictors of Children's Credibility of a Unique Event and an Instance of a Repeated Event" (2008) 32:1 Law & Human Behavior 92; Heather Price, Deborah Connolly, and Heidi Gordon, "Children's Recall of an Instance of a Repeated Event: Does Spacing of Instances Matter?" (2006) 14:8 Memory 977.
75 Don Stuart, Ronald Joseph Delisle, and David M. Tanovich, *Evidence: Principles and Problems* (Toronto: Thomson Reuters, 2010) at 6.
76 *R. v Lalonde* (1971), 15 C.R.N.S. 1 (Ont. H.C.) at 4.
77 Stephen T. Goudge, *Inquiry into Pediatric Forensic Pathology in Ontario,* volume 2 (Toronto: Ministry of the Attorney General of Ontario, 2008) at 90, 137-40.
78 *R. v Mullins-Johnson* (2008), 87 O.R. (3d) 425 at para. 24.
79 Richard L. Lippke, "Punishing the Guilty, Not Punishing the Innocent" (2010) 7:4 J. Moral Philosophy 462.
80 Tiffany Field et al., "Legal Interviewers Use Children's Affect and Eye Contact Cues to Assess Credibility of Their Testimony" (2010) 180:3 Early Child Development & Care 397; Jane Goodman-Delahunty, Anne Cossins, and Kate O'Brien, "Enhancing the Credibility of Complainants in Child Sexual Assault Interviews: The Effect of Expert Evidence and Judicial Directions" (2010) 28:6 Behav. Sci. & L. 769; Louise Ellison, "Closing the Credibility Gap:

The Prosecutorial Use of Expert Witness Testimony in Sexual Assault Cases" (2005) 9:4 Int'l J. Evidence & Proof 239.

81 Fiona E. Raitt, "Expert Evidence as Context: Historical Patterns and Contemporary Attitudes in the Prosecution of Sexual Offences" (2004) 12 Fem. Leg. Stud. 233; Paul Roberts, "Towards the Principled Reception of Expert Evidence of Witness Credibility in Criminal Trials" (2004) 8:3 Int'l J. Evidence & Proof 215; Tony Ward, "Usurping the Role of the Jury? Expert Evidence and Witness Credibility in Criminal Trials" (2009) 13:2 Int'l J. Evidence & Proof 83; David Paciocco, "Coping with Expert Evidence about Human Behavior" (1999) 25 Queen's L.J. 305.

82 Diana Eades, "Lexical Struggle in Court: Aboriginal Australians versus the State" (2006) 10:2 J. Sociolinguistics 153; Diana Eades, *"I don't think it's an answer to the question*: Silencing Aboriginal Witnesses in Court" (2000) 29:2 Language in Society 161; Diana Eades, "Telling and Retelling Your Story in Court: Questions, Assumptions, and Intercultural Assumptions" (2009) 20:2 Current Issues in Criminal Justice 209; Nigel Stobbs, "An Adversarial Quagmire: The Continued Inability of the Queensland Criminal Justice System to Cater for Indigenous Witnesses and Complainants" (2007) 6:30 Indigenous Law Bulletin 30.

83 Martine B. Powell, "PRIDE: The Essential Elements of an Effective Forensic Interview with an Aboriginal Person" (2000) 35:3 Australian Psychologist 186.

84 *Ibid.* at 188.

85 David Nash, "Aborigines in Court: Foreigners in Their Own Land" (1979) 4 Legal Service Bulletin 105.

86 Powell, *supra* note 83 at 187.

87 *Ibid.* at 187.

88 *Ibid.* at 189.

89 Eades, "Telling and Retelling Your Story in Court," *supra* note 82 at 225.

90 Powell, *supra* note 83 at 189-90.

Chapter 8: The Investigative Stage

1 *Canadian Charter of Rights and Freedoms,* Part 1 of the *Constitution Act, 1982,* being Schedule B to the *Canada Act 1982* (U.K.), 1982, c. 11.

2 *R. v Edwards*, [1996] 1 S.C.R. 128 at 145-46.

3 *Ibid.* at 145.

4 *Hunter v Southam*, [1984] 2 S.C.R. 145 at 160-62 [*Hunter*].

5 *Ibid.* at 167-68.

6 *R. v Harrison*, [2009] 2 S.C.R. 494.

7 *R. v Collins*, [1987] 1 S.C.R. 265 at 278-279.

8 *Hunter, supra* note 4 at 161.

9 *R. v Borden*, [1994] 3 S.C.R. 145.

10 *R. v Silviera*, [1995] 2 S.C.R. 297 at 370-71.

11 *R. v Ruiz* (1991), 68 C.C.C. (3d) 500 (N.B.C.A.) at 509.

12 *R. v Law* (2002), 48 C.R. (5th) 199 (S.C.C.).

13 *Cloutier v Langlois*, [1990] 1 S.C.R. 158 at 186.

14 *R. v Golden*, [2001] 3 S.C.R. 679 at para. 89 [*Golden*].

15 *Ibid.* at para. 90-101.

16 Glen Luther, "Police Power and the Charter of Rights and Freedoms: Creation or Control?" (1986-87) 51 Saskatchewan L. Rev. 217 at 218. Section 9 of the *Charter* reads: "Everyone has the right not to be arbitrarily arrested or detained." See also James Stribopoulos, "In Search of Dialogue: The Supreme Court, Police Powers, and the *Charter*" (2005) 31 Queen's L.J. 1.

17 *R. v Storrey*, [1990] 1 S.C.R. 241 at 249.

18 *R. v Stillman*, [1997] 1 S.C.R. 607 at 660.

19 *R. v Mentuck* (2001), 205 D.L.R. (4th) 512 (S.C.C.) at 537.

20 William B. Newell, *Crime and Justice among the Iroquois Nations* (Montreal: Caughnawaga Historical Society, 1965) at 47-51.

21 Douglas George-Kanentiio, *Iroquois Culture and Commentary* (Santa Fe, NM: Clear Light Publishers, 2000) at 99.

22 Arthur C. Parker, *An Analytical History of the Seneca Indians* (Rochester, NY: New York State Archaeological Association, 1926) at 29.
23 Newell, *supra* note 20 at 53-54.
24 *First Nations Policing Agreements* (Ottawa: Solicitor General of Canada, Ministry Secretariat, 1992). Robert H.D. Head, *Policing for Aboriginal Canadians: The R.C.M.P. Role* (Ottawa: Royal Canadian Mounted Police, 1993).
25 Lysane Cree, "Mohawk Community-Based Policing" (1999) 14:3 Canadian Human Rights Foundation Newsletter 12.
26 Robert Depew, "Policing Native Communities: Some Principles and Issues in Organizational Theory" (July 1992) 34 Can. J. Crim. 461 at 463.
27 Chris Murphy and Don Clairmont, *First Nations Police Officers Survey* (Ottawa: Solicitor General of Canada, Minister Secretariat, Ottawa, 1996) at 41-42. For an anecdotal example of this theme, see "Police Look to Native Traditions to Curb Crime" (2008) 15:7 Alberta Sweetgrass 3.
28 "Crime Gangs Get Free Roam on Canadian Indian Reserves," *Boston Globe* (1 February 2004) A6.
29 Benoit Aubin, "A Chief in Exile," *Maclean's* (23 February 2004) 26.
30 *R. v Kokesch*, [1990] 3 S.C.R. 3 at 29.
31 *R. v Jobidon*, [1991] 2 S.C.R. 714.
32 *R. v Ewanchuk*, [1999] 1 S.C.R. 330.
33 *R. v Pohorestsky*, [1987] 1 S.C.R. 945 at 949; *R. v Greffe*, [1990] 1 S.C.R. 755 at 795.
34 For border crossings, see *R. v Simmons*, [1988] 2 S.C.R. 495 at 528-29 [*Simmons*]. For airport terminals, see *R. v Monney*, [1999] 1 S.C.R. 652 at 678-79.
35 *Customs Act*, R.S. 1985, c. 1 (2nd. supp.), s. 98.
36 *R. v Patrick*, [2009] S.C.J. no. 17.
37 For the scope of school authority searches, see *R. v M. (M.R.)*, [1998] 3 S.C.R. 393 at 421-22. For a recent statement on the scope of police authority to conduct searches within school, see *R. v A.M.* (2008), 293 D.L.R. (4th) 187 (S.C.C.).
38 *Hopi Tribe v Kahe*, 21 Indian L. Rep. 6079 (Hopi Tribal Ct. 1994).
39 *Ibid.* at 6079.
40 *Simmons, supra* note 34 at 528.
41 *M. (M.R.), supra* note 37 at 414.
42 Tammy Landau, "Policing and Security in Four Remote Aboriginal Communities: A Challenge to Coercive Models of Police Work" (1996) 38:1 Can. J. Criminology & Crim. Just. 1.
43 *R. v Hatchard*, [1993] 1 C.N.L.R. 96 (Ont. Ct. Just.). *Indian Act*, S.C. 1985, c. I-5.
44 *Criminal Code*, R.S.C. 1985, c. 46.
45 *Hatchard, supra* note 43 at 97.
46 Royal Commission on Aboriginal Peoples, *Bridging the Cultural Divide: A Report on Aboriginal People and Criminal Justice in Canada* (Ottawa: Minister of Supply and Services Canada, 1996) at 261.
47 *Golden, supra* note 14.
48 *R. v Hebert*, [1990] 2 S.C.R. 151 at 173-75 [*Hebert*].
49 *R. v Grant*, [2009] 2 S.C.R. 353 at para. 44 [*Grant*].
50 *Ibid.* at 173-75; *R. v Noble*, [1997] 1 S.C.R. 874 [*Noble*].
51 *Grant, supra* note 49 at 164.
52 *R. v Broyles*, [1991] 3 S.C.R. 595 at 609-12.
53 *R. v Chambers*, [1990] 2 S.C.R. 1293 at 1316; *Noble, supra* note 50.
54 *R. v S. (R.J.)*, [1995] 1 S.C.R. 451 at 561.
55 *British Columbia Securities Commission v Branch*, [1995] 2 S.C.R. 3 at 46-47.
56 *R. v S. (R.J.), supra* note 54. *Thomson Newspapers Ltd. v Canada (Director of Investigation and Research, Restorative Trade Practices Commission)*, [1990] 1 S.C.R. 425 at 480; quoted in S. (R.J.), *supra* note 54 at 504.
57 *Hebert, supra* note 48 at 179-80.
58 *Ibid.* at 180.
59 *R. v Amway of Canada Ltd.*, [1989] 1 S.C.R. 21.
60 *Hebert, supra* note 48 at 174.

61 *Indian Civil Rights Act*, 25 U.S.C., s. 1301-3.
62 Rights of Members of Indian Tribes: Hearing before the Subcommittee on Indian Affairs of the House Committee on Interior and Insular Affairs, 90th Congress, 2nd Sess. (1968). For a brief history, see Kent McNeil, "Aboriginal Governments and the *Charter*: Lessons from the United States" (2002) C.J.L.S. 73 at 78-85.
63 *McNeil, supra* note 62. Rights of Members of Indian Tribes, *supra* note 62 at 127.
64 Jonathan Rudin and Dan Russell, *Native Alternative Dispute Resolution Systems: The Canadian Future in Light of the American Past* (Mississauga, ON: Ontario Native Council on Justice, 1993) at 50 [emphasis added].
65 *R. v Lyons*, [1987] 2 S.C.R. 307 at para. 74.
66 *Ibid.* at para. 84-85.
67 *R. v Swain*, [1991] 1 S.C.R. 933 at 975-77.
68 *Ibid.* at 986-88.
69 *R. v Hanneson* (1989), 71 C.R. (3d) 249 (Ont. C.A.). The Court held that a violation of the right to counsel did not insulate the person detained from a subsequent prosecution for obstructing justice where the inadmissable statements are the *actus reus* of the offence.
70 *R. v B. (K.G.)*, [1993] 1 S.C.R. 740 at 819.
71 *R. v P. (M.B.)* (1994), 29 C.R. (4th) 209 (S.C.C.) at 227-28.
72 *Noble, supra* note 50.
73 Karl Llewellyn and Edward Adamson, *The Cheyenne Way: Conflict and Case Law in Primitive Jurisprudence* (Norman, OK: University of Oklahoma Press, 1941) at 118-19.
74 *R. v Bartle*, [1994] 3 S.C.R. 173, at 194-96; *R. v Brydges*, [1990] 1 S.C.R. 190.
75 *Ibid.* at 198.
76 *R. v Pozniak*, [1994] 3 S.C.R. 310 at 319.
77 *R. v Evans*, [1991] 1 S.C.R. 869 at 891.
78 *Ibid.* at 893.
79 *R. v Prosper*, [1994] 3 S.C.R. 236 at 274 [*Prosper*].
80 *R. v Manninen*, [1987] 1 S.C.R. 1233 at 1241 [*Manninen*].
81 *Ibid.* at 1242.
82 *Prosper, supra* note 79 at 275.
83 *Ibid.* at 266-70.
84 *R. v Tremblay*, [1987] 2 S.C.R. 435 at 439.
85 *R. v Playford* (1987), 40 C.C.C. (3d) 142 (Ont. C.A.) at 155.
86 *R. v Smith*, [1991] 1 S.C.R. 714 at 728-29.
87 *R. v Sinclair*, [2010] 2 S.C.R. 310.
88 David Tanovich, "Charting the Constitutional Right of Effective Assistance of Counsel in Canada" (1994) 36 Criminal L.Q. 404.
89 Alan Young, "Adversarial Justice and the Charter of Rights: Stunting the Growth of the 'Living Tree'" (1997) 39 Criminal L.Q. 362 at 365.
90 *Manninen, supra* note 80 at 1242-43.
91 *R. v Ross*, [1989] 1 S.C.R. 3 at 14.
92 Ontario Professional Organizations Committee, *Report of the Professional Organization Committee (Ministry of the Attorney General of Ontario)* (Toronto: Ministry of the Attorney General of Ontario, 1980) at 26. Quoted in *Pearlman v Manitoba Law Society Judicial Committee*, [1991] 2 S.C.R. 869 at 887.
93 *Code of Offences and Procedures of Justice for the Mohawk Nation at Akwesasne*, Draft no. 10.
94 See, for example, Law Society of British Columbia, *Law Society Rules* (Vancouver: Law Society of British Columbia, 2012), Rule 2-27.
95 *Ibid.*, Rules 2-30, 2-32, and 2-47.
96 *Ibid.*, Rule 2-44.
97 See, for example, Law Society of British Columbia, *Professional Conduct Handbook* (Vancouver: Law Society of British Columbia, 2011), s. 3.
98 Larry Chartrand, "The Appropriateness of a Lawyer as Advocate in Contemporary Aboriginal Justice Initiatives" (August 1995) 33 Alta. L. Rev. 874. For a similar critique, see Troy Chalifoux, "A Need for Change: Cross-Cultural Sensitization of Lawyers" (1994) 32 Alta. L. Rev. 762.

99 Yvonne Boyer, "Community-Based Justice Initiatives of the Saskatoon Tribal Council" in Wanda D. McCaslin (ed.), *Justice as Healing: Indigenous Ways* (St. Paul, MN: Living Justice Press, 2005) 196 at 202.

100 *Ibid.* at 203.

101 *Ibid.* at 202. For a similar assertion that those involved with a social conflict may want to assume primary roles in a restorative resolution with a corresponding exclusion of justice professionals, see Susan Olson and Albert Dzur, "The Practice of Restorative Justice: Reconstructing Professional Roles in Restorative Justice Programs" (2003) Utah L. Rev. 57.

102 Paul Jonathan Saguil, "Ethical Lawyering across Canada's Legal Traditions" (2010) 9:1 Indig. L.J. 157.

103 To be fair, law society codes of professional conduct already temper the duty of advocacy with other ethical duties. British Columbia's *Professional Conduct Handbook, supra* note 97, outlines the ethical duties to treat the court, other lawyers, witnesses, and clients for the other side with respect and courtesy (Chapter 1) as well as an ethical duty to avoid dishonourable conduct (Chapter 2, s. 1).

104 *R. v Anunga*, [1976] 11 A.L.R. 412 (N.T.S.C.).

105 A.C. Hamilton and C.M. Sinclair, *Report of the Inquiry into the Administration of Justice and Aboriginal People* (Winnipeg: Government of Manitoba, Public Inquiry into the Administration of Justice and Aboriginal People, 1991).

106 *Justice on Trial* (Edmonton: Task Force on the Criminal Justice System and Its Impact on the Indian and Metis People of Alberta, 1991).

107 Law Reform Commission of Canada, *Aboriginal People and Justice Administration: A Discussion Paper* (Ottawa: Department of Justice, 1991).

108 Native Counseling Services of Alberta, online: http://www.ncsa.ca.

109 They also provide a court workers' program. Aboriginal Legal Services of Toronto, online: http://www.aboriginallegal.ca/court_work.php.

110 Frank Pommersheim, *Braid of Feathers: American Indian Law and Contemporary Tribal Life* (Berkeley: University of California Press, 1995) at 70-71.

111 *Red Cliff Band of Lake Superior Chippewas Tribal Law and Constitution*, Ch. 4, s. 24.

112 Chartrand, *supra* note 98.

113 For a similar argument on the potential roles of defence counsel during victim-offender mediation programs, see Jennifer Gerarda Brown, "The Use of Mediation to Resolve Criminal Cases: A Procedural Critique" (1994) 43 Emory L.J. 1247 at 1287-91.

114 Boyer, *supra* note 99.

Chapter 9: The Final Resolution

1 *Canadian Charter of Rights and Freedoms*, Part I of the *Constitution Act, 1982*, being Schedule B to the *Canada Act 1982*, (U.K.), c. 11.

2 See, for example, *Smith v R*, [1987] 1 S.C.R. 1045 [*Smith*]; *Steele v Mountain Institution*, [1990] 2 S.C.R. 1385; *R. v Goltz*, [1991] 3 S.C.R. 485; *R. v Latimer*, [2001] 1 S.C.R. 3.

3 *Canadian Bill of Rights*, S.C. 1960, c. 44. *R. v Miller and Cockriell*, [1977] 2 S.C.R. 680 [*Miller and Cockriell*].

4 *Miller and Cockriell, supra* note 3. See also Michael Jackson, "Cruel and Unusual Treatment or Punishment" (1982) 17 U.B.C. L. Rev., Charter Edition 189.

5 *United States v Burn*, [2001] 1 S.C.R. 283.

6 *Ibid.* at paras. 124-43.

7 *Ibid.* at paras. 50-57.

8 *Ibid.* at para. 78.

9 *Ibid.* at paras. 96-102.

10 *Ibid.* at para. 103.

11 Austin Sarat, *When the State Kills: Capital Punishment and the American Condition* (Princeton, NJ: Princeton University Press, 2002).

12 Michael Cousins, "Aboriginal Justice: A Haudenosaunee Approach" in Wanda D. McCaslin (ed.), *Justice as Healing: Indigenous Ways* (St. Paul, MA: Living Justice Press, 2005) 141 at 150-51.

13 *Smith, supra* note 2 at 1073-74.
14 *Kindler v Canada (Minister of Justice)*, [1991] 2 S.C.R. 779; *Suresh v Canada (Minister of Citizenship and Immigration)*, [2002] 1 S.C.R. 3.
15 Michael Jackson, "Locking Up Natives in Canada" (1988-1989) 23 U.B.C. L. Rev. 215 at 272.
16 *Thomas v Norris*, [1992] 2 C.N.L.R. 139 (B.C.S.C.).
17 "Dance to the Death: A Secretive Ritual Practised by Some Native Peoples on Canada's West Coast Is Intended to Seek Power from the Spirits That Will Help the Dancer through Life," *Hamilton Spectator* (16 April 2005) F6.
18 "Recent Native Longhouse Initiation Deaths Spark Investigation, Explanation," *Canadian Press Newswire* (13 January 2005).
19 "Dance to the Death," *supra* note 17.
20 *Ibid.*
21 Emma LaRocque. "Re-examining Culturally Appropriate Models in Criminal Justice Applications" in Michael Asch (ed.), *Aboriginal and Treaty Rights in Canada: Essays on Law, Equality, and Respect for Difference* (Vancouver: UBC Press, 1997) 75; Sherene Razack, *Looking White People in the Eye: Gender, Race, and Culture in Courtrooms and Classrooms* (Toronto: University of Toronto Press, 1998).
22 *R. v Joseph Murray Jungarai* (1981), 9 N.T.R. 30 (N.T.S.C.) at 31-32.
23 *R. v Joseph Murray Jungarai* (2 November 1981) (N.T.S.C.) [unreported].
24 *R. v Joseph Murray Jungarai* (4 June 1982) (F.C. Aust.) [unreported].
25 *R. v Jadurin* (1982), 7 A. Crim. R. 182.
26 *Ibid.* at 187.
27 *R. v Minor* (1992), 59 A. Crim. R. 227 at 238.
28 *Ibid.* at 237.
29 *R. v Mamarika* (1982), 63 F.L.R. 202.
30 John Chesterman, "Balancing Civil Rights and Indigenous Rights: Is There a Problem?" (2002) 8:2 Aust. J.H.R. 125 at 142.
31 Australian Law Reform Commission, *The Recognition of Aboriginal Customary Laws*, Report no. 31, volume 2 (Canberra, Australia: Australian Government Publishing Service, 1986) at 366-67.
32 *R. v Clarkson*, [1986] 1 S.C.R. 383 at 394-95 [*Clarkson*].
33 Placing value on the sanctity of the human body also resonates in other aspects of the Court's jurisprudence. For example, consent to serious bodily harm is not a lawful defence for someone charged with assault. See *R. v Jobidon*, [1991] 2 S.C.R. 714.
34 Geoffrey Scarre, "Corporal Punishment" (2003) 6 Ethical Theory & Moral Practice 295 at 307.
35 "Malaysia Urged to End Brutal Punishments after Women Caned," *States News Service* (17 February 2010); "Womens' Groups Protest Caning of Women in Malaysia," *Indo-Asian News Service* (18 February 2010).
36 "Malaysia Spares the Rod for Muslim Woman Convicted for Drinking Beer," *Asian Political News* (5 April 2010).
37 Andrew Heavens, "Police Break Up Rally for Woman on Trial for Wearing Pants: Tear Gas Fired at Khartoum Protest against Possible Flogging for Breach of Dress Code," *Globe and Mail* (5 August 2009) A2.
38 Hung-En Sung, "Nonfatal Violence-Related and Accident-Related Injuries among Jail Inmates in the United States" (2010) 90:3 Prison Journal 353; Deanna M. Perez et al., "Individual and Institutional Characteristics Related to Inmate Victimization" (2010) 54:3 Int'l J. Offender Therapy & Comparative Criminology 378; Nancy Wolff and Jing Shi, "Type, Source, and Patterns of Physical Victimization: A Comparison of Male and Female Inmates" (2009) 89:2 Prison Journal 173; Benjamin Steiner, "Assessing Static and Dynamic Influences on Inmate Violence Levels" (2009) 55:1 Crime & Delinquency 134; Melissa Sisco and Judith Baker, "Beyond Predicting the Risk of Sexual Victimization in Prison: Considering Inmate Options and Reporting Avenues for Addressing an Inherent Problem" (2007) 6:3 Criminology & Public Policy 573; Mark T. Berg and Matt DeLisi, "The Correctional Melting

Pot: Race, Ethnicity, Citizenship, and Prison Violence" (2006) 34:6 J. Crim. Justice 631; Ian O'Donnell and Kimmett Edgar, "Routine Victimisation in Prisons" (1998) 37:3 How. J. Crim. Justice 266.

39 Meredith Huey Dye, "Deprivation, Importation, and Inmate Suicide: Combined Effects of Institutional Conditions and Inmate Composition" (2010) 38:4 J. Crim. Justice 796.
40 Stefan Fruehwald and Patrick Frottier, "Death behind Bars" (2002) 167:10 Can. Medical Association Journal 1127.
41 *International Covenant on Civil and Political Rights*, 16 December 1966, adopted by United Nations General Assembly Resolution 2200A (XXI).
42 *Osbourne v Jamaica*, Communication no. 759/1997.
43 United Nations Human Rights Committee, 15 March 2000, UN Doc. A/55/40 *GAOR*, (vol. II), 138, para. 9.1.
44 *Tyrer v United Kingdom* (1978), (E. Ct. H.R.), Series A, no. 26.
45 David Cayley, *The Expanding Prison: The Crisis in Crime and Punishment and the Search for Alternatives* (Toronto: House of Anansi Press, 1998) at 219-20 and 290.
46 Numerous writers, both past and contemporary, have articulated theories of social contract. Famous examples include Thomas Hobbes, *Leviathan*, ed. J.C.A. Gaskin (New York: Oxford University Press, 1998); John Locke, *Second Treatise of Government*, ed. Peter Laslett (Cambridge: Cambridge University Press, 1960); Jean-Jacques Rousseau, *The Social Contract*, ed. Maurice Cranston (Baltimore, MD: Penguin Books, 1968); John Rawls, *A Theory of Justice* (Cambridge, MA: Belknap Press, 1971).
47 Garrett Hardin, "The Tragedy of the Commons" (1968) 162 Science 1243; John M. Parrish, *Collective Responsibility and the State* (Conference Papers, American Political Science Association, Annual Meeting, 2007) [unpublished]; Todd R. Clear, "The Punitive Paradox: Desert and the Compulsion to Punish" (1996) 33:1 J. Research in Crime & Delinquency 94.
48 *R. v Strachan*, [1988] 2 S.C.R. 980 at 1005.
49 *Ibid.* at 1005-6.
50 *R. v Collins*, [1987] 1 S.C.R. 265.
51 Dale Gibson, *The Law of the Charter: General Principles* (Calgary: Carswell, 1986) at 236-46, cited in *Collins, ibid.* at 282.
52 *Collins, supra* note 50 at 282.
53 *Ibid.*
54 *Ibid.* at 284-86.
55 *R. v Stillman*, [1997] 1 S.C.R. 607 at 655.
56 *Ibid.* at 663-64.
57 *Ibid.* at 664-65.
58 *Ibid.* at 668.
59 *R. v Grant*, [2009] 2 S.C.R. 353 *[Grant]*.
60 *R. v Buhay* (2003), 10 C.R. (6th) 205 at para. 59 *[Buhay]*.
61 *R. v Seiben* (1987), 56 C.R. (3d) 225 (S.C.C.); *R. v Hamill* (1987), 56 C.R. (3d) 220 (S.C.C.); *R. v Sanelli* (1990), 74 C.R. (3d) 281 (S.C.C.); *R. v Wong* (1990), 1 C.R. (4th) 1 (S.C.C.).
62 *Grant, supra* note 59 at para. 75; *R. v Wise* (1992), 11 C.R. (4th) 253 (S.C.C.); *R. v Silviera*, [1995] 2 S.C.R. 297; *R. v Feeney* (1997) 115 C.C.C. (3d) 129 (S.C.C.).
63 *Grant, supra* note 59 at para. 74; *Clarkson, supra* note 32; *R. v Burlingham*, [1995] 2 S.C.R. 206 *[Burlingham]*; *Buhay, supra* note 60.
64 *Grant, supra* note 59 at para. 75.
65 *Ibid.* at para. 76.
66 *Ibid.* at para. 91.
67 *Ibid.* at para. 97.
68 *Ibid.* at para. 109.
69 *Ibid.* at para. 114.
70 *Ibid.* at para. 122.
71 *Ibid.* at para. 81.
72 *Ibid.* at para. 83.
73 *Ibid.* at para. 86.

74 *Code of Offences and Procedures of Justice for the Mohawk Nation at Akwesasne,* Draft no. 10.
75 *Criminal Code,* R.S.C. 1985, c. 46.
76 *R. v Thomsen,* [1988] 1 S.C.R. 640.
77 *R. v Manninen,* [1987] 1 S.C.R. 1233 at 1242.
78 *R. v Playford* (1987), 40 C.C.C. (3d) 142 (Ont. C.A.) at 155.
79 *R. v Prosper,* [1994] 3 S.C.R. 236 at 276.
80 See *R. v Mills,* [1986] 1 S.C.R. 863. A court having that competent jurisdiction often depends upon a statutory grant of jurisdiction over the offence and the accused, as is the case with provincial criminal courts (at 955-56) or appeal courts (at 958-59). Perhaps Mr. X would have to apply to a court of superior jurisdiction. Courts of superior jurisdiction in each province have all of the historic jurisdiction of the high court in England, subject to statutory limitations, and are therefore courts of competent jurisdiction under section 24. The superior court jurisdiction will not displace the jurisdiction of other courts of limited jurisdiction (at 956).
81 *R. v Johnstone,* 2009 SKPC 133.
82 Kathy L. Brock, "Polishing the Halls of Justice: Sections 24(2) and 8 of the *Charter of Rights*" (1992-93) 2 N.J.C.L. 265 at 270.
83 Steven M. Penney, "Unreal Distinctions: The Exclusion of Unfairly Obtained Evidence under S. 24(2) of the Charter" (1994) 32 Alta. L. Rev. 782 at 797.
84 Jamie Cameron, "Dialogue and Hierarchy in Charter Interpretation: A Comment on *R. v. Mills*" (2000) 38 Alta. L. Rev. 1051 at 1064. *Dagenais v Canadian Broadcasting Corporation,* [1994] 3 S.C.R. 835.
85 Jennifer Koshan "Aboriginal Women, Justice and the Charter: Bridging the Divide?" (November 1998) 32 U.B.C.L. Rev. 23 at 51.
86 *R. v Andersen,* 2010 ABPC 325; *R. v Blackwood,* [2009] O.J. 5393 (Sup. Ct. Just.); *R. v Blake,* 2009 ONCA 1; *R. v Bryce,* [2009] O.J. 3640; *R. v Chuhaniuk,* 2010 BCCA 403; *R. v Crocker* (2009), 69 C.R. (6th) 107; *R. v Cuttell* (2009), 247 C.C.C. (3d) 247; *R. v D.B.M.* (2009), 282 N.S.R. (2d) 64; *R. v Fildan* (2009), 69 C.R. (6th) 65; *R. v Foy,* 2010 BCSC 112; *R. v Hubar-Rook,* 2010 ABPC 283; *R. v T.O.,* 2010 ONCJ 334; *R. v Graham,* 2010 ONSC 119; *R. v Huddlestone,* 2009 BCPC 404; *R. v Johnson,* 2010 ONSC 6186; *R. v Karanouh,* 2009 ONCJ 579; *R. v Kisil,* 2009 ONCJ 424; *R. v Mahmood,* [2009] O.J. 3192 (Sup. Ct. Just.); *R. v Mason,* [2009] O.J. 4468 (Sup. Ct. Just.); *R. v McIntosh,* 2010 SKPC 22; *R. v Meija* (2009), 14 Alta. L.R. (6th) 368; *R. v Melynchuk* (2010), 209 C.R.R. (2d) 63 (Alta. P.C.); *R. v Mudryk,* 2009 ABPC 253; *R. v Nagassar,* 2010 ONSC 6032; *R. v Nother,* 2009 ONCJ 624; *R. v Pillott* (2009), 14 Alta. L.R. (5th) 112; *R. v Quesnelle,* [2009] O.J. 5445 (Sup. Ct. Just.); *R. v Ramage* (2010) 257 C.C.C. (3d) 61; *R. v Rego,* 2009 ONCJ 612; *R. v Rempel* (2010), 252 Man. R. (2d) 108 (Prov. Ct.); *R. v Roemer,* 2010 ONSC 430; *R. v Rusnak,* 2009 ABPC 258; *R. v Simpson,* [2009] O.J. 5452 (Sup. Ct. Just.); *R. v Skuce,* [2009] B.C.J. 2289; *R. v Tse,* [2009] B.C.J. 2632; *R. v Usher,* 2010 BCPC 210; *R. v Vinohoran,* [2009] O.J. 4037 (Sup. Ct. Just.); *R. v Ward,* 2010 BCCA 1; *R. v White,* 2009 BCPC 312; *R. v Xhango,* 2010 ONCJ 503; *R. v Blanchard,* 2011 NLCA 33; *R. v Sing,* 2011 ONSC 3124; *R. v Johnson,* 2011 ABPC 179 [*Johnson*]; *R. v Charlton,* 2011 BCSC 805; *R. v Tuduce,* 2011 ONSC 2749.
87 *R. v Alexander* (2010), 209 C.R.R. (2d) 34 (Ont. S.C.); *R. v D.C.,* 2010 SKPC 132; *R. v Fiddler,* [2010] S.J. 545; *R. v Gaba* (2010), 211 C.R.R. (2d) 265 (B.C.S.C.); *R. v Gerun,* 2009 ABPC 224; *R. v Kur,* 2010 ONCJ 295; *R. v Morgan,* 2010 ONSC 4258; *R. v Soto* (2010), 209 C.R.R. (2d) 191 (Ont. C.J.); *R. v Strilec* (2010), 256 C.C.C. (3d) 403 (B.C.C.A.); *R. v Sunshine,* 2010 BCSC 45; *R. v Way* (2010), 358 N.B.R. (2d) 119 (Q.B.); *Johnson, supra* note 86.
88 *R. v Leitner,* 2009 BCPC 402; *R. v Knight,* 2010 ONCJ 400; *R. v Quan,* [2010] O.J. no. 2641; *R. v Schmidt* (2010), 27 Alta. L.R. (5th) 352 (Q.B.); *R. v Sotana,* 2010 BCSC 267; *R. v Zaba,* 2010 SKPC 85.
89 *R. v Blazevic,* 2010 ONCJ 137; *R. v Ciachurski,* 2009 BSCS 1467; *R. v Dhillon,* 2010 ONCA 582; *R. v E. Star International Inc.,* 2009 ONCJ 576; *R. v Fernandes,* [2009] O.J. 5218 (Sup. Ct. Just.); *R. v Goodwin,* 2009 ABQB 710; *R. v Huynh,* 2010 BCSC 1553; *R. v J.A.J.,* 2009 ONCJ 467; *R. v Jaswal,* 2010 ABPC 366; *R. v MacFarlane,* 2009 ONCJ 489; *R. v Nguyen,* [2009] O.J. 4565 (Sup. Ct. Just.); *R. v N.N.,* 2009 ONCJ 508; *R. v Peacock,* 2009 ONCJ 479; *R. v Rusnov,* 2009 ONCJ 564; *R. v Sandhu,* 69 C.R. (6th) 137 (Ont. Sup. Ct. Just.); *R. v Sandypoint,* 2009

SKPC 108; *R. v Watson,* 2010 ONSC 448; *R. v Vu* (2010), 2010 BCSC 1260; *R. v Koczab,* 2011 MBQB 70; *R. v Puleio,* 2011 ONCJ 260.

90 *R. v A.K.,* 2009 ONCJ 578; *R. v Adams* (2010), 211 C.R.R. (2d) 360 (Nfld. S.C.); *R. v Adhofer,* 2010 ABPC 235; *R. v Appleby,* 2009 ABPC 301; *R. v Armstrong,* [2009] O.J. 5617 (Sup. Ct. Just.); *R. v Avila,* 2010 ONCJ 512; *R. v Banks,* 2010 ONCJ 553; *R. v Beattie* (2009), 69 C.R. (6th) 92 (Ont. Sup. Ct. Just.); *R. v Bruno,* 2009 ABPC 232; *R. v Carriero* (2010), 210 C.R.R. (2d) 65; *R. v Churko,* 2010 SKPC 5; *R. v Comber,* 2009 ONCJ 418; *R. v Dinwall,* 2010 ONCJ 5207; *R. v Dupras,* 2010 ABPC 138; *R. v Epp,* 2010 SKPC 89; *R. v Erickson,* 2009 BCPC 365; *R. v Erickson* (2010), 353 Sask. R. 132 (P.C.); *R. v Farahanchi,* 2010 NSPC 57; *R. v Fynn,* 2010 ONCJ 543; *R. v Forster,* 2009 ABPC 278; *R. v Givens,* 85 M.V.R. (5th) 218 (B.C.S.C.); *R. v Hamilton,* 2010 YKTC 75; *R. v Henry,* 2010 ONSC 5206; *R. v Hoang,* 2010 BCPC 230; *R. v J.K.,* 2010 ONCJ 232; *R. v Judge,* 2010 ONCJ 488; *R. v Kerr,* 2010 ONCJ 189; *R. v Khan,* 2010 ONCJ 404; *R. v LaFontaine,* 2010 ONSC 21; *R. v Lee,* 2009 ONCJ 434; *R. v Losier* (2010), 361 N.B.R. (2d) 217; *R. v MacKay,* 2009 ONCJ 510; *R. v MacKenzie,* 2009 SKQB 415; *R. v Mai,* 2010 BCPC 159; *R. v Meijid,* 2010 ONSC 5532; *R. v Mellors,* 2010 BCPC 211; *R. v Menzies,* 2009 MBQB 250; *R. v Mohmedi,* 2009 ONCJ 533; *R. v Nguyen,* 2010 ONSC 1520; *R. v Ogbaldet,* 2010 ONCJ 477; *R. v Osolky,* 2009 ONCJ 445; *R. v Payette* (2010), 259 C.C.C. (3d) 178 (B.C.C.A.); *R. v Perry,* 2010 ABPC 350; *R. v Reddy,* 2010 BCCA 11; *R. v Ryan* (2010), 210 C.R.R. (2d) 307 (Nfld. Prov. Ct.); *R. v Sergalis,* [2009] O.J. 4823; *R. v Shaw,* [2009] O.J. 4142; *R. v Sheppard,* 2010 ABPC 200; *R. v Smith,* 2010 ONCJ 28; *R. v Smith,* 2010 ONCJ 641; *R. v Snider,* 2009 BCPC 300; *R. v Solomon,* [2009] O.J. 4578; *R. v Stritharan,* 2010 ONCJ 466l; *R. v Valinquette,* 2010 BCSC 1423; *R. v Vijayam,* 2010 ONCJ 537; *R. v Waters,* 2010 ABQB 607; *R. v Whyte,* 2009 ONCJ 389; *R. v Ross,* 2011 ABPC 695; *R. v Henderson,* 2011 ONSC 2392; *R. v Pengchanh,* 2011 BCSC 484; *R. v Hatton,* 2011 ABQB 242; *R. v Main,* 2011 ABQB 290; *R. v Hatzel,* 2011 SKQB 49; *R. v Walters,* 2011 ONSC 2316; *R. v Phillips,* 2011 ONSC 3890; *R. v McAnuff,* 2011 ONSC 2760; *R. v Weibe,* 2011 SKPC 70; *R. v Boyd,* 2011 BCPC 137; *R. v McPhail,* 2011 ONCJ 315; *R. v Castillo,* 2011 ONSC 3257.

91 *R. v Martin* (2010), 361 N.B.R. (2d) 251 (C.A.); *R. v Rosales,* 2010 ONSC 1992; *R. v Stanton* (2010), 254 C.C.C. (3d) 421 (B.C.C.A.); *R. v Trieu,* 2010 ONCJ 518; *R. v Guenter,* [2011] O.J. no. 2233 (Sup. Ct. J.); *R. v Guce,* 2011 ONSC 2331;

92 L. Timothy Perrin et al., "If It's Broken, Fix It: Moving beyond the Exclusionary Rule: A New and Extensive Empirical Study of the Exclusionary Rule and a Call for a Civil Administrative Remedy to Partially Replace the Rule" (1998) 83 Iowa L. Rev. 669.

93 *Ibid.* at 676. This finding was based on National Institute of Justice, *The Effects of the Exclusionary Rule: A Study in California 2* (Washington, DC: Department of Justice, 1982). This study stated that 32.5 percent of all felony drug arrests cleared for prosecution in 1981 to the Los Angeles County Prosecutor's Office were rejected after an initial review because of search and seizure problems. See also Harry M. Caldwell and Carol A. Chase, "The Unruly Exclusionary Rule: Heeding Justice Blackmun's Call to Examine the Rule in Light of Changing Judicial Understanding about Its Effects outside the Courtroom" (1994) 78 Marq. L. Rev. 45. This article argues that even though suppression hearings are unsuccessful 80 to 90 percent of the time, defence counsel still go for them often with the hopes of wearing down the prosecution and wringing concessions (at 50-51).

94 Perrin et al., *supra* note 92. It is also based National Institute of Justice, *supra* note 93. The study found that 46 percent of individuals freed in California in 1976 and 1977 as a result of the exclusionary rule went on to commit additional crimes within twenty-four months of their release.

95 Raymond A. Atkins and Paul H. Rubin, "Effects of Criminal Procedure on Crime Rates: Mapping Out the Consequences of the Exclusionary Rule" (Emory University Department of Economics, Working Papers, November 1998).

96 Silvia Mendes, "Certainty, Severity, and Their Relative Deterrent Effects: Questioning the Role of Risk in Criminal Deterrence Theory" (2004) 32:1 Pol'y Studies J. 59.

97 Rupert Ross, *Returning to the Teachings: Exploring Aboriginal Justice* (Toronto: Penguin Books Canada, 1996) at 227-32; and David Cayley, *The Expanding Prison: The Crisis in Crime and Punishment and the Search for Alternatives* (Toronto: House of Anansi Press, 1998) at 325-27.

98   Steven M. Penney, "Unreal Distinctions: The Exclusion of Unfairly Obtained Evidence under
     S. 24(2) of the Charter" (1994) 32 Alta. L. Rev. 782 at 792. *Kuruma v The Queen*, [1955] A.C.
     197 (P.C.); *R. v Sang*, [1980] A.C. 402 (H.L.).
99   *R. v Wray*, [1971] S.C.R. 272.
100 J.A.E. Pottow, "Constitutional Remedies in the Criminal Context: A Unified Approach to
     Section 24" (2000) 43:4 Crim. L.Q. 43 459; (2000) 44:1 Crim. L.Q. 34; and (2000) 44:2
     Criminal L. Q. 44 223.
101 Quote and case commentary in Alan Robinson "*R. v. Williams and Orrs*: Cigar Store Indians
     and Juvenile Confessions" (1986) Aboriginal Law Bulletin 20.
102 Steven Penney, "Taking Deterrence Seriously: Excluding Unconstitutionally Obtained Evi-
     dence under S. 24(2) of the *Charter*" (2004) 49 McGill L.J. 105 at 121.
103 *R. v Erven*, [1979] 2 S.C.R. 1041.
104 *Burlingham, supra* note 63 at para. 32.
105 Jack Watson, "Curial Incompetence in Criminal Trials: A Discussion of Section 24 of the
     Charter of Rights and Freedoms in the Criminal Trial Context" (Part 1) (1990) 32 Crim.
     L.Q. 162 at 167.
106 *Pottow, supra* note 100 at 67.
107 *R. v Corbett*, [1998] 1 S.C.R. 670; *R. v Harrer*, [1995] 3 S.C.R. 562.
108 *R. v White*, [2000] 2 S.C.R. 417.
109 *Burlingham, supra* note 63 at 263.
110 *R. v Harper*, [1994] 3 S.C.R. 343.
111 *Ibid.* at 353-54.
112 *Violent Crime Control and Law Enforcement Act of 1995,* 108 Stat. 1796.
113 C.T. Walker, "A Critique of the Prima Facie Exclusionary Rule" (1996) 17:1 N.Z.U. L.R. 94.
114 *Burlingham, supra* note 63 at 270.
115 *United States v Calandra*, 414 U.S. 338 (1974).
116 *Mackin v New Brunswick; Rice v New Brunswick*, [2002] 1 S.C.R. 405 at para. 79. See also *R. v
     Mills*, [1999] 3 S.C.R. 668.
117 *R. v 974649 Ontario Inc.,* [2001] 3 S.C.R. 575.
118 *Vancouver (City) v Ward*, [2010] 2 S.C.R. 28.

Chapter 10: Conclusion

1   Carol LaPrairie, *Justice for the Cree: Communities, Crime and Order* (Nemaska, PQ: Cree Regional
     Authority, 1991); Carol LaPrairie, *Exploring the Boundaries of Justice: A Report Prepared for the
     Department of Justice* (Whitehorse: First Nations of the Yukon Territory and Justice Canada,
     1992).
2   Bruce G. Miller, "The Individual, the Collective, and the Tribal Code" (1997) 21:1 Am.
     Indian Culture & Research Journal 185 at 195.
3   *Code of Offences and Procedures of Justice for the Mohawk Nation at Akwesasne*, Draft no. 10.
4   Douglas George-Kanentiio, "Iroquois Justice" (Spring 1995) 1:1 Akwesasne Notes 106.
5   For a detailed history, see Gerald R. Alfred, *Heeding the Voices of Our Ancestors: Kahnawake
     Mohawk Politics and the Rise of Native Nationalism* (Don Mills, ON: Oxford University Press
     Canada, 1995).
6   E. Jane Dickson-Gilmore "'This Is My History, I Know Who I Am': History, Factionalist Com-
     petition, and the Assumption of Imposition in the Kahnawake Mohawk Nation" (1999)
     46:3 Ethnohistory 429.
7   *Ibid.* at 434-35.
8   Miller, *supra* note 2 at 195-97. See also David Milward, "Not Just the Peace Pipe but Also the
     Lance: Exploring Different Possibilities for Indigenous Control over Criminal Justice" (2008)
     23:1 Wicazo Sa Rev. 97.
9   Joyce A. Green, *Cultural and Ethnic Fundamentalism: The Mixed Potential for Identity, Liberation,
     and Oppression*, Scholar Series (Regina: Saskatchewan Institute of Public Policy, 2003) at
     10-11.
10 *Canadian Charter of Rights and Freedoms*, Part I of the *Constitution Act, 1982*, being Schedule
     B to the *Canada Act 1982*, (U.K.), c. 11.

11 Royal Commission on Aboriginal Peoples, *Bridging the Cultural Divide: A Report on Aboriginal People and Criminal Justice in Canada* (Ottawa: Minister of Supply and Services Canada, 1996).

12 *R. v Oakes*, [1986] 1 S.C.R. 103; *Dagenais v Canadian Broadcasting Corporation*, [1994] 3 S.C.R. 835.

13 Leslie Jane MacMillan, "Colonial Traditions, Co-optations, and Colonial Indigenous Legal Consciousness" (2011) 36:1 Law & Social Inquiry 171.

14 Dwayne Trevor MacDonald, "Resistance or Engagement? A Pair of Indigenous Writers Come to Very Different Conclusions about Dialogue with the White Community" (2006) 14 Literary Rev. Canada 8 at 9.

15 Scott Clark, "The Nunavut Court of Justice: An Example of Challenges and Alternatives for Communities and for the Administration of Justice" (2011) 53:3 Can. J. Crim. 343 at 364-65; Harry Blagg, *Crime, Aboriginality, and the Decolonisation of Justice* (Sydney, Australia: Hawkins Press, 2008).

16 James W. Zion and Elsie Zion, "'Hazho' Sokee' – Stay Together Nicely': Domestic Violence under Navajo Common Law" (1993) 25:2 Arizona St. L.J. 407.

17 Rupert Ross, *Returning to the Teachings: Exploring Aboriginal Justice* (Toronto: Penguin Books Canada, 1996).

18 My discussion here is based on private conversations that I have had with DeLloyd Guth.

19 Miller, *supra* note 2 at 34-37.

Bibliography

Aboriginal Justice Strategy Summative Evaluation: Final Report (Ottawa: Department of Canada, Evaluation Division, 2007).

Aboriginal Peoples in Canada in 2006: Inuit, Metis, and First Nations, 2006 Census (Ottawa: Statistics Canada, 2006).

Aboriginal Peoples and Criminal Justice: Equality, Respect and the Search for Justice, Report no. 34 (Ottawa: Law Reform Commission of Canada, 1991).

Aboriginal Witnesses in Queensland's Criminal Courts (Brisbane: Queensland Criminal Justice Commission, Goprint, 1996).

"Aboriginals Deserve Equal, Not Special, Treatment: Overplaying the Race Card Is in No One's Interest." *Globe and Mail* (29 April 1999) A12.

Acorn, Annalise. *Compulsory Compassion: A Critique of Restorative Justice* (Vancouver: UBC Press, 2004).

Albrecht, Berit. "Multicultural Challenges for Restorative Justice: Mediators' Experiences from Norway and Finland" (2010) 11:1 J. Scandinavian Stud. Criminology & Crime Prevention 3.

Alfred, Gerald R. *Heeding the Voices of Our Ancestors: Kahnawake Mohawk Politics and the Rise of Native Nationalism* (Don Mills, ON: Oxford University Press Canada, 1995).

Alfred, Taiaiake. *Peace, Power, Righteousness* (London: Oxford University Press, 2008).

Andersen, Chris. "Governing Aboriginal Justice in Canada: Constructing Responsible Individuals and Communities through 'Tradition'" (1999) 31 Crime, Law & Social Change 303.

Annexstad, W. James. "The Detention and Prosecution of Insurgents and Other Non-Traditional Combatants: A Look at the Task Force 134 Process and the Future of Detainee Prosecutions" (2007) 410 Army L. 72.

Arbour, Jane M. "The Protection of Aboriginal Rights within a Human Rights Regime: In Search of an Analytical Framework for Section 25 of the Canadian Charter of Rights and Freedoms" (2003) 21 Sup. Ct. L. Rev. (2d) 3.

Asch, Michael, and Patrick Macklem. "Aboriginal Rights and Canadian Sovereignty: An Essay on *R. v. Sparrow*" (1991) 29:2 Alta. L. Rev. 517.

Asher, Brad. *Beyond the Reservation: Indians, Settlers, and the Law in Washington Territory, 1853-1889* (Norman: University of Oklahoma Press, 1999).

Ashworth, Andrew. "Responsibilities, Rights and Restorative Justice" (2002) 43:3 Brit. J. Crim. 578.

Ashworth, Andrew, and M. Hough. "Sentencing and the Climate of Opinion" (1996) Crim. L. Rev. 761.

Atkins, Raymond A., and Paul H. Rubin. "Effects of Criminal Procedure on Crime Rates: Mapping Out the Consequences of the Exclusionary Rule" (Emory University Department of Economics, Working Papers, November 1998).

Atkins, Scott. "Racial Segregation, Concentrated Disadvantage, and Violent Crime" (2009) 7 J. Ethnicity in Crim. Justice 30.

Atkinson, Judy. "Violence against Aboriginal Women: Reconstitution of Community Law – The Way Forward" (1990) 2:46 Indigenous Law Bulletin 6.

Aubin, Benoit. "A Chief in Exile." *Maclean's* (23 February 2004) 26.

Austin, Raymond D. *Navajo Courts and Navajo Common Law: A Tradition of Tribal Self-Governance* (Minneapolis, MN: University of Minnesota Press, 2009).

Australian Law Reform Commission. *The Recognition of Aboriginal Customary Laws*, Report no. 31, volume 2 (Canberra, Australia: Australian Government Publishing Service, 1986).

"Badly Formed Sentences." *Ottawa Citizen* (5 April 2001) A14.

Bagaric, Mirko, and John Morss. "International Sentencing Law: In Search of a Justification and a Coherent Framework" (2006) 6:2 Int'l Crim. L. Rev. 191.

Baker, Thomas, and Alex R. Piquero. "Assessing the Perceived Benefits: Criminal Offending Relationship" (2010) 38:5 J. Crim. Justice 981.

Banks, Christopher B. "Security and Freedom after September 11" (2010-11) 13:1 Public Integrity 5.

Bansen, Ira. "Doing the Crime and Doing the Time." *CBC Reality Check Team* (5 January 2006).

Barnett, Randy. "Restitution: A New Paradigm of Criminal Justice" (1977) 87 Ethics 279.

Barnsley, Paul. "Author Reveals SIGA 'Mistakes'" (2001) 18:8 Windspeaker 3.

Baron, Stephen W., and Leslie W. Kennedy. "Deterrence and Homeless Male Youths" (1998) 40:1 Can. J. Crim. 27.

Barratt, Monica. "Cannabis Law Reform in Western Australia: An Opportunity to Test Theories of Marginal Deterrence and Legitimacy" (2005) 25:4 Drug & Alcohol Rev. 321.

Barrett, Emma, Katherine A. Mills, and Maree Teeson. "Hurt People Who Hurt People: Violence amongst Individuals with Comorbid Substance Abuse Disorder and Post-Traumatic Stress Disorder" (2011) 36:7 Addictive Behaviors 721.

Barsh, Russell Lawrence, and Sákéj Henderson. "The Supreme Court's *Van der Peet* Trilogy: Naïve Imperialism and Ropes of Sand" (1997) 42 McGill L.J. 993.

Bayda, Justice E.D. "The Theory and Practice of Sentencing: Are They on the Same Wavelength?" (1996) 60 Sask. L. Rev. 317.

Bazemore, Gordon. "Young People, Trouble and Crime: Restorative Justice as a Normative Theory of Informal Social Control and Social Support" (2001) 33:2 Youth & Society 199.

Bell, Catherine. "New Directions in the Law of Indigenous Rights" (1998) 77 Can. Bar Rev. 36.

Bell, Diane. "Aboriginal Women and the Recognition of Customary Law in Australia." In Bradford W. Morse and Gordon R. Woodman (eds.), *Indigenous Law and the State* (Dordrecht, Holland: Foris Publications, 1988) 297.

Bennett, Christopher. *The Apology Ritual* (Cambridge: Cambridge University Press, 2008).

Berg, Mark T., and Matt DeLisi. "The Correctional Melting Pot: Race, Ethnicity, Citizenship, and Prison Violence" (2006) 34:6 J. Crim. Justice 631.

"Berlusconi Fiddles, Italy Burns" 388:5859 Economist (19 July 2008) 59.

Bibas, Stephanos. "Transparency and Participation in Criminal Procedure" (2006) 81:3 N.Y.U. L. Rev. 911.

Bierschbach, Richard A., and Alex Stein. "Deterrence, Retributivism, and the Law of Evidence" (2007) 93:6 Va. L. Rev. 173.

"Bill Doesn't Reflect Crime Rate Drop." *Kitchener-Waterloo Record* (26 July 2010) A6.

Blagg, Harry. *Crime, Aboriginality, and the Decolonisation of Justice* (Sydney, Australia: Hawkins Press, 2008).

"Blame the Judges" 49:16 Africa Confidential (1 August 2008) 6.

Bluehouse, Philmer, and James Zion. "Hozhooji Naat'aanii: The Navajo Justice and Harmony Ceremony" (1993) 10:4 Mediation Q. 328.

Blumoff, Theodore. "Justifying Punishment" (2001) 14 C.J.L.S. 161.

Borrows, John. "Domesticating Doctrines: Aboriginal Peoples after the Royal Commission" (2001) McGill L.J. 615.

–. *Recovering Canada: The Resurgence of Indigenous Law* (Toronto: University of Toronto Press, 2002).

–. "Tracking Trajectories: Aboriginal Governance as an Aboriginal Right" (2005) 38 U.B.C. L. Rev. 285.

Boyer, Yvonne. "Community-Based Justice Initiatives of the Saskatoon Tribal Council." In Wanda D. McCaslin (ed.), *Justice as Healing: Indigenous Ways* (St. Paul, MN: Living Justice Press, 2005) 196.

Bracken, Denis C., Lawrence Deane, and Larry Morrissette. "Desistance and Social Marginalization: The Case of Canadian Aboriginal Offenders" (2009) 13:1 Theoretical Criminology 61.

Bradford, William C. "Reclaiming Indigenous Autonomy on the Path to Peaceful Coexistence: The Theory, Practice, and Limitations of Tribal Peacemaking in Indian Dispute Resolution" (2000) Notre Dame L. Rev. 551

Bradshaw, William, David Roseborough, and Mark S. Umbreit. "The Effect of Victim-Offender Mediation on Juvenile Offender Recidivism: A Meta-Analysis" (2006) 24:1 Conflict Resolution Q. 87.

Braithwaite, John. "In Search of Restorative Jurisprudence." In Lode Walgrave (ed.), *Restorative Justice and the Law* (Devon, UK: Willan, 2002) 150.

Braithwaite, John, and Stephen Mugford. "Conditions of Successful Reintegration Ceremonies: Dealing with Juvenile Offenders" (1994) 34 Brit. J. Crim. 139.

Bridges, George, and James A. Stone. "Effects of Criminal Punishment on Perceived Threat of Punishment: Toward an Understanding of Specific Deterrence" (1986) 23:3 J. Research in Crime & Delinquency 207.

Brinott, Simon, and Henry Mares. "The History and Theory of the Adversarial and Inquisitorial Systems of Law" (2004) 16:3 Legaldate 1.

Brock, Kathy L. "Polishing the Halls of Justice: Sections 24(2) and 8 of the *Charter of Rights*" (1992-93) 2 N.J.C.L. 265.

Brown, Jennifer Gerarda. "The Use of Mediation to Resolve Criminal Cases: A Procedural Critique" (1994) 43 Emory L.J. 1247.

Bryant, Marian E. "Tsuu T'ina First Nations: Peacemaker Justice System." *Law Now* (February/March 2002) 14.

Bryden, Joan. "Limit Native Government, Former Chief Justice Warns." *Kitchener-Waterloo Record* (16 March 1992) A1.

Brzozowski, Jodi-Anne, Andrea Taylor Butts, and Sara Johnson. *Victimization and Offending among the Aboriginal Population in Canada* (Ottawa: Canadian Centre for Justice Statistics, 2006).

Burnett, Ros, and Catherine Appleton. *Joined-Up Youth Justice: Tackling Youth Crime in Partnership* (Lyme Regis, UK: Russell Publishing, 2004).

Bushway, Shawn D., and Peter Reuter. "Deterrence, Economics, and the Context of Drug Markets" (2011) 10:1 Criminology & Pub. Pol'y 183.

Butler, Paul. "One Hundred Years of Race and Crime" (2010) 100:3 J. Criminal L. & Criminology 1043

Cairns, Alan. *Citizens Plus: Aboriginal Peoples and the Canadian State* (Vancouver: UBC Press, 2000).

Caldwell, Harry M., and Carol A. Chase. "The Unruly Exclusionary Rule: Heeding Justice Blackmun's Call to Examine the Rule in Light of Changing Judicial Understanding about Its Effects outside the Courtroom" (1994) 78 Marq. L. Rev. 45.

Calhoun, Avery, and William Pelech. "Responding to Young People Responsible for Harm: A Comparative Study of Restorative and Conventional Approaches" (2010) 13:3 Contemporary Justice Rev. 287.

Cameron, Angela. "Sentencing Circles and Intimate Violence: A Feminist Perspective" (2006) 18:2 C.J.W.L. 479.

–. "Stopping the Violence: Canadian Feminist Debates on Restorative Justice and Intimate Violence" (2006) 10:1 Theoretical Criminology 49.

Cameron, Jamie. "Dialogue and Hierarchy in Charter Interpretation: A Comment on *R. v. Mills*" (2000) 38 Alta. L. Rev. 1051.

Canada. Aboriginal Corrections Policy Unit. *The Four Circles of Hollow Water*. Aboriginal Peoples Collection. Ottawa: Ministry of the Solicitor General, 1997.

–. Special Joint Committee of the Senate and of the House of Commons on the Constitution. *Proceedings and Evidence of the Special Joint Committee of the Senate and of the House of*

Commons on the Constitution. Ottawa: Queen's Printer, 1981.

Canada Human Rights Commission. *Still a Matter of Rights: A Special Report of the Canadian Human Rights Commission on the Repeal of Section 67 of the Canadian Human Rights Act* (Ottawa: Minister of Public Works and Government Services, 2008).

Carlsmith, Kevin M. "On Justifying Punishment: The Discrepancy between Words and Actions" (2008) 21:2 Social Justice Research 119.

–. "The Roles of Retribution and Utility in Determining Punishment" (2006) 42:4 Journal of Experimental Social Psychology 437.

Carswell, Margaret. "Social Controls among the Natives Peoples of the Northwest Territories in the Pre-Contact Period" (1984) 22 Alta. L. Rev. 303.

Carter, Mark. "Of Fairness and Faulkner": Colloquy on "Empty Promises: Parliament, the Supreme Court, and the Sentencing of Aboriginal Offenders" (2002) 65 Sask. L. Rev. 63.

Case, Patricia F. "The Relationship of Race and Criminal Behavior: Challenging Cultural Explanations for a Structural Problem" (2008) 34 Critical Sociology 213.

Cayley, David. *The Expanding Prison: The Crisis in Crime and Punishment and the Search for Alternatives* (Toronto: House of Anansi Press, 1998).

Chalifoux, Troy. "A Need for Change: Cross-Cultural Sensitization of Lawyers" (1994) 32 Alta. L. Rev. 762.

Chartrand, Larry. "The Appropriateness of a Lawyer as Advocate in Contemporary Aboriginal Justice Initiatives" (August 1995) 33 Alta. L. Rev. 874.

Chase, Steven. "Conservative Majority Would Hustle Crime Bills into Law All at Once: Harper Vows to Enact Omnibus Legislation within 100 Days of Taking Office." *Globe and Mail* (7 April 2011).

Chauhan, Preeti, and N. Dickon Reppucci. "The Impact of Neighbourhood Disadvantage and Exposure to Violence on Self-Report of Antisocial Behavior among Girls in the Juvenile Justice System" (2009) 38 J. Youth & Adolescence 401

Chauhan, Preeti, N. Dickon Reppucci, and Eric N. Turkmeier. "Racial Differences in the Associations of Neighbourhood Disadvantage, Exposure to Violence, and Criminal Recidivism among Female Juvenile Offenders" (2009) 27:4 Behav. Sci. & L. 351.

Cheloukhine, Serguei, and Joseph King. "Corruption Networks as a Sphere of Investment Activities in Modern Russia" (2007) 40:1 Communist & Post-Communist Studies 107.

Chesterman, John. "Balancing Civil Rights and Indigenous Rights: Is There a Problem?" (2002) 8:2 Aust. J.H.R. 125.

Christie, Gordon. "Aboriginal Citizenship: Sections 35, 25 and 15 of Canada's *Constitution Act, 1982*" (2003) 7:4 Citizenship Studies 481.

–. "A Colonial Reading of Recent Jurisprudence: *Sparrow*, *Delgamuukw*, and *Haida Nation*" (2005) 24 Windsor Y.B. Access Just. 17.

–. "Justifying Principles of Treaty Interpretation" (2000) 26 Queen's L.J. 143.

–. "Law, Theory, and Aboriginal Peoples" (2003) 2 Indigenous L.J. 67.

Christie, Nils. "Conflicts as a Property" (1977) 17:1 Brit. J. Crim. 1.

Cid, Jose. "Is Imprisonment Crimogenic? A Comparative Study of Imprisonment Rates between Prison and Suspended Sentence Sanctions" (2009) 6:6 Eur. J. Criminology 459.

Clark, Scott. "The Nunavut Court of Justice: An Example of Challenges and Alternatives for Communities and for the Administration of Justice" (2011) 53:3 Can. J. Crim. 343.

Clear, Todd R. "The Punitive Paradox: Desert and the Compulsion to Punish" (1996) 33:1 J. Research in Crime & Delinquency 94.

Clough, Alan R., Kylie Kim San Lee, and Katherine M. Conigrave. "Promising Performance of a Juvenile Justice Diversion Programme in Remote Aboriginal Communities, Northern Territories, Australia" (2008) 27 Drug & Alcohol Rev. 433.

Coker, Donna. "Enhancing Autonomy for Battered Women" (1999) 47 U.C.L.A. L. Rev. 1.

Connolly, Deborah, et al. "Perceptions and Predictors of Children's Credibility of a Unique Event and an Instance of a Repeated Event" (2008) 32:1 Law & Human Behavior 92.

Contreras, Kate Spilda. "Cultivating New Opportunities: Tribal Government Gaming on the Pechunga Reservations" (2006) 50:3 American Behavioral Scientist 315.

Cook, Kimberly J. "Doing Difference and Accountability in Restorative Justice Conferences" (2006) 10:1 Theoretical Criminology 107.

Cook, Tim. "Grieving Grandmother Calls for Change: Saskatchewan Reserve Where Young Sisters Froze to Death Needs Alcohol Ban, Counseling, She Says." *Globe and Mail* (4 February 2008) A7.

Corntassel, Jeff. "Indigenous Governance amidst the Forced Federalism Era" (2009) 19:1 Kan. J.L. & Pub. Pol'y 47.

Cornwell, David. *Criminal Punishment and Restorative Justice: Past, Present and Future* (Winchester, UK: Waterside Press, 2006).

Costello, Nancy A. "Walking Together in a Good Way: Indian Peacemaker Courts in Michigan" (1999) 76 U. Det. Mercy L. Rev 875.

"Cotler to Table Bills Inspired by Cadman." *Vancouver Sun* (28 September 2005) A1.

Cousins, Michael. "Aboriginal Justice: A Haudenosaunee Approach." In Wanda D. McCaslin (ed.), *Justice as Healing: Indigenous Ways* (St. Paul, MN: Living Justice Press, 2005) 141.

Couture, J., et al. *A Cost-Benefit Analysis of Hollow Water's Community Holistic Circle Healing Process* (Ottawa: Ministry of the Solicitor General, 2001).

Coyle, Michael. "Defending the Weak and Fighting Unfairness: Can Mediators Respond to the Challenge?" (1998) 36 Osgoode Hall L.J. 625.

–. "Traditional Indian Justice in Ontario: A Role for the Present?" (1986) 24 Osgoode Hall L.J. 605.

Crawford, Adam, and Tim Newburn. *Youth Offending and Restorative Justice: Implementing Reform in Youth Justice* (Devon, UK: Willan Publishing, 2003).

Cree, Lysane. "Mohawk Community-Based Policing" (1999) 14:3 Canadian Human Rights Foundation Newsletter 12.

"Crime Gangs Get Free Roam on Canadian Indian Reserves." *Boston Globe* (1 February 2004) A6.

"Crime, Time and Race," editorial. *Globe and Mail* (16 January 1999) D6.

Criminal Intelligence Service of Canada. *2003 Annual Report on Organized Crime in Canada* (Ottawa: Criminal Intelligence Service Canada, 2003).

Cunliffe, Emma, and Angela Cameron. "Writing the Circle: Judicially Convened Sentencing Circles and the Textual Organization of Criminal Justice" (2007) 19:1 C.J.W.L. 1.

Currie, Alberta, et al. *The 2007 National Justice Survey: Tackling Crime and Public Confidence* (Ottawa: Department of Justice Canada, 2007).

Cutting Crime: The Case for Justice Re-Investment (London: House of Commons Justice Committee, 2009).

"Dad Guilty in Freezing Deaths to Be Sentenced: Saskatchewan Man's Punishment to Be Determined by Aboriginal Sentencing Circle." *Edmonton Sun* (8 January 2009) 7.

Dagny, Leonard. "When Offenders and Victims Sit Down and Talk" (2010) 20:9 C.Q. Researcher 206.

Daly, Kathleen. "Mind the Gap: Restorative Justice in Theory and Practice." In Andrew Von Hirsch, Julian V. Roberts, and Anthony Bottoms (eds.), *Restorative Justice and Criminal Justice: Competing or Reconcilable Paradigms?* (Oxford: Hart Publishing, 2003) 219.

–. "Restorative Justice and Sexual Offences: An Archival Study of Court and Conference Cases" (2006) 46 Brit. J. Crim. 334.

–. "Revisiting the Relationship between Retributive and Restorative Justice." In Heather Strang and John Braithwaite (eds.), *Restorative Justice: Philosophy to Practice* (Dartmouth, UK: Ashgate, 2000) 33.

"Dance to the Death: A Secretive Ritual Practised by Some Native Peoples on Canada's West Coast Is Intended to Seek Power from the Spirits That Will Help the Dancer through Life." *Hamilton Spectator* (16 April 2005) F6.

David, Diane E. "Law Enforcement in Mexico City: Not Yet under Control" (2003) 37:2 N.A.C.L.A. Report on the Americas 17.

Davis, Robert C. "Brooklyn Mediation Field Test" (2009) 5:1 J. Experimental Criminology 25.

de Beus, Kimberly, and Nancy Rodriguez. "Restorative Justice Practice: An Examination of Program Completion and Recidivism" (2007) 35:3 J. Crim. J. 337.

De Córdoba, José, and David Luhnow. "Mexican Officials Allege Drug Cartel Infiltrated Attorney General's Office." *Wall Street Journal* (eastern edition) (28 October 2008) A8.

DeFina, Robert, and Lance Hannon. "For Incapacitation, There Is No Time Like the Present: The Lagged Effects of Prisoner Re-entry on Property and Violent Crime Rates" (2010) 39:6 Social Science Research 1004.

Department of Indian Affairs and Northern Development. *The Government of Canada's Approach to Implementation of the Inherent and the Negotiation of Aboriginal Self-Government* (Ottawa: Minister of Public Works and Government Services Canada, 1995).

Depew, Robert. "Policing Native Communities: Some Principles and Issues in Organizational Theory" (July 1992) 34 Can. J. Crim. 461.

de Smith, Stanley A., Lord Woolf, and Jeffrey Jowell. *Judicial Review of Administrative Action* (5th edition) (London: Sweet and Maxwell, 1995).

Dhami, Mandeep K., and Penny Joy. "Challenges to Establishing Volunteer-Run, Community-Based Restorative Justice Programs" (2007) 10:1 Contemporary Justice Rev. 9.

Dickason, Olive Patricia. *A Concise History of Canada's First Nations* (Don Mills, ON: Oxford University Press, 2006).

Dickson, Timothy. "Section 25 and Intercultural Judgment" (2003) 61 U.T. Fac. L. Rev. 141.

Dickson-Gilmore, E. Jane. "'This Is My History, I Know Who I Am': History, Factionalist Competition, and the Assumption of Imposition in the Kahnawake Mohawk Nation" (1999) 46:3 Ethnohistory 429.

DiManno, Rosie. "Jail Only Just Term in Freezing Deaths." *Toronto Star* (9 January 2009) A2.

Dioso, Rachel, and Anthony Doob. "An Analysis of Public Support for Special Consideration of Aboriginal Offenders at Sentencing" (2001) 43:3 Can. J. Crim. 405.

Doak, Jonathan. "Victims' Rights in Criminal Trials: Prospects for Rehabiliation" (2005) 32:2 J.L. & Society 294.

Domink-Bachmann, Sascha. "Control Order Post-911 and Human Rights in the United Kingdom, Australia, and Canada: A Kafkaesque Dilemma?" (2010) 15:2 Deakin L. Rev. 131.

Doolin, Katherine. "But What Does It Mean? Seeking Definitional Clarity in Restorative Justice" (2007) 71:5 J. Crim. L. 427.

Du Vaal, Kathleen. "Cross-Cultural Crime and Osage Justice in the Western Mississipi Valley, 1700-1826" (2007) 54:4 Ethnohistory 697.

Dzur, Albert W., and Susan M. Olson. "The Value of Community Participation in Restorative Justice" (2004) 35:1 J. Social Philosophy 91.

Eades, Diana. "'I don't think it's an answer to the question': Silencing Aboriginal Witnesses in Court" (2000) 29:2 Language in Society 161.

–. "Lexical Struggle in Court: Aboriginal Australians versus the State" (2006) 10:2 J. Sociolinguistics 153.

–. "Telling and Retelling Your Story in Court: Questions, Assumptions, and Intercultural Assumptions" (2009) 20:2 Current Issues in Criminal Justice 209.

Earring-Chosa, Georgina. "Loss of a Language: Forgotten through Time" (2009) 29:1 Tribal College J. 44.

Edwards, Ian. "Victim Participation in Sentencing: The Problems of Incoherence" (2001) 40:1 How. L.J. 39.

Eitle, David E., Stewart J. D'Alessio, and Lisa Stolzenberg. "Economic Segregation, Race, and Homicide" (2006) 87:3 Social Sci. Q. 638.

Ellison, Louise. "Closing the Credibility Gap: The Prosecutorial Use of Expert Witness Testimony in Sexual Assault Cases" (2005) 9:4 Int'l J. Evidence & Proof 239.

Ethical Principles for Judges (Ottawa: Canadian Judicial Council of Canada, 1998).

"Father of Two Girls Who Froze to Death Needs Treatment, Not Jail, Judge Hears." *CBC News* (13 February 2009).

Fawcett, J.E.S. *The Application of the European Convention on Human Rights* (Oxford: Clarendon Press, 1969).

Field, Rachael. "Victim-Offender Conferencing: Issues of Power Imbalance for Women Juvenile Participants" (2004) 11:1 Murdoch U.E.J.L.

Field, Tiffany, et al. "Legal Interviewers Use Children's Affect and Eye Contact Cues to Assess Credibility of Their Testimony" (2010) 180:3 Early Child Development & Care 397.

Finkler, Harald. "Community Participation in Socio-Legal Control: The Northern Context" (1992) 34 Can. J. Crim. 503.

First Nations Policing Agreements (Ottawa: Solicitor General of Canada, Ministry Secretariat, 1992).

Fiske, Jo-Anne, and Betty Patrick. *Cis Dideen Kat: The Way of the Lake Babine Nation* (Vancouver: UBC Press, 2000).

Fiss, Tanis. "Special Treatment Can't Right Wrongs to Aboriginals." *Guelph Mercury* (9 January 2004) A9.

Fitzgerald, Jacqueline. "Does Circle Sentencing Reduce Aboriginal Offending?" (2008) 115 Contemporary Issues in Crime & Justice 1.

Flanagan, Thomas. *First Nations, Second Thoughts* (Montreal and Kingston: McGill-Queen's University Press, 2000).

Fowler, Alan, and Kasturi Sen. "Embedding the War on Terror: State and Civil Society Relations" (2010) 41:1 Development & Change 1.

Fowlie, Jonathan. "Liberals to Ramp Up War on Meth." *Vancouver Sun* (12 December 2005) A1.

Fox, Chris, Kevin Alberton, and Frank Wharburton. "Justice Reinvestment: Can It Deliver More for Less?" (2011) 50:2 How. J. Crim. Just. 119.

Fruehwald, Stefan, and Patrick Frottier. "Death behind Bars" (2002) 167:10 Can. Medical Association Journal 1127.

Fulkerson, Andrew. "The Use of Victim Impact Panels in Domestic Violence Cases: A Restorative Justice Approach" (2001) 4:3-4 Contemporary Justice Rev. 355.

Gagnon, Lysiane. "A Telling Take on Yellow Quill." *Globe and Mail* (22 June 2009) A15.

Garland, David. *The Culture of Control: Crime and Social Order in Contemporary Society* (Oxford: Oxford University Press, 2001).

George-Kanentiio, Douglas. *Iroquois Culture and Commentary* (Santa Fe, NM: Clear Light Publishers, 2000).

–. "Iroquois Justice" (Spring 1995) 1:1 Akwesasne Notes 106.

Gerber, Theodore P., and Sarah E. Mendelson. "Public Experiences of Police Violence and Corruption in Contemporary Russia: A Case of Predatory Policing?" (2008) 42:1 L. & Soc'y Rev. 1.

Gewurz, Ilan G. "(Re)Designing Mediation to Address the Nuances of Power Imbalance" (2001) 19:2 Conflict Resolution Q. 135.

Gibbins, Roger. "Citizenship, Political, and Intergovernmental Problems with Indian Self-Government." In J. Rick Ponting (ed.), *Arduous Journey: Canadian Indians and Decolonization* (Toronto: McClelland and Stewart, 1986) 369.

Gibbs, Meredith. "Using Restorative Justice to Resolve Historical Injustices of Indigenous Peoples" (2009) 12:1 Contemporary Justice Rev. 45.

Gibson, Dale. *The Law of the Charter: General Principles* (Calgary: Carswell, 1986).

Gill, Terenia Urban. "A Framework for Understanding and Using ADR" (1996-97) 71 Tul. L. Rev. 1313.

Goldkamp, John S. "Optimistic Deterrence Theorizing" (2011) 10:1 Criminology & Public Policy 115.

Goodman-Delahunty, Jane, Anne Cossins, and Kate O'Brien. "Enhancing the Credibility of Complainants in Child Sexual Assault Interviews: The Effect of Expert Evidence and Judicial Directions" (2010) 28:6 Behav. Sci. & L. 769.

Gora, Christopher. "Jury Trials in the Small Communities of the Northwest Territories" (1993) Windsor Y.B. Access Just. 156.

Goren, Suzanne. "Healing the Victim, the Young Offender, and the Community via Restorative Justice: An International Perspective" (2001) 22 Issues in Mental Health Nursing 137.

Gosse, Richard. "Charting the Course for Aboriginal Justice Reform through Aboriginal Self-Government." In Richard Gosse, James Youngblood Henderson, and Roger Carter (eds.), *Continuing Poundmaker and Riel's Quest: Presentations Made at a Conference on Aboriginal Peoples and Justice* (Saskatoon: Purich Publishing, 1994) 1.

Gottschalk, Marie. "The World's Warden: Crime, Politics and Punishment in the United States" (2008) 55:4 Dissent 58.

Goudge, Stephen T. *Inquiry into Pediatric Forensic Pathology in Ontario*, volume 2 (Toronto: Ministry of the Attorney General of Ontario, 2008).

Graham, Jennifer. "Father of Frozen Girls Jailed, Judge Hands Man Prison Term Despite Sentencing Circle Decision." *Calgary Sun* (7 March 2009) 7.

Grauwiler, Peggy, and Linda G. Mills. "Moving beyond the Criminal Justice Paradigm: A Radical Restorative Justice Approach to Intimate Abuse" (2004) 31:1 J. Sociology & Welfare 49.

Gray-Kanatiiosh, Barbara, and Pat Lauderdale. "The Great Circle of Justice: North American Indigenous and Contemporary Justice Programs" (2007) 10:2 Contemporary Justice Rev. 215.

–. "The Web of Justice: Restorative Justice Has Presented Only Part of the Story" (2006) 21:1 Wicazo Sa Rev. 29.

Green, Joyce A. *Cultural and Ethnic Fundamentalism: The Mixed Potential for Identity, Liberation, and Oppression*, Scholar Series (Regina: Saskatchewan Institute of Public Policy, 2003).

Green, Ross Gordon. "Aboriginal Community Sentencing and Mediation: Within and Without the Circle" (1997) 24 Man. L.J. 77.

Grekul, Jana, and Patti Laboucane-Benson. "Aboriginal Gangs and Their (Dis)placement: Contexualizing Recruitment, Membership and Status" (2008) 50:1 Can. J. Criminology & Crim. Justice 59.

Gromet, Dena M., and John M. Darley. "Punishment and Beyond: Achieving Justice through the Satisfaction of Multiple Goals" (2009) 43:1 L. & Soc'y Rev. 1.

Gustafson, Kaaryn. "The Criminalization of Poverty" (2009) 99:3 J. Crim. L. & Criminology 643.

Haig-Brown, Celia. "Continuing Collaborative Knowledge Production: Knowing When, Where, How, and Why" (2001) 22:1 J. Intercultural Stud. 19.

Haist, Matthew. "Deterrence in a 'Sea of Just Deserts': Are Utilitarian Goals Achievable in a World of 'Limiting Retributivism'?" (2009) 99:3 J. Crim. L. & Criminology 789.

Hamilton, A.C., and C.M. Sinclair. *Report of the Inquiry into the Administration of Justice and Aboriginal People* (Winnipeg: Government of Manitoba, Public Inquiry into the Administration of Justice and Aboriginal People, 1991).

Hampton, Robert J., et al. "Evaluating Domestic Violence Interventions for Black Women" (2008) 16:3 J. Aggression, Maltreatment, & Trauma 330.

Harasymiw, Bohdan. "Policing, Democratization and Political Leadership in Postcommunist Ukraine" (2003) 36:2 Can. J. Pol. Sci. 319.

Hardin, Garrett. "The Tragedy of the Commons" (1968) 162 Science 1243.

"Harper Government's Abolition of Early Parole Act Receives Royal Assent: Criminals Convicted of White Collar Crimes Will No Longer Be Released from Prison after Serving Only One-Sixth of Their Sentence." *Marketwire* (24 March 2011).

Harris, Nathan. "Reintegrative Shame, Shaming, and Criminal Justice" (2006) 62:2 J. Social Issues 327.

Harris, Nathan, Lode Walgrave, and John Braithwaite. "Emotional Dynamics in Restorative Conferences" (2004) 8:2 Theor. Crim. 191.

Harrison, Anne, Muriel Meric, and Alan Dickson. *Justice and Healing at Sheshatshit and Davis Inlet* (Ottawa: Peace Brigades International, 1995).

Hay, Carter, et al. "The Impact of Community Disadvantage on the Relationship between the Family and Crime" (2006) 43 Juvenile Crime & Delinquency 326.

Hayes, Hennessey. "Assessing Reoffending in Restorative Justice Conferences" (2005) 38:1 Aust. Crim. & N.Z. J. 77.

Hazard, Geoffrey C., and Dana C. Remus. "Advocacy Revalued" (2011) 159:3 U. Penn. L. Rev. 751.

Head, Robert H.D. *Policing for Aboriginal Canadians: The R.C.M.P. Role* (Ottawa: Royal Canadian Mounted Police, 1993).

Heavens, Andrew. "Police Break Up Rally for Woman on Trial for Wearing Pants: Tear Gas Fired at Khartoum Protest against Possible Flogging for Breach of Dress Code." *Globe and Mail* (5 August 2009) A2.

Heckert, D. Alex, and Edward Gondolf. "The Effect of Perceptions of Sanctions on Batterer Program Outcomes" (2000) 37:4 J. Research in Crime & Delinquency 369.

Hedderman, Carol. *Building on Sand: Why Expanding the Prison Estate Is Not the Way to "Secure the Future,"* Briefing 7 (Leicester, UK: Centre for Crime and Justice Studies, 2008).

Heinamaki, Leena. "Inherent Rights of Aboriginal Peoples in Canada: Reflections of the Debate in National and International Law" (2006) 8 Int'l Community L. Rev. 155.

Henderson, Sákéj. "Constitutional Powers and Treaty Rights" (2000) Sask. L. Rev. 719.

–. "Indigenous Legal Consciousness" (2002) 1 Indigenous L.J. 1.

Henman, Ralph, and Grazia Mannozzi. "Victim Participation and Sentencing in England and Italy: A Legal and Policy Analysis" (2003) 11:3 Eur. J. Crime, Crim. L. & Crim. J. 278.

Herman, Michel G. "The Dangers of ADR: A Three-Tiered System of Justice" (1989-90) 3 J. Contemporary Legal Issues 117.

Hetzer, Wolfgang. "Corruption as Business Practice? Corporate Criminal Liability in the European Union" (2007) 15:3-4 Eur. J. Crime, Crim. L. & Crim. Justice 383.

Hinton, Leanne. "Language Loss and Revitalization in California: Overview" (1998) 32 Int'l J. Sociology of Language 132.

Hobbes, Thomas. *Leviathan,* edited by J.C.A. Gaskin (New York: Oxford University Press, 1998).

Hoffman, W.J. "Curious Aboriginal Customs" (1879) 13:1 American Naturalist 6.

Hogg, Peter. *Canadian Constitutional Law* (5th edition) (Toronto: Carswell, 2007).

–. *Constitutional Law of Canada* (2nd edition) (Toronto: Carswell, 1985).

Hogg, Peter, and Mary Ellen Turpel-Lafond. "Implementing Aboriginal Self-Government: Constitutional and Jurisdictional Issues" (1997) 74 Can. Bar. Rev. 187.

Hogg, Russell. "Penality and Modes of Regulating Indigenous Peoples in Australia" (2001) 3:3 Punishment & Society 355.

Holcombe, Sarah. "The Arrogance of Ethnography: Managing Anthropological Research Knowledge" (2010) 2 Australian Aboriginal Stud. 22.

Hooghe, Marc, et al. "Unemployment, Inequality, Poverty and Crime: Spatial Distribution Patterns of Criminal Acts in Belgium, 2001-06" (2011) 51:1 Brit. J. Crim. 1.

Hopkins, Quince C., Mary Koss, and Karen Bachar. "Applying Restorative Justice to Ongoing Intimate Violence: Problems and Possibilities" (2004) 23:1 St. Louis Univ. Pub. L. Rev. 289.

"How Flexible Should the Law Be against Criminal Corporate Executives?" 52:4 Beijing Rev. 46.

Huey Dye, Meredith. "Deprivation, Importation, and Inmate Suicide: Combined Effects of Institutional Conditions and Inmate Composition" (2010) 38:4 J. Crim. Justice 796.

Hughes, Patricia, and Mary Jane Mossman. "Re-Thinking Access to Criminal Justice in Canada: A Critical Review of Needs and Responses" (2002) 13 Windsor Rev. Legal Soc. Issues 1.

Hunt Peacock, John, Jr. "Lamenting Language Loss at the Modern Language Association" (2006) 30:1-2 Am. Indian Q. 138.

Isaac, Thomas. "Canadian Charter of Rights and Freedoms: The Challenge of the Individual and Collective Rights of Aboriginal People" (2002) 21 Windsor Y.B. Access Just. 431.

Jackson, Michael. "Cruel and Unusual Treatment or Punishment" (1982) U.B.C. L. Rev., Charter Edition 189.

–. "In Search of the Pathways to Justice: Alternative Dispute Resolution in Aboriginal Communities" (1992) U.B.C. L. Rev., Special Edition on Aboriginal Justice 147.

–. "Locking Up Natives in Canada" (1988-1989) 23 U.B.C. L. Rev. 215.

Jackson, Moana. *The Maori and the Criminal Justice System, He Whaipaanga Hou: A New Perspective,* Part 2 (Auckland, New Zealand: New Zealand Department of Justice, 1988).

Jacobs, Mindelle. "Don't Impair Justice." *Ottawa Sun* (9 December 2008) 15.

Joh, Elizabeth E. "Custom, Tribal Court Practice, and Popular Justice" (2000-01) 25 Am. Indian L. Rev 117.

John Howard Society of Alberta. *Halfway House: Executive Summary* (Edmonton: John Howard Society of Alberta, 2001).

Johnson, Daniel. "From Destruction to Reconciliation: The Potential of Restorative Justice" (2004) 23:1-2 J. Religion & Spirituality in Social Work 83.

Justice on Trial (Edmonton: Task Force on the Criminal Justice System and Its Impact on the Indian and Metis People of Alberta, 1991).

Karp, David, Gordon Bazemore, and J.D. Chesire. "The Role and Attitudes of Restorative Board Members: A Case Study of Volunteers in Community Justice" (2004) 50:4 Crime & Delinquency 487.

Karr, Steve M. "Now We Have Forgotten the Old Indian Law: Choctaw Culture and the Evolution of Corporal Punishment" (1998-99) 23 Am. Indian L. Rev. 409.

Keesing, Roger. *Custom and Confrontation: The Kwaio Struggle for Cultural Autonomy* (Chicago: University of Chicago Press, 1992).

Kendall, Joan. "Circles of Disadvantage: Aboriginal Poverty and Underdevelopment in Canada" (2001) 31:1-2 Am. Rev. Can. Stud. 43.

Kenney, Scott J., and Don Clairmont. "Using the Victim as Both Sword and Shield" (2009) 38:3 J. Contemporary Ethnography 279.

Kinner, Stuart A., and M.J. Milloy. "Collateral Consequences of an Ever-Expanding Prison System" (2011) 183:5 C.M.A.J. 632.

Kinsella, Alex. "Punishment Deserved." *Waterloo Region Accord* (20 February 2009) A8.

Kitai, Rinat. "Protecting the Guilty" (2003) 6 Buff. Crim. L.R. 1163.

Kitty, Jennifer. "Gendering Violence, Remorse, and the Role of Restorative Justice: Deconstructing Public Perceptions of Kelly Ellard and Warren Glowatski" (2010) 13:2 Contemporary Justice Rev. 155.

Kleck, Gary, et al. "The Missing Link in General Deterrence Research" (2005) 43:3 Criminology 623.

Knoll, Douglas E., and Linda Harvey. "Restorative Mediation: The Application of Restorative Justice Practice and Philosophy to Clergy Sexual Abuse Cases" (2008) 17:3-4 J. Child Sexual Abuse 377.

Knox, George W. *The Problem of Gangs and Security Threat Groups in American Prisons Today: Recent Research Findings from the 2004 Prison Gang Survey* (Peotone, IL: National Gang Crime Research Center, 2004).

Koshan, Jennifer. "Aboriginal Women, Justice and the Charter: Bridging the Divide?" (November 1998) 32 U.B.C. L. Rev. 23.

Kurki, L., and Kay Pranis. *Restorative Justice as Direct Democracy and Community Building* (St. Paul, MN: Minnesota Department of Corrections, Community and Juvenile Services Division, 2000).

Kwochka, Daniel. "Aboriginal Injustice: Making Room for a Restorative Paradigm" (1996) 60 Saskatchewan L. Rev. 153.

Lajeunesse, Therese. *Evaluation of the Hollow Water Community Holistic Circle Healing Project* (Ottawa: Solicitor General of Canada, 1996).

Landau, Tammy. "Policing and Security in Four Remote Aboriginal Communities: A Challenge to Coercive Models of Police Work" (1996) 38:1 Can. J. Criminology & Crim. Just. 1.

Lane, Phillip. "Mapping the Healing Journey: First Nations Research Project on Healing in Canadian Aboriginal Communities." In Wanda D. McCaslin (ed.), *Justice as Healing: Indigenous Ways* (St. Paul, MN: Living Justice Press, 2005) 369.

LaPriarie, Carol. "Aboriginal Crime and Justice: Explaining the Present, Exploring the Future" (1992) 34 Can. J. Crim. 281.

–. "Aboriginal Over-Representation in the Criminal Justice System: A Tale of Nine Cities" (2002) 44:2 Can. J. Crim. 181.

–. "Community Justice or Just Communities? Aboriginal Communities in Search of Justice" (1995) Can. J. Crim. 521

–. *Examining Aboriginal Corrections in Canada* (Ottawa: Aboriginal Corrections, Ministry of the Solicitor General, 1996).

–. *Exploring the Boundaries of Justice: A Report Prepared for the Department of Justice* (Whitehorse: First Nations of the Yukon Territory and Justice Canada, 1992).

–. "The Impact of Aboriginal Justice Research on Policy: A Marginal Past and an Even More Uncertain Future" (1999) Can. J. Crim. 249.

–. *Justice for the Cree: Communities, Crime and Order* (Nemaska, PQ: Cree Regional Authority, 1991).

LaPrairie, Carol, and E. Jane Dickson-Gilmore. *Will the Circle Be Unbroken? Aboriginal Communities, Restorative Justice, and the Challenges of Conflict and Change* (Toronto: University of Toronto Press, 2005).

Large, Norma. "Healing Justice: The Tsuu T'ina First Nation's Peacemaker Court Throws Out Punitive Justice and Restores the Ancient Tradition of ... Talking." *Alberta Views* (May/June 2001) 20.

LaRocque, Emma. "Re-examining Culturally Appropriate Models in Criminal Justice Applications." In Michael Asch (ed.), *Aboriginal and Treaty Rights in Canada: Essays on Law, Equality, and Respect for Difference* (Vancouver: UBC Press, 1997) 75.

Latimer, Jeff, Craig Dowden, and Danielle Muise. *The Effectiveness of Restorative Justice Programs: A Meta-Analysis* (Ottawa: Department of Justice, Research and Statistics Division, 2001).

Law Reform Commission of Canada. *Aboriginal People and Justice Administration: A Discussion Paper* (Ottawa: Department of Justice, 1991).

–. *Studies on Diversion*, Working paper no. 7 (Ottawa: Law Reform Commission of Canada, 1975).

Law Society of British Columbia. *Law Society Rules* (Vancouver: Law Society of British Columbia, 2012).

–. *Professional Conduct Handbook* (Vancouver: Law Society of British Columbia, 2011).

Leonardy, Matthias R.J. *First Nations Criminal Jurisdiction in Canada* (Saskatoon: Native Law Centre, University of Saskatchewan, 1998).

"Letters to the Editor Column." *Winnipeg Sun* (20 January 2009) 8.

Liebmann, Marian. *Restorative Justice: How It Works* (London: Jessica Kingsley Publishers, 2007).

Lilles, Judge Heino. "Tribal Justice: A New Beginning" (Paper delivered to a conference titled Achieving Justice: Today and Tomorrow, Whitehorse, Yukon, 3-7 September 1991) [unpublished].

Lin, Brian. "Preserving Native Languages" (2005) 8:10 Raven's Eye 6.

Lippke, Richard L. "Punishing the Guilty, Not Punishing the Innocent" (2010) 7:4 J. Moral Philosophy 462.

Llewellyn, Karl, and Edward Adamson. *The Cheyenne Way: Conflict and Case Law in Primitive Jurisprudence* (Norman: University of Oklahoma Press, 1941).

Locke, John. *Second Treatise of Government*, edited by Peter Laslett (Cambridge: Cambridge University Press, 1960).

Lokanan, Mark. "An Open Model for Restorative Justice: Is There Room for Punishment?" (2009) 12:3 Contemporary Justice Rev. 289.

Lomasky, Loren. "Classical Liberalism and Civil Society." In Simone Chambers and Will Kymlicka (eds.), *Alternative Conceptions of Civil Society* (Princeton, NJ: Princeton University Press, 2002) 50.

London, Ross D. "The Restoration of Trust: Bringing Restorative Justice from the Margins to the Mainstream" (2003) 16:3 Criminal Justice Studies 175.

Lorden, Michael. *Mas Oyama: The Legend, the Legacy* (Burbank, CA: Unique Publications, 2000).

Losoncz, Ibolya, and Graham Tyson. "Parental Shaming and Adolescent Delinquency" (2007) 40:2 Aust. Crim. & N.Z. J. 161.

Lussier, Patrick, David P. Farrington, and Terrie E. Moffitt. "The Abusive Man? A Forty-Year Prospective Longtitudinal Study of the Development Antecedents of Intimate Partner Violence" (2009) 47:3 Criminology 741.

Luther, Glen. "Police Power and the Charter of Rights and Freedoms: Creation or Control?" (1986-87) 51 Saskatchewan L. Rev. 217.

Lutz, Donald S. "The Iroquois Confederation Constitution: An Analysis" (1998) 28:2 Publius: The Journal of Federalism 99.

Lysyk, Kenneth. "The Rights and Freedoms of the Aboriginal Peoples of Canada (Sections 25, 35, and 37)." In W. Tarnopolsky and G.A. Beaudoin (eds.), *The Canadian Charter of Rights and Freedoms: Commentary* (Toronto: Carswell, 1982) 470.

MacDonald, Dwayne Trevor. "Resistance or Engagement? A Pair of Indigenous Writers Come to Very Different Conclusions about Dialogue with the White Community" (2006) 14 Literary Rev. Canada 8.

MacDonald, Kelly. *Literature Review: Implications of Restorative Justice in Cases of Violence against Aboriginal Women and Children* (Vancouver: Aboriginal Women's Network, 2001).

MacMillan, Leslie Jane. "Colonial Traditions, Co-optations, and Colonial Indigenous Legal Consciousness" (2011) 36:1 Law & Social Inquiry 171.

–. *Koqqwaja'ltimk: Mi'kmaq Legal Consciousness* (Ph.D. dissertation, Department of Anthropology, University of British Columbia 2002).

Mainville, Besse. "Traditional Native Culture and Spirituality: A Way of Life That Governs Us" (2010) 8:1 Indigenous L.J. 1.

"Malaysia Urged to End Brutal Punishments after Women Caned." *States News Service* (17 February 2010).

"Malaysia Spares the Rod for Muslim Woman Convicted for Drinking Beer." *Asian Political News* (5 April 2010).

Mandamin, Leonard. "Aboriginal Justice Systems." In Royal Commission on Aboriginal Peoples, *Aboriginal Peoples and the Justice System, Report of the National Round Table on Aboriginal Justice Issues* (Ottawa: Supply and Services, 1993).

Maniadaki, Katerina, and Efthymios Kakouros. "Social and Mental Health Profiles of Young Male Offenders in Detention in Greece" (2008) 18 Crim. Behavior & Mental Health 207.

Marlowe, Douglas, et al. "Perceived Deterrence and Outcomes in Drug Courts" (2005) 23:2 Behav. Sci. & L. 183.

Maruna, Shadd. "Lessons for Justice Reinvestment from Restorative Justice and the Justice Model Experience" (2011) 10:3 Criminology & Public Pol'y 661.

Matthews, Shelly Keith, and Robert Agnew. "Extending Deterrence Theory" (2008) 45:2 J. Research in Crime & Delinquency 91.

Maxson, Cheryl, Kristy Matsuda, and Karen Hennigan. "'Deterrability' among Gang and Non-Gang Juvenile Offenders: Are Gang Members More (or Less) Deterrable Than Other Juvenile Offenders?" (2011) 57:4 Crime & Delinquency 516.

McElrea, Judge F.M.W. "Restorative Justice: The New Zealand Youth Court – A Model for Development in Other Courts?" (1994) 4 J. Judicial Administration 36.

McGillivray, Anne, and Brenda Comaskey. *Black Eyes All of the Time: Intimate Violence, Aboriginal Women, and the Justice System* (Toronto: University of Toronto Press, 1999).

McLean, Candis. "A Spoon-Fed Mentality" (2002) 29:15 Newsmagazine 8.

–. "Twenty-Dollar Bribes" (2002) 29:4 Newsmagazine 14.

McNeil, Kent. "Aboriginal Governments and the *Canadian Charter of Rights and Freedoms*" (1996) 34:1 Osgoode Hall L.J. 61.

–. "Aboriginal Governments and the *Charter*: Lessons from the United States" (2002) C.J.L.S. 73.

–. "The Constitutional Rights of the Aboriginal Peoples of Canada" (1982) 4 Sup. Ct. L. Rev. 255.

McPherson, C.B. *The Political Theory of Possessive Individualism* (Oxford: Clarendon Press, 1962).

Mekka, Pakel. "Collective Agents and Moral Responsibility" (2007) 38:3 J. Social Philosophy 456.

Mendes, Silvia. "Certainty, Severity, and Their Relative Deterrent Effects: Questioning the Role of Risk in Criminal Deterrence Theory" (2004) 32:1 Pol'y Studies J. 59.

"A Messy Prescription for Native Offenders." *Globe and Mail* (12 August 2002) A12.

Miller, Bruce G. "The Individual, the Collective, and the Tribal Code" (1997) 21:1 Am. Indian Culture & Research Journal 185.

–. *The Problem of Justice: Tradition and Law in the Coast Salish World* (Lincoln: University of Nebraska Press, 2001).

Miller, J.R. *Skyscrapers Hide the Heavens: A History of Indian-White Relations in Canada* (Toronto: University of Toronto Press, 2000).

Milward, David. "Making the Circle Stronger: An Effort to Buttress Aboriginal Use of Restorative Justice in Canada against Recent Criticisms" (2008) 4:3 Int'l J. Punishment & Sentencing 124.

–. "Not Just the Peace Pipe but Also the Lance: Exploring Different Possibilities for Indigenous Control over Criminal Justice" (2008) 23:1 Wicazo Sa Rev. 97.

Mohan, John. "Own Up and Bring Our Sanity Back." *Portage Daily Graphic* (15 April 2009) 4.

Moore, Shelby A.D. "Understanding the Connection between Domestic Violence, Crime, and Poverty: How Welfare Reform May Keep Battered Women from Leaving Abusive Relationships" (2003) 12 Texas J. Women & Law 451.

Monture-Angus, Patricia. *Journeying Forward: Dreaming First Nations' Independence* (Halifax: Fernwood Publishing, 1999).

Morgan, Lewis. *League of the Iroquois*, ed. Herbert M. Lloyd, vol. 1 (New York: Dodd, Mead, and Company, 1901).

Morris, Allison, and Loraine Gelsthorpe. "Re-visioning Men's Violence against Female Partners" (2000) 39:4 How. L.J. 412.

Morse, Bradford W., Robert Groves, and D'Arcy Vermette. *Balancing Individual and Collective Rights: Implementation of Section 1.2 of the Canadian Human Rights Act* (Ottawa: Canadian Human Rights Commission, 2008).

Murphy, Chris, and Don Clairmont. *First Nations Police Officers Survey* (Ottawa: Solicitor General of Canada, Minister Secretariat, 1996).

Murrell, Amy R., Karen A. Christoff, and Chris R. Henning. "Characteristics of Domestic Violence Offenders: Associations with Childhood Exposure to Violence" (2007) 22 J. Family Violence 523.

Nagin, Daniel, and Raymond Paternoster. "Personal Capital and Social Control: The Deterrence Implications of a Theory of Individual Differences in Criminal Offending" (1994) 32:4 Criminology 581.

Nagin, Daniel, and Greg Pogarsky. "Integrating Celerity, Impulsivity, and Extralegal Sanction Threats into a Model of Deterrence: Theory and Evidence" (2001) 39:4 Criminology 865.

Nahanee, Theresa. "Dancing with a Gorilla: Aboriginal Women, Justice, and the *Charter*." In Royal Commission on Aboriginal Peoples, *Aboriginal Peoples and the Justice System: Report on the Round Table on Aboriginal Justice Issues* (Ottawa: Minister of Supply and Services, 1993) 359.

Nash, David. "Aborigines in Court: Foreigners in Their Own Land" (1979) 4 Legal Service Bulletin 105.

National Institute of Justice. *The Effects of the Exclusionary Rule: A Study in California 2* (Washington, DC: Department of Justice, 1982).

"Native Representation on Juries to Be Reviewed." *Hamilton Spectator* (12 August 2011) A8.

Nesper, Larry. "Negotiating Jurisprudence in Tribal Court and the Emergence of a Tribal State: The Lac Du Flambeau Ojibwe" (2007) 48:5 Current Anthropology 675.

Newell, William B. *Crime and Justice among the Iroquois Nations* (Montreal: Caughnawaga Historical Society, 1965).

Niemeyer, Mike, and David Schicor. "A Preliminary Study of a Large Victim/Offender Reconciliation Program" (1996) 60 Federal Probation 30.

Nugent, William, et al. "Participation in Victim-Offender Mediation and Reoffense: Successful Replication?" (2001) 11:1 Research on Social Work Practice 5.

"Nunavut Unveils 'Prudent' $1.3B Budget." *CBC News* (8 March 2010).

Oberg, Kalvervo. "Crime and Punishment in Tlingit Society" (1934) 36:2 Am. Anthropologist 145.

O'Connel, Daniel, et al. "Decide Your Time: Testing Deterrence Theory's Certainty and Celerity Effects on Substance-Abusing Probationers" (2011) 39:3 J. Crim. Justice 261.

O'Donnell, Ian, and Kimmett Edgar. "Routine Victimisation in Prisons" (1998) 37:3 How. J. Crim. Justice 266.

Olson, Susan, and Albert Dzur. "The Practice of Restorative Justice: Reconstructing Professional Roles in Restorative Justice Programs" (2003) Utah L. Rev. 57.

Ontario Judicial Appointments Advisory Committee. *Policies and Process* (Toronto: Ontario Courts, 2005).

Ontario Professional Organizations Committee. *Report of the Professional Organization Committee (Ministry of the Attorney General of Ontario)* (Toronto: Ministry of the Attorney General of Ontario, 1980).

Orge, Kathleen. "Cultural Knowledge under Siege" (May 2004) Ontario Birchbark 8.

Owen, Simon. "A Crack in Everything: Restorative Possibilities of Plea-Based Sentencing Courts" (2011) 48 Alta. L. Rev. 847.

Paciocco, David. "Coping with Expert Evidence about Human Behaviour" (1999) 25 Queen's L.J. 305.

–. *Getting Away with Murder: The Canadian Criminal Justice System* (Toronto: Irwin Law, 1999).

Pachula, Chassidy et al. "Using Traditional Spirituality to Reduce Domestic Violence within Aboriginal Communities" (2010) 16:1 J. Alternative & Complementary Medicine 89.

Packer, Herbert. *The Limits of the Criminal Sanction* (Stanford, CA: Stanford University Press, 1968).

Palys, Ted, and Winona Victor. "'Getting to a Better Place': Qwi:Qwelstom, the Sto:lo, and Self-Determination." In Law Commission of Canada (ed.), *Indigenous Legal Traditions* (Vancouver: UBC Press, 2007) 12.

Parker, Arthur C. *An Analytical History of the Seneca Indians* (Rochester: New York State Archaeological Association, 1926).

Parker, Shafer, Jr. "Self-Government or Gangsterism?" (1996) 23:27 Alberta Report 27.

Parrish, John M. *Collective Responsibility and the State Collective Responsibility and the State* (Papers from the annual meeting of the American Political Science Association, 2007) [unpublished].

Paternoster, Raymond. "How Much Do We Really Know about Criminal Deterrence" (2010) 100:3 J. Crim. L. & Criminology 765.

Pauktuutit Inuit Women's Association. *Setting Standards First: Community-Based Justice and Corrections in Inuit Canada* (Ottawa: Pauktuutit, 1995).

Penney, Steven. "Taking Deterrence Seriously: Excluding Unconstitutionally Obtained Evidence under S. 24(2) of the *Charter*" (2004) 49 McGill L.J. 105.

–. "Unreal Distinctions: The Exclusion of Unfairly Obtained Evidence under S. 24(2) of the Charter" (1994) 32 Alta. L. Rev. 782.

Perez, Deanna M., et al. "Individual and Institutional Characteristics Related to Inmate Victimization" (2010) 54:3 Int'l J. Offender Therapy & Comparative Criminology 378.

Perreault, Samuel. *The Incarceration of Aboriginal People in Adult Correctional Services* (Ottawa: Statistics Canada, 2009).

Perrin L., Timothy, et al. "If It's Broken, Fix It: Moving beyond the Exclusionary Rule: A New and Extensive Empirical Study of the Exclusionary Rule and a Call for a Civil Administrative Remedy to Partially Replace the Rule" (1998) 83 Iowa L. Rev. 669.

Petney, William F. *The Aboriginal Rights Provisions in the Constitution Act, 1982* (Ottawa: University of Ottawa Press, 1987).

Pizarro, Jessenia M., and Jean Marie McGloin. "Explaining Gang Homicides in Newark, New Jersey: Collective Behavior or Social Disorganization?" (2006) 34:2 J. Crim. Justice 195.

Pogarsky, Greg, Kim KiDeuk, and Ray Paternoster. "Perceptual Change in the National Youth Survey: Lessons for Deterrence Theory and Offender Decision-Making" (2005) 22:1 Justice Q. 1.

Pogarsky, Greg, Alex Piquero, and Ray Paternoster. "Modeling Change in Perceptions about Sanction Threats: The Neglected Linkage in Deterrence Theory" (2004) 20:4 J. Quantitative Criminology 343.

Polgreen, Lydia. "Nigeria Reassigns Corruption Fighter, Motive Is Hazy." *New York Times* (29 December 2007) 3.

"Police Look to Native Traditions to Curb Crime" (2008) 15:7 Alberta Sweetgrass 3.

Pommersheim, Frank. *Braid of Feathers: American Indian Law and Contemporary Tribal Life* (Berkeley, CA: University of California Press, 1995).

Poor, Tim. "Singapore Caning Brings Outpouring of Agreement Here." *Washington Post* (10 April 1994) 1A.

Porter, Robert. "Strengthening Tribal Sovereignty through Peacemaking: How the Anglo-American Legal Tradition Destroys Indigenous Societies" (1996-97) 28 Colum. H.R.L. Rev. 235.

Pottow, J.A.E. "Constitutional Remedies in the Criminal Context: A Unified Approach to Section 24" (2000) 43:4 Crim. L.Q. 459; (2000) 44 Crim. L.Q. 44:1 34; and (2000) 44:2 Crim. L.Q. 223.

Poulson, Barton. "A Third Voice: A Review of Empirical Research on the Psychological Outcomes of Restorative Justice" (2003) Utah L. Rev. 167.

Powell, Martine B. "PRIDE: The Essential Elements of an Effective Forensic Interview with an Aboriginal Person" (2000) 35:3 Australian Psychologist 186.

Price, Heather, Deborah Connolly, and Heidi Gordon. "Children's Recall of an Instance of a Repeated Event: Does Spacing of Instances Matter?" (2006) 14:8 Memory 977.

Pridemore, William Alex. "A Methodological Addition to the Cross-National Empirical Literature on Social Structure and Homicide: A First Test of the Povery-Homicide Thesis" (2008) 46:1 Criminology 133.

Prison Justice Day Committee. *Behind Bars in Canada: The Costs of Incarceration* (Vancouver: Prison Justice Day Committee, 2008).

Pritchard, Dean. "Perv Elder Spared Jail." *Winnipeg Sun* (28 July 2010) 3.

Purdy, Chris. "Healing Won't Happen in Jail: Life of Spiritual Guidance Needed, Say Elders, but a Judge Will Get the Final Say." *Globe and Mail* (14 February 2009) A8.

Purvin, Diane M. "Weaving a Tangled Safety Net: The Intergenerational Legacy of Domestic Violence and Poverty" (2003) 9 Violence against Women 1263.

Pve, Clifton. "Language Loss among the Chilcotin" (1992) 93 Int'l J. Sociology of Language 75.

Quirk, Hannah. "Identifying Miscarriages of Justice: Why Innocence in the UK Is Not the Answer" (2007) 70:5 Modern L. Rev. 759.

Radelet, Michael L., and Traci L. Lacock. "Do Executions Lower Homicide Rates: The Views of Leading Criminologists" (2009) 99:2 J. Crim. L. & Criminology 489.

Raitt, Fiona E. "Expert Evidence as Context: Historical Patterns and Contemporary Attitudes in the Prosecution of Sexual Offences" (2004) 12 Fem. Leg. Stud. 233.

Rawls, John. *A Theory of Justice* (Cambridge, MA: Belknap Press, 1971).

Razack, Sherene. *Looking White People in the Eye: Gender, Race, and Culture in Courtrooms and Classrooms* (Toronto: University of Toronto Press, 1998).

"Recent Native Longhouse Initiation Deaths Spark Investigation, Explanation." *Canadian Press Newswire* (13 January 2005).

Reed, Elizabeth, et al., "Experiences of Racial Discrimination and Relation to Violence Perpetration and Gang Involvement among a Sample of Urban African American Men" (2010) 12:3 J. Immigrant & Minority Health 319.

Reilly, John. *A Judge's Struggle for Justice in a First Nations Community* (Calgary: Rocky Mountain Books, 2010).

Research Framework for a Review of Community Justice in Yukon: Community Justice – Peacemaker Diversion Project (Whitehorse, YT: Department of Justice, 2003).

Richland, Justin B. "'What Are You Going to Do with the Village's Knowledge?' Talking Tradition, Talking Law in Hopi Tribal Court" (2005) 39 L. & Soc'y Rev. 235.

Ritters, Alison, and Jennifer Chalmers. "The Relationship between Economic Conditions and Substance Abuse and Harms" (2011) 30:1 Drug & Alcohol Rev. 1.

Roach, Kent. "Changing Punishment at the Turn of the Century: Restorative Justice on the Rise" (2000) 42 Can. J. Crim. 239.

–. "Criminology: Four Models of the Criminal Process" (1999) 89 J. Crim. L. & Criminology 671.

Roberts, Julian V., and Loretta J. Stalans. *Public Opinion, Crime and Criminal Justice* (Boulder, CO: Westview Press, 2006).

–. "Restorative Sentencing: Exploring the Views of the Public" (2004) 17:3 Social Justice Research 315.

Roberts, Paul. "Towards the Principled Reception of Expert Evidence of Witness Credibility in Criminal Trials" (2004) 8:3 Int'l J. Evidence & Proof 215.

Robinson, Alan. "*R. v. Williams and Orrs:* Cigar Store Indians and Juvenile Confessions" (1986) Aboriginal Law Bulletin 20.

Roche, Declan. *Accountability in Restorative Justice* (Oxford: Oxford University Press, 2003).

Rosen, Mark D. "Multiple Authoritative Interpreters of Quasi-Constitutional Federal Law: Of Tribal Courts and the *Indian Civil Rights Act*" (2000) 69 Fordham L. Rev. 479.

Ross, Rupert. *Returning to the Teachings: Exploring Aboriginal Justice* (Toronto: Penguin Books Canada, 1996).

Rossner, Meredith. "Emotions and Interaction Ritual: A Micro Analysis of Restorative Justice" (2011) 51 British J. Criminology 95

Rousseau, Jean-Jacques. *The Social Contract,* edited by Maurice Cranston (Baltimore, MD: Penguin Books, 1968).

Roy, Sudipto. "Two Types of Juvenile Restitution Programs in Two Midwestern Counties: A Comparative Study" (1993) 57 Federal Probation 48.

Royal Commission on Aboriginal Peoples. *Bridging the Cultural Divide: A Report on Aboriginal People and Criminal Justice in Canada* (Ottawa: Minister of Supply and Services Canada, 1996).

–. *Restructuring the Relationship,* volume 2, part 1, chapter 3 "Governance" (Ottawa: Royal Commission on Aboriginal Peoples, 1993).

Royal Commission on the Donald Marshall, Jr., Prosecution (Halifax: Province of Nova Scotia, 1989).

Rudin, Jonathan. "One Step Forward, Two Steps Back: The Political and Institutional Dynamics behind the Supreme Court of Canada's Decisions in *R. v. Sparrow, R. v. Van der peet,* and *Delgamuukw*" (1998) 13 J.L. & Soc. Pol'y 67 at 85.

Rudin, Jonathan, and Kent Roach. "Broken Promises: A Response to Stenning and Roberts' Colloquy on 'Empty Promises: Parliament, the Supreme Court, and the Sentencing of Aboriginal Offenders'" (2002) 65:1 Sask. L. Rev. 1.

Rudin, Jonathan, and Dan Russell. *Native Alternative Dispute Resolution Systems: The Canadian Future in Light of the American Past* (Mississauga, ON: Ontario Native Council on Justice, 1993).

Rugge, Tanya, James Bonta, and Suzanne Wallace-Capretta. *Evaluation of the Collaborative Justice Project: A Restorative Justice Program for Serious Crime, 2002-2005* (Ottawa: Public Safety and Emergency Preparedness Canada, 2005).

Ryals, John S., Jr. "Restorative Justice: New Horizons in Juvenile Offender Counseling" (2004) J. Addictions & Offender Counseling 18.

Ryan, Joan. *Doing Things the Right Way* (Calgary: University of Calgary Press, Arctic Institute of North America, 1995).

Sabates, Ricardo. "Educational Attainment and Juvenile Crime: Area-Level Evidence Using Three Cohorts of Young People" (2008) 48 Brit. J. Crim. 395.

Saguil, Paul Jonathan. "Ethical Lawyering across Canada's Legal Traditions" (2010) 9:1 Indig. L.J. 157.

Salisbury, Emily, Kris Henning, and Robert Holdford. "Fathering by Partner-Abusive Men: Attitudes on Children's Exposure to Interparental Conflict and Risk Factors for Child Abuse" (2009) 14:3 Child Maltreatment 232.

Sanders, Douglas. "The Rights of Aboriginal Peoples of Canada" (1983) 61 Can. Bar. Rev. 314.

Sapers, Howard. *Annual Report of the Office of the Correctional Investigator 2005-2006* (Ottawa: Minister of Public Safety, 2006).

Sarat, Austin. *When the State Kills: Capital Punishment and the American Condition* (Princeton, NJ: Princeton University Press, 2002).

Sarnoff, Susan. "Restoring Justice to the Community: A Realistic Goal?" (2001) 65:1 Federal Probation 3.

"Saskatchewan's First Aboriginal Police Force Faces Questions of Conduct." *First Nations Drum* (September 2007) 23.

Sawatsky, Jarem. *The Ethic of Traditional Communities and the Spirit of Healing Justice: Studies from Hollow Water, the Iona Community, and Plum Village* (Philadelphia, PA: Jessica Kingsley Publishers, 2009).

Scarre, Geoffrey. "Corporal Punishment" (2003) 6 Ethical Theory & Moral Practice 295.

Sekaqualptewa, Pat. "Evolving the Hopi Common Law" (2000) 9 Kan. J.L. & Pub. Pol'y 761.

–. "Key Concepts in the Finding, Definition, and Consideration of Custom Law in Tribal Lawmaking" (2007-08) 32:2 Am. Indian L. Rev. 319.

Shepherd, Jonathan. "Criminal Deterrence as a Public Health Strategy" (2001) 358:9294 Lancet 1717.

Shepherd, Robert, and Russell Diablo, "A Government-First Nations Dialogue on Accountability: Re-establishing Understanding on the Basics of a Complex Relationship" (2005) 15:2 Native Studies Rev. 61.

Sherman, Lawrence, and Heather Strang. *Restorative Justice: The Evidence* (London: Smith Institute, 2009).

Sherman, Lawrence, Heather Strang, and Daniel Woods. *Recidivism Patterns in the Canberra Reintegrative Shaming Experiments* (Canberra, Australia: Reintegrative Shaming Experiments, 2000) [unpublished].

Shermer, Lauren O'Neill, Karen C. Rose, and Ashley Hoffman. "Perceptions and Credibility: Understanding the Nuances of Eyewitness Testimony" (2011) 27:2 J. Contemporary Criminal Justice 183.

Simpson, Leanne R. "Anticolonial Strategies for the Recovery and Maintenance of Indigenous Knowledge" (2004) 28:3-4 Am. Indian Q. 373.

Singh Bati, Avinashi, and Alex R. Piquero. "Estimating the Impact of Incarceration on Subsequent Offending Trajectories: Deterrent, Crimogenic, or Null Effect?" (2008) 98:1 Criminology 207.

Sisco, Melissa, and Judith Baker. "Beyond Predicting the Risk of Sexual Victimization in Prison: Considering Inmate Options and Reporting Avenues for Addressing an Inherent Problem" (2007) 6:3 Criminology & Public Policy 573.

Slattery, Brian. "First Nations and the Constitution: A Question of Trust" (1992) 71 Can. Bar. Rev. 261.

Small, Deborah. "The War on Drugs Is a War on Racial Justice" (2001) 68:3 Social Research 896.

Smith, Carolyn A., Timothy O. Ireland, and Terrence B. Thornberry. "Adolescent Maltreatment and Its Impact on Young Antisocial Behavior" (2005) 29:10 Child Abuse & Neglect 1099.

Smith, Dawn, Colleen Varcoe, and Nancy Edwards. "Turning around the Intergenerational Impact of Residential Schools on Aboriginal People: Implications for Health Policy and Practice" (2005) 37:4 Can. J. Nursing Research 38.

Smith, Kevin B. "The Politics of Punishment: Evaluating Political Explanations of Incarceration Rates" (2004) 66:3 J. Politics 925.

Smith, Linda Tuwihai. *Decolonizing Methodologies: Research and Indigenous Peoples* (New York: Zed Books, 1999).

Smitz, Cristin. "SCC Wrong Forum for Native Land Claims: Bastarache." *Lawyers Weekly* (19 January 2001) 20:34.

Snackens, Sonja, and Crystal Beyens. "Sentencing and Prison Overcrowding" (1994) 2:1 Eur. J. Crim. Pol'y & Research 84.

Soldwedel, Arne F. "Testing Japan's Convictions: The Lay Judge System and the Rights of Criminal Defendants" (2008) 41:5 Vand. J. Transn'l. L. 1417.

"Sorry's Not Enough." *National Post* (28 June 1999) A19.

Sousa, Cindy, et al. "Longitudinal Study on the Effects of Child Abuse and Childrens' Exposure to Domestic Violence, Parent-Child Attachments, and Antisocial Behavior in Adolescence" (2011) 12:2 Asia Pacific J. Anthropology 146.

Souza, Karen A., and Mandeep K. Dhami. "A Study of Volunteers in Community-Based Restorative Justice Programs" (2008) 50:1 Can. J. Crim. 31.

Spano, Richard, Joshua D. Frielich, and John Bolland. "Gang Membership, Gun Carrying, and Employment: Applying Routine Activities Theory to Explain Violent Victimization among Inner City, Minority Youth Living in Extreme Poverty" (2008) 25:2 Justice Q. 381.

Spano, Richard, Craig Rivera, and John Bolland. "The Impact of Timing of Exposure to Violence on Violent Behavior in a High Poverty Sample of Inner City African American Youth" (2006) 35 J. Youth & Adolescence 681.

Spohn, Cassia. "The Deterrent Effect of Imprisonment and Offenders' Stake in Conformity" (2007) 18:1 Crim. Justice Pol'y 31.

Stahlkopf, Christina. "Restorative Justice, Rhetoric or Reality? Conferencing with Young Offenders" 12:3 Contemporary Justice Rev. 231.

Standing Committee on Justice and Solicitor General, House of Commons. *Report of the Standing Committee on Justice and Solicitor General on Its Review of Sentencing, Conditional Release and Related Aspects of Corrections, Taking Responsibility.* (Ottawa: Solicitor General, 1988).

Steel, Kevin. "No Love for Indian Democracy" (1998) 25:36 Alberta Report 9.

Stein, Karin. *Public Perception of Crime and Justice in Canada: A Review of Opinion Polls* (Ottawa: Department of Justice Canada, 2001).

Steiner, Benjamin. "Assessing Static and Dynamic Influences on Inmate Violence Levels" (2009) 55:1 Crime & Delinquency 134.

Stenning, Phillip, and Julian V. Robert. "The Sentencing of Aboriginal Offenders in Canada: A Rejoinder," Colloquy on "Empty Promises: Parliament, the Supreme Court, and the Sentencing of Aboriginal Offenders'" (2002) 65:1 Sask. L. Rev. 75.

Stobbs, Nigel. "An Adversarial Quagmire: The Continued Inability of the Queensland Criminal Justice System to Cater for Indigenous Witnesses and Complainants" (2007) 6:30 Indigenous Law Bulletin 30.

Strang, Heather. *Repair or Revenge? Victims and Restorative Justice* (Oxford: Clarendon Press, 2002).

Strang, Heather, et al. "Victim Evaluations of Face-to-Face Restorative Justice Conferences: A Quasi-Experimental Analysis" (2006) 62:2 J. Social Issues 281.

Stribopoulos, James. "In Search of Dialogue: The Supreme Court, Police Powers, and the *Charter*" (2005) 31 Queen's L.J. 1.

Stuart, Barry. *Building Community Justice Partnerships: Community Peacemaking Circles* (Ottawa: Department of Justice, Canada, 1997).

Stuart, Don, Ronald Joseph Delisle, and David M. Tanovich. *Evidence: Principles and Problems* (Toronto: Thomson Reuters, 2010).

Stubbs, Julie. "Domestic Violence and Women's Safety: Feminist Challenges to Restorative Justice." In Heather Strang and John Braithwaite (eds.), *Restorative Justice and Family Violence* (Cambridge: Cambridge University Press, 2002).

Stuesser, Lee. *An Advocacy Primer* (2nd edition) (Scarborough, ON: Thomson Carswell, 2005).

Sung, Hung-En. "Nonfatal Violence-Related and Accident-Related Injuries among Jail Inmates in the United States" (2010) 90:3 Prison Journal 353.

Sussman, Steve, et al. "Prediction of Violence Perpetration among High-Risk Youth" (2004) 28:2 Am. J. Health Behavior 134.

Sutherland, Dannia, Cecilia E. Casaneuva, and Heather Ringeisen. "Young Adult Incomes and Mental Health Problems among Transition Age Youth Investigated for Maltreatment during Adolescence" (2009) 31:9 Child & Youth Services Rev. 947.

"Systemic Racism." *Ottawa Citizen* (1 May 1999) B5.

Szablowinski, Zenon. "Punitive Justice and Restorative Justice as Social Reconciliation" (2008) 49:3 Heythrop Journal 18.

Tanovich, David. "Charting the Constitutional Right of Effective Assistance of Counsel in Canada" (1994) 36 Criminal L.Q. 404.

Tauri, Juan, and Allison Morris. "Re-forming Justice: The Potential of Maori Processes" (1997) 30:2 Austl. Crim. & N.Z. J. 149.

Thwaites, Reuben G. (ed.). *The Jesuit Relations and Allied Documents*, volume 43 (Cleveland, OH: Burrows Brothers, 1897).

Tittle, Charles, Ekaterina Botchkovar, and Alena Antonaccio. "Criminal Contemplation, National Context and Deterrence" (2011) 27:2 J. Qualitative Criminology 225.

Tomporowski, Barbara. *Exploring Restorative Justice in Saskatchewan* (MA thesis, Department of Social Studies, University of Regina, 2004).

Totten, Mark. "Aboriginal Youth and Violent Gang Involvement in Canada: Quality Prevention Strategies" (2009) 3 I.P.C. Review 135.

"Trying Times for Taiwan's Judiciary." *Global Agenda* (31 January 2009) 10.

Tsuji, Leonard. "Loss of Cree Traditional Ecological Knowledge in the Western James Bay Region of Northern Ontario, Canada: A Case Study of the Sharp-Tailed Grouse, *Tympanachus phasianellus phasianellus*" (1996) 26:2 Can. J. Native Stud. 283.

Turner, Dale. *This Is Not a Peace Pipe: Towards a Critical Indigenous Philosophy* (Toronto: University of Toronto Press, 2006).

Turpel-Lafond, Mary Ellen. "Aboriginal Peoples and the Canadian Charter: Interpretive Monopolies, Cultural Differences" (1989-90) Can. H.R. Y.B. 3.

Turpel-Lafond, Mary Ellen, and Patricia Monture-Angus. "Aboriginal Peoples and Canadian Criminal Law: Rethinking Justice," Special edition on Aboriginal Justice (1992) 26 U.B.C. L. Rev. 239.

Umbreit, Mark S. *Victim Meets Offender: The Impact of Restorative Justice and Mediation* (Monsey, NY: Willow Tree Press, 1994).

Umbreit, Mark S., Robert B. Coates, and Betty Vos. "Restorative Justice Circles: An Exploratory Study" (2003) 6:3 Contemporary Justice Rev. 265.

–. "Restorative Justice Dialogue: A Multi-Dimensional, Evidence-Based Practice Theory" (2007) 10:1 Contemporary Justice Rev. 23.

Ungar, Mark. "Contested Battlefields: Policing in Caracas and La Paz" (2003) 37:2 N.A.C.L.A. Report on the Americas 30.

Unterberger, Betty Ellen. "Self-Determination." In Alexander Deconde (ed.), *American Encyclopedia of Foreign Policy* (2nd edition) (New York: Schribner, 2002).

Vacca, James S. "Crime Can Be Prevented If Schools Teach Juvenile Offenders to Read" (2008) 30:9 Children & Youth Services Rev. 1055.

Van Dorn, Richard A., and James Herbert Williams. "Correlates Associated with Escalation of Delinquent Behavior in Incarcerated Youths" (2003) 48:4 Social Work 523.

van Wormer, Katherine. "Restorative Justice: A Model for Personal and Societal Empowerment" (2004) 23:4 J. Religion & Spirituality in Social Work 103.

–. "Restorative Justice as Social Justice for Victims of Gendered Violence: A Standpoint Feminist Perspective" (2009) 54:2 Social Work 107.

Varna, Kimberly N., and Anthony Doob. "Deterring Economic Crimes: The Case of Tax Evasion" (1998) 40:2 Can. J. Crim. 165.

Vermette, D'Arcy. "Colonialism and the Suppression of Aboriginal Voice" (2008-09) 40 Ottawa L. Rev. 225.

Waldram, James. *The Way of the Pipe* (Peterborough, ON: Broadview Press, 1997) 44.

Walker, C.T. "A Critique of the Prima Facie Exclusionary Rule" (1996) 17:1 N.Z.U. L.R. 94.

Walker, Loren, and Leslie A. Hayashi. "Pono Kaulike: A Hawaii Criminal Court Provides Restorative Justice Practices for Healing Relationships" (2007) 71:3 Federal Probation 18.

Wall, Steven. "Collective Rights and Individual Autonomy" (2007) 117 Ethics 234.

Wallingford, Jayne. "The Role of Tradition in the Navajo Judiciary: Reemergence and Revival" (1994) 19 Okla. City U.L. Rev. 141.

Ward, Tony. "Usurping the Role of the Jury? Expert Evidence and Witness Credibility in Criminal Trials" (2009) 13:2 Int'l J. Evidence & Proof 83

Ward, Tony, and Robyn Langlands. "Repairing the Rupture: Restorative Justice and the Rehabilitation of Offenders" (2009) 14:3 Aggression and Violent Behavior 205

Wareham, Jennifer, Denise Paquette Boots, and Jorge M. Chavez. "A Test of Social Learning and Intergenerational Transmission among Batterers" (2009) 37:2 J. Crim. Justice 163.

Warner, Barbara D., Elizabeth Back, and Mary L. Ohmer. "Linking Informal Social Control and Restorative Justice: Moving Social Disorganization Theory beyond Community Policing" (2010) 13:4 Contemporary Justice Rev. 355.

Watson, Jack. "Curial Incompetence in Criminal Trials: A Discussion of Section 24 of the Charter of Rights and Freedoms in the Criminal Trial Context" (Part 1) (1990) 32 Crim. L.Q. 162.

Weisbrot, David. "Comment on the ALRC Discussion Paper: *Customary Law*" (1981) 1:1 Aboriginal Law Bulletin 3.

Weisburd, David, Elin Waring, and Ellen Chayet. "Specific Deterrence in a Sample of Offenders Convicted of White Collar Crimes" (1995) 33:4 Criminology 587.

Whannock, Karen. *Aboriginal Courts in Canada* (Vancouver: Scow Institute, 2008).

–. "A Tale of Two Courts: The New Westminister First Nations Court and the Colville Tribal Court" (2011) 44 U.B.C. L. Rev. 99.

Wheeldon, Johannes. "Finding Common Ground: Restorative Justice and Its Theoretical Construction(s)" (2009) 12:1 Contemporary Justice Rev. 91.

White, Rob. "Community Corrections in Criminal Justice" (2004) 16:1 Current Issues in Criminal Justice 42 at 47.

Wildsmith, Bruce. *Aboriginal Peoples and Section 25 of the Canadian Charter of Rights and Freedoms* (Saskatoon, SK: Native Law Centre, University of Saskatchewan, 1988).

–. "Treaty Responsibilities: A Co-Relational Model," Special Edition on Aboriginal Justice (1992) U.B.C. L. Rev. 324.

Wilkins, Kerry. "But We Need the Eggs: The Royal Commission, the Charter of Rights and the Inherent Right of Aboriginal Self-Government" (1999) 49 U.T.L.J. 53.

Williams, Frank D., and Marilyn P. McShane. *Criminological Theory* (3rd edition) (Englewood Cliffs, NJ: Prentice Hall. 1999).

Williamson, Linda. "Different Strokes for Different Folks: This Is Social Engineering Disguised as Justice for All." *Toronto Star* (30 April 1999) 17.

Wilson, Robin J., Bria Huculak, and Andrew McWhinnie. "Restorative Justice Innovations in Canada" (2002) 20 Behav. Sci. & L. 363.

Wolff, Mark J. "Spirituality, Culture and Tradition: An Introduction to the Role of Tribal Courts and Councils in Reclaiming Native American Heritage and Sovereignty" (1994-95) 7 St. Thomas L. Rev 761.

Wolff, Nancy, and Jing Shi. "Type, Source, and Patterns of Physical Victimization: A Comparison of Male and Female Inmates" (2009) 89:2 Prison Journal 173.

"Womens' Groups Protest Caning of Women in Malaysia." *Indo-Asian News Service* (18 February 2010).

Wright, Bradley R.E., et al. "Does the Perceived Risk of Crime Deter Criminally Prone Individuals: Rational Choice, Self-Control and Crime" (2004) 41:2 J. Research in Crime & Delinquency 180.

Yazzie, Robert. "The Navajo Response to Crime." In Wanda D. McCaslin (ed.), *Justice as Healing: Indigenous Ways* (St. Paul, MN: Living Justice Press, 2005) 121.

Yessine, Annie K., and James Bonta. "The Offending Trajectories of Youthful Aboriginal Offenders" (2009) 51:4 Public Safety Canada 435.

Young, Alan. "Adversarial Justice and the Charter of Rights: Stunting the Growth of the 'Living Tree'" (1997) 39 Criminal L.Q. 362.

Zdenkowski, George. "Customary Punishment and Pragmatism: Some Unresolved Dilemmas" (1993) Indigenous Law Bulletin 33.

Zedner, Lucia. "Securing Liberty in the Face of Terror: Reflections from Criminal Justice" (2005) 32:4 J.L. & Soc'y 507.

Zellerer, Evelyn, and Chris Cunneen. "Restorative Justice, Indigenous Justice, and Human Rights." In Gordon Bezemore and Mara Schiff (eds.), *Restorative Community Justice: Repairing Harm and Transforming Communities* (Ottawa: Anderson Publishing, 2001) 245.

Zernova, Margarita. *Restorative Justice: Ideals and Realities* (Hampshire, UK: Ashgate Publishing, 2007).

Zimring, Franklin E., and David T. Johnson. "Public Opinion and the Governance of Punishment in Democratic Political Systems" (2006) 605:1 Ann. Am. Acad. Pol. & Soc. Sci. 265.

Zion, James. "Taking Justice Back: American Indian Perspectives." In Royal Commission on Aboriginal Peoples, *Aboriginal Peoples and the Justice System: Report of the National Round Table on Aboriginal Justice Issues* (Ottawa: Supply and Services, 1993) 309.

Zion, James W., and Elsie Zion. "'Hazho' Sokee' – Stay Together Nicely': Domestic Violence under Navajo Common Law" (1993) 25:2 Arizona St. L.J. 407.

Zlotkin, Norman. *Unfinished Business: Aboriginal Peoples and the 1983 Constitutional Conference*, Discussion Paper no. 15 (Kingston, ON: Institute of Intergovernmental Relations, Queen's University, 1983).

Legislation

Canada
An Act Relating to Self-Government for the Sechelt Indian Band, S.C. 1986, c. 27.
Canadian Bill of Rights, S.C. 1960, c. 44.
Canadian Charter of Rights and Freedoms, Part I of the *Constitution Act, 1982*, being Schedule B to the *Canada Act 1982*, (U.K.), c. 11.
Canadian Human Rights Act, R.S.C. 1985, c. H-6.
Code of Offences and Procedures of Justice for the Mohawk Nation at Akwesasne, Draft no. 10.
Constitution Act, 1867, (U.K.), 30 and 31 Victoria, c. 3.
Constitution Act, 1982, being Schedule B to the *Canada Act 1982*, (U.K.), c. 11.
Corrections and Conditional Release Act, S.C. 1992, c. 20.
Criminal Code, R.S.C. 1985, c. 46.
Customs Act, R.S. 1985, c. 1 (2nd. supp.).
Indian Act, S.C. 1985, c. I-5.
Nisga'a Final Agreement (Ottawa: Library of Parliament, 1999).
Sechelt Agreement-in-Principle (Vancouver: Library of the Legislature of British Columbia, 1999).
Tsawwassen Final Agreement (Vancouver: Government of British Columbia, 2006).
Tsawwassen First Nation Final Agreement Act, Bill 40, 3rd Session, 38th Parliament, 2007.

United States
Absente Shawnee Tribe of Oklahoma Tribal Code (circa 1999).
Blackfeet Tribal Code (circa 1999).
Chitimaca Comprehensive Codes of Justice (last amended 15 April 2003).
Colville Tribal Law and Order Code, 7 N.T.C. s. 606.
Ely Shoshone Tribal Law and Order Code (last revised 2000).
Hopi Indian Tribe Law and Order Code.
Indian Civil Rights Act, 25 U.S.C. s. 1301-3.
Law and Order Code of the Fort McDowell Yavapai Community, Arizona, adopted by Resolution no. 90-30.
Major Crimes Act, 18 U.S.C. s. 1153.
Nation Bill of Rights, N.N.C. s. 1, et seq. (2005).
Oglala Sioux Tribe: Law and Order Code.
Red Cliff Band of Lake Superior Chippewas Tribal Law and Constitution.
Stockbridge-Munsee Tribal Code.
Violent Crime Control and Law Enforcement Act of 1995, 108 Stat. 1796.

International
Declaration of the Rights of Indigenous Peoples, UN General Assembly, 7 September 2007, Doc. A/61/L.67.
International Covenant on Civil and Political Rights, 16 December 1966, adopted by United Nations General Assembly Resolution 2200A (XXI).
United Nations Human Rights Committee, 15 March 2000, UN Doc. A/55/40 GAOR, (vol. II).

Legislative Committees, Debates, and Documents
Ontario Judicial Appointments Advisory Committee. *Policies and Process* (Toronto: Ontario Courts, 2005).
Rights of Members of Indian Tribes: Hearing before the Subcommittee on Indian Affairs of the House Committee on Interior and Insular Affairs, 90th Congress, 2nd Sess. (1968).
Wabanaki Compact, 1725, Article 6, in a letter, with enclosures, of Lt. Governor Dummer of New England to Duke of Newcastle, Secretary of States, Calendar of State Papers, Colonial

Series (America and West Indies), vol. 35 (8 January 1726), UK Public Records Office, Colonial Office Papers, Series 5/898.

Jurisprudence

Canada
Adler v The Queen in Right of Ontario, [1996] 3 S.C.R. 609.
Augustine and Augustine v The Queen; Barlow v The Queen, [1987] 1 C.N.L.R. 20.
British Columbia Securities Commission v Branch, [1995] 2 S.C.R. 3.
Campbell v British Columbia (A.G.), [2000] 8 W.W.R. 600 (B.C.S.C.).
Cloutier v Langlois, [1990] 1 S.C.R. 158.
Dagenais v Canadian Broadcasting Corporation, [1994] 3 S.C.R. 835.
Delgamuukw v British Columbia, [1997] 3 S.C.R. 1010.
Guerin v The Queen, [1984] 2 S.C.R. 335.
Haida v British Columbia (Minister of Forests), [2004] 3 S.C.R. 511.
Hunter v Southam, [1984] 2 S.C.R. 145.
Irwin Toy Ltd. v Quebec (A.G.), [1989] 1 S.C.R. 927.
Kindler v Canada (Minister of Justice), [1991] 2 S.C.R. 779.
Mackin v New Brunswick; Rice v New Brunswick, [2002] 1 S.C.R. 405.
Mitchell v Canada (Minister of National Revenue), [2001] 1 S.C.R. 911.
Pearlman v Manitoba Law Society Judicial Committee, [1991] 2 S.C.R. 869.
R. v 974649 Ontario Inc., [2001] 3 S.C.R. 575.
R. v A.K., 2009 ONCJ 578.
R. v A.M. (2008), 293 D.L.R. (4th) 187 (S.C.C.).
R. v Adams (2010), 211 C.R.R. (2d) 360 (Nfld. S.C.)
R. v Adhofer, 2010 ABPC 235.
R. v Alexander (2010), 209 C.R.R. (2d) 34 (Ont. S.C.).
R. v Amway of Canada Ltd., [1989] 1 S.C.R. 21.
R. v Andersen, 2010 ABPC 325.
R. v Appleby, 2009 ABPC 301.
R. v Armstrong, [2009] O.J. 5617 (Sup. Ct. Just.).
R. v Atkins (2002), 5 C.R. (6th) 400 (Ont. C.A.).
R. v Avila, 2010 ONCJ 512.
R. v B. (K.G.), [1993] 1 S.C.R. 740.
R. v Badger, [1996] 1 S.C.R. 771.
R. v Banks, 2010 ONCJ 553.
R. v Barrett, [1995] 1 S.C.R. 752.
R. v Bartle, [1994] 3 S.C.R. 173.
R. v Bear (1993), 90 Man. R. (2d) 286 (Q.B.).
R. v Beattie (2009), 69 C.R. (6th) 92 (Ont. Sup. Ct. Just.).
R. v Bell (1930), 53 C.C.C. 80 (Alta. C.A.).
R. v Bencardino (1973), 24 C.R.N.S. 173 (Ont. C.A.).
R. v Big M Drug Mart Ltd., [1985] 1 S.C.R. 295.
R. v Blackwood, [2009] O.J. 5393 (Sup. Ct. Just.).
R. v Blake, 2009 ONCA 1.
R. v Blanchard, 2011 NLCA 33.
R. v Blazevic, 2010 ONCJ 137.
R. v Borden, [1994] 3 S.C.R. 145.
R. v Boyd, 2011 BCPC 137.
R. v Broyles, [1991] 3 S.C.R. 595.
R. v Bruno, 2009 ABPC 232.
R. v Bryce, [2009] O.J. 3640.
R. v Burns, [1994] 1 S.C.R. 656.
R. v Brydges, [1990] 1 S.C.R. 190.
R. v Burlingham, [1995] 2 S.C.R. 206.
R. v Buhay (2003), 10 C.R. (6th) 205 (S.C.C.).
R. v Cappo, [2005] S.J. no. 720 (C.A.).

R. v Carriero (2010), 210 C.R.R. (2d) 65.
R. v Castillo, 2011 ONSC 3257.
R. v Chambers, [1990] 2 S.C.R. 1293.
R. v Charlton, 2011 BCSC 805.
R. v Chaulk, [1990] 3 S.C.R. 1303.
R. v Chuhaniuk, 2010 BCCA 403.
R. v Churko, 2010 SKPC 5.
R. v Ciachurski, 2009 BSCS 1467.
R. v Clarkson, [1986] 1 S.C.R. 383.
R. v Collins, [1987] 1 S.C.R. 265.
R. v Comber, 2009 ONCJ 418.
R. v Corbett, [1998] 1 S.C.R. 670.
R. v Crocker (2009), 69 C.R. (6th) 107.
R. v Cullen (1989), 52 C.C.C. (3d) 459 (Ont. C.A.).
R. v Cuttell (2009), 247 C.C.C. (3d) 247.
R. v D.B.M. (2009), 282 N.S.R. (2d) 64.
R. v D.C., 2010 SKPC 132.
R. v Daviault, [1994] 3 S.C.R. 63.
R. v Demeter (1975), 25 C.C.C. (2d) 417 (Ont. C.A.).
R. v Desnomie (2005), Sask. R. (C.A.).
R. v Dhillon, 2010 ONCA 582.
R. v Dinwall, 2010 ONCJ 5207.
R. v Downey, [1992] 2 S.C.R. 10.
R. v Dupras, 2010 ABPC 138.
R. v E. Star International Inc., 2009 ONCJ 576.
R. v Edwards, [1996] 1 S.C.R. 128.
R. v Epp, 2010 SKPC 89.
R. v Erickson, 2009 BCPC 365.
R. v Erickson (2010), 353 Sask. R. 132 (P.C.).
R. v Erven, [1979] 2 S.C.R. 1041.
R. v Evans, [1991] 1 S.C.R. 869.
R. v Ewanchuk, [1999] 1 S.C.R. 330.
R. v F.A. (1993), 30 C.R. (4th) 333 (Ont. Ct. of Justice (Gen. Div.)).
R. v Farahanchi, 2010 NSPC 57.
R. v Fatt, (1986) 54 C.R. (3d) 281 (N.W.T.S.C.).
R. v Feeney (1997) 115 C.C.C. (3d) 129 (S.C.C.).
R. v Fernandes, [2009] O.J. 5218 (Sup. Ct. Just.).
R. v Fiddler, [2010] S.J. 545.
R. v Fildan (2009), 69 C.R. (6th) 65.
R. v Forster, 2009 ABPC 278.
R. v Foy, 2010 BCSC 112.
R. v Fynn, 2010 ONCJ 543.
R. v Gaba (2010), 211 C.R.R. (2d) 265 (B.C.S.C.)
R. v Gerun, 2009 ABPC 224.
R. v Gingell (1996), 50 C.R. (4th) 326 (Y. Terr. Ct.).
R. v Givens, 85 M.V.R. (5th) 218 (B.C.S.C.).
R. v Gladstone, [1996] 2 S.C.R. 723.
R. v Gladue, [1999] 1 S.C.R. 688.
R. v Golden, [2001] 3 S.C.R. 679.
R. v Goltz, [1991] 3 S.C.R. 485.
R. v Goodwin, 2009 ABQB 710.
R. v Graham, 2010 ONSC 119.
R. v Grant, [2009] 2 S.C.R. 353.
R. v Greffe, [1990] 1 S.C.R. 755.
R. v Guce, 2011 ONSC 2331.
R. v Guenter, [2011] O.J. no. 2233 (Sup. Ct. J.).

R. v H.R. (1997), 205 A.R. 226 (Prov. Ct.).
R. v Hamill (1987), 56 C.R. (3d) 220 (S.C.C.).
R. v Hamilton, 2010 YKTC 75.
R. v Hanemaayer (2008), 234 C.C.C. (3d) 3 (Ont. C.A.).
R. v Hanneson (1989), 71 C.R. (3d) 249 (Ont. C.A.).
R. v Harper, [1994] 3 S.C.R. 343.
R. v Harrer, [1995] 3 S.C.R. 562.
R. v Harrison, [2009] 2 S.C.R. 494.
R. v Hatchard, [1993] 1 C.N.L.R. 96 (Ont. Ct. Just.).
R. v Hatton, 2011 ABQB 242.
R. v Hatzel, 2011 SKQB 49.
R. v Hebert, [1990] 2 S.C.R. 151.
R. v Henderson, 2011 ONSC 2392.
R. v Henry, 2010 ONSC 5206.
R. v Horse, [1988] 1 S.C.R. 187.
R. v Horseman, [1990] 3 C.N.L.R. 95 (S.C.C.).
R. v Hubar-Rook, 2010 ABPC 283.
R. v Huddlestone, 2009 BCPC 404.
R. v Hunter (1997), 52 Alta. L.R. (3d) 359 (Prov. Ct.).
R. v Huynh, 2010 BCSC 1553.
R. v J.A.J., 2009 ONCJ 467.
R. v J.K., 2010 ONCJ 232.
R. v Jaswal, 2010 ABPC 366.
R. v Jobidon, [1991] 2 S.C.R. 714.
R. v Johnson, 2011 ABPC 179.
R. v Johnson, 2010 ONSC 6186.
R. v Johnstone, 2009 SKPC 133.
R. v Judge, 2010 ONCJ 488.
R. v K.I., [1990] N.W.T.R. 388 (S.C.).
R. v Kapp, [2008] 2 S.C.R. 483.
R. v Karanouh, 2009 ONCJ 579.
R. v Keegstra, [1990] 3 S.C.R. 697.
R. v Kendall (1987), 57 C.R. (3d) 249 (Ont. C.A.).
R. v Kerr, 2010 ONCJ 189.
R. v Khan, 2010 ONCJ 404.
R. v Kisil, 2009 ONCJ 424.
R. v Knight, 2010 ONCJ 400.
R. v Koczab, 2011 MBQB 70.
R. v Kokesch, [1990] 3 S.C.R. 3.
R. v Kur, 2010 ONCJ 295
R. v LaFontaine, 2010 ONSC 21.
R. v Lalonde (1971), 15 C.R.N.S. 1 (Ont. H.C.).
R. v Latimer, [2001] 1 S.C.R. 3.
R. v Law (2002), 48 C.R. (5th) 199 (S.C.C.).
R. v Lee, 2009 ONCJ 434.
R. v Leitner, 2009 BCPC 402.
R. v Lemky, [1996] 1 S.C.R. 757.
R. v Leon-Uzarraga (1998), 123 C.C.C. (3d) 291 (B.C.C.A.).
R. v Losier (2010), 361 N.B.R. (2d) 217.
R. v Lyons, [1987] 2 S.C.R. 307.
R. v M. (M.R.), [1998] 3 S.C.R. 393.
R. v M. (R.E.), [2008] 3 S.C.R. 3.
R. v MacDonald, [1977] 2 S.C.R. 665.
R. v MacFarlane, 2009 ONCJ 489.
R. v MacKay, 2009 ONCJ 510.
R. v MacKenzie, 2009 SKQB 415.

R. v Mahmood, [2009] O.J. 3192 (Sup. Ct. Just.).
R. v Mai, 2010 BCPC 159.
R. v Main, 2011 ABQB 290.
R. v Manninen, [1987] 1 S.C.R. 1233.
R. v Marshall, [1999] 3 S.C.R. 456 [*Marshall (no. 1)*].
R. v Marshall, [1999] 3 S.C.R. 533 [*Marshall (no. 2)*].
R. v Martin (2010), 361 N.B.R. (2d) 251 (C.A.).
R. v Mason, [2009] O.J. 4468 (Sup. Ct. Just.).
R. v McAnuff, 2011 ONSC 2760.
R. v McDonald, [1960] S.C.R. 186.
R. v McFadden (1981), 28 C.R. (3d) 33 (B.C.C.A.).
R. v McIntosh, 2010 SKPC 22.
R. v McNamara (No. 1) (1981), 56 C.C.C. (2d) 193 (Ont. C.A.).
R. v McPhail, 2011 ONCJ 315.
R. v Meija (2009), 14 Alta. L.R. (6th) 368.
R. v Meijid, 2010 ONSC 5532.
R. v Mellors, 2010 BCPC 211.
R. v Melynchuk (2010), 209 C.R.R. (2d) 63 (Alta. P.C.).
R. v Mentuck (2001), 205 D.L.R. (4th) 512 (S.C.C.).
R. v Menzies, 2009 MBQB 250.
R. v Miller and Cockriell, [1977] 2 S.C.R. 680.
R. v Mills, [1986] 1 S.C.R. 863.
R. v Mills, [1999] 3 S.C.R. 668.
R. v Mohmedi, 2009 ONCJ 533.
R. v Monney, [1999] 1 S.C.R. 652.
R. v Morgan, 2010 ONSC 4258.
R. v Morin (1995), 134 Sask. R. 120 (C.A.).
R. v Morris (2004), B.C.A.C. 235.
R. v Mudryk, 2009 ABPC 253.
R. v Mullins-Johnson (2008), 87 O.R. (3d) 425.
R. v N.N., 2009 ONCJ 508.
R. v Nagassar, 2010 ONSC 6032.
R. v Nepoose (1985), 85 Alta. L.R. (2d) 18 (Q.B.).
R. v Nguyen, [2009] O.J. 4565 (Sup. Ct. Just.).
R. v Nguyen, 2010 ONSC 1520.
R. v Nicholas and Bear, [1989] 2 C.N.L.R. 131 (N.B.Q.B.).
R. v Noble, [1997] 1 S.C.R. 874.
R. v Nother, 2009 ONCJ 624.
R. v Nowegijick, [1983] 1 S.C.R. 29.
R. v Oakes, [1986] 1 S.C.R. 103.
R. v Ogbaldet, 2010 ONCJ 477.
R. v Osolin, [1993] 2 S.C.R. 313.
R. v Osolky, 2009 ONCJ 445.
R. v P. (M.B.) (1994), 29 C.R. (4th) 209 (S.C.C.).
R. v P. (N.A.) (2002), 8 C.R. (6th) 186 (Ont. C.A.).
R. v P. (P.N.) (1993), 81 C.C.C. (3d) 525 (Nfld. C.A.).
R. v Pamajewon, [1996] 2 S.C.R. 821.
R. v Patrick, [2009] S.C.J. no. 17.
R. v Payette (2010), 259 C.C.C. (3d) 178 (B.C.C.A.).
R. v Pauchay, [2009] 2 C.N.L.R. 314 (Sask. P.C.).
R. v Peacock, 2009 ONCJ 479.
R. v Pengchanh, 2011 BCSC 484.
R. v Perry, 2010 ABPC 350.
R. v Phillips, 2011 ONSC 3890.
R. v Pillott (2009), 14 Alta. L.R. (5th) 112.
R. v Playford (1987), 40 C.C.C. (3d) 142 (Ont. C.A.).

R. v Pohorestsky, [1987] 1 S.C.R. 945.
R. v Pollock (2004), 23 C.R. (6th) 98 (Ont. C.A.).
R. v Powley, [2003] 2 S.C.R. 207.
R. v Pozniak, [1994] 3 S.C.R. 310.
R. v Prosper, [1994] 3 S.C.R. 236.
R. v Puleio, 2011 ONCJ 260.
R. v Quan, [2010] O.J. no. 2641.
R. v Quesnelle, [2009] O.J. 5445 (Sup. Ct. Just.).
R. v Ramage (2010), 257 C.C.C. (3d) 61.
R. v Reddy, 2010 BCCA 11.
R. v Redhead (1995), 42 C.R. (4th) 252.
R. v Rego, 2009 ONCJ 612.
R. v Rempel (2010), 252 Man. R. (2d) 108 (Prov. Ct.).
R. v Roemer, 2010 ONSC 430.
R. v Rosales, 2010 ONSC 1992.
R. v Rose, [1998] 3 S.C.R. 262.
R. v Ross, [1989] 1 S.C.R. 3.
R. v Ross, 2011 ABPC 695.
R. v Ruiz (1991), 68 C.C.C. (3d) 500 (N.B.C.A.).
R. v Rusnak, 2009 ABPC 258.
R. v Rusnov, 2009 ONCJ 564.
R. v Ryan (2010), 210 C.R.R. (2d) 307 (Nfld. Prov. Ct.).
R. v S. (A.) (2002), 165 C.C.C. (3d) 426 (Ont. C.A.).
R. v S. (R.J.), [1995] 1 S.C.R. 451.
R. v Sandhu, 69 C.R. (6th) 137 (Ont. Sup. Ct. Just.).
R. v Sandypoint, 2009 SKPC 108.
R. v Sanelli (1990), 74 C.R. (3d) 281 (S.C.C.).
R. v Sappier; R. v Gray, [2006] 2 S.C.R. 686.
R. v Schmidt (2010), 27 Alta. L.R. (5th) 352 (Q.B.).
R. v Seiben (1987), 56 C.R. (3d) 225 (S.C.C.).
R. v Sergalis, [2009] O.J. 4823.
R. v Shaw, [2009] O.J. 4142.
R. v Sheppard, [2002] 1 S.C.R. 869.
R. v Sheppard, 2010 ABPC 200.
R. v Silviera, [1995] 2 S.C.R. 297.
R. v Simmons, [1988] 2 S.C.R. 495.
R. v Simon, [1985] 2 S.C.R. 387.
R. v Simpson, [2009] O.J. 5452 (Sup. Ct. Just.).
R. v Sinclair, [2010] 2 S.C.R. 310.
R. v Sing, 2011 ONSC 3124.
R. v Sioui, [1990] 3 C.N.L.R. 127.
R. v Skuce, [2009] B.C.J. 2289.
R. v Smith, [1991] 1 S.C.R. 714.
R. v Smith, 2010 ONCJ 28.
R. v Smith, 2010 ONCJ 641.
R. v Snider, 2009 BCPC 300.
R. v Solomon, [2009] O.J. 4578.
R. v Sotana, 2010 BCSC 267.
R. v Soto (2010), 209 C.R.R. (2d) 191 (Ont. C.J.).
R. v Sparrow, [1990] 1 S.C.R. 1075.
R. v Stanton (2010), 254 C.C.C. (3d) 421 (B.C.C.A.).
R. v Stevenson (1971), 5 C.C.C. (2d) 415 (Ont. C.A.).
R. v Stillman, [1997] 1 S.C.R. 607.
R. v Storrey, [1990] 1 S.C.R. 241.
R. v Strachan, [1988] 2 S.C.R. 980.
R. v Strilec (2010), 256 C.C.C. (3d) 403 (B.C.C.A.).

R. v Stritharan, 2010 ONCJ 466l.

R. v Sunshine, 2010 BCSC 45.

R. v Swain, [1991] 1 S.C.R. 933.

R. v T.O., 2010 ONCJ 334.

R. v Taylor and Williams (1981), 34 O.R. (2d) 360 (C.A.).

R. v Teneycke (1996), 108 C.C. (3d) 53 (B.C.C.A.).

R. v Thomsen, [1988] 1 S.C.R. 640.

R. v Tremblay, [1987] 2 S.C.R. 435.

R. v Trieu, 2010 ONCJ 518.

R. v Tse, [2009] B.C.J. 2632.

R. v Tuduce, 2011 ONSC 2749.

R. v Usher, 2010 BCPC 210.

R. v Valente, [1985] 2 S.C.R. 673.

R. v Valinquette, 2010 BCSC 1423.

R. v Van der Peet, [1996] 2 S.C.R. 507.

R. v Vanezis (2006), 43 C.R. (6th) 116 (Ont. C.A.)

R. v Vijayam, 2010 ONCJ 537.

R. v Vinohoran, [2009] O.J. 4037 (Sup. Ct. Just.).

R. v Vu (2010), 2010 BCSC 1260.

R. v W.D. [D.W.], [1991] 1 S.C.R. 742.

R. v Walters, 2011 ONSC 2316.

R. v Ward, 2010 BCCA 1.

R. v Waters, 2010 ABQB 607.

R. v Watson, 2010 ONSC 448.

R. v Way (2010), 358 N.B.R. (2d) 119 (Q.B.).

R. v Weibe, 2011 SKPC 70.

R. v Wells, [2000] 1 S.C.R. 207.

R. v West (1992), Docket no. Prince George 21151 (B.C.S.C.).

R. v White, [2000] 2 S.C.R. 417.

R. v White, 2009 BCPC 312.

R. v Wholesale Travel Group Inc., [1991] 3 S.C.R. 154.

R. v Whyte, [1988] 2 S.C.R. 3.

R. v Whyte, 2009 ONCJ 389.

R. v Wigglesworth, [1987] 2 S.C.R. 541.

R. v Wise (1992), 11 C.R. (4th) 253 (S.C.C.).

R. v Wong (1990), 1 C.R. (4th) 1 (S.C.C.).

R. v Wray, [1971] S.C.R. 272.

R. v Xhango, 2010 ONCJ 503.

R. v Yooya, [1995] 2 W.W.R. 135 (Sask. Q.B.).

R. v Zaba, 2010 SKPC 85.

Reference re Bill 30, An Act to Amend the Education Act (Ontario), [1987] 1 S.C.R. 1148.

Reference re Rumeration of the Judges of the Provincial Court of Prince Edward Island; Reference re Independence and Impartiality of Judges of the Provincial Court of Prince Edward Island; R. v Campbell; R. v Ekmecic; R. v Wickman; Manitoba Provincial Judges Assn. v Manitoba (Minister of Justice), [1997] 3 S.C.R. 3.

Reference re Remuneration of Judges of the Provincial Court of Prince Edward Island; Reference re Independence and Impartiality of Judges of the Provincial Court of Prince Edward Island; R. v Campbell; R. v Ekmecic; R. v Wickman; Manitoba Provincial Judges Assn. v Manitoba (Minister of Justice), [1998] 1 S.C.R. 3.

Reference re Section 94(2) of the Motor Vehicle Act, B.C., [1985] 2 S.C.R. 486.

Smith v R. [1987] 1 S.C.R. 1045.

Steele v Mountain Institution, [1990] 2 S.C.R. 1385.

Steinhauer v The Queen, [1985] 3 C.N.L.R. 187 (Alta. Q.B.).

Suresh v Canada (Minister of Citizenship and Immigration), [2002] 1 S.C.R. 3.

Thomas v Norris, [1992] 2 C.N.L.R. 139 (B.C.S.C.).

Thomson Newspapers Ltd. v Canada (Director of Investigation and Research, Restorative Trade Practices Commission), [1990] 1 S.C.R. 425.
United States v Burn, [2001] 1 S.C.R. 283.
Vancouver (City) v Ward, [2010] 2 S.C.R. 28.

United States
Evans v Gore, 253 US 245, 247-48 (1920).
Jones v Meehan, 175 U.S. 1 (1899).
Malone v City of Poway, 746 F2d 1375, 1376 (9th Cir. 1982).
United States v Calandra, 414 U.S. 338 (1974).
United States v Will, 449 US 200, 213-14 (1980).

Native American Courts
Boos v Yazzie, No. A-CV-35-90 (Navajo, 24 September 1990).
Crow Tribe of Indians v Bull Tail, 2000 Crow 8 (Crow, 12 October 2000).
Fort Peck Assiniboine and Sioux v Howard, No. 057 (Fort Peck, 11/38/1988).
Hopi Tribe v Kahe, 21 Indian L. Rep. 6079 (Hopi Tribal Ct. 1994).
St. Peter v Colville Confederated Tribes, 2 CCAR 2 (Colville Confederated, 28 September 1993).
Thompson v Yazzie, No. SC-CV-21-06 (Navajo, 14 July 2006).

Australia
Laws v Australian Broadcasting Tribunal (1990), 93 A.L.R. 435.
R. v Anunga, [1976] 11 A.L.R. 412 (N.T.S.C.).
R. v Jadurin (1982), 7 A. Crim. R. 182.
R. v Joseph Murray Jungarai (1981), 9 N.T.R. 30 (N.T.S.C.).
R. v Joseph Murray Jungarai (2 November 1981) (N.T.S.C.) [unreported].
R. v Joseph Murray Jungarai (4 June 1982) (F.C. Aust.) [unreported].
R. v Mamarika (1982), 63 F.L.R. 202.
R. v Minor (1992), 59 A. Crim. R. 227.

United Kingdom
Kuruma v The Queen, [1955] A.C. 197 (P.C.).
R. v Sang, [1980] A.C. 402 (H.L.).
Woolmington v Director of Public Prosecutions, [1935] A.C. 462 (H.L.).

International
Osbourne v Jamaica, Communication no. 759/1997.
Tyrer v United Kingdom (1978), Series A, no. 26 (E. Ct. H.R.).

Index

974649 Ontario Inc., R. v, 211

Aboriginal Charters of rights: communities drafting own, 76-77; community court judges' knowledge of, 88-90, 95-96; constitutional balancing and, 89; culturally sensitive interpretations of legal rights and, 89; exclusion of evidence in, 207, 208; federal government and, 74; knowledge of, 182; remedies in, 206-7; search and seizure in, 162, 164; and s. 24 of Charter, 89

Aboriginal court systems. *See* community courts

Aboriginal judges. *See* community court judges

Aboriginal justice: accuracy/perceived credibility gap in, 152-53; adversarial justice vs., 19, 142, 216; Canadian initiatives, 27-32; Charter and, 3-5, 73, 108-9, 117, 138-39, 214; cohesive vision of, 213, 214; collective power vs. individual liberty and, 50; and common law standards of fairness, 117-18; and community reconciliation, 23; competing visions of, 212-13; constitutional balancing of laws within, 70-71; crime control vs. due process models and, 55-57; *Criminal Code* and, 26-27; cross-examination and, 142, 216; and customary laws/values, 56; defence lawyers and, 177-78; differing values regarding, 212-13; diversionary programs in, 28; diversity among, 79, 172-73; economic bases of communities and, 129; Elders in, 108-9; elites and, 60-61; evidence in, 135, 145-46, 200-5; exclusion of evidence and, 211, 218; fact-determining processes in, 31; failure to come to agreement in, 127-28; federal government and, 44-45; as healing-based, 100; incarceration in, 24-25; *Indian Act* and, 26; individual rights vs., 3-4, 56, 59, 71; and individual rights vs. collective good, 57; inherent rights and, 32; and lawyers, 177-78, 182; legislation regarding, 26-27; liberal legal rights vs., 56-57, 214; limitations on, 31-32; offence bifurcation and, 31; and police, 158; political obstacles to, 40-47; power and, 56, 59, 129; and presumption of innocence, 131-34; prior to European contact, 158-59; prisoners' friends in, 182, 217; proof of guilt beyond reasonable doubt and, 139; public demands for incarceration and, 44; punishment in, 21-25, 186-88; RCAP and, 4-5; and reasonable person standard, 202-3; restorative justice compared to, 10-11, 21; and right against unreasonable search and seizure, 158; safeguards in, 118; "tough on crime" policies and, 41, 42-44; transitory phase in development of, 129; treaty rights and, 39-40; truth in, 203; victims' rights in, 106. *See also* restorative justice

Aboriginal Legal Services of Toronto, 29, 179

Aboriginal offenders: advocates for, 103-4; background/systemic factors and, 27; community-based sentences, 27; courts for, 29; incarceration and, 16-17, 27, 31, 36, 44, 45-48, 192; judges and, 27; marginalized, 103; over-incarceration of, 3; politicians and, 41; power differential and, 103; and procedural fairness, 102-3; right to counsel, 103-4; sentencing of, 26-27, 41, 45. *See also* offenders

Aboriginal peoples of Australia. *See* Australian Aboriginal peoples

programs, 28; procedural fairness and, 106; and proof of guilt beyond reasonable doubt, 130

public opinion: on exclusion of evidence, 198; on incarceration, 43-44; on restorative justice, 44, 46; on sentencing, 45-48

punishment(s): in Aboriginal justice systems, 21-25; Aboriginal peoples and, 86, 186-88; in *Akwesasne Justice Code*, 90; certainty/swiftness of, 12, 16-17, 110; and collective good, 196-97; and deterrence, 8-9, 11-12; and efficiency in criminal process, 54-55; just deserts theory of, 8-9; justifications for, 8-9; and pain, 191; peacemaking vs., 23; presumption of innocence and, 132; and proof of guilt beyond reasonable doubt, 133; reliability vs. efficiency and, 54-55; restorative justice and, 23-24, 56, 109-10; retribution and, 8, 191; social contract theory and, 196-97; in Western justice systems, 7-9, 11-21

Puyallups, gift-giving to victims, 10

Queensland Criminal Justice Commission, 148

Quigley, Tim, 46

R. v 974649 Ontario Inc., 211
R. v Amway of Canada Ltd., 167
R. v Anunga, 179
R. v Badger, 38, 39
R. v Burlingham, 210, 211
R. v Chaulk, 140, 141
R. v Collins, 198, 199, 202, 203, 204, 210
R. v Daviault, 149
R. v Downey, 139-40, 141
R. v Edwards, 156, 161, 162-63, 164, 165
R. v Fatt, 137
R. v Gladstone, 35
R. v Gladue, 27, 29, 146
R. v Golden, 157, 161, 164
R. v Grant, 165-66, 199, 202, 203-4, 210
R. v Gray, 33
R. v Harper, 210
R. v Hatchard, 163
R. v Hebert, 166-67
R. v Jadurin, 189
R. v Joseph Murray Jungarai, 189
R. v Kapp, 66-67
R. v K.I., 137
R. v Lyons, 105, 169-70, 179, 180
R. v M. (M.R.), 163
R. v M. (R.E.), 115-16
R. v Mamarika, 190

R. v Manninen, 175-76
R. v Marshall (no. 1), 38, 39
R. v Marshall (no. 2), 39
R. v Mentuck, 158
R. v Miller and Cockriell, 184
R. v Mills, 89-90, 105-6
R. v Minor, 189-90
R. v Noble, 172
R. v Oakes, 69-70, 71, 139, 215
R. v Osolin, 142
R. v Pamajewon, 32
R. v Rose, 142
R. v Ross, 176
R. v S. (R.J.), 166
R. v Sang, 206
R. v Sappier, 33
R. v Sheppard, 115-16, 117
R. v Simmons, 162-63
R. v Smith, 186
R. v Sparrow, 35-36, 39, 41
R. v Stillman, 158
R. v Storrey, 158
R. v Swain, 141-42, 170
R. v Valente, 80
R. v Van der Peet, 32, 33-34, 48
R. v Wells, 27
R. v Wholesale Travel Group Inc., 140
R. v Williams and Orrs, 207

Ragueneau, Father, 51

Razack, Sherene, 107-8, 188

reasonable expectations of privacy: in Aboriginal justice systems, 217; Aboriginal vs. Western, 164-65; and community well-being, 163-64; right against unreasonable search and seizure and, 156, 161; social cost, 162-63

recidivism: restorative justice and, 19, 119-20, 122; sentencing circles and, 119; sexual abuse and, 20; victim-offender mediation and, 19

Red Cliff Band of Lake Superior Chippewas Tribal Law and Constitution, 180

Reference re Bill 30, An Act to Amend the Education Act (Ontario), 65

Reference re Section 94(2) of the Motor Vehicle Act, B.C., 65

rehabilitation: correctional programs and, 30-31; deterrence vs., 9; and restorative justice, 9; retribution vs., 9

Reilly, John, 53

relationship reparation: adversarial justice systems and, 18-19; capital punishment and, 185, 188; offender reintegration and, 11; restorative justice and, 10-11, 121

LAW AND
SOCIETY

David R. Boyd
The Right to a Healthy Environment: Revitalizing Canada's Constitution (2012)

Shelley A.M. Gavigan
Hunger, Horses, and Government Men: Criminal Law on the Aboriginal Plains, 1870-1905 (2012)

Steven Bittle
Still Dying for a Living: Corporate Criminal Liability after the Westray Mine Disaster (2012)

Jacqueline D. Krikorian
International Trade Law and Domestic Policy: Canada, the United States, and the WTO (2012)

Michael Boudreau
City of Order: Crime and Society in Halifax, 1918-35 (2012)

Lesley Erickson
Westward Bound: Sex, Violence, the Law, and the Making of a Settler Society (2011)

David R. Boyd
The Environmental Rights Revolution: A Global Study of Constitutions, Human Rights, and the Environment (2011)

Elaine Craig
Troubling Sex: Towards a Legal Theory of Sexual Integrity (2011)

Laura DeVries
Conflict in Caledonia: Aboriginal Land Rights and the Rule of Law (2011)

Jocelyn Downie and Jennifer J. Llewellyn (eds.)
Being Relational: Reflections on Relational Theory and Health Law (2011)

Grace Li Xiu Woo
*Ghost Dancing with Colonialism: Decolonization and Indigenous Rights
at the Supreme Court of Canada* (2011)

Fiona Kelly
*Transforming Law's Family: The Legal Recognition of Planned Lesbian
Motherhood* (2011)

Colleen Bell
The Freedom of Security: Governing Canada in the Age of Counter-Terrorism (2011)

Andrew S. Thompson
In Defence of Principles: NGOs and Human Rights in Canada (2010)

Aaron Doyle and Dawn Moore (eds.)
Critical Criminology in Canada: New Voices, New Directions (2010)

Joanna R. Quinn
The Politics of Acknowledgement: Truth Commissions in Uganda and Haiti (2010)

Patrick James
*Constitutional Politics in Canada after the Charter: Liberalism, Communitarianism,
and Systemism* (2010)

Louis A. Knafla and Haijo Westra (eds.)
Aboriginal Title and Indigenous Peoples: Canada, Australia, and New Zealand (2010)

Janet Mosher and Joan Brockman (eds.)
Constructing Crime: Contemporary Processes of Criminalization (2010)

Stephen Clarkson and Stepan Wood
A Perilous Imbalance: The Globalization of Canadian Law and Governance (2009)

Amanda Glasbeek
Feminized Justice: The Toronto Women's Court, 1913-34 (2009)

Kimb Brooks (ed.)
Justice Bertha Wilson: One Woman's Difference (2009)

Wayne V. McIntosh and Cynthia L. Cates
Multi-Party Litigation: The Strategic Context (2009)

Renisa Mawani
*Colonial Proximities: Crossracial Encounters and Juridical Truths in British
Columbia, 1871-1921* (2009)

James B. Kelly and Christopher P. Manfredi (eds.)
*Contested Constitutionalism: Reflections on the Canadian Charter of Rights
and Freedoms* (2009)

Catherine Bell and Robert K. Paterson (eds.)
Protection of First Nations Cultural Heritage: Laws, Policy, and Reform (2008)

Hamar Foster, Benjamin L. Berger, and A.R. Buck (eds.)
The Grand Experiment: Law and Legal Culture in British Settler Societies (2008)

Richard J. Moon (ed.)
Law and Religious Pluralism in Canada (2008)

Catherine Bell and Val Napoleon (eds.)
First Nations Cultural Heritage and Law: Case Studies, Voices, and Perspectives (2008)

Douglas C. Harris
Landing Native Fisheries: Indian Reserves and Fishing Rights in British Columbia, 1849-1925 (2008)

Peggy J. Blair
Lament for a First Nation: The Williams Treaties of Southern Ontario (2008)

Lori G. Beaman
Defining Harm: Religious Freedom and the Limits of the Law (2007)

Stephen Tierney (ed.)
Multiculturalism and the Canadian Constitution (2007)

Julie Macfarlane
The New Lawyer: How Settlement Is Transforming the Practice of Law (2007)

Kimberley White
Negotiating Responsibility: Law, Murder, and States of Mind (2007)

Dawn Moore
Criminal Artefacts: Governing Drugs and Users (2007)

Hamar Foster, Heather Raven, and Jeremy Webber (eds.)
Let Right Be Done: Aboriginal Title, the Calder *Case, and the Future of Indigenous Rights* (2007)

Dorothy E. Chunn, Susan B. Boyd, and Hester Lessard (eds.)
Reaction and Resistance: Feminism, Law, and Social Change (2007)

Margot Young, Susan B. Boyd, Gwen Brodsky, and Shelagh Day (eds.)
Poverty: Rights, Social Citizenship, and Legal Activism (2007)

Rosanna L. Langer
Defining Rights and Wrongs: Bureaucracy, Human Rights, and Public Accountability (2007)

C.L. Ostberg and Matthew E. Wetstein
Attitudinal Decision Making in the Supreme Court of Canada (2007)

Chris Clarkson
Domestic Reforms: Political Visions and Family Regulation in British Columbia, 1862-1940 (2007)

Jean McKenzie Leiper
Bar Codes: Women in the Legal Profession (2006)

Gerald Baier
Courts and Federalism: Judicial Doctrine in the United States, Australia, and Canada (2006)

Avigail Eisenberg (ed.)
Diversity and Equality: The Changing Framework of Freedom in Canada (2006)

Randy K. Lippert
Sanctuary, Sovereignty, Sacrifice: Canadian Sanctuary Incidents, Power, and Law (2005)

James B. Kelly
Governing with the Charter: Legislative and Judicial Activism and Framers' Intent (2005)

Dianne Pothier and Richard Devlin (eds.)
Critical Disability Theory: Essays in Philosophy, Politics, Policy, and Law (2005)

Susan G. Drummond
Mapping Marriage Law in Spanish Gitano Communities (2005)

Louis A. Knafla and Jonathan Swainger (eds.)
Laws and Societies in the Canadian Prairie West, 1670-1940 (2005)

Ikechi Mgbeoji
Global Biopiracy: Patents, Plants, and Indigenous Knowledge (2005)

Florian Sauvageau, David Schneiderman, and David Taras, with Ruth Klinkhammer and Pierre Trudel
The Last Word: Media Coverage of the Supreme Court of Canada (2005)

Gerald Kernerman
Multicultural Nationalism: Civilizing Difference, Constituting Community (2005)

Pamela A. Jordan
Defending Rights in Russia: Lawyers, the State, and Legal Reform in the Post-Soviet Era (2005)

Anna Pratt
Securing Borders: Detention and Deportation in Canada (2005)

Kirsten Johnson Kramar
Unwilling Mothers, Unwanted Babies: Infanticide in Canada (2005)

W.A. Bogart
Good Government? Good Citizens? Courts, Politics, and Markets in a Changing Canada (2005)

Catherine Dauvergne
Humanitarianism, Identity, and Nation: Migration Laws in Canada and Australia (2005)

Michael Lee Ross
First Nations Sacred Sites in Canada's Courts (2005)

Andrew Woolford
Between Justice and Certainty: Treaty Making in British Columbia (2005)

John McLaren, Andrew Buck, and Nancy Wright (eds.)
Despotic Dominion: Property Rights in British Settler Societies (2004)

Georges Campeau
From UI to EI: Waging War on the Welfare State (2004)

Alvin J. Esau
The Courts and the Colonies: The Litigation of Hutterite Church Disputes (2004)

Christopher N. Kendall
Gay Male Pornography: An Issue of Sex Discrimination (2004)

Roy B. Flemming
Tournament of Appeals: Granting Judicial Review in Canada (2004)

Constance Backhouse and Nancy L. Backhouse
The Heiress vs the Establishment: Mrs. Campbell's Campaign for Legal Justice (2004)

Christopher P. Manfredi
Feminist Activism in the Supreme Court: Legal Mobilization and the Women's Legal Education and Action Fund (2004)

Annalise Acorn
Compulsory Compassion: A Critique of Restorative Justice (2004)

Jonathan Swainger and Constance Backhouse (eds.)
People and Place: Historical Influences on Legal Culture (2003)

Jim Phillips and Rosemary Gartner
Murdering Holiness: The Trials of Franz Creffield and George Mitchell (2003)

David R. Boyd
Unnatural Law: Rethinking Canadian Environmental Law and Policy (2003)

Ikechi Mgbeoji
Collective Insecurity: The Liberian Crisis, Unilateralism, and Global Order (2003)

Rebecca Johnson
Taxing Choices: The Intersection of Class, Gender, Parenthood, and the Law (2002)

John McLaren, Robert Menzies, and Dorothy E. Chunn (eds.)
Regulating Lives: Historical Essays on the State, Society, the Individual, and the Law (2002)

Joan Brockman
Gender in the Legal Profession: Fitting or Breaking the Mould (2001)

Printed and bound in Canada by Friesens

Set in Stone by Artegraphica Design Co. Ltd.

Copy editor: Stacy Belden

Proofreader: Dianne Tiefensee

Indexer: Noeline Bridge